A FIRESIDE BOOK

PUBLISHED BY SIMON & SCHUSTER

NEW YORK   LONDON   TORONTO   SYDNEY   TOKYO   SINGAPORE

HOME WATERS

• • •

A FLY-FISHING ANTHOLOGY

Edited by

GARY SOUCIE

FIRESIDE
SIMON & SCHUSTER BUILDING
ROCKEFELLER CENTER
1230 AVENUE OF THE AMERICAS
NEW YORK, NEW YORK 10020

DESIGNED BY DIANE STEVENSON, SNAP • HAUS GRAPHICS
MANUFACTURED IN THE UNITED STATES OF AMERICA

1   3   5   7   9   10   8   6   4   2

LIBRARY OF CONGRESS CATALOGING IN PUBLICATION DATA
HOME WATERS : A FLY-FISHING ANTHOLOGY / EDITED BY GARY SOUCIE.
P.   CM.
"A FIRESIDE BOOK."
1. FLY-FISHING.   I. SOUCIE, GARY.
SH456.H64   1992
799.1'2—DC20   91-26101
                                        CIP

ISBN 0-671-68747-6

Home Waters *is dedicated to*
the memory of my mother,
Marie Soucie,
who nearly always put up with
my preference for fishing, over chores

◆   ◆   ◆

CONTENTS

Introduction · 9

Home Water   Nick Lyons · 13
Going Home   William Cowper Prime · 17
On Turniptown Creek   Jimmy Carter · 19
The Ritual   Chuck and Sharon Tryon · 26
A Long Way from Home   Stephen J. Bodio · 32
Where the Heart Is   Robert F. Jones · 38
The Consolation of the
  Pond   George Reiger · 46
West Fork   Caroline Gordon · 50
To Know a River . . .   Roderick L. Haig-Brown · 55
Worming Murphy Creek   John Engels · 62
A Stream for Anglers   W. H. H. Murray · 67
Into Big Timber Creek   Stewart Hardison · 69
The Family Pool   John Gierach · 74
The Upper Reaches of
  Lone Tree Creek   Ron Spomer · 84
Battenkill Seasons   Craig Woods · 88
My Best Hour of Fishing   Henry Williamson · 93
A Woman's Place   Judy Muller · 96
Solitaire   Ted Kerasote · 101
Private Waters: Rolling
  Your Own Farm Pond   Vance Bourjaily · 108
The Pageant of the
  Seasons   John Waller Hills · 120
A Fly-Fisherman's Peace   Geoffrey Norman · 125
Just a Spring Creek   Charles F. Waterman · 127
A Home by the River   W. D. Wetherell · 132
The Marquesas: February
  29, 1988   John N. Cole · 136
A River's Tale   Justin Askins · 155
The Same River Twice   David Quammen · 161
Something More   David Seybold · 167
The Vicar's Pool   J. P. Wheeldon · 175

Dancing on the Spine of
  Time   Harry Middleton · 184
The Gift of Creeks   Peter Steinhart · 189
Smack-dab in the Middle
  of the Rock   Paul Quinnett · 193
The Cottage by the
  Itchen   Viscount Grey of Fallodon · 200
Seasons Now and Then   Russell Chatham · 203
Wild Dogs Couldn't Drag
  Me Away   Michael Levy · 215
Drifting Down the River
  of My Mind   Lionel Atwill · 222
Lime Creek   Steven J. Meyers · 226
Making Time   Thomas R. Pero · 236
The Cleveland Wrecking
  Yard   Richard Brautigan · 239
A Place at Dawn   Datus C. Proper · 245
The Creek   Tony Dawson · 251
My Fishing Pond   Stephen Leacock · 257
Runoff   Thomas McGuane · 261
Menunketesuck Justice   Edward R. Ricciuti · 269
Love Affair   Dennis Bitton · 274
Night Shift   Steven A. Griffin · 279
In The Enchanted   Ted Williams · 284
The Finest Trout in the
  River   Harry Plunket Greene · 298
Mother's Day   Margot Page · 301
Timeless River   Jack Samson · 303
The Approaching Storm   Jeanette Foster · 309
Home River   Paul Schullery · 314
The Man without a River   Gary Soucie · 325
Contributors'
  Biographies · 333

INTRODUCTION

◆ ◆ ◆

THE NOTION OF HOME WATER IS ALMOST AS OLD AS FLY-FISHING ITSELF. In the beginning, at least, and on the other side of the Atlantic, it was tied very tightly to another of fly-fishing's early notions: private water. *Home water* has always had a particularly British ring to it. The Brits have certainly taken to the notion of home water. Throughout the British Isles, on private salmon river after private trout stream, there are even home pools. Often located virtually in the shadow of the castle keep, these are spots where the laird and his guests could take their sport without overexerting on the trail.

On our side of the Atlantic, private waters haven't played so large a role in the development of fly-fishing, and home water has taken on a more democratic meaning. Meanings, actually, because today's fly-fishers harbor many different notions of home water. For some, steeped in the British tradition, it means club water—private, exclusive, expensive. For most, though, home water means public water; for them, privacy, exclusivity, and privilege are not deeded or inherited from without, but felt within. Home water is personal water in the psychic rather than the legal or proprietary sense.

Some fly-fishermen take the term quite literally; their home waters flow by their dooryards or are located just down the road a piece. Others engage in wishful thinking: "If only I could afford the time and expense to fish more often out in . . ."—you fill in the place. Still others have home waters of the imagination, the perfect waters they haven't yet found but plan to retire to someday. When I called Ted Kerasote to ask him to contribute to this anthology, he offered me two pieces: one on his literal home water, the one that runs by his house in Wyoming, and the other on his "psychic home water," the Río Chimehuin in Argentina. Home is, after all, where the heart is, in fishing as well as in homily. The term *home water* is almost exclusive to fly-fishing, but other anglers have their secret spots and honey holes. Every fisherman, I figured—every fly-fisherman, certainly—has his or her home water.

But Keith Gardner, editor of *Fishing World* magazine, quickly disabused me of this notion in his letter declining my invitation to contribute something. In wonderfully wry, self-deprecating humor he wrote:

Dear Gary:

Your invitation to contribute to Home Waters *forced me to examine both my files and my conscience, and I found that I seldom return more than once to any water and the quality of the experience invariably declines on repetition.*

This so perfectly describes a shallow, superficial character devoid of profound or substantive interests that I would be ashamed to admit it except that self-delusion and hypocrisy are even more contemptible than frivolity.

Thank you for the opportunity to add to my awareness of the miserable wretch that I am. Obviously, I am not a fit contributor to Home Waters.

In defense of us airheads with lamentable attention spans it might be said that we fish a lot of fascinating waters worldwide and our knowledge of the sport and its implications can be, theoretically at least, as broad as it is shallow.

Good luck with your project,

Keith

His letter gave me pause as well as a chuckle. It suddenly dawned on me that here I was, editing an anthology on home waters, and I didn't have one. Not even a very strong candidate. The irony of it really had me twisted out of shape for a while. I tried to rationalize myself into adopting Long Island's Connetquot River. But how can you have a home water so nearby that you don't fish as often as you fish trout streams a thousand miles away? I almost convinced myself that the Sava–Bohinjka, in the Julian Alps of Slovenia, was my psychic home water. In the end I gave up. I began to wonder about my wretched, shallow, superficial character.

Perhaps its lack of true universality is one of home water's special attractions. You don't just happen upon home water, you have to earn it with attention and devotion, by investing time and spirit.

◆   ◆   ◆

The contributors to this volume have limned the depths and breadths of home water. Here you will find creeks and rivers, ponds and lakes, waters large and small, still and swift, homely and exotic, past and present. Some of the writers have chosen to disguise their home waters; others have precisely located them. There are first-person, experiential pieces; philosophical ruminations; paeans of place; confessionals; humor; remembrances of times and places past; character sketches; fiction; conservation alerts. In length alone, they run the gamut, from just over four hundred words to that many more than eight thousand. I asked those who contributed original material to let their stories find their natural lengths.

In selecting previously published pieces and inviting writers to contribute original material, I have striven for a mix of the familiar and the unknown. I think you will be delighted to encounter some old favorites, some perhaps only dimly remembered, and to discover some new voices that speak with eloquence and authority. Some who are not represented here wanted to contribute, but couldn't find the time in their busy schedules. Quite a few articles and sketches that belong here were omitted because there simply wasn't enough room or budget to include them. Still, the only thing that really nettles me is my failure to find enough women to fairly reflect what has been happening to fly-fishing in recent years. Women are taking to the sport in droves, bringing fresh blood and new ideas, and sometimes a stronger conservation ethic. As time passes, I predict, you will see a great many more women's names among the bylines in fishing magazines. There are five good ones in this volume: Jeanette Foster, Caroline Gordon, Judy Muller, Margot Page, and Sharon Tryon.

◆   ◆   ◆

Most of the reprinted material is unaltered from its original form. In some cases, though, I have had to change punctuation and capitalization and usage to give this book a unified character. In a few of the book excerpts, it was necessary to omit a paragraph or two that made no sense out of their original context. And I've had to correct a few mistakes and lapses that eluded editors who were apparently less conscientious than the ones I was fortunate to have at Fireside Books: Sydny Miner and Kara Leverte, and my copy editor, Steve Boldt.

In a handful of cases, I worked with the authors to disassemble their books and stitch them back together to create what are essentially new pieces that are better suited to this anthology. I want especially to thank three fine writers—Steven J. Meyers, Craig Woods, and Harry Middleton, men whose work hardly needs improvement—for humoring me in this regard. If you have read the books whence their contributions came (and you definitely should), you might have only the vaguest sense of déjà vu, so altered and rearranged are their works. The redoubtable Ted Williams took two articles he'd published several years before and rewrote them as one, adding considerable new material in the process.

◆   ◆   ◆

I really had fun, editing this anthology. I *almost* didn't mind all those otherwise-fishable hours spent with my nose in a book or bent over the keyboard or a manuscript, blue pencil sharpened and at the ready. (Actually, I tend to edit with a red marker pen, but *blue pencil* is traditional editorial shoptalk.) I especially enjoyed discovering writers and works that are new to me if not to the world.

Enough said. I hereby lay down said blue pencil cum red marker with the intention of taking up the graphite rod. The waters are waiting.

Gary Soucie
New York City
Midsummer, 1990

HOME WATER

• • •

NICK LYONS

"At a certain season of our life," says Henry Thoreau, "we are accustomed to consider every spot as the possible site of a house." We want roots. We want an end to the gray, grinding transitoriness of our lives. By extension, at a certain season every fly-fisherman considers what might best become his "home water."

It could be a private pond, a half mile or ten miles of private trout water, a cove in a lake, a section of a shoreline, a couple of bends of a public river that everyone else and his brother consider their home water, too. But something in us hungers for the familiar, the known, the pleasure of fishing water that we know like the freckles on our arms.

There is nothing surprising in this. We can only love what we know well, and "first sight" rarely satisfies. We like the comfortable feeling of fishing up a stretch of water we've fished thirty times before; there was a good brown behind that boulder, another in the riffle near those rhododendrons. A Haystack worked well there in early June, the Gray Fox Variant after that, and a Whitlock Hopper all summer. The fallen tree seems farther downstream this year, perhaps because of the March flood; perhaps that orange flash, near the deeply undercut bank, that hint of a truly big brown trout, will reveal itself more fully this year. Home water is intimate water. There is that about it which you know and no one else knows in quite the same way; there is that about it which infects your dreams, like wine in water, touching every part.

Take such memories and multiply them five, ten, twenty times—until the place becomes an extension of your imagination and you're not entirely sure whether or not some of the times you fished it were real or only dreamed. Hemingway, in his story "Now I Lay Me," has a young man stave off fear of death during the war by fishing in his dreams a river he knew well as a boy. He would "fish its whole length very carefully" in his mind, "fishing very carefully under all the logs, all the turns of the bank, the deep holes and the clear shallow stretches." Sometimes he would fish four or five different streams in the night; sometimes, later, he would confuse the actual with the dreamed.

◆   ◆   ◆

There is a special pleasure in fishing new water, matching the general knowledge we have about a particular kind of water to a new and specific challenge. The pleasure of fishing "old" water is different: the water has a history with us; we know how to prompt out some of its secrets; it is the same but, this season, boasts slight changes—and these slight variations in what is remembered are the lovelier for their delicate newness. The Green Drake will hatch in the afternoons in early June on such water, and as you fish up the river, the layers of old memories drift back, fueled by recollection, expectation, that new color to the water, the difference in the air, the presence of caddis, too, this time, new-fallen logs, and a fish that splash-rises near a boulder you can't remember, the fish's head the size of a dog's.

Often you'll achieve a special level of excellence on such home water. Lefty Kreh once told me that he'd bet on the knowledgeable local fisherman, on his home water, to catch more and larger fish than the acknowledged pro, fishing it for the first few times, any day. And when the "pro" and the "local" are combined, the skill can be awesome. I used to love to watch Art Flick fish up the riffles and pockets of the Schoharie, flicking his Gray Fox Variant into a score of remembered pockets. He was like a vacuum cleaner. He'd take eight, ten fish for every one I or Mike Migel—with whom we often fished—would raise.

I've had half a dozen pools over the years that I thought of as home water, though I fish none of them today. There was one on the East Branch of the Croton that I fished Opening Days for a hundred years when I was a kid; but it got pounded to death by overfishing, and its conformation changed radically when the huge tree, which formed holding pockets upstream and down, was washed away. A part of us gets washed away at such times, too. There's another pool, on another East Branch, that I fished with good friends for ten years, after a halcyon day that was never repeated. I kept trying to make that one a home; I kept coming back to it with the most romantic readiness—and it always sent me packing.

Some years ago I felt that I was in for the season of my life when

I wanted a more permanent brand of home water. I was in no position financially to buy water, and I knew only vaguely about a number of clubs I might join. In the end I became a member of one that I had fished as a guest ten years earlier; it was old, storied water, long in private hands, and the fee wasn't quite stiff enough to sting. Many of the runs and riffles and pools had names like Oak Run and Hemlock Riffle and Frying Pan Pool, and the first spring before the season started, my nerves buzzed with anticipation. I liked the idea of getting to know it well, every foot of it. I liked the idea of fishing it early and late, year after year.

Early one morning in late May, I started at six A.M. and fished the whole length of it, hungry to know it all. I started out at the down-stream wire with the orange POSTED sign slung in the middle, in sneak-ers (so I could travel fast), and fished a dry fly to where the uppermost orange sign hung, three miles upriver. I fished the long, flat pools and runs beneath the overhanging hemlocks; I lingered at the pools with names that had grown greater through public print and at pockets that had no names. I fished hard and intensely, and since it was early, and during the week, I met no one. I had my home water to myself, just as I'd always dreamed.

What a memorable day that was, filled with discovery: the gray-ness when I started; the slowly twisting mists; the first fish that came sluggishly into the flat where the current broke; the sight of those cruising browns—making waves—in the Frying Pan Pool, neither of which I raised; the way the river came alive at nine-thirty with a storm of caddis; and then the deliberate hatch of Sulphurs at eleven, and how I could only take two fish from ten that were working.

On other days, when I came back, I went to sections I wanted to know better, that had revealed enough of their mystery to make me hunger for more. I remember lovely days: a spinner fall at the Bridge Pool, when a dozen fish were high in the water and sipping with great selectivity; an afternoon when the riffles danced with caddis and every fish there rose to my fly; a morning when the Sulphurs came, and then kept coming, and I took nine trout and walked away, smiling like a baboon, from a pool still pocked with the rises of trout.

Getting to know the water better, I scored better; discovering some secrets, I pursued others; I loved the water and I shared it with a few close friends, and in the winter I dreamed fifty times of fishing it, from POSTED sign to POSTED sign, and those dreams mingled with days I actually spent on the water.

And then I quit the club.

At first I could not tell precisely why. Was it my chronic rest-

lessness? Was it some wild thing in me that wants never to be ritualized or standardized or muzzled? And why would I think the club was
doing that to me?

I don't know.

Oh, I know I'll miss it. I know when I've spent a fruitless day
banging away at some stretch of unknown water, whose only denizens
may be muskrats for all I know, I'll wish I were back there, fishing
water I'd grown to love so much. I'll miss it when I find a dozen guys
pounding a favorite pool on public waters with spinning lures. I know,
too, that I won't miss it when I turn the corner of some new stream
and see water and challenges that make me shiver with pleasure, that
have me talking to myself.

I don't really know why I quit the club—except that, possibly, I
found home water too comfortable. Or maybe I'd rather be hunting for
new home water.

GOING HOME

• • •

WILLIAM COWPER PRIME

THE SUN HAS GONE DOWN. THE STARS ARE BEGINNING TO BE VISIBLE. The breeze has died away, and there is no ripple on the lake, nor any sound in the tree-tops. Let us go home.

The contentment which fills the mind of the angler at the close of his day's sport is one of the chiefest charms in his life. He is just sufficiently wearied in body to be thoughtful, and the weariness is without nervousness, so that thoughts succeed each other with deliberation and calm, not in haste and confusion. The evening talk after a day of fishing is apt to be memorable. The quiet thinking on the way home is apt to be pleasant, delicious, sometimes even sacred.

I am not sure but that many anglers remember with more distinctness and delight their going home after days of sport than the sport itself. Certainly the strongest impressions on my own mind are of the last casts in the twilight, the counting of the day's results on the bank of lake or river, the homeward walk or ride, and, best of all, the welcome home. For the sportsman's home is where his heart is; and most earnestly do I recommend all lovers of the rod to find their sport, if they can do so, where they can be accompanied by wives and daughters, even by children. On this account, if on no other, every one must be glad to see the formation of clubs whose arrangements include accommodations for the families of members.

There is no more graceful and healthful accomplishment for a lady than fly-fishing, and there is no reason why a lady should not in every respect rival a gentleman in the gentle art.

Shall I ever forget a day along one of the Connecticut streams, of which I have spoken in this volume, when four of us—a lady, two boys, and myself—took a superb basket of trout, and the lady beat us all? What a surprise it was when I saw her, far off across a meadow, standing alone, with her light rod bending as she gave the butt to a strong fish, to keep him from a last rush down the rapid! I hastened to her assistance, but it was useless; for before I reached her he lay on the grass, two pounds and three-quarters exactly, the noblest trout I ever saw taken from a Connecticut brook.

Make your home, therefore, as near as may be to your sport, so, at the least, that you may always find it when the day is done.

ON TURNIPTOWN CREEK

◆ ◆ ◆

JIMMY CARTER

BELOW ME, PERHAPS FIFTY FEET AWAY, IS A QUIET POOL, ROCK STREWN, from which multiple gushes of white water flow over and through large granite boulders. The pool is fed by a series of waterfalls that drop about thirty feet in all, tumbling down the streambed from an almost horizontal rocky ledge just about level with my eyes. Now, in early September, I can barely see the highest falls through the leafy branches of rhododendron, red maple, white pine, black gum, alder, hemlock, dogwood, and wild honeysuckle. The first leaves are just beginning to fall, and after each gust of wind through the narrow valley we can see a few of them floating down the creek like small red and yellow boats. In a few weeks the leaves will be gone, and the upper waterfall will be in full view.

This is Turniptown Creek, which rises five miles east of our cabin in the north Georgia mountains and continues on a fairly straight course until it runs into the Ellijay River. Rosalynn and I have walked the entire distance, during different seasons of the year, and I confess it is gratifying to find that our waterfalls are twice as high as and more beautiful than any others on the creek. There are a number of houses, mostly weekend cottages, built far upstream from us, but when we go downstream, we see no buildings of any kind. In most places there is not even a path; when the water is high during the winter and early spring, it is impossible to wade down the creek and very difficult to make much progress at all without frequent detours up the steep hills to get around the precipitous rock formations that keep the water in its bounds.

◆ ◆ ◆

After leaving the White House in 1981 we were burdened with duties and overrun with visitors. Rosalynn and I had not spent more

than two or three days at a time either alone or without pressing
responsibilities for more than fifteen years. When some friends, John
and Betty Pope, showed us this property, there was no doubt that it
was a place where we could nurture our privacy.

With the Popes as partners we made the plans for our cabin. The
buried electric power lines, drinking water supply, and waste disposal
system were designed to change the natural site as little as possible.
Today even the traces of these are gone, and we believe that the place
is as beautiful as it was when we found it.

While we were still building, I asked the state game and fish
biologists if there were any trout in the stream. They reported that it
was too small to have been stocked with hatchery trout, but they
would be glad to bring a few fish to the stream if I ever wanted them.
Brook trout were about gone in this region, they said, and rainbows
very rarely reproduced naturally in north Georgia. This was disheart-
ening news, but did not detract from my pleasure in the site's natural
loveliness.

The following July, when we finished construction, we went up
to spend our first few days at the small cabin. It was remarkably cool,
often fifteen degrees less than reported on the Chattanooga radio
stations, and delightful to sit on the front porch that extends out
toward the bank of the stream.

On this visit I was able to examine the creek more closely. I
found a good population of mayfly, caddis, and stonefly nymphs under
the stones in the creekbed, so I knew the water was pure and cold
enough for trout. Late one afternoon Rosalynn and I were observing
a small hatch of white mayflies. When I referred to my entomology
book, *Stenonema ithaca,* easily imitated by a small Light Cahill fly
pattern, was the nearest match I could make. Somewhat disappointed
because there were no wild trout in the stream, I went down and sat
on a large rock at the base of the pool and watched the small insects
emerging from the water and fluttering on top. A few of them were
darting back and forth, three or four inches above the surface of the
water. Suddenly, there was an explosive rise not ten feet away, and an
eight-inch trout came up out of the water to take one of the airborne
mayflies. In all my life, it was the most memorable rise of a wild fish,
exceeding in my mind even the soaring leap of a mighty blue marlin
off the coast of Anegada Island in the eastern Caribbean.

When I reported this momentous event to one of the old-time
fishermen in the community, he replied, "Yep. Turniptown has always
had a pretty good crop of native rainbows."

A few weeks later I had a call from my young Montana friend
Rich McIntyre, whose Timberline company specialized in the reha-

bilitation of trout habitat. After exchanging pleasantries, he said, "I hear you've built a mountain cabin on a creek, and I want to make a small contribution to the enterprise. I'll be on the East Coast soon with one of my biologists. If you like, I'll take a look at your stream and give you some advice on how to improve it."

Of course I accepted his offer immediately. Within a few weeks we were together in our creek. To inventory the fish, Rich had brought along a small electric shocking outfit whose generator was powered by a gasoline motor carried in his backpack. With the two electrodes and a dip net, we moved upstream from one pool or crevasse to another. The weak electric current was not strong enough to injure the fish, but would stun them for a moment so that, if we were very quick, we could scoop up some of them before they recovered.

Within a couple of hours we had caught ninety-nine trout, all rainbows, ranging in size from three to ten inches. We saw a few larger ones, but they escaped. Rich examined each fish, weighed and measured it, took a scale or two to determine its age, and quickly returned it to the water. He also assessed the population of insects, sculpins, minnows, creek chubs, and other potential trout food. Although quite pure with a fair population of insects, Turniptown Creek could not support many trout, or very large ones, because the granite streambed produced minimal nutrients, unlike those where limestone or chalk deposits would always provide a much richer menu and water that was less acidic. At least the many bubbling waterfalls kept the oxygen content high.

All in all, I was pleased. I later followed Rich's advice by arranging small rock dams to deepen some of the pools in order to make better holding basins for the times during the late summer when the stream was at its lowest and warmest stage.

Since then, Rosalynn and I have enjoyed fishing and also observing the creek closely at different times of the year. We've learned more about trout habits and insect hatches in addition to studying the bird and animal population along its banks. Two black bear came down the valley while the cabin was being built, and sometimes we see their tracks on the sand and gravel bars. There are also some ruffed grouse and a number of white-tailed deer. Late one evening we opened the cabin door and watched a small flock of wild turkeys calmly walking just in front of us, not thirty feet away, cross the water, and disappear up the mountain.

◆   ◆   ◆

Turniptown Creek is in what was once the gold-producing area of Georgia, and there are many legends recorded in the county history books about an Indian chief named White Path, who owned a number of black slaves in the early nineteenth century and became quite wealthy from his mining operations.

Some of these tales seem far-fetched, but it's interesting to stretch one's imagination enough to believe them. In any case, several miles below us, not far from our stream, was the large cabin where White Path lived before he and other members of his tribe were forced to leave the Southeast on the "Trail of Tears" and suffer a torturous migration to the government's Indian reservations in Oklahoma. The chief died on this march, never to reach the unwanted destination.

One morning we were hiking up a steep incline in front of our cabin when we came to a strange path in the forest. Unlike the numerous old logging trails that crisscross all the woodlands in north Georgia, this one was shaped more like a ditch and seemed to follow a level contour around the mountain. We decided to follow its generally westward direction and soon realized that it was descending very gradually but at a constant rate. At a few places where it crossed a small stream or drain, there was a kind of viaduct constructed of rock, with the man-made ditch continuing across it. This path was obviously a sluice of some kind, quite old, with some trees as large as eighteen inches in diameter growing in it.

As we followed the waterway farther and farther on subsequent exploratory visits, we finally reached the point where it disappeared into the ground, about ten feet below a huge oak tree. We were perplexed, disappointed that our theories about a long waterway had been disproved. But when we scraped away some loose dirt, a tunnel was revealed.

I felt like a kid in an adventure story. We searched the other side of the hill and, about a hundred yards away, found where the sluice emerged. After some reluctance and half-bantering remarks about bear dens and snake condominiums, we crawled down into the tunnel and, bending over, walked safely through to the other end. Farther westward there were three other similar arteries dug through the hills.

Eventually the waterway ended near, but high above, Turniptown Creek, overlooking excavations that had obviously been ancient placer mines. It now seemed obvious that the channeled water, at high pressure, had been used to wash the dirt and stones from the gold flakes and nuggets. Later, when we described our explorations to the proprietor of a nearby antique shop, she gave us a large and ancient nozzle that she said was used for this very purpose. Now on the ground alongside our cabin, it is a reminder of mountain history.

◆   ◆   ◆

With telephones, mail delivery, and word processors, our days at the cabin are usually about as busy as those in Plains, but there are no passers-by and visitors are rare. In this different atmosphere we find more time to read, meditate, study, and explore. With field guides to trees, birds, mammals, nests, mushrooms, wild flowers, ferns, rocks, and minerals and a good collection of other nature books, it is much easier to learn about the relatively isolated community around us.

We have especially enjoyed getting to know some of our neighbors, who are friendly but taciturn, inclined to respect the privacy of others, worshipping in religious services that are more emotional and fundamental in character than those to which we are accustomed. We have been to a few square dances and other social events, and we shop at the country stores and nearby roadside stands to buy fresh corn, tomatoes, apples, and cider. On our long hikes we often stop by to visit families who greet us from their yards, and sometimes leave with fresh vegetables, some blackberry preserves, sourwood honey, a woven basket, or maybe an invitation to fish in their pond.

Just over the mountain from our cabin, within easy walking distance, is the Turniptown Missionary Baptist Church, where we have worshipped on some of the first and third Sundays. There is a regular membership of about fifty, most of whom have amazing musical ability. On our first visit, the pastor began calling on various people to leave their pews and come to the front to play instruments or sing. Before the service was over, almost every member had participated in the extemporaneous program, often with the performers and congregation laughing, choked with tears, or on a few occasions, actually racked with loud sobbing. They knew each other and related the words of a selected hymn to either a happy event or a tragedy in the lives of those who were singing. One lady sitting behind us leaned forward every now and then to whisper: "That man gave up drinking and was saved last month" or "They just lost their mama" or "They've been separated but are living together again" or "The little girl up there has leukemia." Although we didn't know the people personally, we responded with a few tears of our own.

After two hours it was time for some invited guests to arrive at our cabin, and so we had to leave, long before the service was over. I stood to apologize to the congregation for our premature departure, and, partially to compensate, I later turned for them on my lathe a pair of mahogany collection plates.

Walking the steep trail back among the tall trees, Rosalynn and I wondered why the service in the little mountain church had moved us so profoundly. It seemed that we had participated in a ceremony from olden times. Some of the hymns were little changed from their origins in England or pre-Revolutionary days, preserved down through the generations by the unshakable religious beliefs and customs of mountaineer ancestors. The surprising public display of unabashed laughter and tears—deep emotions that resonated among all their Christian brothers and sisters—had demonstrated the closeness of family members and their ties with others in this isolated rural community.

In such a setting, companionship from family or caring neighbors was available whenever it was needed, but total solitude could always be found just a few steps from one's door. We felt that meditation among the rolling mountains and deep valleys, the cathedral-like forests and pristine bubbling brooks, all served to keep these people especially close to nature and reminded them unceasingly of God's miraculous creation. Regardless of one's faith or beliefs, it would not be possible to absorb these impressions without being moved.

◆   ◆   ◆

In some ways, our place on Turniptown Creek completes a circle in my life, bringing me back to many of the outdoor experiences of childhood in south Georgia that I enjoyed with my mother and father. Our children and grandchildren are already sharing this love for the outdoors. It multiplies our pleasure to have them picnicking with us on a flat rock in the middle of the creek, with the small babies in their bassinets shaded from the sun by an overhanging ledge of stone. Together, our older grandchildren stand with us under a waterfall; help to identify mountain trees, shrubs, and flowers; explore the hills and swamps; pull a trout from the stream; or sit on the front porch to hear recollections of bygone times and loved ones long gone. All of us know that this place will be theirs someday, perhaps to share with later generations. Here in this mountain valley even the awareness of our own mortality does not detract from the reassuring contemplation of the cycles of nature. The words of Ecclesiastes come to mind:

> A generation goes and a generation comes,
> But the earth remains forever.
> Also, the sun rises and the sun sets;
> And hastening to its place it rises there again.
> Blowing toward the south,
> Then turning toward the north,
> The wind continues swirling along;
> And on its circular courses the wind returns.
> All the rivers flow into the sea,
> Yet the sea is not full.

To the place where the rivers flow,
There they flow again.
. . . .
That which has been is that which will be,
And that which has been done is that which will be done.
So, there is nothing new under the sun.

It is good to realize that, if love and peace can prevail on earth, and if we can teach our children to honor nature's gifts, the joys and beauties of the outdoors will be here forever.

THE RITUAL

• • •

CHUCK AND SHARON TRYON

"**Mornin', neighbor.**"

"Howdy, young feller," came the reply.

"You Mr. Smith?" I inquired. *If he isn't, the mailbox lied.*

"That's right, son," he confirmed.

"How are you today, Mr. Smith?"

"Gonna live to see the sunset," he responded with a chuckle.

"Better'n some folks, I guess." I glanced around, then blurted out, "Things look pretty dry." *Safe conversation,* I figured. *If it's not too wet on the farm, it's too dry.*

"Worst ever," Mr. Smith agreed. "Cows been givin' powdered milk for a month now." His eyes twinkled mischievously.

"Sounds bad, all right. Folks back the way say their chickens been layin' hard-boiled eggs, been so hot." *I can play that game, too.*

"I reckon that's so," he replied with a sly grin.

"Cigar?" I offered. Imported. Expensive.

"Thank ya, son." Mr. Smith studied it, then broke the seal and sniffed. "Mighty fine," he allowed, slipping it into his shirt pocket with the pencils, pens, and tire gauge.

A bony old black-and-tan, ears full of ticks and cockleburs, and dancing with fleas, ambled over and covetously sniffed my leg like it was a brand-new fireplug. "Good-lookin' dog," I mumbled nervously.

"That's ol' Buck. Best nose in the valley in his day. Gettin' down in his hindquarters now, though."

"Shame," I sympathized. "Bet you've had a lotta good times with him."

"Yep. Don't find one like him but once in a lifetime. He mostly protects the place from caterpillars and June bugs nowadays."

Ol' Buck's nose was still working my leg over excitedly. *Not so down in his hindquarters he can't get one leg up, I'll bet.*

It was time to make my move. "Folks say there might be some fishin' 'round here," I probed. "Any truth to that?"

"Hmmm. Dunno, son. Used to be, long time ago. Don't hear much of it anymore, though." He scratched the back of his neck and gazed into the distance. "Better the next valley over, most folks say."

"Pretty little creek back at the bridge," I persisted.

"Yeah. Awful low, though, dry like it is. A few minnys and such. Snakey, too."

"Hmmm. Wouldn't have guessed it." *He's playing games with me now.*

"Back in 'thirty-eight, worst flood I ever saw," he continued. "Covered this whole valley." His hand swept the landscape, then pointed. "Got up in the house there. Took half the barn away. Not a fence left on the place. Hard to imagine, lookin' at it now."

"Musta been some hard times," I sympathized again.

"Yup. Coulda been worse, though. Folks kinda hung together back then, what with the Depression and all. Helped each other out. Not like today, everybody just lookin' out for themselves. We've had our ups and downs here, all right, but it's been a good life."

Fine old gentleman, I thought. *Bet he's got some real tales to tell.*

"Hey! You two gonna stand out there in the sun all day? Get up here on the porch and have some lemonade."

It was Mrs. Smith calling from the door. She was everybody's idea of the perfect grandmother. Small and weathered, silver hair in a bun, but with a sparkle in her eye and a lilt in her slightly brassy voice.

"Comin', Momma," Mr. Smith called back.

"You two just sit down there, and I'll be right back."

She disappeared inside.

Rocking chairs. Old, with frayed cane bottoms and backs. Squeaky. The porch deck squeaks, too. *It's cool in the shade. I wish I could sit here forever.* Ol' Buck ambled over, crumpled in a heap, laid his chin on my foot, and gazed soulfully into my eyes.

Mrs. Smith reappeared. "Here you are, young man. Don't be bashful. There's plenty more."

Lemonade, with huge chunks of pulp floating in it. Ice tinkled against the glass as I swirled it. My fingers traced little pictures in the frost on the outside.

"Where you from, son?" Mr. Smith inquired.

"Missouri," I responded. "Ozark Mountains. Beautiful country."

"Whatcha doin' way out here?" he went on.

"Just trying to get away from it all for a while," I explained. "Does a fella good to blow off the dust every now and then. Get his head back in order. Listen to the birds sing. Watch some sunsets. Drink some old-fashioned lemonade. Maybe catch a fish or two. Makes life worth livin'.''

"How did you come to find us?" Mrs. Smith asked.

"I like to get off the beaten path, ma'am. Prowl the back roads, away from the crowds. Just never cared for all the touristy things most folks do. A fella in town said this was kind of a quiet corner of the county, with nice people and beautiful scenery. So here I am."

"We don't ask for much out here," she said gently. "Just the chance to see another day, a crop in the fall, church on Sunday, and seein' the young'uns as often as we can. We have four children—two sons and two daughters. Three grandchildren, too, and a great-grandchild due next month. You have children?"

"Oh, yes, ma'am," I replied. "A daughter, too. Full of mischief. We love her dearly. Here's a picture."

"Oh, she's cute as a ladybug. You're a very lucky young man."

"Yes, ma'am," I agreed.

"That a fishin' pole in the back of your car?" Mr. Smith broke in.

"Yes, sir," I responded. "Never leave home without it. Always a chance I might stumble onto something."

"Looks like one o' them fancy fly poles," he observed.

"Yeah, it's a fly rod, all right," I admitted. "Nothin' fancy about it, really. Had it forever. Most of the shine wore off years ago. It's kinda like Ol' Buck here—just real comfortable to have around. Caught a lotta fish in its day."

"Cookie?" Mrs. Smith offered.

Chocolate chip. Still warm, kinda gooey. "Thank you, ma'am. Mmm. Wummerfoo."

"Breeze sure feels good," Mr. Smith digressed.

"Smells good, too," I added. "Been mowin' hay?"

"Down by the creek," he replied. "Clover. Just fixin' to go back when you drove in."

Uh-oh, I thought. "Don't let me keep you from anything."

"That's all right, son. I've got time. What kinda fish you catch, mostly?"

"Oh, I like 'em all, sir. Bass, sunfish, trout. I like trout most of all, I guess."

"Why's that?" he asked.

"Y'know, I've thought a lot about that. I guess it's because they're so beautiful. You ever hold a little brook trout in your hand and study it? The sides are sky blue, with little crimson spots all over, and the belly's the brightest orange you've ever seen. Fins are, too, and they've got a coal-black edge on 'em. It's just like holding a handful of sunsets. They smell different, too. Not strong like most fish. Sorta like that clover on the breeze, with maybe a hint of talcum powder thrown in. There's other kinds, too—rainbows, cutthroats, browns. I love 'em all, but brookies are my favorite."

"Just catch little fish?" he chided.

I laughed. "Seems so, sometimes. Oh, I manage a bigger one every now and then. 'Bout like most folks, I guess. No better, no worse. I don't worry about it too much. Just the fun of trying for the big ones is enough."

"Nothin' better than a platter full o' fresh-caught fish, with some home-fried potatoes, an ear o' sweet corn, and a pot o' coffee brewed the old-fashioned way with egg shells in the bottom."

"You're sure right about that," I agreed. "I don't keep many fish anymore, though. A few bluegills, sometimes, but most others I put back."

"Why's that?" Mr. Smith asked.

"Well, sir, I finally figured out I'd have a lot more fun the second time I went somewhere if I didn't take 'em all home the first time. Lot more folks fishing now than there used to be, and there's only so many fish to go around. So I've kinda worked out a deal, especially with the trout. If they'll show me a good time, let me catch 'em every now and then, put up a good fight, I'll return the favor by letting 'em go. Seems fair enough for both of us."

Mr. Smith studied the porch deck for a moment, chin in hand. "Stay where you are," he directed. "I'll be right back."

He slipped inside, then reappeared with that little grin on his face again. "Let's take a walk, son. Wanna show you something. Might's well bring that fly pole along."

He led me around the house and through the back gate. It squeaked, too, just like the rocking chairs. Through the clover. Grasshoppers crackled. A crow called. It was still cool, but the afternoon promised to be a scorcher.

"Over this way," he motioned. We bore left, toward the fence.

The old gentleman stepped down on one strand of wire and lifted the one above it. "Go ahead," he invited. Through, I returned the favor.

"Step softly now," he cautioned. "Don't wanna shake the ground too much. Let's stop here."

We were at the creek. The same one back at the bridge. It was a little bigger here, but not by much. The morning sun filtered through maples vibrant with autumn color. A scarlet leaf spiraled lazily to the water, then drifted slowly away, spinning a little in the soft breeze. The only sounds were the drone of unseen insects, the clatter of grasshoppers, and the crow's insistent caw.

My host pointed to the far bank. "See that big hemlock leaning out over there? Look under it. Must be four feet deep. Fulla roots, too."

"Looks fishy," I remarked.

" 'Tis," he replied. "There's a trout under there big enough to chew your leg off. I call him Ol' Fred. First caught Ol' Fred six, maybe seven, years ago when he was just a little tyke. A few times since then, too, but the last was a couple years ago."

"Are you sure he's still there?" I questioned.

"Oh, yeah," Mr. Smith assured me. "I came down here last week with a jar fulla grasshoppers. Snuck up above there on my belly, laid still for a few minutes, then started flippin' 'em in so they'd drift right to him. First couple got by, but the third one never had a chance. Musta fed him a dozen or more. Ol' Fred's a real sucker for grasshoppers, all right. Here—give this a try."

A hopper. Deer hair. Size 8. *So that's what he went in the house for.* "Why, you crafty ol' rascal," I scolded. "You've been sandbaggin' me all along, haven'tcha? Here—why don't you show me how it's done?"

He grinned again, only bigger this time, like a wise little leprechaun. "No, no, no, son. Thanks, but I've had my turn at him, and I'll have more. Crawl up there real slow, now," he instructed. "Watch your shadow. What size tippet ya got?"

"Six-X," I said confidently.

"Too light," he admonished. "He'll be in the roots before you can turn him. Better go to three-X. Drift it downstream so he sees the hopper first. Just as the water gets deep there, give it a little twitch, then let it go."

Nerves. The worst I'd ever had. Casting blindly in the hope a big trout's there is one thing. Casting to a monster you know is there is something else. In front of an audience, worse yet. One little slip, and it's all over. I had ten thumbs and wrists of rubber.

After what seemed an eternity, I was ready. New tippet on, the hopper secured to its end. *Careful now, take it slow and easy. There's a stump I can crouch behind. Okay, let's sit a minute and calm down. Sidearm cast, rod low so he doesn't see it. Soft delivery, not too close. Here goes. Look out, Fred.*

No one could have been more amazed by the luck of my cast than I was. *E-e-e-asy. Pay out line. A little twitch right about here.*

A nose. A big nose. Lots of white under it, and an enormous shadow behind it. Not fast or violent. Just slow and deliberate, like something awesomely final.

Set the hook . . . now! Hang on. Get him outa there quick, before he's in the roots.

It was finished almost as soon as it had begun. A powerful lunge, one, two, three throbs telegraphed up the line, then—nothing.

Slowly, a shroud of reality settled over me. Nerves again, worse than before. My breath was ragged, my stomach felt awful. It was over. Or had I just imagined it?

Mr. Smith was at my side, his hand on my shoulder. "You did fine, son. Letter perfect. Wish I could do as well. Feel terrible, though, don'tcha?"

"Yeah," I stammered. "I'll never see another one like that again. Darn!"

"I can't tell ya how many times he's done the same thing to me," the old gentleman said softly. "But ya know, I've never forgotten a one of 'em. And you won't forget this one, either. Ol' Fred's still there, and there'll be another day.

"Soon's ya settle down, we'll have some more lemonade. Better yet, why not stay for lunch? If you thought Momma's cookies were good, you won't believe what she can do with a slab o' ham, some sweet corn, and tomatoes fresh outa the garden. And then, when your stomach's back in order, I'll take ya down around the bend and introduce ya to Ol' Fred's granddaddy."

A LONG WAY
FROM HOME

◆ ◆ ◆

STEPHEN J. BODIO

I DIDN'T MOVE TO MY PERCH ON THE EDGE OF THE MAGDALENA MOUN-tains in southwestern New Mexico for the trout fishing. But it's where I do much of my fishing now. As Thomas McGuane wrote in *The Heart of the Game*, "Hunting in your own back yard becomes with time, if you love hunting, less and less expeditionary."

What I don't want to do here is reinforce coastal prejudices about what kind of place the high plateaus here are. (Or then again, maybe I do; I mean, I don't want you to *move* here.) This is important: *I do not live in the desert.* Easterners in particular seem to think that the Southwest is like Phoenix without swimming pools—hundred-plus-degree temperatures, saguaro cacti, bare rock mountains, all-terrain vehicles, warm winters, sleepy Mexicans, taciturn cowboys, nuclear tests, Edward Abbey . . . You can name your own clichés.

If you are to understand fly-fishing here, you must first understand what manner of place I inhabit.

First, it's high country. If you leave the Rio Grande Valley at Socorro to take the only paved road west in a stretch of approximately 125 miles of state highway—the only way to get to Magdalena—you start your climb to the edge of the Rio's rift at an altitude of 4,500 feet above sea level.

Then you go up for twenty-six miles—steeply for the first half, then up an incline so slow it almost seems you are driving across a brown pool table. When you top out at the beginning of this subtly inclined part, you have already reached six thousand feet of altitude; by the time you reach Magdalena you will have have added another five hundred.

To your left, if it is winter, the Magdalenas look like the Alps, their jagged peaks covered with snow. They should: South Baldy, the highest peak, almost achieves eleven thousand feet. If you live in Magdalena, you live on a dry, grassy plain that is the same height as the tallest mountains in my native New England, staring south at those Pleistocene peaks. Remember the adjective *Pleistocene*, and let me wander a little further afield.

The second thing about this country—call it the Gila country for convenience—is that, even though it is cold and more likely to snow here in May or October than in Boston, it is dry. Oh, most winters you get a winter-long snowpack on the peaks that is deep enough to require snowshoes or cross-country skis. And when you venture up the mountain canyons in the spring, through meadows, under hundred-foot-tall ponderosas and Douglas firs (*not a desert, remember?*), you might think that the little stream cutting its way through the bottom would be ideal for small native trout.

But that's in April, when the snow is melting. Come back in June and the stream will have disappeared, leaving nothing but dry rocks and sand-rimmed puddles where, if you are very lucky, you may find the fresh print of an invisible mountain lion.

The stream will return, often bigger than it was in spring, after the daily thunderstorms of July and August. Sometimes, if it's a very wet year, it may flow, at least in a trickle, until winter freezes it solid.

What is going on here, besides modern cycles of drought or heat, is that these mountains have slowly been drying out since the time of the last glaciation. If Folsom man had been a fly-fisherman, he doubtless could have cast a fly over native cutthroats in Hop Canyon, not five miles by air from my house. However, since he was still dealing with imperial mammoths, oversized bison, saber-toothed cats, and dire wolves, he may not have had the leisure to contemplate catch-and-release fishing. Yes, there were trout here once, and not that long ago, either.

The next thing to think about in this country is that it is very big. There are enormous distances between very small towns, and to my southwest four paved roads enclose an area rather bigger than Connecticut that is inhabited by only 2,700 people. As you move southwest in this block, the forested mountain ranges become bigger, with smaller open plains between them. If you run along the pavement on the eastern or southern edge, you will never see water except in the Rio Grande, which, dozing under huge cottonwoods, is rather like the Nile in miniature—static most of the year and intensely diverted to agriculture. All of the old tributaries that lead down to it are barren, dry canyons, "sand rivers" that only flow in the spring or after thunderstorms. This, perversely, is a reason to treasure the high country.

Nobody goes there but locals—what could attract an Interstate tourist cruising Route 25 in his Winnebago to those distant blue mesas shimmering in the summer heat?

Well, for one thing, Canadian temperatures in July. And for another, trout. Native cutts, monster browns, stocked rainbows. The Magdalenas, perched on the plateau's edge, are too narrow and too exposed to hold enough water for permanent streams. Their next neighbors to the southwest, the San Mateos, are lusher and probably lost their trout later. But keep on pushing, almost against logic, to the southwest. When you reach about one hundred miles in any of several bearings from Magdalena, you will find the true remnants of the Pleistocene: blue spruce, willow, aspen. And streams. And more than one kind of good fishing.

Somewhat arbitrarily, I call any water that I can reach by taking one paved road a piece of "home" water. By this definition there are three such points: Quemado Lake, the Rio Grande, and the San Francisco River. And since Quemado Lake is—well, I'll tell you in a moment—I'll add one more, one I can reach by way of a 125-mile *unpaved* road: Willow Creek, which in its modest way may be the best of all.

◆   ◆   ◆

Quemado Lake is a high-country impoundment about ninety miles from Magdalena that can be reached by way of the main highway, a picturesque two-lane that travels across the Continental Divide and through three tiny towns. Although it is man-made, it is "pretty"—a still, blue cup surrounded by tall ponderosas. All my neighbors go there for what they call trout fishing.

Now, I am far from a fly snob or, for that matter, a trout snob; I have written elsewhere of my love for catfish and live bait. But, for me, the method and what I hate to call the ambience have to be appropriate to the quarry. I don't ground-sluice prairie chickens, hunt sparrows with my peregrine falcon, or use my 10-bore for Mearns' quail.

At Quemado, there is a parking lot. Half of it is usually full of trailers and RVs. The fishermen and -women, many of them friends of mine, sit in chairs along the lakeside with two or more spinning rods propped beside them. The preferred baits are Velveeta and "fireballs." The trout are often sixteen inches long, grain-fed piscine cattle, and, you know, I'd just as soon go to the Safeway. It's only twenty-six miles away, and freezing doesn't seem to do too much to harm the taste of hatchery fish that are so slow-witted and voracious they seem to spend no more than a week in the little lake's artificial "freedom." I suspect they're *scared* of insects.

And even if they weren't, fly-fishing for such fish is preposterous. You can't dignify supermarket fishing by using fancy tools. My friends have the right idea.

So, ascending: the Rio Grande. I don't use the fly rod much on the Big River, either. Whether the Rio is a "natural" river is a moot question, but it *is* full of fish, large and small, of many species, all wild. My favorite quarry there are monster catfish, and tying a fly to mimic a ten-inch salamander would be an odd proposition, even if I owned a rod heavy enough to cast it. Still, there are times in the spring when you can take a little boat up into the flooded cottonwoods, where the river begins to give way to the head of Elephant Butte Reservoir, and imagine yourself to be in some Deep South bayo, minus the alligators and most of the mosquitoes. You can take the eight-weight Fenwick and some hairy poppers made from the hair of last year's deer and entice splashy strikes from largemouth bass guarding their beds. Or you can take a handful of old shad flies that first saw service on Massachusetts tidal streams a decade past and work the runoff-swollen ditches for gleaming metallic yellow bass that are like tiny, deep-bodied, lemon stripers. (For that matter, the Montana painter, writer, and angler Russell Chatham insists that someday we will take a boat and penetrate Elephant Butte's immense reaches, where we will refine saltwater fly-fishing techniques for stripers and transform "desert" reservoir fishing. I'll do it, when the time comes. But there's something purely shocking to a kid who grew up in the last glory days of the New England striper surf to *see* a striped bass in New Mexico, never mind catch one on a fly. . . .)

So, back to the high country again, a hundred and more miles west into the plateau, to the San Francisco, one of the Gila River's headwaters. This is pure New Mexico fly-fishing, right down the middle. Which is to say it's good, it's consistent, the fish are big, and it looks, as they say here, *real different.* For instance: rock walls, often more than a hundred feet high, over the stream. There are few trees except on sandbars, and those mostly willows and young cottonwoods that will be swept away by the next flood, or tropical-looking walnuts hung with curtains of wild grape in the rare broad stretches.

But also: roaring water, deep holes, the energizing smell of wet air. And birds everywhere: familiar, tipsy spotted sandpipers; tropical tanagers and Scott's orioles like Christmas ornaments; vermilion fly-catchers like coals from the woodstove that snap up insects in repetitive motions, mechanical-toy predators; swallows looping, like crosses between falcons and dragonflies; herons groaning in protest, lumbering into the air, then levitating upstream.

And fish! I fish streamers here, and Woolly Buggers, and big hairy nymph-type deals I tie myself. With them, I catch nice rainbows and the occasional killer brown. Also, to my entire delight, smallmouth bass, which I have been in love with since I lived on the Saco River in Maine and caught them on minnow imitations trolled behind my canoe in the dusk. And once in a while—on the same flies—a muscular and graceful channel cat. While I stoutly maintain that it's an affectation to try to catch a catfish on a fly, I can't suppress a giggle of pleasure when I see one rolling in the wash with a fly designed for New England lakes dangling amidst the whiskers. Variety is the spice of life—in the catching, as well as in the later, and most pleasing, eating.

◆   ◆   ◆

But the best of my home waters, not in quantity or size or culinary reward, or almost anything but pure aesthetics, is this last: Willow Creek. I only get up there a couple of times a year because I'm busy and poor and it's a long, grueling four-wheel trip to the Gila's deep mountain stream. Still, that's best, too: I can remember how sick I got of a diet of stripers, quahogs, lobsters, and mussels—how occasionally tiresome even the rituals of obtaining them became—when I lived for a year in a one-room shack on the New England coast and of necessity did nothing but hunt and fish and gather and worry.

Willow Creek is caviar from the Caspian. It's tiny; you don't need waders. It's brushy and foggy and cold and surrounded by dank stands of fir and wet meadows full of a rare, semiaquatic subspecies of garter snake. It looks as though it should have grizzlies, which indeed it should; we lost our last ones here in the thirties, and some inspired maniac should put them back.

There are a few stocked trout here, trickling down from a remote high-country lake. But the real fish here are eight-inch native cutthroats. Like most small-stream native trout, they resemble cloisonné ornaments and have deep-red flesh. However, despite my unregenerate piscivory, I rarely keep one; they have a hard enough time surviving near-glacial winters and periodic, scouring floods. Come to think of it, though, they do a lot better here than the big, soft stockers, and they have been here a lot longer.

The fishing is unrefined by spring-creek standards. I use mostly terrestrials. Apart from being the natives' most natural summer food source, terrestrials delight me because they look like something real—a grasshopper, an ant, a beetle—without leading me down the tiresome and time-consuming path of hatch-matching. And if your heart doesn't thrill to see one of these parakeet-brilliant little dinosaurs hit a perfect grasshopper on the surface with an audible *bap!* then you are not welcome to fish with me or brag about your fishing.

◆   ◆   ◆

Are these my home streams forever? I don't know. They say there's some great fishing across the Big River near Ruidoso, where Sierra Blanca towers twelve thousand feet above real desert. But there are Texans there and condos and German elk hunters who pay five thousand dollars a head to shoot semitame elk. It's interesting, but I feel I leave my *querencia,* my heart's home, when I cross the Rio Grande.

Being that odd kind of homeless person that every writer is, I know that I might someday pull up stakes and go someplace where there are more water, more trout, and grouse—Taos, maybe, where the Rio Grande resembles a monstrous version of the San Francisco, or even Montana, where a by-no-means-rich friend of mine just bought a place with a stream the size of Willow Creek running through it. I hear there is a great falconry in Idaho, and steelhead on the borders. . . .

And yet, I have something here, a whole life in a wild place, and things to do. My diverse enthusiasms, from Gila cutts to horses to gyrfalcons to books, and even New York City, can all be indulged here at the appropriate times. I do not envy the city-bound, even though they have more money than I, fly to Iceland and Yellowstone to go fishing, and have more entertainment than I can find at the Golden Spur Bar. And I know some of them envy me. Here, a hundred miles from some of my home water, I have learned a few things that I can not even wholly comprehend yet. One of them is that home, and home water, can be a long way from home.

WHERE THE
HEART IS

● ● ●

ROBERT F. JONES

MY FIRST LOVE WAS COLD AND BROWN AS OLD IRON, STRONG ENOUGH
during breakup to gnaw away the roots of old cottonwoods along her
banks and send them tumbling like drowned ogres, groaning and
crackling and shaggy with skinned bark as they rolled through tan
foam down toward Lake Michigan. Great ice floes ran with them,
packing up at times in the shallows to form cold, brown lakes that
flooded the low-lying woods on either bank, then carrying away finally
with a roar like coupling freight cars. Huge slabs of ice flipped
skyward—a giant's tiddlywinks—along with sords of mallards and
springs of teal, spooked by the explosions. Men ran the river in flood-
time in the heavy, cedar-ribbed canvas canoes of the day. I remember
standing with my father on a newly built Federal Works Project bridge
one raw April morning in 1941 and watching the canoeman dodging
among the ice floes, racing the drowned trees downriver. I was not
quite seven years old, and I clutched my dad's hand for all I was worth.
He grinned down at me out of his mustache: "Say, Bobby, don't you
just love a big wild river?"

But in summer—all the summers of my boyhood—the river was
calm and deep-voiced, slow-spoken as a good schoolmaster: clear of
meaning but swift when it came to corrections. It taught me a lot.
How to pole a flimsy, jerrybuilt raft of basswood logs and scrap lumber
(*Poseidon* was her magical name) down swift, deep runs, and the best
way (there was no easy way) to skid her through mud banks; how to
remove leeches (we called them bloodsuckers) with a sprinkle of salt
rather than yanking them off with part of your hide; how to trap
muskrats and raccoons and opossums and once a mink in the dead of
winter in bankset number 1 and 1½ steel traps, and how to skin them
out, stretch them, and salt them down. In the woods beside the river
I could be Tarzan or Jim Bridger ("Old Gabe, the Blanket Chief"); in

the river itself I could be a South Seas pearl diver plumbing the depths (all six feet of them) for nacreous treasure or a UDT frogman scouting the reefs of Tarawa under enemy fire. The nacreous treasure was actually freshwater-mussel shell; the reefs, glacial gravel—no matter, they were good enough for me.

The fish were better, though. No pretense, no imagination, was necessary to start my heart racing when their long, dark shadows lanced out from the bankside shadows and disappeared upstream in the wink of an eye. When I'd seen enough dragonflies disappear in a sudden, violent splash, enough leopard frogs vanish in midkick, leaving only evanescent and rapidly widening concentric circles on the water to remember them by; when I noticed that often in early summer at dawn and at dusk the river's smooth surface was pocked with interlocking rise rings as if by an invisible ball-peen hammer, I knew I had to take action. I "liberated" an old rod of my dad's from the attic—an 8½-foot Heddon, all cracked varnish and rusty snake guides, with an ancient Pflueger fly reel—blew half a summer's lawn-mowing earnings on a new HDG oiled-silk fly line and a supply of gut leaders, "borrowed" a few bass bugs, dries, streamers from the paternal fly box, and sallied forth one sultry June morning. The fly rod was couched like a bamboo lance as I spurred my fat-wheeled Schwinn charger down to the riverside tilting grounds on my Quest for the Aqueous Grail.

That day was a revelation. So far, I'd only fished "Up North," during the two or three weeks each summer when my folks rented a cottage on one or another of Wisconsin's myriad lakes. I'd graduated from cane poles, worms, and panfish—bluegills, rock bass, yellow perch, and crappies: tasty little buggers, all of them—to a plug-casting rod for bass, pike, and walleyes. Soon after my tenth birthday the previous spring, my dad had started me on the fly rod, casting short distances from a rowboat for nesting sunfish in the shallows of nearby Okauchee Lake. It was the perfect fly-rod kindergarten: bushy dry flies thrown at close range to plenty of visible, stationary, and aggressive targets. Where the nests were close together, even a flubbed cast would usually produce an exciting strike and often an inadvertent hookup. Nothing builds confidence in a kid quicker than catching a lot of fish. Soon he's casting without thinking about it—none of this boring "elbow-in, locked-wrist, one-o'clock, drift, powerstroke" bullshit—and just getting the fly where he wants it when he wants it, regardless of range, wind, or difficulty of lie. He's ready for the real thing: bright trout in moving water.

Ground fog hung low on the water as I approached the river that morning. The sun loomed huge and dull red through mist-shrouded popples; a great blue heron creaked off in high dudgeon as I pushed through the alders and waded out knee-deep on a gravel bar. I was wearing high-cut canvas Keds with my Levis tucked into my socktops to discourage bloodsuckers, and the water felt chilly. A pair of mallards came toward me out of the mist, spotted me, squawked, and hurriedly reversed course upstream. Fish were rising out there in the fog. I tied on a big, fat Adams for openers, worked out a reasonable length of fly line, and with my teeth starting to chatter like Carmen Miranda's castanets, delivered. The fly alighted out of sight in the mist, a straight-enough cast, but then the line started coming back at me on the water, crooked as a snake. Something splashed out there and the line jerked. I struck—and picked up nothing but slack. I stripped in line like a mad masturbator. Nothing.

I'd learned my first lesson about running water.

It took me all morning to figure out natural drift, even longer to overcome the drag imparted to my Adams the moment the line started to belly downstream. (Years later, I read somewhere that the procedure I formulated that morning was called mending line, and whole chapters were devoted to it in the sacred fly-casting texts.) As a result, I caught only one fish that morning—a five-inch creek chub (but a game little rascal!)—before the sun burned off the fog and put down the rise.

But my luck improved with my skill through the course of that summer. I learned to trail streamers down through the riffles into long, slow pools, then retrieve them with rapid jerks and frequent pauses that sometimes produced pickerel, and once a twenty-inch northern. I discovered (to my disappointment) that suckers will take a dry fly, right off the top of the water—thirteen in a row one morning off a deep, riprap, outside bend that I was sure had to hold a big trout. I experimented with deer-hair bugs—gaudy green and yellow and black monstrosities of my own devising—until I found the back eddies and current edges where bass hung out: tough, chunky bronzebacks for the most part, none of them bigger than about a pound, but as game a gang of scrappers as ever bent a rod; and now and then a bigger, tougher, broader-shouldered largemouth.

Not until summer's end, though, did I hook a trout. I'd begun by that time to wonder if, indeed, there were trout in the river. Maybe it was too warm for them. I thought I'd seen them occasionally, sipping flies from the surface when the caddises came off in droves at dusk, or flashing their sides butter-yellow as they grubbed for nymphs in the deep, gravel-bedded pools. But I didn't yet know how to tie, much less fish, a nymph, and my casting was still too clumsy to raise one to a dry fly. I'd about given up.

Then I came to the river at dusk, on the last day of summer.

School had resumed and with it, football practice. I had the beginnings of a charley horse in one leg, both elbows were skinned (along
with the bridge of my nose—no face masks in that era of leather
helmets), and I could taste grass, mixed with mud or blood, in the
back of my throat. It had rained earlier in the week, one of those cold,
slashing rains out of the northwest where winter lurks year-round,
followed by a cold, coin-bright high out of Canada that left the lawns
silver at sunup and withered the last tomatoes in the victory gardens.
The river glinted cold as brass under a gunmetal sky; the weakening
sun looked bilious. A big fish was rising steadily at the head of a run
upstream of me, along the other bend of a back eddy. Head-and-tail
rises, three or four a minute, then a pause for maybe a minute or two,
then the rises again. As I waded up into casting range, I saw mayfly
duns coming down between me and the bank. Big duns with smoky
wings, placid on the water until they were ready to take flight, when
they started twitching and skipping to get off the water. I tied on a big
Mahogany Drake, about a number 10. My dad had given me a handful
of them that very morning. "They used to come off about now on the
Wolf," he said. "The trout went crazy for them, big browns. But I
don't know if Mahoganies happen down here."

"That's okay," I said. "I don't even know if *trout* happen down
here. They haven't happened to me yet."

"They will," he said, grinning through his mustache.

I stood shivering within forty feet of the riser. The water was up
to my crotch, and I could feel the current flapping my soaked jeans,
scouring the gravel from under my sneakers. A dirty-black cloud with
rain in its teeth scudded over the setting sun. The riser was resting
now, and I took advantage of his break to work out line until I had the
range. *Okay, he's been down a minute.* . . . I dropped the fly just where
I wanted it, upstream and a bit to the left of the riser, so that the curve
of the eddy would dead-drift it over his lie. I flipped in a tad of
upstream mend and focused on the floating silhouette of the fly—big
and black as a pirate ship in that gloomy light.

The fish took me by surprise—the huge head suddenly surfacing,
the open-and-shut slash of the jaws, the downward swoop of dorsal
and tail left me paralyzed for a second or two. Thank God it did,
otherwise in my eagerness I might have taken the fly right out of his
mouth. When I tightened on him, I felt something heavy and solid
and vibrant, but only for the instant it took him to feel the bite of the
hook. Then he exploded. A great muscular, shining shape—black and
old gold, head shaking in a flurry of pewter-colored water—erupted
once, twice, then twice more as he raced upstream. At first I thought
it must be a smallmouth, the biggest I'd hooked in the river. But the

afterimage of the jump showed spots on his sides—big maroon and black spots the size of dimes. *Dear God, let it be a brown.* And it was. Ten minutes later I'd worn him down and worked him in to the shallows. He was on his side now, and I could see his hooked jaw working, the shabby fly firm in the corner of his mouth. I had no landing net, so I got the toe of my sneaker under him and, with a punt that would have done the Green Bay Packers proud, levitated him into the willow scrub. I pounced on him like a fumble. I was shaking, but not from the cold.

I'd like to tell you how I unhooked him tenderly, gently; how I carried him in both hands back to the water and worked him back and forth in the current until his gills were pulsing, until I felt him squirming in my hands; I'd like to tell you how he finally burst away from me with a contemptuous flirt of his tail, a golden tail as broad as my hand is long. But that would be a lie, because I didn't. Catch-and-release would come later, much later, along with maturity. Instead, I brained him with the haft of my bone-handled Case knife, ran him up to where I'd left my bike in the roadside weeds, and pedaled as fast as I could back home—forgetting even my fly rod there on the bank—with the big fish glassy-eyed in the basket, bent and stiffening but with both his head and tail sticking over the edges, to show him off to my folks. He was twenty inches long, fat as butter, and pushed four pounds on my dad's spring scale. We ate him that night for supper.

◆   ◆   ◆

That was forty-five years ago, on the Menomonee River in southern Wisconsin, just west of Milwaukee. I remember it clear as a crystal, honor bright. It was my first "home water," and first things last forever. The Menomonee's dead now—outflanked by the surge of suburban expansion, silted up six inches deep over its ancient gravel beds, home only to carp and the occasional bullhead. It was moribund even when I last lived in Milwaukee, after college and three years in the U.S. Navy. That was in 1959, and I remember driving along the river one bleak fall day shortly after my return, indulging in sweet melancholy, savoring memories (as only a young man can) of old loves now blighted, probing the irrecoverable past the way you would an aching tooth: just to suffer a little (but not too much). I saw a county maintenance truck parked on the shoulder, signs reading MEN WORKING IN TREES, and heard the snarl of chain saws. I stopped and walked down to the river. A gang of workmen across the shallow stream was "removing" a huge, blighted elm tree. I remembered that tree from of old: It had stood, alive, in the middle of an impenetrable thicket of popple and briars. We'd hacked our way into it one winter when we were trapping this stretch of the river, and we'd measured the elm's girth at breast height by our arm spans. We hugged the old tree around its circumference, about sixty feet of hugs. Now the tree was dead, and the rocks in the river were trailing long tendrils of green slime in the weak, silty current. The chain saws yowled and a crow flapped past, peering down curiously.

For me, at least, the Menomonee died in that moment. But not the love for home water. I've known many fisheries since then, east and west, north and south, across the seas and in them. Beaverkill, Willowemoc, and Delaware; Penobscot, Housatonic, and Spruce Creek. Madison, Bitterroot, Henry's Fork; the Frying Fan and the South Platte, above Decker's. The Togiak, the Situk, and the Ogilvie north of Dawson. Even the Tongariro and the Mararoa and the feeders of Lake Te Anau in New Zealand; even the bonefish flats and tarpon passes of the Caribbean: from Andros to Roatán to Parismina and back up to the Dry Tortugas. All of that could have been home water for me, as it was to the locals I fished with. But you have to live there for it to take: know the birds and trees and the texture of weather through many seasons, know the old-timers who live in that country and something of its legends, the good spots to stop in after a day on the water for a beer or a cup of coffee or half an hour of good, gritty, down-home talk. Only then do the quiet places—runs and pools, riffles and nymphing holes—take on the necessary resonance.

Right now my home water is the Mettawee River in southwestern Vermont. It's a quiet, unassuming little freestoner that runs through farmland, among worn-down old mountains, breaking now and then over time-smoothed slate ledges, full of small rainbows and a few brown trout. Word has it the trout are wild: Vermont doesn't stock the Mettawee, and the fish sure don't act or look like stockies. So far, the river has maintained its fecundity. There's lots of bugs—a good Hen-drickson hatch, loads of caddises and stoneflies, a steady, summer-long production of Blue-winged Olives. From time to time I see March Browns on the water—not enough to provoke a rise of trout, though. Early one season I saw a big hatch of Quill Gordons, but that was a few years back and it hasn't been repeated. There's a little bit of every-thing on the Mettawee, and a lot of smallish trout eager to play. Worm-flingers and hardware types work it hard after a spate of rain, but that's a hazard everywhere, nowadays. At least there are no canoes—it's too shallow most of the year. There's plenty of POSTED signs, though—more every year.

So it's a peaceful little river—one that, like sleep, "knits up the raveled sleave of care, the death of each day's life, sore labor's bath, balm of hurt minds . . ." And that's what home water is all about.

◆   ◆   ◆

A hot summer day in late June, getting on toward three o'clock. Lots of daylight left. I jounce down a two-track through fields of cow corn, headed for the river. It's not a fat-wheeled Schwinn anymore, but a clapped-out half-ton GMC pickup with eighty thousand up-and-down miles on the odometer. I park near the bank—good, no other vehicles. The river crashes down toward me through a narrow granite gorge, but I know that above it lies a quieter stretch of deep pools alternating with pocket water and sinuous riffles, flanked by high, rocky, pine-topped bluffs. It will be still in there, no wind, no other anglers. And very hot. Too hot for chest-highs, so I'll wade wet, as much for old times' sake as comfort.

I joint up the rod—graphite now, not battered bamboo, an Orvis 8½-foot, 2¾-ounce "Western Two"—and pull on my vest, then head up a narrow, winding footpath along the left bank, through young pines and briars, to the head of the gorge. Along the way a woodcock jumps almost from underfoot and twitters off, dodging through the pine tops. I file away the memory for autumn.

At the top of the gorge, the river widens, gathering itself for the plunge, and I squat at the edge, watching. There's nothing coming off the water, only a few caddis flies, straw-yellow in the sunlight, dive-bombing the riffles to oviposit. It's not a dry-fly kind of day. I string up the rod, clinch on a number 14 Gold-ribbed Hare's Ear nymph, add a single split shot a foot and a half above the fly, and wade out into the river. To hell with a strike indicator—the fly line is fluorescent yellow, and if I can't see it twitch to a trout's quick, invisible touch down there on the bottom, I don't deserve to catch him.

The water is cold, refreshingly so on such a hot day, about sixty or sixty-two degrees Fahrenheit, I'd guess. I used to carry a stream thermometer and record water temperatures assiduously, copying them into my fishing log, comparing them with hatches, then comparing both with data from seasons past. Pretending to make a science out of what should be no more than a pleasant sport. Or is it an art? No, let's not get grandiose. Then, one cold day on the Yellow Branch of the Nulhegan, a couple of years ago in the Northeast Kingdom of upstate Vermont, the thermometer slipped from my numb fingers and rolled away into the current. I never replaced it, never really missed it.

Dredging the channels with my nymph, I work slowly upstream from pool to pool. Getting into it now, the hypnotic focus of upstream nymphing, feeling the split shot tick the bottom as it bounces downstream, imagining the Hare's Ear down there, trailing just behind, swirling and eddying now and then, up and down, sideways, flashing its golden, chitinous come-on to the trout, its hackles stirring in the current like the legs and gills of some hapless, helpless aquatic larva being swept downstream: *Come and eat me, Mister Trout!*

I pause at the bottom of a long, deep, fast run that over the years has always produced at least one good-sized fish, sometimes three or four. There's a bit of a breeze stirring the tops of the white pines on the bluff to my left, but still no wind down on the river. Behind the pines, I know, starts the old cemetery. A friend of mine is buried up there, a guy I'd gotten to know since I moved to Vermont ten, no, eleven years ago. He wasn't a fisherman or a bird hunter, but he was a helluva fine guy anyway—a gentleman and a winning driver of harness-racing horses. I think of him buried up there, on the bluff overlooking the river, whenever I fish past. Not a bad place to spend eternity.

I flip the weighted nymph up into the head of the run and strip back line under my rod finger as it ticks back down to me, keeping the rod high over my head and parallel to the water, watching the yellow fly line for that telltale twitch. Once, twice, three times the nymph probes the channel, and on the fourth dead drift the line jumps six inches upstream. I set the hook. Something heavy, vibrant, almost electric, shoots its charge up leader and line and rod into my arm. The old fire lights in my heart. The line cuts up through the water and the surface erupts once again, old but always new, forever thrilling, and a bright, broad-sided rainbow trout vaults into the sunlight in a scatter of spray, the red stripe down his flanks and gill covers brilliant in the air. The Menomonee strikes again, only now it's called the Mettawee.

Home water is where the heart is.

THE CONSOLATION OF THE POND

. . .

GEORGE REIGER

To UNDERSTAND HOW I CAME BY MY LITERAL HOME WATER, YOU SHOULD know that I'm a refugee from the American dream—or at least that part of it that tends toward conventional notions of success.

Disillusionment for me began early, in a glorified cram school whose principal interest in students was in what we could do to drive up the institution's Ivy League acceptance curve. I found variations on this theme in college and graduate school, and further disappointment in my early career as a teacher and, later, as a magazine editor.

All the while, I was writing and even occasionally selling what I wrote. I tried science and science fiction, political history and natural history, short stories, long stories, plays, and a novel. But parents, teachers, and friends all assured me that it was impossible to make a living free-lancing unless I were either very good or very lucky— implying that I was neither. They urged me to settle down. "You can always use your writing in business or law," they said. "Or save it for your retirement."

By the time I was twenty-five, I knew that each story and book I'd already postponed would never get written. And two tours in Vietnam and a Purple Heart had confirmed my suspicion that life is too brief and too fragile to spend the prime of it doing only what others expect of you.

In 1969, I began an editorial apprenticeship at a do-it-yourself magazine—no intellectual magazine would then touch a supposedly bloodstained veteran—with the hope of eventually taking my writing skills and editorial contacts to a farm in Virginia where I could be, as Captain John Smith told prospective colonists, "master of my own labor and land."

After two years of working in New York, and with a new wife

who was making a comparable income at a book publisher's, I was again tempted to postpone my leap into space. Editing other people's work is much easier than wrestling with one's own, and moving outside commuter radius of New York City would put me beyond the usual editorial safety lines. But I crossed my fingers and made the leap. Many of my former colleagues still distrust my judgment in deciding to move to the rural South. ("What do you read?" they ask. "The same as you do," I reply, "books and magazines." "What do you talk about?" they ask. "The same as you," I reply, "nothing.")

Before flinging himself over the edge of the abyss, a free-lance writer must make for himself a sturdy hang glider (meaning dependable markets). If he succeeds in doing this, however, he can ride the uncertain thermals of literary life for a career that is more deeply satisfying than any city-bound editor's. Furthermore, an impecunious free-lance living in a rural setting can afford a lifestyle that better-paid urbanites cannot.

Take my tackle shed, for example. Although my annual income wouldn't cover the initiation fee for some posh fishing clubs, where wealthy anglers keep their tackle in small private lockers, I have an entire outbuilding dedicated to angling gear and oddities. I acquired the shed for nothing and brought it across a field from a neighboring farm. I paid Norman West, our local harness-racer and house-mover, forty dollars to put the structure on a travois, drag it over the intervening ground, jack it up over a new foundation, and drop it into place. For a few hundred dollars more, I had the building patched up, painted, electrified, and even insulated so I can putter about there in the heat of summer or the cold of winter.

A club fisherman is mostly limited to the private waters his fraternity owns or leases: typically, less than a mile of stream, or a small lake. By contrast, for five dollars—the cost of an Accomack County fishing license—and the permission of landowners, I have seven large private ponds to fish that are less than thirty minutes from my home, and a dozen more within the county.

Christopher, my twelve-year-old son, and I load our small canoe into the back of my pickup and are fishing on the best of these ponds—sometimes with a bass or bluegill on one or both of our lines— less than twenty minutes after walking out the back door. We start fishing as early as the first warm spell in February and stay on fresh water until late May. Then we take a summer break to pursue flounder in the marshes and tuna offshore, returning to the farm ponds in September and October. By that time, the biting flies are gone and the mosquitoes are only half as bad as they are in June. We start with small spinners in February, step up to streamers in March, and graduate to hair bugs in April and May. In September and October, when crickets and grasshoppers are abundant, we switch to poppers.

My neighbors are mostly saltwater fishermen, so Christopher and I rarely encounter other anglers. I further discourage competition by showing around articles concerning the high levels of pesticides that are now found in farm-pond fishes. My neighbors, who can't imagine fishing except to keep and eat what you catch, wonder why my son and I continue fishing for such contaminated fare. (In fact, my family rarely eats the freshwater fish we catch, not only because we're concerned about carcinogens, but because we find freshwater fish bland fare alongside the crabs, oysters, clams, periwinkles, flounder, weakfish, spot, mackerel, tuna, wahoo, and dolphinfish we catch in nearby coastal waters.)

We enjoy releasing the bass and bluegills—but not where they were caught. Thanks to Virginia's freshwater angling regulations, we can fish for bass and bluegills year-round and keep any size, so long as we don't keep more than five bass and fifty bluegills per angler per day. Christopher and I sit in our canoe with five-gallon buckets in front of each of us. We fill our buckets with water, then with fish, as we cast our way around neighbors' ponds. We bring the fish back alive and put them into one of the four ponds I've dug on our farm.

Two of these ponds are more like runoff sumps, and one is an irrigation canal. Fish survive in them, but don't thrive in them. However, the largest pond, the one within sight of the house, is a thing of cornucopian beauty that is enjoyed by herons, egrets, mergansers, cormorants, ospreys, and otters as much as by us—which is the reason my son and I must make frequent spring trips to our neighbors' ponds to replace the bass, bluegills, and occasional white crappie that disappear down the gullets of herons, egrets, mergansers, cormorants, ospreys, and otters.

The eight-inch bass that Christopher and I catch each spring and release into our home water can be scrappy half-pounders by fall. Two- and three-pounders may eventually reach weights of more than five pounds, but we've never caught any bigger than that. Either such lunkers outwit us or, more likely, the shallow edges of the three islands in our two and a half acres of water provide insufficient food for really big bass to develop.

One autumn, I was able to amaze guests by "calling" bass whenever we walked down to the pond. Of course, I always went to the same spot with a supply of crickets I had found under a piece of tin roofing left on the ground for that very purpose, or with a supply of mummichog "minnows" from the marsh. I'd make appropriate "hawgcalling" sounds as I approached the pond. The bass would congregate, probably because they'd felt our footfalls through their lateral-line organs. The first tossed cricket or minnow would be taken with a rush. By the sixth or seventh bait, the water would be churned white by the bass' feeding frenzy. For added effect, I'd admonish "Boris" or "Belinda" not to be too greedy.

I stopped doing it when I realized I'd trained an osprey to come as well. After my guests and I would move away from the edge of the pond, the osprey would move in to take advantage of the incautious bass.

◆ ◆ ◆

I like to share my neighbors' ponds with my son in the spring, but try to reserve our home water for him and his friends in the fall, long after the wood ducks and mallards that nest in boxes around the edge of the pond have fledged their broods and gone. Some days, however, I need to get away from the house and office and fish the pond by myself. Although I don't always return with a solution to whatever problem compelled me to seek solace there, I do return better able to handle whatever the real world throws my way. The pond is a good place to escape without ducking my responsibilities altogether. I'm still close enough to the house to see the Federal Express truck drive up, but too far away to hear the phone ring.

Fly-fishing is wonderful therapy. The mesmerizing repetition of casting, the concentration on targets, the pondering of all possibilities—these work to drive other, less immediate, and often darker thoughts from my mind.

The pleasure of fishing my home water begins when I drop a popper an inch away from a snag that is sixty or seventy feet away. The pleasure grows as I sit and wait. On a still day, with the canoe barely moving from where I made the cast, the suspense may build through half a minute before I twitch the lure. Whether the water explodes with the rush of a yearling fish or the popper is surreptitiously slurped under with barely a ripple by an older and wiser bass, each subsequent surge and leap is as exhilarating to me today as when I felt my first largemouth at the end of a line more than forty years ago.

Best of all, no matter how much pressure or sorrow I left ashore, everything's bearable when I return. The consolation of my pond is like that of a good woman: she isn't very demanding, but you do have to tend to her various, sometimes subtle, needs. Her finite, diminutive size offers infinite companionship and surprise to someone who still doesn't know whether he's a writer who enjoys fishing or an angler who needs to write.

WEST FORK

◆ ◆ ◆

CAROLINE GORDON

IT SEEMED TO ME THAT FEBRUARY WOULD NEVER END. I HAD ALREADY resolved that I would go fishing the first day the weather permitted and had anticipated the season by buying myself a new rod. I spent a great deal of time those dreary winter afternoons going over my tackle or walking about on the spongy lawn estimating how long it would take the water courses to get back to normal.

Then, on March 3, just as I thought the back of the cold spell was broken, came a tremendous storm. Mr. Fayerlee coming in about four o'clock from attending to some lambs reported that "there was a very queer sky out there." Tom and I hurried out and stood for some minutes on the porch watching a darkish gray cloud roll up from the northwest. As we turned to go in the house the snow began falling. It fell all that afternoon and throughout the night. When we got up the next morning it was banked even with the porch floor, and it would lie three or four feet deep, Mr. Fayerlee said, in the valleys. It was out of the question for school to keep; most of the scholars lived two or three miles from the schoolhouse; so I did not even attempt to make the trip that morning.

◆ ◆ ◆

A warm wind sprang up on Friday and the snow began to melt. But the ground was still covered when I started out on Saturday to ride down to Peacher's Mill for the mail. . . . The wind had changed in the night and there was a light crust of sleet over the road. The old mare kept her footing but I had to ride very slowly. We were over an hour traversing the two miles to the mill.

It was from the top of a high hill that I had my first glimpse of the stream—a shallow stretch lying between the bridge and the mill pond and off to the right in a clump of trees and miller's tall, whiteverandaed house. There were no signs of life about the mill, so I rode up to the house. The miller himself came out on the porch and informed me that there was no mail; the road between Peacher's and Gloversville was still impassable and the boy had not been able to get through. He invited me to come in and warm myself before starting back but I assured him that I was warm enough and got on my horse again to go home.

As I stood on the porch talking to him I got a sight of the stream flowing dark beneath its crust of snow and ice and the fancy suddenly came upon me to have a look at it before I went home. I rode on back to the mill, hitched my horse, and made my way down the slippery bank.

The stream makes a turn immediately above the mill pond. I was confronted almost at once with an ideal formation, a bold limestone bluff on one side, on the other, low ground that was in all probability a sand bar. A man could hardly ask for more. But I was eaten by curiosity to know what the rest of the stream was like. I scrambled along the muddy bank holding onto the bushes until I had rounded the bend. I stood here for some minutes sizing things up. The more I saw the better I liked the prospect. The water flowing strongly broke here and there over ridges of ice. That meant riffles. I judged that along here it would be only shoe-mouth deep in some places and yet all along were dark patches that must be pools. The bank I had been walking on shelved suddenly. I had to descend and walk for some way on the ice that edged the stream. I was able to make my way up the creek for over a mile in this way. What I saw continued to delight me. Recurring over and over was the same ideal formation of bold lime-stone bluff and sand bar and nearly always room between the water and the bluff to make your way.

It was nearing four o'clock by this time and I knew that it would be dark long before I got home. I made my way back as best I could. On the path I stopped once to look back. From there the whole surface of the stream seemed sheathed in ice, black water breaking through only occasionally. But it seemed to me that it was flowing even more strongly in the short time I had been there and at the edges of the stream chunks of ice were breaking continually from their moorings. It could not be long now until the whole stream was free. I turned and made my way up the hill. Lights were on in the miller's house and as I was about to get on my horse he called to me from the porch. The boy had come with the mail. I rode back to the house and took the packet for Merry Point. There were three letters in it for me from Molly.

◆   ◆   ◆

Four days of perfect sunshine cleared the snow off the ground in what seemed a miraculously short time. Winter was gone, as suddenly as it had come. All this time I had been observing the weather impatiently. The moon would change on the fifteenth of March. I was determined to get in some fishing before it was full. Tuesday was cool and clear with no wind blowing. I thought that if the weather would only continue like that through the night I might go fishing Wednesday morning, and I asked Mrs. Fayerlee to lay a package of sandwiches and a flask of cold coffee on the dining-room table for me before she went to bed Tuesday night as I was determined to make the try if conditions were at all favorable.

◆   ◆   ◆

I arrived at the crest of the hill and started down into the little valley. The prospect was very different from that which had greeted my eyes a week ago. The sumacs and willows along the bank were already showing green and the mill which had lain cold and silent, still banked with snow, was going full blast now. The miller, his garments dusted white with meal, came to the door as I rode up. I exchanged a few words with him. He averred that living right there on the banks of the creek he had not wet a line in forty years. I replied that it was perhaps too late for him to start now, hitched my horse at his rack and hurried down the slippery path. I had thought that I had surveyed the stream carefully enough when I was here before but I saw now that I had not fully realized its possibilities. It was actually the likeliest water I had ever come upon, and half a dozen people, no, seven, counting the half-witted boy of Joe Turner's, had assured me that nobody had ever cast a fly in it!

I sat down on a log, got out my fly book and solemnly weighed the possibilities. I used the method of exclusion. All the flies went promptly back into the book except three: a Royal Coachman, a Black Gnat, and Old Speck. (Cecil Morrison had taught me to tie the original Old Speck in my faraway youth. I reckon she took five hundred pounds of fish before she petered out on me. I have her made-to-order these days, red and white Guinea feathers tied on a No. 1 hook.) All the time I was looking over those flies I knew it was a work of supererogation. Old Speck was the only one worthy of the virgin stream.

I was anxious to get away from the mill pond as soon as possible, so I at once started wading up-stream. I never cast at random, but only when my eye discerns some object near which fish may be hiding. And I was in a mood to be hard to please that day. I had waded several hundred yards before I came upon a pool that took my fancy. It was a beauty, at least four feet across and five or six feet deep. An old log protruded from the bank and made a deep shadow half-way across the pool. I knew they ought to be lurking in that shadow. Young willows growing breast high screened the bank. I stepped up behind them and cast. No luck. My own fault. I had cast a little short, just grazing the edge of the shadow. I bent nearer, keeping the bushes still in front of me. The water boiled as he came forward in a savage rush. An old Little Mouth. He must have weighed four pounds. I cast again, hoping to get his mate. But she was too wary, or I too inexpert. The fly lit again and again but never a strike to break the calm surface of the pool. I looked farther up-stream and saw what I thought was likelier water, a longer, deeper pool; one of those that lying between a bluff and a sand bar nearly always harbor fish.

I took two sizeable bass there and during the next two or three hours I fished half a dozen more pools, approaching each one with rising excitement. I had taken four bass by this time, all of them Little Mouth. I was too ignorant to realize that I was likely to take only Little Mouth that day—for the Little Mouth and Big Mouth inhabit differ-ent kinds of water—but I hoped fervently that the luck would hold. A Big Mouth bass is all right but a three-pound Little Mouth is a chicken hawk and chain lightning—no other fish of its size can give you a better fight.

It was twelve o'clock by this time. I rested under the shade of a sycamore while I ate the ham sandwiches and drank the coffee that Mrs. Fayerlee had given me. After lunch I waded up-stream another mile, fishing half a dozen good pools on the way. I had a creelful of fine bass by this time and might have called it a day but I was devoured by curiosity to know just how much of this likely water there was and I passed over two or three pools in my haste to find out what was around the next bend.

The sun was going down but it was still light when I rounded the bend and came upon a pool whose image will always remain indelibly imprinted on my memory. A crest of foamy water flowing very swift struck a limestone ledge that ran clear across the creek. The high waters pouring over this miniature natural dam had hollowed out a deep pool and the ledge or rock running a little obliquely across the stream gave a twist to the current—it was the most beautiful eddy I had ever seen, shoe-mouth deep above and below and the pool fully twenty feet across and over six feet deep. I backed off from it and sat down on the sand and for some minutes feasted my eyes on the sight—the likeliest water I had ever come upon. I knew they were there!

When I had a little mastered my excitement I bent Old Speck on a six-foot leader, took the rod in my teeth and crawled up to the pool. I lay down on my left side and made dry casts till I had got out about thirty feet of line and then cast to the far side of the pool. A Little Mouth struck like a flash of lightning. The fight was on. I raised myself on one elbow and played him. I dared not rise for if a Little Mouth once sees you it is all off. After a sharp fight I landed him, a two-and-a-half-pound bronze warrior. I rested a few minutes and then lying in the same position I made another cast. No luck this time. Another and still another and then a bass struck savagely. It was a female, larger and stronger than the first bass, his mate probably. I landed her after an even sharper fight. The next fish I hooked must have been a six-pounder. He whipped that pool to foam. I saw I could do nothing with him lying down so I gave him the butt of the rod. He snapped the leader like a pack thread. I was wet with sweat by this time and shaking with fatigue. I knew I had to rest again. I crawled back out of sight carefully, got up and walked around a bit to unlimber myself and then went back. I got two more this time, one two pounds and other other about the same size as the first two.

Dark comes swiftly in the spring. I had been walking about to stretch my cramped muscles and was about to go back to the pool and repeat the same procedure that I had engaged in now half a dozen times when I suddenly realized that it had got so dark that I could hardly see. I was very tired too and had three or four miles to wade back to the mill. There was no help for it. I would have to leave. I reeled in my line, unjointed my rod, put Old Speck back in the fly book and started back the three or four miles to the mill. I remember wading with hardly a glance past pools that had seemed fascinating a few hours before. The image of that perfect spot was so sharp in my memory that I could not look with interest at any other water. It seemed almost too much that I would have to wait until another Saturday rolled around before I could fish it again.

◆　　◆　　◆

I did fish it again, on the next and many successive Saturdays. I came finally to know all that water intimately—to this day I could make you a chart of every mile between McCaulay's and Peacher's Mill. I was the first man ever to cast a fly into Big West Fork . . . and I felt for it an affection I had never felt for any other stream, not even excepting Camp Creek, beloved of my youth.

TO KNOW
A RIVER . . .

RODERICK L. HAIG-BROWN

A RIVER IS WATER IN ITS LOVELIEST FORM; RIVERS HAVE LIFE AND SOUND and movement and infinity of variation; rivers are veins of the earth through which the lifeblood returns to the heart. Rivers can attain overwhelming grandeur, as the Columbia does in the reaches all the way from Pasco to the sea; they may slide softly through flat meadows or batter their way down mountain slopes and through narrow canyons; they may be heavy, almost dark, with history, as the Thames is from its mouth at least up to Richmond; or they may be sparkling fresh on mountain slopes through virgin forest and alpine meadows.

Lakes and the sea have great secret depths quite hidden from man and often almost barren of life. A river too may have its deep and secret places, may be so large that one can never know it properly; but most rivers that give sport to fly-fishermen are comparatively small, and one feels that it is within the range of the mind to know them intimately—intimately as to their changes through the seasons, as to the shifts and quirks of current, the sharp runs, the slow glides, the eddies and bars and crossing places, the very rocks of the bottom. And in knowing a river intimately is a very large part of the joy of fly-fishing.

One may love a river as soon as one sets eyes upon it; it may have certain features that fit instantly with one's conception of beauty, or it may recall the qualities of some other river, well-known and deeply loved. One may feel in the same way an instant affinity for a man or a woman and know that here is pleasure and warmth and the foundation of deep friendship. In either case the full riches of the discovery are not immediately released—they cannot be; only knowledge and close experience can release them. Rivers, I suppose, are not at all like human beings, but it is still possible to make apt comparisons; and this is one: understanding, whether instinctive and immediate or devel-

oping naturally through time or grown by conscious effort, is a necessary preliminary to love. Understanding of another human being can
never be complete, but as it grows toward completeness, it becomes
love almost inevitably. One cannot know intimately all the ways and
movements of a river without growing into love of it. And there is no
exhaustion to the growth of love through knowledge, whether the
love be for a person or a river, because the knowledge can never
become complete. One can come to feel in time that the whole is
within one's compass, not yet wholly and intimately known, but there
for the knowing, within the last little move of reaching; but there will
always be something ahead, something more to know.

I have known very few rivers thoroughly and intimately. There is
not time to know many, and one can know only certain chosen
lengths of the few. I know some miles of the Dorsetshire Frome and of
the little river Wrackle that cuts away from the Frome by Stratton Mill
and rejoins it farther down, because I grew up with them and had all
the quick, instinctive learning power of the very young when I fished
there. It was a happy and proud thing to know those streams, and the
knowing paid great dividends in fish; it paid even greater dividends in
something that I can still recapture—sheer happiness in remembering
a bend or a run or the spread below a bridge as I saw them best,
perhaps open in sunlight with the green weeds trailing and a good fish
rising steadily, or perhaps pitted by rain under a gray sky, or white and
black and golden, opaque in the long slant of the twilight. I knew
those streams through fishing them, through cutting the weeds in
them, through shooting ducks and snipe all along them, through
setting night lines in them, through exploring them when the hatches
were down and the water was very low. I carry them with me wherever
I go and can fish them almost as well sitting here as I could were I
walking the meadow grass along their banks six thousand miles from
here.

I learned other waters almost as easily, though more superficially,
when I was very young. The lower reaches of the Frome, between
Wool and Wareham, where we used to fish for salmon, were harder to
know than the best of the trout water because the river was deeper and
darker and slower down there, more secret within itself. But I fished
with a man who knew all the secrets, and we used the prawn a lot,
fishing it deep down and slow, close to bottom and close under the
banks. Fish lay where he said they should lie and took hold as he said
they would take, and one remembered and fished it that way for
oneself until the knowledge was properly one's own. I think I could
still start at Bindon Mill and work on all the way down to the Salmon
Water without missing so very many of the good places. And then,

perhaps, I could walk back along the railroad track toward evening with a decent weight of salmon on my back.

I knew the little length of narrow carrier in Lewington's field by the bakery at Headbourne Worthy; it was so small and clear that one couldn't help knowing it and so difficult that one had to know it. I knew where each fish lay and why, how he would rise and when, what chance of ground would hide me during the cast, what tuft of grass would probably catch my fly on each attempted recovery. And Denis and I knew the narrow part of Avington Lake where the great pike lay under the shadow of the rank weeds; we knew the schools of roach and rudd and the few solitary trout; we had seen the big carp and the slow black tench; we knew, almost, where each little one- or two-pound pike had his hunting ground.

The winter days at Avington, under the tall, bare beeches and ashes and sycamores, were very good. There were always mallards to be seen in hundreds, always herons, sometimes a peregrine falcon chasing the mallards; the cock pheasants were richer, burnished gold against the gold of fallen beech leaves, and rabbits sometimes rustled the leaves softly, unaware that we were fishing near them. The rank, thick weed banks of the bottom showed clearly, green through the shallow water of the narrow part of the lake. We cast our big spoons and phantoms and wagtails far out, letting them into the unrippled water as gently as we could, then brought them twinkling back over the dark mystery of the weed beds. Sometimes a big pike was lying out over the weeds, and we tried and tried to tempt him. Sometimes one appeared suddenly behind the spoon, followed it, and took or turned away. Sometimes—and this was best and surest of all—there was a heavy flash and a swirl as the spoon passed over a known lie, then the pull and the lunging fight.

The first western river I learned was the Nimpkish, the seven twisting miles of it that lie between the lake and the sea. I learned the best of the trout pools first, wading the round and slippery rocks in an old pair of calked shoes, letting the swift water climb up to the pockets of my shirt and sometimes letting it knock me down and carry me half the length of a pool before I could find a way out of it. Then I learned the tyee pools and the cutthroat trout runs of the tidal reaches. Taking the canoe up to go over the traps, lining the big skiff through to the lake, fishing for steelhead, watching the salmon runs, I learned more of it and felt it my own. But I never really knew the river as one can know a river. I don't know, even today, just how and when the steelhead run there, nor more than a fraction of their lying places. And I never could solve the secrets of Ned's Canyon and Wright's Canyon or that third one of the long, slow, deep pools on the river;

they were so big, and I knew so many other places to catch fish, that it was hard to give them time. But I once wrote a book that had the Nimpkish for a heroine, and I saw and learned so much of her for myself through five or six years that I feel my faulty knowledge has given me a full love of her. Whenever I think of a western fishing river, one typical of all the best things that western fishing can offer, I think of the Nimpkish; and I expect I always shall.

The Campbell I know almost as a man should know a river. I don't know the whole story, or anything like the whole story; but the outlines of plot and characterization are clear and definite, much of the detail is filled in, and each new detail fits neatly into an appointed place as I learn it. The Campbell is a little like the Nimpkish, yet most unlike it. Both rivers are broad and clear and swift, with broken, white water, rare, smooth pools, and rocky beds. But the Campbell runs only three or four miles to salt water from the foot of its great Elk Falls, beyond which salmon and steelhead and cutthroat trout from the sea cannot pass. The Nimpkish is a highway to all the miles of Nimpkish Lake and the Kla-anche River and Woss Lake, to the Hustan River and the chain of lakes beyond that, and to all the tributary streams of the watershed. The Campbell draws to itself a noble run of winter steelhead, a run of fine cutthroats, a queer little run of small summer steelheads; it has its great tyees, its dying run of humpbacks, a fair run of cohos and dogs in some years, but no more than an occasional sockeye, probably a stray from some other parent stream. The Nimpkish has all the runs that the Campbell has in fullest strength and adds to them a fine run of true summer steelheads, a wonderful sockeye run, and a fabulous dog-salmon run. The Campbell is the simpler river of the two, easier to know and understand for all those reasons. Nimpkish is more wonderful, more impressive, more beautiful; but Campbell—and not simply because I live within sight and sound of her—is the better of the two to love.

I can mark the months on the Campbell and tell myself, at least to my own satisfaction, what will be happening in the river during each one of them. In January the steelhead are running well; in February the cutthroats are spawning; in March and April the winter steelheads spawn; in May the little summer steelhead should be in the Island Pools, most of the humpback fry will already have found their way to the sea, and the flying ants will hatch out; in August it is time to go to the Canyon Pool and look for the big cutthroats; in September the tyees are in the river; during October the cohos will come; in December the steelhead again. I know the May-fly and stonefly nymphs that I will find under the rocks and the caddises that will crawl over the bottom in the different months; I know the rocks that the net-winged midges will blacken with their tiny cases, the places where the bright-green cladophora will grow richly, and where and when the rocks will be slippery with brown diatom growth. Some of these things, perhaps, are not important to know if one only wishes to catch fish; but they have their part in the pleasure of fishing.

I find I am quite often wrong about the Campbell even now. I may say that it is too early for the fish to be in, then go up and find them there. I can't always judge when the freshets are coming, but that, perhaps, is no more than saying I'm not an infallible weather prophet. Perhaps it is truer to say that I often find new things about the river than that I am often wrong about her; and sometimes I suddenly realize things that I have known for quite a long time almost unconsciously. It is years, for instance, since I first knew that I could kill fish well in August with the fly I call Silver Brown. I tied the fly to imitate coho fry, which are the only numerous salmon fry in that month. In spring, when the river is full of many kinds of fry, the Silver Brown does not do so well for me, and I use the Silver Lady, which has a paler wing and a more complicated tying. I changed over with comparatively little thought, and the true inference of the change only came to me this year—trout may at times feed rather selectively on fry of different species.

Apart from bullheads and sticklebacks, one can expect some five or six different species of fry in the Campbell. Cutthroat fry and coho fry are so much alike that no sensible fish would bother to distinguish between them; it is reasonable to use the Silver Brown as an imitation of both. But humpback fry are like no other fry, trout or salmon; they are, for instance, quite without parr marks, their bellies are brightest silver, their backs generally bluish. I remember that I have fished a fly with long blue hackles for wings and often killed well with it during the humpback run. From there it is only a step to the making of a special humpback imitation; I think I shall start with something of this sort: tail—green swan; body—flat silver tinsel; hackle—scarlet and quite small; wing—blue hackles, back to back enclosing a white strip and perhaps a strand or two of blue herl; cheeks—pale blue chatterer. When I fish the river again in springtime, I shall use that fly.

If a coho–cutthroat imitation and a humpback imitation, why not imitations of the others in their days and seasons? The Silver Lady, perhaps, is sufficiently like spring salmon and steelhead fry. Yet the spring salmon fry has a light brown in its back and an impression of palest pink about him which the steelhead fry has not. It might make all the difference one day. So I shall build a fly with a tail of pink swan, a silver body, and wings of barred summer duck enclosing yellow swan; and if that isn't good, I shall try grizzled hackles, preferably from

a Plymouth cock with a touch of Red Game in him, set back to back
with light-red hackles between them.

None of that is desperately important or highly significant, and I
suppose I should feel ashamed of having waited ten or fifteen years to
think of it. What I really feel is a good measure of gratitude to the
Campbell for having at last brought home to me the rather obvious
point that, if it is worth trying for exact imitation of sedges and May
flies, it is worth trying for reasonably exact imitations of salmon and
trout fry. In time I shall think of dressings for the green color that is
dominant in the backs of dog-salmon fry and the olive-grass green of
the young sockeye's back. I may catch very few more fish through my
efforts than I should have caught without them, but it's going to be
fun.

I fish the Campbell with a sense of ownership fully as strong as
that of any legitimate owner of fishing rights in the world, not because
I do own any part of the river, nor even because I should like to or
should like to keep other people away from it; I should not care to do
either of these things. The sense of ownership grows simply from
knowing the river. I know the easiest ways along the banks and the
best ways down to the pools. I know where to start in at a pool, where
to look for the fish in it, how and where I can wade, what point I can
reach with an easy cast, what lie I can barely cover with my strongest
effort. This is comfortable and pleasant and might well begin to seem
monotonous sooner or later were it not something of an illusion. I
have a fair idea of what to expect from the river, and usually, because
I fish it that way, the river gives me approximately what I expect of it.
But sooner or later something always comes up to change the set of my
ways. Perhaps one day, waiting for a friend to fish down a pool, I start
in a little farther up than usual and immediately hook a fish where I
had never been able to hook one before. A little more of the river
becomes mine, alive and productive to me. Or perhaps I notice in
some unusual slant of light what looks to be a glide of water along the
edge of a rapid; I go down to it and work my fly through, and whether
or not a fish comes to it, more of the river is known and mine.

For years I have promised myself to fish through the sort of half
pool below the Sandy Pool. It starts almost opposite my own line fence
and is little more than a smoothing off of the long rapid that runs right
down to the Highway Bridge; but there are many big rocks in it and—I
can say this now—some obvious holding water. I fished it twice this
spring. On the first evening I caught two or three fair-sized cutthroats,
and once a really good fish broke water at the fly. I went down earlier
on the second evening. A three-pound cutthroat came to my first cast.
There was a slow silver gleam as the fly came around on the second

cast, a solid heavy pull, and the 2X gut was broken. I put up heavier gut and hooked a clean steelhead that ran me almost to the end of the backing. I hooked two others along the pool that evening, both of them too close to their spawning; but the pool is the Line Fence Pool now, something so close to home and so obvious that I took ten years to learn about it, a discovery as well worthwhile as any I have ever made.

One discovers other things than new pools and new fish lies in old pools. One learns to mark one's casts by such things as the kidney stones and the flat rock in General Money's Pool in the Stamp, one learns to hope for the sight of a pileated woodpecker crossing the river in swooping flight at this place, a flock of mergansers at that place, a dipper against black rocks and rippled water somewhere else, deer coming down to eat moss on the rocks at the water's edge in hard weather. All these things are precious in repetition, and, repeated or no, they build the river for one. They are part of the background of knowing and loving it, as is every fish hooked, every cast fished through, every rock trodden. And men and women come strongly into it. Here, I can remind myself, was where Ann sat that first day we came up the river together, and here it was that she loved the September sun the year before Valerie was born. Here we stopped and Letcher made us an old-fashioned before we went on to the Canyon Pool that day. Here Buckie brought his first fish to the bank, here I gaffed Sandy's first steelhead for him, here Tommy hooked one last winter, there it was that the big fish took Reg's line across the roots of the cedar tree. . . .

I still don't know why I fish or why other men fish, except that we like it and it makes us think and feel. But I do know that if it were not for the strong, quick life of rivers, for their sparkle in the sunshine, for the cold grayness of them under rain and the feel of them about my legs as I set my feet hard down on rocks or sand or gravel, I should fish less often. A river is never quite silent; it can never, of its very nature, be quite still; it is never quite the same from one day to the next. It has its own life and its own beauty, and the creatures it nourishes are alive and beautiful also. Perhaps fishing is, for me, only an excuse to be near rivers. If so, I'm glad I thought of it.

WORMING
MURPHY CREEK

◆ ◆ ◆

JOHN ENGELS

I N 1943, WHEN I WAS TWELVE, I WOULD GET UP EARLY TO GO TROUT
fishing in Murphy Creek, a small-to-medium river outside Pound,
Wisconsin. I would get up sometimes before first light and go quietly
outside, rig up the old steel, telescoping rod, and fill a can with damp
moss and populate the moss with hard, shiny redworms from the worm
bed in the ell of the house right near the leaky outside water faucet.

The smell of those early mornings when I would be out gathering
worms is what I remember best: clean, damp, a hint of mold to it, not
mildew, though nothing rank about it—swamp smell, a cool basement
in the middle of July, fresh-spaded soil, sweet fern underfoot—that
sort of thing.

I was dedicated, and up by five o'clock morning after morning
that summer, for I had a long walk, nearly five miles, to the creek,
down Highway 64, then off to the left on County Z and on into the
swamp for another half mile or so till I came on Murphy Lake, from
which the creek originated and descended, and I could turn downstream and fish back to the road.

I never caught much in the way of memorable—which in those
days meant *big*—fish. The inhabitants of Murphy Creek were small—
little native brook trout, a nine-incher among whom was a giant. I
fished worms as I had learned on the wonderful bass and bluegill lakes
of Notre Dame. I used small hooks, 14s and 16s, and hooked the
worms lightly. I fished the bait unweighted on a 4X tippet, using an
old telescoping True Temper rod at first, and then later, owing to my
Uncle Vince's beneficence, a 7½-foot South Bend fly rod, my first. I
cast or dapped the fly, or let it drift with the various twists and coilings
of the currents, down into the big pools, along the deep undercuts of
the clay and sand banks. I did great slaughter.

I became, in fact, what some might call a storied angler, consulted as an authority by my peers, referred to (I liked to think) in hushed and respectful tones by my elders in the Golden West Tavern where I would stop on my way home with my limit catches of eight-inch brookies, to swill cream soda and engulf French fries. Already my moral underpinnings were, if only slightly, undermined.

But for the most part I was an innocent, and therefore bound to fall. I was accustomed to sally forth on my early-morning expeditions to Murphy Creek filled with buoyant self-confidence, utterly unself-critical, not yet afflicted with bad habits of self-analysis or the inspection of motivations. To this day I know trout fishermen who have—or seem to have—an absolute assurance as to the value of what they do, and the manners in which they do it. This is a quality with which I have had no firsthand experience, except for that brief period that summer when I was twelve and could catch trout whenever I wanted.

Though I was a successful trout fisherman early on, I was not a serious angler. I had not yet come to regard trout fishing in the light of its dangers, its emphasis on personal inadequacy, its great threat to the personal self-esteem of the angler. By "serious angler" I do not mean one especially successful at catching fish, or especially devoted to the sport, nor even to its practice (two different things altogether), but one who, while he is fishing, feels that in this endeavor a great deal, most of it undefinable, is at stake, so much so that to "fail" involves an affirmation of his personal unworthiness, whereas to "succeed" is a testimony to a character and personality of quality so high as to exceed the ordinary capacity of human beings to define it. What is meant by to "fail" and to "succeed," further, the truly serious angler will be quite unable to say.

But I began by saying I was an early riser. It was not only that I was eager to get on the river, but also that I liked the stillness of things at that time of day, liked looking up through my breath in the cold mornings at the cold sky, seeing the flat ribbons of pink and orange light grow over the tips of the cedars and pines, smelling a long way off the fresh rankness of the swamp, hearing at a distance the noise of the stream, finding it hard sometimes to tell the water noise from the wind in the hemlocks, being able to tell by the sound of the water just what level of spate the river might be in, often seeing near the creek at the edge of the swamp a big red fox I thought must have taken to waiting for me, which, just as I passed, would cut in front of me, moving very fast, passing close, then vanishing into the cedars like a red spark.

I loved Murphy Creek. I loved it because I knew it so well, was intimate with it, knew every mood, every detail of its physical being, and yet could never fully anticipate what it might do on any given day, could never dominate it. But I came to terms with it; for the most part it felt friendly toward me, I think. I loved coming onto one of its big dark pools and finding a school of dace skittering crazily along the surface, and then everything going still again. I liked seeing that and knowing something big was at work in that pool, and it might pay me to walk upstream and bait up a small hook with a tiny piece of red-worm and catch a small dace, cut the tail off, and throw the rest back into the river where it would turn and bump downstream along the bottom giving back little golden measures of light; then thread the chubtail onto a bigger hook and let it drift down into the pool where it would swing back and forth in the brown-red water in short, silvery arcs, the sun rising higher and higher, maybe a deerfly buzzing in persistent narrowing circles around my head, the day growing warmer, my shirt sticking to my back, the air heavy with the sweetness of crushed ferns and hemlock needles; and nothing happening, nothing at all.

But every once in a while the life of the river would manifest itself, a school of dace, or a big fish jumping, more likely flashing deep in the pool, rising once in a while to boil at something on the surface, the thick, dark-green, black-spotted back porpoising, the rise-rings spreading to splash at the edges of the bank.

Murphy Creek was just a little too small in most places to wade properly, though for all its general narrowness it was often deep and powerfully swift. After a couple of harrowing experiences, I became wary of flowing water and have remained so to this day. I was some-times even—inexplicably, out of the blue—spooked by it, over-whelmed by visions of myself caught in the current and swept far downstream into the rapids, maybe pinned in an undercut or against a rock and held there until the river dropped, by that time nothing but a bone and a scrap of yellow shirt.

I was accustomed to thinking about and being intimidated by what I imagined to be the life of those big pools, the trout turning and swimming in tremendous spurts against the press and power of water, cavernously gaping, the white linings of their mouths clearly visible through six feet of water, flaring out the ruffs of the red gills, hearing the water roar about them like a storm, tasting the stony water in their throats: I used to wonder, and still do, what it might be like to have to hold myself against such a river day and night for the rest of my life.

Those are the sorts of things I used to think of while walking out of the swamp of Murphy Creek back to County Z. Because I had not yet learned self-irony, I used sometimes to permit myself fantasies, images of myself in heroic poses: leaning back, for instance, against a heavily bowed Leonard, fighting the huge rainbow slowly, artistically, from my Hardy St. John. I could see myself fighting the big fish with confidence and bringing him to the net while Ray Bergman, passing along the bank, stopped to watch, amazed at the coolness of this young boy engaged in epic struggle with a trout the likes of which he, Ray Bergman himself, had never seen. I could see the rod strain more heavily, the green mesh of the net trail downstream, and then there would be a flurry of spray, and a six-pound rainbow would be doubled on itself in the net, great gills flaring and heaving.

But I would be dignified, not let out whoops or run for the bank, and Ray would call to me, "Well done, young feller!" And I would see him from the corner of my eye making notes in a little blue notebook. And so on.

But much, much later in my career, when I had begun to lose a certain sense of possibility, when I had stopped imagining, for instance, that I might be taken for Ernest Schwiebert fishing size 24 *Paraleptophlebia* nymphs upstream, I began to develop more appropriate attitudes, to feel, for one, that at all times my equipment was not what it should be, or, if irrefutably adequate, that I did not know and would never learn how to use it, or knowing abstractly how to use it, was nevertheless hopelessly inept.

I began also to feel displeasure at certain democratic notions, such as that the wilderness river should be shared by all, by me with, even, rafters, canoeists, swimmers, mad wielders of portable stereo radios. I began to have deep anxieties about being on the river *on time*, to fear I would be late, that someone else would be on *my* pool, that I would have to recognize someone else's rights when it was perfectly clear to me that mine were, *ad naturem*, primary and paramount. I began to feel old, dark urges stirring just beneath the skin, began to understand the force of difficulty with which civilized behavior is maintained at the sight of a raft heading around the bend toward me and the pool where I had been for the past half-hour casting to a selective brown. I especially began to enjoy seeing David Huddle or John Reiss or Syd Lea in low, vulgar spasms of envy as I coolly played and landed what seemed even to me an indecently large fish that I had absolutely accidentally hooked, might even call upstream to one of them that the fish I had just taken was a fourteen-inch brown when in fact it was a ten-inch fallfish.

I came to the realization one day that the sport had assumed such power over me that I actually felt guilty when not indulging in it. I felt undutiful; sometimes—as against any tyranny—mutinous.

But worst of all I have felt—having prepared myself, so to speak, purified myself, prostrated myself before the altar, studied, read the holy books, practiced the rites—I have felt despair, the total loss of

faith: I have, in the midst of an uncharacteristically flawless performance over an obliging trout on a perfect stream in the midst of a
glorious day, been suddenly overwhelmed by the absurdity of the
situation, the innate stupidity of the contest, of the beast, the inher-
ent haplessness and bad judgment of the angler, the power of chance
that informs the whole pointless ceremony. It is hard to have to think
such things when one has invested forty years of one's life and, it
seems, about half one's income in the venture.

But in those days I was free of doubt and given to great, uncomplicated dreams. And when I would finally come out of the swamp
bearing such a vision in my head, exhausted and fly-bitten, muddy and
sweaty, the hour late and the dark having come on, the sound of the
woods all around me, the wind so loud in the hemlocks as to make the
whole forest seem to vibrate, behind me somewhere the whole oxbow
flashing with the big night-feeding browns, ashine with schools of
frenzied dace, it seemed to me that nowhere in all time had anything
so wonderful been invented.

I would look up and see nothing, no stars, only hemlock and pine
interlocked. In time I would come to the clearing by County Z and
look up again to meet, this time, the great cool eye of the moon that
had swum up through the lock and tangle of the trees, for the rest of
the night to hold steady over wherever I might be, bright in the whole
clear sweep and current of the sky over Murphy Creek.

A STREAM
FOR
ANGLERS

♦ ♦ ♦

W. H. H. MURRAY

I KNOW A STREAM AMONG THE HILLS, WHICH GLIDES DOWN STEEP declines, flows across level stretches and tumbles over rocky verges into dark ravines. Over it are white birches, and firs, and fragrant cedars, some spruces, tall and straight, and here and there an oak or mountain ash. The breezes, born of cool currents that pour downward from upper heights, where snow whitens yet, blow along this stream among the mountains full of ozone, brewed in the upper atmospheres, and which the nose of the climber drinks as the Homeric gods drank their wine, leisurely, because it is so strong and pure. In the spruces along this stream live two big, brown owls that doze through the day, and if you will sit for an hour and listen you will hear them mutter and murmur in their dreams; dreaming of mice in the meadow, and young chickens in the lowlands, I fancy. On the largest oak, old and gnarled, at the end of a dead bough, a white-headed eagle sits watchfully. Twenty feet below him his mate is hovering over four eggs in a huge nest made of dry sticks. Their eyes have seen more suns rise and set than mine, and will see the crimson long after mine are closed forever, doubtless. All men are their foes, yet they live on. All men are my friends, still I must die. Queer, isn't it?

There are anglers on this mountain stream, but only I know them. They fish each day, and each day fill their creels, and yet they use no rods, nor lines, nor hooks, nor flies, nor bait. It is because I have never fished this hidden stream myself that I have seen them fish it. Poachers? Nay. This brook is their preserve, and I would be a poacher on their rights should I cast line across it. Who are these strange anglers that angle so strangely?

The oldest of them is a snapping turtle, and a great angler he is in truth. I ambushed him as he lay asleep on a log one day, and on his back was written "A.D. 1710." That makes him one hundred and eighty years old—an age that all good anglers ought to live to. Do you tell me "That was a lie; he couldn't be so old"? It may be so—I won't quarrel with you, friend. Regard it as a bit of history, and I will agree with you. But he is a great angler, this old turtle, and has caught more trout than any angler who reads this passage—ten to one, I warrant.

The best angler of them all—better than the watersnake or the kingfisher, or the mountain cat, or the turtle, wise as he is—is an old brown mink. He is so old that his face is gray and his fur shabby, but he is a wise old angler. Six days I watched him come to the stream, and six good half-pound trout did I see the old gray veteran sit and eat on the cool, damp ledge against which the whirling bubbles ran. It was a sight to see him wash himself after his repast! And after he had thoroughly washed his mouth and cleansed his hands, he would stand and look into the deep, dark pool for a moment, contemplatively, as I fancied. Perhaps he is a deacon among the minks! Who knows? Isn't a good angler as good as a deacon, anyway?

There is a bit of meadow on the stream enclosed with a fringe of white birches and cedar growths; and amid the green grasses of it are cranberry vines, and bunches of beaver cups; white and blue flowers speck it with color, and the earth odors are strong over it. It is pleasant to stand in it and breathe in the aboriginal scents of wild roots and uncultivated mould. The untameable in me fraternizes so lovingly with this rare bit of untamed nature. This little mountain meadow, from whose stretch the beaver, with their sharp teeth, cut the trees centuries ago, is so real and genuine that it charges its influence to the very core of me. It is so natural that it makes me more so.

The old beaver dam is still there, and over it the water pours with soft noises into a deep and wide pool. On one side of this dark bit of water is a great rock. Its front is covered with thick mosses very rich in color. Across it wanders a vine with little red berries strung on it. Can you see the old beaver dam, the pool, the big rock, the moss, the running vine and the shining red berries? Yes? Very likely you can; but, oh, you who have such eyes to see—you cannot see the huge trout whose home that dark, deep pool is, and which I have seen so many times as he rose for the bug or grub that I tossed him. And once as I lay on the edge of the pool, hidden in the long grasses, I saw him at play, having a frolic all by himself, and, oh, he made that space of gloomy water iridescent as he flashed and flew through it. Where is he? Do you really wish to know? Well, I will be good and tell you. He is where I found him.

INTO BIG TIMBER CREEK

◆ ◆ ◆

STEWART HARDISON

The last mountain lion in North Carolina was reportedly killed in the western part of the state in 1900. But even today, rumors circulate among the hill people that the big cats are still "out there." Though these rumors are rarely based on anything more than a far-off scream in the night or a pair of eyes gleaming in a car's headlights or sometimes a mysteriously mauled coon dog, they will not die. And while I doubt whether a conclusive shred of evidence will ever be found, the rumors live for me. Admittedly this belief is an act of faith; it makes little sense to think a mountain lion could be prowling the almost suburbanized mountains of North Carolina.

But however irrational this belief is—call it hope even—I still persist in believing. For the mountain lion, like a hawk sailing high in a thermal, is one of those curious fragments of the natural world that can loom in a man's mind and become the very essence, symbol, of what is wild. And as the idea of wilderness becomes increasingly elusive, this symbol, or any particular natural symbol, becomes more and more important.

These symbols help fill the growing void in that part of a man's heart that is reserved for what is wild. That is why I believe in a mountain lion that rationally can't exist, and that is one reason why I enjoy fishing for trout. For the trout, to me, is one of those symbols. Only it is a symbol that I can see, experience. And when I'm on a remote stream and see a wild trout holding in a clear swirl of current, his every spot distinct and his spread fins the color of sunlight and reflected pebbles, then I have the heartening feeling that nature, at least somewhere, is having her say.

Aside from actually catching a trout and the sometimes intricate ritual involved in doing it, I believe that what fires a trouter's heart the most is the place he fishes. And when I think of trout fishing in North

Carolina, I think of a place called Big Timber Creek. Shortly, I will try to tell you something about that place, but for now I must confess to you that I have fictionalized its name. Admittedly, I do this partly out of angler's greed. But there is another reason, too. And this is the fact that Big Timber Creek, like any good trout stream, is a fragile watercourse of living things. Should this watercourse be exposed to a sudden and dramatic increase in fishing or other recreational pressure, these living things and the aesthetics entwined with them could be irretrievably damaged. I want no part in that.

Like numerous other North Carolina trout streams, Big Timber Creek's entire watershed lies within the boundaries of a national forest. Even so, it is easy to get to; gravel roads follow the ridge crests above it, and one even spurs off to give access to its headwaters. Also, the heavily traveled Blue Ridge Parkway curves around a mountain above the upper end of its valley. There is even a pull-off so that tourists may park their cars and view the panorama at leisure. But few cars stop. Evidently, it's just another hazy, green gorge and, by the time a vacationing family has traveled a couple of hundred miles of parkway, they are sick of pretty scenery anyway.

Yet, despite its easy access and close proximity to a major recreational highway, Big Timber Creek remains lost to all but a few. Fortunately, it lacks the kind of epic grandeur—towering mountain peaks, misty waterfalls, sheer cliffs of oblivion, and so forth—that attracts people in hordes. So, curiously, whatever it might lack in geological scale it gains in green seclusion.

When I go in for trout, I prefer to walk in, following a switchback trail that leads in some four miles below the one access road. It's become a kind of prelude, this trek down the ridge, and I enjoy the building anticipation in hearing the faint roar of water grow louder as the trail descends, constantly turning back on itself as it winds through tunnels of overhanging laurel and across mushy spring pools and in and out of timbered hollows. Because of the dense timber, you're upon the stream suddenly. It's not large, but open enough for pleasurable fly-casting.

When I hit the stream, I always head up (an instinct as normal to anglers as salmon) and walk half a mile to a spot where the stream splits around a grassy island and riffles, in two channels, into a wide pool. It's beautiful water—a green glide of smooth current down either side and a submerged bar of pebbles and sand in the middle. It is also forgiving water, a good place to cast out the hindering anticipation that is chronic in the first few minutes of fishing. For if a trout doesn't take in the near run, it's a simple matter to lay a line across a bar and fish the opposite run. Usually one or the other will produce a fish.

This particular day is no exception. After greasing my fly, a number 18 Adams, I work line into the air with a quick series of false casts, then shoot a long curl upstream into the near run of current. Before the fly can ride a yard, it's taken in a quick slurp, and a fat rainbow, a nine-incher with scarlet-pink sides, bores against the rod. After netting him, I release him. Browns predominate, but there are also rainbows and, in the highest headwaters, brook trout or "speckles" as the mountain people call them.

Moving upstream, I come to a long, narrow run that sweeps in tight against the laureled bank. It is deeply shaded and I can see feeding activity. Wading in very slowly, I make one exploratory cast. Nothing. So I strip in line and wait, studying the water for a possible clue. Up and down the trout are dimpling the surface with their rings, but I can see no insects. Midges, I suspect, and dig in my vest for a one-pound-test tippet.

Unlike other eastern waters, a southern Appalachian stream has comparatively little aquatic insect life. The trout, for the most part, feed on various terrestrial insects and assorted stream food—minnows, crayfish, snails, and salamanders. Consequently, fly selection is seldom a fussy matter. But not so now and, after tying on the platinum fine tippet, I open my midge box. Through the acetate lids covering the different compartments, I see several dozen flies in sizes 20 to 24. Scarcely larger than dust motes, they're marvels of fly-tying art. I select a number 22 Quill Gordon and after a painstaking half-blood knot begin false casting.

When I can feel the curl of line pulling in the air, I take a careful step forward for better positioning. But it's a mistake. For no sooner have I lifted my foot than a trout shoots off, only feet from me, and churns directly up the run leaving a V-shaped wake. The feeding stops. Now there's nothing to do but wait. I light a cigarette (very carefully) and smoke it down before the first rise appears again. Feeling too eager, I decide to give the trout some more time, knowing that one more such performance will put them down for good.

Then, to my surprise and horror, I see another trout, this one scarcely six feet from my boot. I know he's seen me because he's holding perfectly still in the shallow current. It's the same as when the bird sees the stalking cat and the cat knows he's been seen and they play a game of psych-out. Only it's me and the trout. So I stand motionless, fearful that the slightest move on my part will launch him on a panic dash up the run. He's a nice brown, perhaps thirteen inches, and I can see his every spot and the quiverous spread of his fin—beautiful but a bother. Then, get this, he eases upstream to a rock a few feet away, turns on his side, and wiggles under the rock. I am dumbstruck. I know trout have the uncanny ability to hide in a trickle of water. But half eel?

With the pool crier out of my way, I start to work out line. When twenty feet is in the air, I lay it on the water. Even at that distance the tiny fly is invisible. I will have to react to any rise in the general vicinity of my tippet. But no strike. So I pick up the line, lengthen it in the air, and lay it back down half a dozen feet upstream. I keep doing this until I'm forty feet out, about the limit I'm willing to go for fear of hanging on my backcast. And still no strike, though the trout continue to rise. Fortunately my casting has not put them down.

The tension builds and I go from the gray Quill Gordon to a brown Dark Cahill, repeating the casting cycle with each. And each fly fails to draw a rise. Finally, my one-pound tippet whittled to a few inches, I tie on a cream-colored Light Cahill. My first cast draws a rise, but I miss. Quickly, before my concentration breaks, I roll the line back out, make two savage false casts to lengthen it, and shoot for the head of the run. My line is on the water for a second or two when there is a dimple above it. Gently, I raise the rod and feel the sharp, delicious surge of a hooked trout.

Because of my light tippet, it's ten minutes before he lies curled in the net, a brown of about fifteen inches, his heavy sides measled with pea-sized red and black spots. I release him in a gentle current and watch him hold over the pebbly bottom, gathering strength with each pump of his gills. Finally, he moves away.

I change to a larger pattern and fish casually, eventually coming to a tight, deep pool of fast water where there is a large, blocklike rock jutting from the bank. It is perfect to sit on, and, deciding I need a break, I do. Here, the rhododendron and alders spread over the stream and, though it's nearly noon, the sun does not blaze, but filters through their foliage in soft splinters of yellow light. I lay my rod on the rock and light a cigarette, feeling satisfied.

Almost at my feet, a small rainbow flashes up for a bug and disappears into the deep current. I watch for him or another, but no trout shows and I'm left studying the myriad whorls of current that race through the run. They change colors as the weak sunlight refracts through—deep blue then green then sunlight-brown and back to blue with the flickering quickness of a strobe light. It's mesmeric, psyche-delic even, and I have to look away into the shaded forest to refocus my eyes.

But then, like the elusive depth of turbulent water, the blue gloom of the alder jungle becomes infectious, transfixing, and random; past images experienced on Big Timber Creek begin to leap out—the eerily human print of a bear track in sand, spring snow sifting through the laurel, a silent rattler coiling back on itself, a puzzled doe snorting for my scent. I look around at the woods and water and rocks, knowing I'm not in wilderness but nevertheless awed at the intimation of wildness. This intimation is so deep and elusive, it can only be absorbed as the rattler absorbs the weak sunlight that filters through the forest canopy with unblinking eyes. And for a moment I feel that this, here and now, is the way it was when the continent was green. Back when.

THE FAMILY POOL

◆ ◆ ◆

JOHN GIERACH

THE FAMILY POOL IS IN THE CHEESMAN CANYON STRETCH OF THE SOUTH Platte River in Colorado. This is an old favorite fishing spot of mine—the pool in particular and the canyon in general—so I naturally thought about trying to disguise it here. That sort of thing is entirely permissible when writing about fishing, as long as you don't get too cute or too superior about it.

I considered it, but then realized that in this case I didn't have to worry about revealing the spot. After all, this particular section of the Platte is a kind of showpiece trout river. It has been designated by the state Division of Wildlife as a Gold Medal stream, and by the U.S. Fish & Wildlife Service as an irreplaceable, Class 1 Fishery; it is the state's oldest and best-known catch-and-release area (to hold up your end of an angling conversation in Colorado you have to have fished it), and the fight over the proposed Two Forks Dam project has brought it to national attention.

In old newspapers you can find photos of various dignitaries and celebrities who have fished the canyon or, more likely, the water below it that's easier to get to. President Bush has never fished it, but I know he's been invited.

Some years ago a friend of mine sent an article on Cheesman Canyon to a national outdoor magazine and the editor wrote back, "Christ! Don't you guys in Colorado fish anywhere else?"

In other words, it's a famous river, and I guess I'd have trouble referring to it as "a pretty good trout stream somewhere in the Rockies" with a straight face.

◆ ◆ ◆

In a part of the country known for pretty canyons, Cheesman is an unusually handsome one. It's steep-sided, narrow, deep, and raw-looking with sparse stands of spruce and pine where it isn't littered with fabulously huge, lichen-covered granite boulders that have come loose and plowed their way down from the canyon walls.

I have never gotten used to the size of these rocks. You're supposed to feel insignificant when you look at something like the night sky, but what does it for me is a lopsided pile of five boulders, each one bigger than my house.

The stream stairsteps down through this in riffles and smooth, green pools, making some of the most luxurious pocket water you'll ever see. A series of fisherman's trails now runs the length of it, but there are places where the footing is skimpy and dizzying, especially in those spots where the trail leads you high above the river and the gravelly scree that passes for soil wants to crumble away under your feet.

From those vantage points—on days when the light is good and the wind is down—you can usually spot fish in the pools, although you learn that when conditions are such that you can see them, they are damned hard to catch.

The Family Pool itself is near the bottom of the canyon. When you hike in on the Gill Trail and begin to work your way upstream, it's about the sixth obviously good hole you come to. I could tell you to look for the big rock, but that probably wouldn't help much.

I don't know for sure how it got its name, but I have a theory: The pool isn't properly a pool at all, like some of the other placid holes in the canyon, but more of a braided run at the end of a long riffle. Trout feed well in the faster water there, and the current helps to mask flies that are a little too big, not to mention slightly sloppy casts and drifts that are less than absolutely perfect. When you're standing on the trail above it, the Family Pool is one of the places where you usually *can't* spot trout, even on a bright, calm day. Relatively speaking, it's an easy spot to fish, and I think people used to bring their families there so the kids could catch something.

That would have been in the old days when you could kill trout. It's rare to see a family in the canyon anymore. Now it's mostly serious grown men.

It would also have been in the old days when you could have legitimately called the Family Pool—or any other spot in the canyon—"easy." Even before the no-kill rule, a lot of canyon regulars released all their fish, and the fishing got progressively more difficult in the years after the regulations went on, finally leveling out at what I guess must be the upper intelligence level of your average trout. You can still catch them—and sometimes you can do very well because there are a lot of fish in there—but you cannot make many mistakes. The fishing has been described as "highly technical," and beginning fly-fishers have been heard to say they don't think they're ready for the canyon yet.

I know what they mean by that because I wasn't ready the first time, either. I had more or less learned to catch trout with a fly rod and had reached that first plateau where you begin to think, *This is not as hard as some people make it out to be.* Then, after the first few times I sauntered into the canyon—the picture of confidence with store-bought flies and freshly patched waders—I had to admit that maybe it could be pretty damned hard after all, and frustrating, too, because the fish were big and you really wanted them.

I stayed with it, though, and eventually started to catch trout there. I had to, because it's a rite of passage. If you don't crack the canyon, it will be said that you never really got serious about fly-fishing. My first few trout were from the Family Pool, up at the head of it in the fast water where a good old Adams dry fly would pass for the more accurate Blue-winged Olive mayfly dun I later learned to use in the slower water.

I guess the Family Pool was the first spot in the canyon where some of my friends and I actually gained some purchase on what was then the hardest trout fishing we'd ever tried to do. It was also the first place we learned to put a name to. A passing fisherman told us what it was called back when there were few enough other anglers that you could stop and talk to them.

We got into the small, entomologically accurate fly patterns everyone said you needed· (nothing bigger than a size 18) and began carrying boxes of tiny nymphs, floating nymphs, emergers, thorax duns, stillborns, no-hackles, parachutes, and so on.

Those of us who weren't into it already took up fly-tying because we couldn't afford to buy all this stuff. Then we began to argue about whether the trailing nymphal husk on an emerger pattern should be wood duck flank or dun hackle tip. We also worked on our casting a little bit and began carrying spools of 7X tippet material.

This is also where we began to realize that successful trout fishing isn't a matter of brute force or even persistence, but something more like infiltration. Technique is part of it, but so is keeping your head straight and your touch light. We were proud of our successes and became philosophical about them. This was about the time when we all started saying, "Fishing is like life," which of course it is.

For years we'd head to the Family Pool first because—if things were right and no one was on the water ahead of us—it was usually good for a couple of fish. Hooking a few right off the bat would wire us up for the rest of the day, and we'd eventually wander off to other spots that we came to know as the Wigwam Pool, the Ice Box, the Channels, the Flats, the Spring Hole, the Chute, the Holy Water, and a few other places that I really *am not* going to tell you about.

Still, when A.K. or Ed or Jim or I would go down there in separate cars, all we'd ever have to say was, "I'll meet you on the river," without having to specify the Family Pool.

Another nice thing about the Family Pool is that it fishes pretty well in most stream flows, except for the very highest when it becomes the Family Rapids. There are a lot of spots in the canyon that fish nicely in one kind of flow, but not so well in others. I don't have a problem with that. In fact, it's fun to be able to look at how high the river is and sort of figure where you might be able to catch some fish. But it's also handy to know of a place that will probably be good, no matter what—as long as you can get to where you have to be on it.

When you come into the canyon you are on the north side of the river, but if you want to fish the Family Pool you need to be on the south bank. Trust me on this, I've tried it both ways. On the north bank you are standing in the spot you should be casting to and it just won't work.

In normal flows, there are two places to cross the river in this stretch; one below the pool and one above. When the river is running high, it's best to try crossing at the wide riffle upstream. A good wading staff helps. I learned one spring, after nearly drowning, that if the wading is too tense there, then the pool is too high to fish well, anyway.

And when the Family Pool is too high to be good, you probably should have gone to a different river.

◆   ◆   ◆

I know that I first fished the canyon in 1974 because that was three seasons before the catch-and-release regulations went on. Technically, this makes me a veteran: a guy who remembers it from "before"—the main difference between then and now being the number of people. You naturally enjoy this old-timer status, and glorifying the old days a bit seems unavoidable. I do remember when there were more eighteen- and twenty-inch trout in there, but, honestly, there was never a time when they were *all* twenty inches.

The size of the trout and their numbers have fluctuated over the years, and there have actually been some poor to mediocre seasons, although, to be fair, even then the trout in Cheesman Canyon are a little bigger and some are prettier than most. There are those who say the decline had to do with poaching, while others claim it was the fault of the people at the Denver Water Board who do damaging things with the stream flows at crucial times of year. The fisheries biologists I've talked to aren't sure, but they won't rule out the stresses on the fish from continuous, heavy fishing pressure or even natural population cycles. Or for that matter, all of the above plus some other things we don't know about.

The last time I was down there it seemed to me there were fewer trout than in recent years, but some of them were bigger. And so it goes.

A lot of new fishermen began to show up when the no-kill rule went on and we learned, along with the Division of Wildlife, that enlightened regulations can be even more glamorous than good fishing. In this context, there are two extreme kinds of anglers. Some just don't fish a place until it becomes fashionable, while a few others slink away the minute it does. In the long run, there are always more of the former than the latter.

Most of my friends and I fall somewhere in the middle. We bitch about the crowds and have taken to fishing the canyon on weekdays at weird times of the year, but we keep going back, even though now there are people on the water we don't recognize—not so much the individuals as the type.

For instance, there are the guys who carry those pocket counters in their vests. Ask one of them "Are you doing any good?" and he'll whip the thing out and say, "I have taken twenty-seven fish since nine this morning. That would be an average of six-point-seven-five trout per hour."

"Ah . . . ," you say, for lack of a better response.

When we started fishing the canyon together, my friends and I saw the catch-and-release business as more mysticism than game management—an attitude that I know aggravates some fisheries biologists who just don't see the religious implications of it. And there was also something in there about an enlightened lack of competitiveness that would eventually lead us into harmony with ourselves and the environment. We gave this some thought at the time, or at least we directed a lot of talk at it.

Eventually that mellowed to the kind of perspective the Division of Wildlife guys might agree with. You hike in and fish hard and as well as you can. At the end of the day when you climb out of the canyon, you're refreshed from the "quality Colorado outdoor-sports experience," but you're empty-handed, however well you did. Having to release any trout you catch means—in an odd sort of way—that it doesn't matter if you catch any or not.

But of course it *does* matter if you catch fish or not. It's a paradox and, as any fisherman knows, one good paradox can cancel out hours of idealistic wrangling.

You can get better at fishing as time goes by (simply "getting better" is probably the ultimate goal of the sport), but there's a moment when your ideas about it set up and become more or less permanent. Then you spend the rest of your active life trying to balance the way things should be with the way they are. Maybe it has more to do with your age than anything else. I know a number of people whose thoughts on sport solidified—for better or worse—in their early to mid thirties, and that was that.

I think my own vision took shape sometime after I began to catch trout on dry flies in the Family Pool on a fairly regular basis and felt ready for more difficult water. On film it would resemble a trout-fishing documentary starring Thomas McGuane, written by Russell Chatham, and directed by Akira Kurosawa. You're not aware of this kind of thing when it happens, but in retrospect you come to know that it occurred while you were knee-deep in a certain pool on a certain river in September of 1979. You were fishing a number 18 Blue-winged Olive emerger on a 5-weight fly rod that you no longer own.

◆　◆　◆

So the Family Pool has become a kind of focal point for some of us. In a way, it reveals more about our feelings for all this than water we actually fish more often because it's always an event. The place is only a two-and-a-half hour drive and then a short hike from here, but weeks and even months go by when we don't get down there. Still, this is the best trout water any of us fish regularly. It's a treat; a homecoming; also a trip where you take one of your very best fly rods. When we fish it, we're on our best behavior, that is, we're about as serious, careful, and patient as we ever get.

It also comes up in conversation a lot. On a cool, overcast day in March, someone is likely to say, out of the blue, "This would be a good time to be fishing the Family Pool," and then someone else will pick it up. "The flow will be about three hundred cubic feet per second [probably lower, actually, but we're fantasizing now], and a midge hatch will be on. Or maybe the mayflies are starting." There's a moment of silence then as we all visualize it. This exchange usually takes place in town, although it's even been known to happen on another trout stream if the fishing is slow.

Don't get me wrong, the fishing can be slow in the Family Pool, too. Because of the crowds in the summer, we now fish it mostly in what some think of as the off-season, that is, roughly from October to late March or early April, which would include the late and the early Blue-winged Olive hatches, with midges in between. It can be cold then, and there's an ancient stone fire ring on the south bank where—I like to think—generations of fishermen have built willow-twig fires for warmth and coffee while waiting for the trout to start rising. The fishing can be surprisingly good between fall and spring, but the hatches can be spotty, and patience is often called for.

I also like to think that if this old, black fire ring had not already been there when we discovered the place, we'd have built one ourselves. This is a good pool that's worth waiting out, and it's also a friendly, domestic sort of spot that encourages coffee breaks, conversation, and the occasional deep thought.

I think it was there that I finally decided to quit smoking, even though I know I'll always dearly love the drug, and even though I didn't tackle the job that very day. It wasn't the constant harping from the Surgeon General that did it or the pointed suggestions of friends or even the fact that the whole culture is encouraging tobacco heads to kick. ("Not a good reason at all," I said of that last one. "What if the culture was encouraging me to help round up the Jews?") The fact is, I've never responded well to criticism. The more people told me I shouldn't do it, the more I thought, *It's a free country—I'll smoke if I want to.*

What it was, finally, was the realization that I am a plodding worker and a slow learner and it's going to take a long life for me to enjoy the few things I'll ever figure out. That, I suppose, is the kind of thing that comes to you on the bank of a difficult but familiar trout stream—not to get sentimental about it or anything.

And there's been some serious talk around that fire, too. In recent years a lot of it has been about the proposed Two Forks Dam project, which, if built, would flood much of the river. At this writing the Environmental Protection Agency has proposed a veto of the project and that veto has been upheld on review. Now the thing goes to Washington for yet another review, and so on. Optimists in the environmental community are choosing to view each step in this horrendously ponderous process as another nail in the coffin.

So lately the talk has been turning to how good it will be to have the canyon back. (It did seem for a while as if we'd already lost it.) Of course we realize that water projects seldom actually die. If the dam proposal finally does go down, there's a good chance of lawsuits, and, if those fail, the whole idea will probably be resurrected in another decade or so. These things never seem to end in a definitive way because there seems to be an unlimited supply of persistent, hard-hearted bureaucrats out there who look at water flowing happily down a trout stream and see nothing but currency washing out to sea. Still, it's looking good for our side, if only because of the volume at which the dam builders are howling.

The party line had been to defend the canyon and the miles of water below as pristine wilderness, although water providers who did their homework—not to mention habitual devil's advocates such as my friend Ed Engle—pointed out that the fishery in question is actually somewhat artificial.

Releases from the existing dam at the head of the canyon keep water temperatures more or less uniform and create a tailwater fishery, or a kind of man-made spring creek. Isn't it a little paradoxical that we're fighting to save a stretch of river from a dam when said river was *created* by a dam?

Well, no, I'd tell Engle. *A thing's origin in the past* (going on a century in the past in this case) *doesn't have anything to do with its quality in the present. And the sketchy historical info indicates that this was a pretty good fishing stream even before Cheesman Dam, although it was cutthroats then instead of browns and rainbows. And the canyon still looks exactly as it has for a million years.*

Goddamn it, Ed, I know you agree with me on this!

But, to Ed, arguing is a sport, sometimes even a contact sport, and, to an outside observer, our friendship would look like a running rhubarb that's been going on for almost twenty years now. The point he's making is valid, though: Isn't it interesting that the logic you apply to the opposition is abrupt and unforgiving, while the reasoning for your own position is fluid, creative, and finds room for infinite subtleties?

About then someone sees a trout rise—or thinks he does—and everyone watches the water. Sure enough, a couple of fish have begun working down in the tail of the pool. "Okay, who's going to try for them first?" And, "What do you suppose they're feeding on?"

No one goes out of his way to make this point, but it's another good one: You must be an environmental activist at some level—there's no way around it that'll still let you live with yourself—but you should never get so grim about it that you stop enjoying what you're supposed to be fighting for. Even if you lose in the end, and some consortium of bastards dams the river, it won't be because you didn't speak up. And for the moment at least, you are still living in the good old days.

◆   ◆   ◆

I moved west in the late 1960s and have lived around Colorado
ever since. Montana, with bigger rivers, fewer people, and harder
winters, beckons occasionally, but I guess I like it here well enough.
I think all I had in mind at the time was to get out of the hot, sticky,
crowded Midwest and become the kind of guy who knew the names of
the pools on a great trout stream; knew the hatches and fly patterns;
knew where to find dry wood for a fire on a cold day; and otherwise just
felt at home. And if that stream wasn't 100 per cent natural, then I'd
know of some that were. They'd involve a longer walk and the trout
wouldn't be as big, but then that's part of what *natural* means when it's
not on a breakfast cereal box.

From that standpoint, I can say that my life has been an unqual-
ified success. I guess I've gotten used to it all by now—even gotten
blasé about some things—but luckily, I still get knocked out by where
I am on a pretty regular basis.

Sometimes it happens when I just walk out my front door at home
to go look in the mailbox. There'll be traffic on the road out front, but
there are some pretty foothills to the south and west and a little creek
across the road with some brown trout in it. These are not the most
gorgeous hills or the most magnificent creek in the Rocky Mountains,
but they are nonetheless *in the Rocky Mountains,* and if you were born
a Midwesterner you'll never outgrow the idea that this is exotic stuff.

Something like a sense of place kicked in when I moved here,
and I realized that I felt genuinely comfortable for the first time in my
life. The air was clear enough; the rocks and trees were the right color;
the water was as cold as I thought it should be. Maybe this was
profound, or maybe it was just the result of watching too many Western movies as a kid. Whatever, it has never worn off.

Not everything that's happened to me out here has been wonderful, but even when things were grim, the scenery was still gorgeous
and the fishing was good. There was always the consolation that I was
a boy from the Midwest who had infiltrated a new environment—
creating only a few ripples in the process—and learned to be at home
in the Rocky Mountains. So, whatever unpleasant crap was happening
to me, I knew it could have been worse—I mean, I could have been
destitute and troubled in Cleveland.

Interestingly, many of the people I fish with now are transplanted
Midwesterners, and I think we all get into this to some degree. After
all, life is going to be the way it is, no matter what, but we live in a
place we like now, and that means a lot to those of us who appreciate
countryside. Even after quite a few years of fishing the Family Pool,

someone is bound to poke the fire during a lull in the conversation and say, as if he'd just noticed, "Shore is purty here, ain't it?"

Relatives back home tell me I speak like that now—with a Western accent—although I can't hear it myself. To me it sounds perfectly normal.

THE UPPER REACHES
OF
LONE TREE CREEK

◆ ◆ ◆

RON SPOMER

An eleven-year-old boy, all but lost in the folds of an adult's old canvas raincoat, squatted beside the rain-swollen street gutter that ran past his father's butcher shop in a South Dakota farm town. The skin of his head glistened through closely cropped hair as he stretched out his hand and dropped a cottonwood stick into the current. For the next two hours the town disappeared as the boy followed the bobbing stick through a wild landscape. It rode the soaring crests of rapids, plunged over cataracts, and swirled in dark backwaters where giant fishes finned in the black depths beneath towering pines.

When the boy came back, he was standing at the edge of a ditch between a cornfield and a gravel road, the last street of the town at his back. The runoff waters had coalesced to the volume of a brook. He stood watching as it carried his stick beyond the cornfields, beyond the barns, beyond the gravel roads.

◆ ◆ ◆

I wonder if I have some form of dyslexia. Whenever I see or hear the word *trout* my brain records *wild*. As in *wilderness*. This has been a defect with me since early childhood when the only fish I'd ever seen were bullheads. I searched for them in the far reaches of Lone Tree Creek, which ran—no, *oozed* would be the more accurate verb— through my uncle's pasture. I had this idea that the farther I got from the farmhouse or road, the bigger the bullheads I'd catch, and maybe, if I went far enough, I'd find trout.

I've been trying to get farther from houses, roads, and bullheads ever since. Considering that most roads in mountain country follow stream courses, this has been no easy task. However, after twenty years of intermittent searching, I think I've finally found the farthest reaches of Lone Tree Creek. No road, no houses, no bullheads. Just lots of wilderness—er, trout.

When I want to catch trout I go to Yellowstone, Marble Canyon, the Bighorn, or the Green below Flaming Gorge. But when I want to go trout fishing, I go to Lone Tree Creek.

It starts on the high ridges, seeping softly from organic earth beneath the roots of ancient hemlocks standing like sanctuary steeples. The water pools in elk hoof prints, trickles under wandering black bears, and detours through thirsty moose or wolverines. Thousands of rivulets join to create hundreds of brooks that buck and plunge down steep canyons. In this country one mountain grows straight up out of the flank of another. Water hasn't had time to wear them down and deposit their detritus into wide, gentle valleys. Here, trout live quicksilver lives between crashing waterfalls. Except in Lone Tree Creek.

In this one special creek, the landscape gentles, the gradient slows, the valley widens. Trout are free to cruise broad, shallow cobble fields for caddis larvae or drift into comfortably deep holes to escape kingfishers and ospreys.

The fish are originals. Native cutthroats as pristine as the wilderness in which they've evolved. They hide against the rocks they resemble, black spots over their fawn-colored backs, shifting like shadows of the current.

When you look into a uniformly shallow section of the stream, open to the sky and no more than a foot deep, you can see it is devoid of fish. If there were any trout you would see them, but you don't, so when you drop your Elk Hair Caddis on the surface, it floats downstream unmolested until you lose sight of it. Lift your rod to move the fly, to see by its wake where it lies, and you meet resistance. There is a quick flash in the water before the fly comes springing back at you.

It doesn't seem right to find trout in such a place at midday, but there they are, right where you don't see them. So your fly becomes your eyes, searching in one narrow scan after another until the trout is revealed in all its splashing, wild panic. For the next few minutes you see it clearly, running up the pool and down, shaking its head and rolling on the surface, and you wonder why you couldn't see it before the hookup. When it calms, you draw it near until it sees your boots and darts between them for refuge, then bolts downstream while you dance to untangle the leader.

There are few classic holding places in Lone Tree Creek, but you search for them eagerly. The best are the heads of deep pools of promise where rowdy gangs of young twelve- to fourteen-inch fish hang out in the agitated water to steal any tidbits washing down. Behind them, where the green water slows over unknown depths, lie bigger fish, fourteen to sixteen inches. They might smash the first number 10 Irresistible you throw at them, or they might watch a number 16 Adams tied parachute style float dead for a minute before sucking it under.

In a few places giant red cedar roots have been washed clear of soil, and you know a big fish is finning smugly within them, but you can't lay a cast past the overhanging branches. You wrap a Blonde Humpy around the lowest limb where it is wet with spray, break it off, and lose another. Then you put a third into the first root before finally bouncing an Irresistible off a wave and into the chute where it is swept downstream and submerged before you can even think about mending. But as you strip it in, a feisty twelve-inch cutthroat leaps from the foam and pounces on it.

Large boulders are surprisingly rare in the stream, but finding one almost always means finding a good fish. Stand beside a fir trunk on the high bank and watch. There. See the flash. Again. A big trout feeding in the flow at the right rear of the rock. You can sneak from downstream and drop the fly just where the water bulges before curling back around the boulder. Perfect. Now it will drift, no need to mend, right down the lane, and there's the flash and here he is!

I've begun thinking of Lone Tree as my backyard creek. It's just one hundred air miles from town, but it takes me seven hours, two hundred miles, and usually a backpack to reach it. I can hike in for the day, but that's not as good. A small tent, a squaw-wood fire, and waiting for the sun to break over the ridge and burn off the dew— that's the meat of it.

By midsummer the trail is obscured by nodding ferns, and you can lose it at the third fork where someone has started a shortcut to an elk camp. Stay to the left there. If you come to a fire-killed cedar fallen across the trail, you're on the right track. Walk around the log or the charred carbon of the 1910 fire will blacken your legs and bottom. You'll cross several feeder streams. Don't grow concerned when the trail veers from the obvious route and climbs a high, dry ridge. This is the final barrier. It will drop quickly through dense Doug-fir forest and unexpectedly deposit you at streamside.

You can start fishing here. There's usually an average-sized fish holding against the upstream bank. I prefer to put on waders, cross over to the big meadow, and carry camp another quarter-mile, dropping it just at the edge of the forest. After setting up the tent and breaking a few dead limbs for firewood, I'm free to fish the day far up the valley and race the night back to camp, splashing clumsily over rocks and boldly through rapids, for there is no trail and you must walk in the stream.

I'll return thirsty, having left under the delusion that a quart of water would carry me through the day. I've never heard of anyone's contracting giardiasis up here, but then I've never met anyone up here, either. The water looks too clear to hide even a *Giardia lamblia* cyst, but I'm not willing to take the risk. I envy my setter swimming the cool water, lapping it leisurely. Why is it dogs can eat and drink even the most putrid-looking stuff and come away smiling?

Last year, in a rare stroke of foresight, I packed one of those water-filtration pumps with me. It weighs less than a quart of water and lets me guzzle brazenly. The freedom of a wild animal.

This pump encouraged me to push farther upstream than I ever had before, past that long, shallow flat, past the two narrow pools where I took the seventeen-incher, into the dark canyon where mossy walls narrow over that cold, dark hole with the hippopotamus boulder in the center, its smooth back shimmering under the surface. I crouch and sneak along the west wall, then under it where eons of water have scoured out a grotto. It is shallow here, the bottom gritty sand, and my splashing echoes in diminuendo, a wet cave sound.

After duck-walking to the mouth of the cavern, I roll-cast a number 6 Joe's Hopper right into the tail-out bubbles. It is the wrong pattern in this forest water, but I want something big.

The fly bounces down the run, spins, catches an eddy, and swirls amid dark backwaters against the far wall. I wait, let it dance, let it tease.

Then a stick swirls into the eddy and bumps against the hopper. It's small and shouldn't foul me, so I wait for it to spin free. It looks almost like a small piece of cottonwood. Could it be? No, there aren't any cottonwoods on this high-mountain stream.

BATTENKILL
SEASONS

◆　◆　◆

CRAIG WOODS

THERE IS A STRETCH OF THE BATTENKILL RIVER, A TROUT STREAM IN southwestern Vermont, that lies across a meadow behind a house my mother and stepfather owned for a number of years. I used to fish it constantly whenever I was in Vermont during my college years. And after I finished college and moved to a nearby town, I fished it even more.

◆　◆　◆

The smell of woodsmoke is in the air, and it makes you think of warm places indoors, sheltered from the elements. The smooth, late-summer smell of freshly mowed fields is gone now, and you don't sweat from the walk into the flat-water stretch above the West Mountain Bridge. It is October, and you know that among the colorful leaves strewn on the water's slick surface, trout will be head-and-tail rising to emerging mayfly nymphs.

You know that the trout will be rising because you were there fishing to them the day before, and the day before that. In fact it's been five days in a row, and most of that time was spent trying to figure out what the fish were feeding on. Now you know that they are feeding on nymphs of a tiny green mayfly—a *Baetis* or *Pseudocloeon* mayfly—with a chunky little body and dark, blue-gray wings. The fly is so small that the imitations you have tied to match it are on size 18 and 20 hooks. All you did was to wrap a fuzzy green dubbing body on the hook shank.

You fish alone and in the middle of the day. You fish alone because it is autumn. You fish in the middle of the day because that is when the small flies hatch and because it will be warm in the Indian-summer sun. After years of fishing the river, you have just come to realize that this hatch in September and October is one of the few

times that you can count on rising trout and a predictable emergence
of flies. Most of the other hatches of the river are so inconsistent these
days that it is hard to catch them right; and when you do find rising
trout, they are superselective.

Some fly-fishermen say that the river is fished out. This is not
true. Biological data gathered by the state fish-and-game agency show
that the populations of trout in the river today compare favorably to
the populations of trout in the river twenty years ago. The trout are
simply becoming harder and harder to catch on flies. And they are
especially difficult to catch on dry flies.

But you think you have the answer now, at least for this hatch.
And you know the pod of trout that you'll try the simple green fly on
contains some good fish.

◆　◆　◆

Sometimes I would come down to my mother and stepfather's
house on a summer evening and leave my car in their driveway and
walk across the meadow and fish until dark. It was best on a June
evening during the Hendrickson hatch. Spinners—spent Hendrickson
mayflies—would fall on the water in large numbers, and trout would
be rising everywhere. When it would be very close to dark, when your
sense of hearing would begin to dominate over sight, the place was
magical. You could hear the slapping and smacking of rising trout, the
gurgle of the stream as it lapped the banks, the soughing of the leaves
in the tree limbs that hung over the river, the whirling of bats in the
air, all underscored by the distant churn of the riffle below the pool.
They were all quiet, lyrical noises.

◆　◆　◆

Everything happens in October. The river and the woods are
alive with activity, with an urgency. Everything moves as it does at no
other time of the year. The woodcock flights are beginning, migrations
from Newfoundland through New England to New Jersey, where the
birds congregate before continuing on to the spots where they will
winter. Ducks and geese are migrating. You seem to notice a change
in your little English setter even before you open the bird season—isn't
there something electric in her gait and overall demeanor when you
work her in the dried grasses and thinning woods that are the grouse
covers you located over the summer? The deciduous trees erupt in
their expression of fruition, and you look for the richness of the
colors—the reds, golds, and yellows—on the mountains to measure
against the amount of rainfall and sunshine in recent weeks to see if
the foliage is as bright or as dull as you guessed it would be. Everything

is happening, changing, moving, preparing for the grip of winter, which is long and hard in these parts.

You are moving, too. There is so much to do in these weeks of October, and you want to move quickly to get to it all—the hunting and the fishing—before it is gone for the winter. You want to make sure that you have gained enough sustenance from your sport to last you for the winter. It is your preparation for the coming grip; the thought that you won't have had enough scares you. You are aggressive—in a special, quiet, human way. But you are moving quickly like your surroundings, and you wish you could suck in everything that's happening to make sure it will last until spring. You begin to think that the term *Mother Nature* doesn't have to be childish and banal after all.

And the trout are moving, too. Mature fish have begun to seek out the spawning areas of clean gravel. They are aggressive in a savage way, eating as much as they can, storing up energy against the rigors of spawning and the demands of survival in the cold months. They have zeroed in on this hatch of small mayflies, and they rise eagerly to the nymphs in the surface film that are struggling to become airborne. The trout will come up—head, dorsal, tail—as long as there are flies to eat.

◆   ◆   ◆

If the fishing was really good, I would fish into the darkness, directing my fly and line toward the sound of the biggest rise, which I would sometimes see as a tiny glint on the otherwise ink-black surface of the stream. If an early moon was up, it was much easier. When my line landed on the water, there would be another glint— this one a quick, narrow streak of light—and I could gauge how close my fly had landed to the rise. When I hooked up to a trout, it was always different from the daytime. It was as though I was invisible, the trout was invisible, and the only reality was the live weight on my line. Trout always felt bigger in the dark.

When I finished fishing, I would walk across the meadow in the darkness and take off my waders and vest at the car and take down the little eight-foot Empress bamboo rod and put everything in the trunk of my car, a 1968 Ford Mustang that my stepfather bought used for me for five hundred dollars while I was in college. I paid him back over time. It was so hard for him to be able to give anything to my brother Jamie or me that I think this used car was something very important to him. I think it was to me.

When I had put everything in the trunk of the car, I would put on my sneakers and walk up to the house, going in through the kitchen. My mother would be finishing putting things away after dinner, and my stepfather would be in the living room watching TV or checking on his investments that were supporting them in their early retirement. My mother would save something from dinner if she knew I would be fishing late, and there was always cold beer in the refrigerator. Though occasionally I would kill trout for them, almost always I released everything I caught. So my stepfather would always make the same joke: "Would you like me to send someone down to the river with a truck to pick up all the fish you caught?"

We would visit while I drank my beer and ate something and they drank after-dinner scotch-and-waters. My stepfather was not an angler, and the thing that impressed my mother most about fishing was that Jamie and I—apparently bereft of any talent in the fine arts— could tie such detailed tiny flies. The house was always warm and inviting, with nice antiques and wide pine floorboards with Persian rugs over them.

◆　　◆　　◆

The trout are rising steadily when you reach the flat. You see some of the hatched-out olive duns floating on the water and some caddis flies in the air. But the trout want nothing to do with these insect forms. They want only to feed on the struggling nymphs a couple of inches below the water's surface. You remember reading a story by Russell Chatham about fly-fishing off Baja for yellowtail. He tells about discovering that the yellowtail are feeding selectively on small baitfish, which doesn't seem to make sense because there must be larger and more plentiful prey to be had. Funny to think, but it is just like that with these trout. They want only the little nymphs.

As you wade across the river, you feel as though you've just about worn a path on the stream bottom because you have fished from precisely the same spot for the last five days, at the head of a gravel bar on the far side of the stream.

The cast is difficult: The fly must land directly upstream from you, it must float down to you just two inches under the surface, and it must be twitched occasionally. You grease the leader to within two inches of the fly and begin to cast to the rising trout.

The leader jumps slightly when the first fish takes, and the trout bulls strongly downstream into the riffle below you. It is a larger fish than you thought it was. You backstep into the shallow water near the gravel bar, and as you do this, the fish moves on the surface. It's about fourteen or sixteen inches long and typical of this river's browns— silver-yellow on the flanks and sleek in shape. You play the fish's runs off the reel, and as the leader cuts through the water, bright leaves wash against it and get caught on the line-to-leader connection. When you bring the fish in, you kill it and clean it in the shallow water. Your hands smell like trout for the rest of the afternoon. It's a good smell.

You fish for four or five hours, and the little nymph works like a charm. The difficulty lies in getting the fish to take your fly instead of one of the many naturals, so you try to call a little extra attention to your imitation by working it slightly just as it passes a fish's nose. Your technique improves as the hours pass. Occasionally the wind gusts and rattles the branches of the oaks that line the upstream bank on your right, and acorns come down to riddle the water as though a handful of pebbles had been thrown into the stream. But it doesn't bother the trout. They keep working steadily. They are locked into their feeding. And you are locked into your fishing. Chipmunks and squirrels rush to gather the fallen bounty that has landed on the stream bank.

It is late afternoon when you leave. You are chilled from standing in the same spot for so long; your feet are numb. But the day's fishing has filled you with a special kind of warmth. You have kept several trout that you and Jane and Samia can have for dinner. None are as large as the first one, but they are all autumn bright, and you know the river can afford to lose them.

When you leave, you realize you will probably not see this stretch of water again until it is high and forbidding with spring snowmelt, a half a year away. The sun is off the valley, and the shadow line is halfway up Red Mountain, moving quickly.

When you leave, the trout are still rising.

◆   ◆   ◆

The last time I went to the stretch of river behind the house, I didn't go there to fish. It was an evening in May, not long after my mother's death, and I went there to sit on the rock on the far side of the river and to watch the trout rise. My stepfather was gone, too. I probably hadn't fished there for three years, but trout dimpled the surface right where they always had. I didn't go there to feel sorry for myself, but I did go there because I wanted to be alone and to be able to watch the trout rise and to look across the meadow at the house and remember a few things.

MY BEST HOUR OF FISHING

❖ ❖ ❖

HENRY WILLIAMSON

EVENING IS THE BEST TIME TO CAST FOR TROUT IN THE SMALL STREAM which runs down the valley, a few yards away from my cottage door. For, as the low sun lengthens the shadows of the oaks in the deer park, the spinners appear over the trout stream.

A spinner is a water fly rising and falling regularly in flight as it prepares to lay its eggs on the water. It is a beautiful, delicate, ethereal creature, subsisting only on air and sunlight during its brief winged life since hatching from the riverbed in the morning. These ephemeral flies live, usually, only a few hours; and at evening you see them rising and falling over the water, dropping their eggs until, exhausted, they sink down and with wings spread flat, drift away with the current, and so out of life—their cycle or racial purpose completed.

I was standing still by the bend of the river, a rod in my hand, and watching the fast run of water slowing up into deeper water below. I was about to make my first cast into the run. The river running through the deer park is only a few miles from its source on Exmoor, and in summer the water is usually low, and generally clear, except when cattle in the morning and afternoon heats have been cooling themselves under the shade of alders. Toward evening any slight cloudiness has settled, however, and the river runs clear, so that in the glides one can see every stone and speck of gravel, every tiny red-spotted samlet of that spring's hatching. During January and the early part of February the water had been high, and salmon coming in from the Atlantic had been able to run much farther up the river than usual at the beginning of the year. As the river became smaller in April, they sought the deepest water they could find. And as the river shrank during May and June, they were forced to spend most of the daylight under the muddy roots of the waterside alders, waiting for twilight and cooler water and safety from the glare of day.

There was a solitary salmon lodged under a clump of roots a few yards below where I was standing at the bend. The water was about two feet deep only—and that salmon was trapped.

I had been watching that fish for more than two months. Its life was one of solitary confinement. When it had first appeared, it had been a bluish silver, and very lively; now it was a pinkish brown and obviously dejected. I could usually see its tail sticking out of the roots about eleven o'clock in the morning, before the shadow of a branch hid it. And if I went to the bridge again about noon, I was likely to see the salmon sidle out of the roots, turn slowly into the shallow current, idle there like a great trout for a few moments, its back fin out of water, and then gather way while it prepared for a leap—a great splash, and it had fallen back, and the narrow river rocked and rippled with the impact. After remaining in midstream for a minute or so, the fish would drift back toward its hiding place, in obvious dejection, and push itself under the roots again.

Now on this particular evening I was standing beside the run, a small seven-foot rod of split cane in my hand. I was about to drop lightly an imitation of a red spinner, tied to a cast of single horsehair, into the run. To a trout this lure of steel and silk and twisted gamecock hackle gave the effect of a live fly; and by this trick I hoped to get my breakfast. But for nearly twenty minutes I had been standing motionless at the bend of the river, hardly daring to move. For when I was about to make my first cast, standing still in water about ten inches deep, the salmon had swum slowly up the run and paused within a few inches of my feet.

Very slowly I turned my head to watch it. After a while it turned on its side and sinuated on the gravel, as though trying to scrape away the itch in its gills—from minute freshwater maggots, which were beginning to cluster there. It actually pushed itself against my left boot. Then it idled awhile, before beginning a series of gentle rolling movements, porpoise-like. Then it swam up the run, pushing waves from bank to bank; and making a slashing turn in water shallower than its own depth, it hurtled down the run again, making a throbbing or thruddling noise as it passed. Entering deeper water again, it leapt and smacked down on its side. Then up it came once more, lifting half of itself out of water, and idled in the run, maintaining its place with the slightest of slow sinuating movements, scarcely perceptible. I saw a bit of crowfoot weed drifting down. As it passed the fish, it was seized, held in its mouth, then blown out suddenly.

Then the salmon turned round violently to seize it again. It was playing with the weed. I stood there more than an hour, the finest fishing hour of my life, watching that lonely salmon playing by itself—a fish a yard long, imprisoned in a few square yards of space, threatened by asphyxiation in warm water, by gaff of poacher, by beak of heron, by eels which would eat it alive, by disease, by otters, by many other dangers. I watched until dusk, when it moved down into deeper water below.

If it survives, if rain comes to widen and deepen the river, that salmon will wait there, or in a like place, until October, when with others it will spawn—which means it will spend itself for the future of its race—and then, in all probability, being a male fish, it will die. Meanwhile it lies there stagnantly throughout the long, hot summer days, waiting until the going down of the sun and twilight and darkness—full of glowing life and stars and cold running water, which is its very life.

A WOMAN'S PLACE

◆ ◆ ◆

JUDY MULLER

A WOMAN'S PLACE IS IN HER HOME WATER. AND FOR THIS WOMAN, THAT means water without men. Or women. Just me and the fish. It took me a long time to come to this realization. I had always fished with *someone:* father, brother, significant others, insignificant others, and friends. And since I'd been fly-fishing since childhood, that added up to a lot of company on a lot of streams.

Not that I don't like a fishing companion or two. It's just that my best-ever fishing experience happened to be the day I first ventured out all by myself. And while I've fished beautiful streams in many places before and after, it is that day and that place that come to mind when I need to take a mental detour from the rat race of the city, even if just for a moment.

Perhaps that is the true test of home water. Lean back at your desk, close your eyes, and wish yourself back to the place where each facet of the day was just right, each facet twinkling like the sun on the water, and then you'll know. "That's the one," you'll say, as the figment of a rainbow leaps across your desk.

As it happens, I stumbled onto my perfect day. I'd like to say that I went to the woods, Thoreau-like, to fish deliberately and alone. Nah. The thought of going fishing alone that weekend was the last thing on my mind. I mean, I hate going to the *movies* alone. I'd invited my fishing friends and even my nonfishing friends. I'd even asked my teenage daughters. No luck. "To hell with them all," I thought, and headed for the little cabin in the Catskills I'd rented for the season.

But behind the bravado was the feeling that I was kidding myself. What fun would it be to fish alone? What would be the point of landing a big, fat trout if no one was there to witness it? And beyond this classic "if a tree falls in the forest" question were more practical matters. My real fear was that I would be incompetent out there all alone. In a crunch, I'd always had someone to consult. What fly to use? What size, what color? Which tippet? Which pool? On the other hand, I realized, there would be no one there to snicker if I spent the entire day snagging rocks and branches. As I set off, then, it seemed pretty much of a wash. No one to appreciate my performance, but no one to ridicule it.

What I did not foresee was the exhilaration that comes from being liberated from this performance anxiety. To demonstrate just how liberating, at least from a female perspective, I digress for a moment to another sort of day on the river. In this case, the Beaverkill. Specifically, the famous Cairns Pool. "To grasp the essence of home waters," a Zen fly-fishing master might say, "is to grasp the essence of crowded waters." Nothing like a bit of yin to help you appreciate the yang.

Cairns Pool in the peak of the season definitely qualifies as yin. I arrived on a lovely summer day with my fishing companion, a significant other of significant fishing skill. Built-in performance anxiety. Add to the mix about seven or eight fishermen lined up on one side of the river. John and I crossed over to the other side to get away from them. And John moved downstream a bit to get away from me. Leaving me alone to face my audience. For make no mistake, that's how I felt: on stage. There I was, facing a lineup of guys, and they were *all* guys, on the other side.

I stepped out on a rock and raised my rod. I felt like an orchestra conductor raising her baton. I also felt a sinking sensation. Literally. The rock I had chosen to step out on was sloped and mossy, and the felt soles on my boots knew they'd finally met their match. I tried to get my footing, to no avail. I slid down into the water, rod raised over my head, like a sinking Statue of Liberty.

Back on the bank, as I emptied the water from my waders, I sneaked a glance across the river. Nary a snicker, nary a flinch. But before this day would end, they would be sorely tested.

Within the hour, we had a caddis hatch and the water came alive with fish. John had worked his way back upstream, and he called out to me to put on a Bivisible, said it was working for him. No one on the other side, I noticed, was having any luck. I didn't have any Bivisibles, so he gave me one of his.

So there I was, ready to make a comeback after my disastrous first act. The hatch was on, the fly was on, and I was on. *Too* on. In my eagerness to prove myself, I missed the first strike. Missed the fish, that is, but got the tree. The upper reaches of the tree. Still not a snicker or sneer from the other side. As I tried in vain to retrieve the fly from the topmost branch, John said, in a remarkably calm voice, "Don't waste time on that, not while a hatch is on. Here, take another." So I frantically tied on another Bivisible, wondering just how many he could possibly have left. I soon got my answer, after placing *that* fly in the *same* tree. I lost the second fly and my cool right about the same time. *"Quick!"* I screamed. "Give me another *Bisexual!"*

That finally proved to be too much for the guy directly across the river. He exploded with laughter. Actually, it was more of an implosion. I mean, you have to figure the guy had been holding it in for about an hour, ever since my initial baptism. The other guys in the lineup turned into a Greek chorus of cackles and snorts.

To say that I was now in a frenzy not unlike that of the fish still feeding in front of me would be an understatement. I tied on one last Bivisible, or at least the last one John would admit to having, and cast it perfectly, if I do say so myself, right into the lineup of feeding trout. And *wham!* I had one on, much to the dismay of the scoffers across the way. For they had yet to catch a thing. This was the fly, all right. No sooner had I released one trout than another was mine for the casting. In my memory, which certainly might be faulty, I recall that each fish was bigger than the one before. As the sun set that day, I looked across the river one more time. No one was laughing.

Now, if I had never gone fishing alone, I probably would rank that day at Cairns Pool right up near the top of Life's Most Satisfying Moments. But to be honest, the satisfaction was rooted in ego and pride and, yes, gender. It was all about proving something to others, which is all right up to a point.

Going beyond that point meant proving something to myself. And I couldn't do that until I'd gone fishing alone. But I didn't know that as I parked my car that solitary day above a beautiful stretch of private water in the Catskills.

(An aside for a moment on the issue of private versus public water. Generally speaking, I believe all waters should be open to all people. Unless, of course, I happen to luck into an invitation to fish private water, in which case I manage to squelch my populist bias. One has to keep an open mind, after all.)

So there I was, all alone, trudging down the path to the river, vest packed to the gills, so to speak, with every conceivable gadget I could possibly need. Yes, Bivisibles, too. My heart may not have been in this fishing-alone thing, but my head was. I'd already adjusted my thinking. I had prepared for any eventuality because there wouldn't be anyone to lean on or filch from.

It happened to be a glorious day. On this clear Catskill stream on this clear, cloudless day, it was hard to believe that New York City was just two hours away. I prefer small streams, streams where I can cast across to banks on the opposite side without much problem, streams with variety: cascading water, riffles, deep pools, and pockets. This spot was made to order. Stepping into the water, I felt the cares of the city and the responsibilities of home float away.

As I listened to the liquid language of the stream as it burbled along, making conversation with everything in its path, I realized I had no *plan*, no schedule. This came as something of a shock. We Type A's always have a schedule, even when we're having fun. But now, with no one along to impress, I had no strategy, no deadline, no quota. It was the most delicious unburdening. Now, I was free to pick and choose my pools, my riffles, my pocket water.

With all that freedom to choose, I chose to do nothing. I stood in the river for quite some time, just thinking about the possibilities. Instead of rushing in where anglers fear to tread, or should fear to tread, I took my time reading the water. It was low and clear. The fish would be spooky. With someone else along, those conditions would be intimidating. "Fast water, dumb fish," that's my motto. But alone, I suddenly considered spooky fish a welcome challenge.

Crossing over to the other side, I took a shortcut across a meadow to start fishing in a pool upstream, a spot where lacy ferns, overhanging pines, and mossy rocks provide a lush frame for a spectacular waterfall. As I stepped into the edge of that picture, and the stream, I was greeted by the roar of the falls and a cool spray. And then it happened. I lost my footing and went down on my waderized keister. Out of habit, I looked around to see if anyone was watching. And then I heard the sound of laughter. Mine.

What is the sound of one voice laughing? A mighty welcome sound. This was the yang, all right. I was free to fall on my ass, free to snag in a tree or two, and, with any luck, free to get into some nice fish before the day was through.

And before the day was through, I would. All of the above. Looking back on it, I can remember a flow of events rather than specific moments. I developed a rhythm to my casting and a method to my madness. *Put your fly right along that log over there,* I'd tell myself. And with no one watching, with no pressure to perform, I'd put the fly right in that spot and watch it drift, sans drag, right over a feeding fish. And nine times out of ten, he would take it. And nine times out of ten, I'd let out a whoop. It didn't matter if that fish were a brookie or a brown, he deserved a whoop before he was released back into current.

There was no hatch on while I was on the stream that day, so I offered up a variety of tempting dry flies. I had the best luck with a

Royal Wulff, the ice-cream sundae of dry flies, a fly that resembles absolutely nothing in nature. Perhaps that's why I like it; it makes no sense. And in a sport where almost everything is overanalyzed, it's reassuring to know that something that makes no sense can be so effective.

One fish still stands out. I caught him on a Royal Wulff, at the tail end of a beautiful pool, at the tail end of my perfect day. A rainbow of considerable girth and energy, he jumped right out of the water, his bands of color flashing in the sun before a spectacular dive and run. I had trouble removing the fly from his mouth and found myself apologizing as I struggled to release him. "I'm-sorry-I'm-sorry-I'm sorry," I muttered like a mantra. Had someone come along, they would surely have thought me mad.

But no one did come along, not for a very long time. Toward dusk, I was crouched near a small pool beneath a large log, talking to and releasing yet another nice rainbow, and then I heard it. A voice other than my own. I looked across the stream, up toward the dirt road on the cliff above, and saw several people standing by their car, watching. I don't know how long they'd been watching, but rather than taking some pleasure from inadvertently performing so well for an audience, I was annoyed. They were interlopers, intruders, *voyeurs*.

And that's when I knew I had crossed over a threshold into a new level of fishing pleasure. I knew this for sure when someone asked me the next day, "So how was the fishing? How many did you catch?" And I couldn't remember.

I had stopped counting.

SOLITAIRE

* * *

TED KERASOTE

SUNDAY. SORE FROM THE PREVIOUS DAY'S CLIMB, WE SIT ON THE DECK and watch the cirrostratus bloom over the Tetons, promising rain by the afternoon. Down from Montana, Ed and Nancy are interested in finding some equine property. Chrislip, my climbing partner who is on holiday between consulting jobs, will be heading back to Colorado soon. Touched by having three friends visit at the same time, I momentarily indulge myself and imagine this northwestern corner of Wyoming as the center of the continent.

But after coffee, Ed and Nancy saddle up their Volvo and return to Bozeman, and Chrislip goes into Jackson on an errand. Left with an abyss of unstructured time, I drift by the study's bookshelves—too filled with other people's emotions—and gravitate to the back room where most of my time-structurers lie: the road bike, the climbing and kayaking gear, and my fishing rods.

Gathering waders and vest, I hesitate a moment and then pick the two-weight, which at one and a half ounces is so light and effortless in the hand that it rarely colors a day astream with purpose. In fact, throwing line with its taut, eight-foot length reminds me more of blowing bubbles than of anything so scientific as duping a trout with a bit of feather and flotsam.

At the eastern border of Grand Teton National Park, the Gros Ventre River turns away from the road, recedes behind a swell of spruce-covered hills, and runs incognito for several miles before re-emerging as a rocky channel behind the Teton Valley Ranch, the small settlement of Kelly, and my house.

Few anglers fish this back bend because to reach it one must wade the Gros Ventre above a small rapid that tumbles directly into a band of cliffs that guard a deep, green pool. Even after you've studied the crossing through polarized glasses and chosen the shallowest line, the ford can be waist-deep, through a strong current. The unfit and the timid usually turn back here.

I am neither. Nonetheless, I have never much liked swimming in fast rivers. Therefore, going with the flow and treading over the rocks with care, I quarter across, reach the other side without incident, then walk a gravel bar to the pools below the cliffs. In one of those moments that still leaven the animistic portion of my soul, the sun unexpectedly emerges from the bank of lowering black clouds and spreads a rich tannic light across the bottom.

Before threading my line through the guides, I turn over some stones in the shallows and find them teeming with the small black cases of Trichoptera caddis larvae, the second stage of the four stages— egg, larva, pupa, and adult—that take this insect from birth to death.

Most anglers, including myself, resist the intrusion of this sort of entomological language into casual excursions. Yet mastery of a task has always produced a specialized vocabulary, and as I've become more sophisticated in matching the insect life of rivers with imitations, the Latin used in taxonomy has become part of my workaday language. I have friends, though, who refute my argument, stating that such pretensions are no more than another symptom of the complex life I live. To them, I can only say that immersion in one's environment has always produced such lexicons. Witness such peoples as the Eskimos, who are routinely viewed by us technocrats as being close to the heart of nature, who have scores of words for what we call nothing more than "snow."

Holding the larvae in my palm, I remember a fishing text informing me that the order Trichoptera comprises about nine hundred species. Feeling inadequate, I guess that this is the genus *Limnephilus*, whose larvae form thick, tubular cases of stone and sand around themselves. Hoping that the trout aren't as fastidious as my old Latin teacher and some other fishermen I know, I tie on two small black flies—one that I bought in New Zealand a couple of years ago and whose name I can no longer remember, and one called simply a Pheasant Tail. Both somewhat resemble the larvae on the river's stones.

Those unfamiliar with fly-fishing may find this grubbing about on the bottom of a river while mumbling Latin flummery a bit disconcerting and certainly not in keeping with the classic view of the fly angler dropping a lovely winged imitation delicately onto the surface of a placid stream dimpled by the rings of rising trout. Yet just as we eat toast rather than croissants most mornings, so, too, these plebian nymphs and larvae provide the bulk of a trout's diet. Those skilled in plumbing the depths of a river with these homely flies take far more fish on far more days than those who hope to lure a trout to the surface for a dramatic strike.

Tackle rigged, I wade across a submerged bar to the tail of the pool that rushes by the cliffs and quiets into a flume of dark green opulence. Wild roses grow on the cliffs, and their pink petals turn in the eddies at the base of the rocks.

I'm bargaining that the pool is home to *Salmo clarki*, the native trout of the Rockies, the cutthroat. Named for the reddish orange slash that extends along each side of its lower jaw, the "cutt" has an olive back, a yellow belly, and a hint of cranberry along its sides, upon which are scattered black spots. In its case, its common name, *cutthroat*, is a bit more accurate than *Salmo*, which means "to leap," which the fish rarely does, and *clarki*, after Captain William Clark, who, like all those individuals who have been honored by having their name given to a species, merely happened upon a creature whose existence antedated its discoverer's by millennia.

As a sport fish the cutthroat gets mixed reviews. Those who like catching numerous fish for the pan enjoy it. Those who are used to the challenge of rainbows or browns find the cutt omnivorous and gullible. In fact, a study in Yellowstone National Park found that wild cutthroat trout were twice as catchable as wild brook trout (and brookies are known for their stupidity) and about eighteen times as catchable as that professor of the salmonids, the brown trout. Nonetheless, in the pan, few fish rival the orange-meated sweetness of a cutthroat, and with respect to the aesthetics of the wild, few sights can match that of this orange, yellow, and green fish swirling close to your net as you stand knee-deep in a stream far from the road.

As I begin to cast upstream, violet-green swallows sweep from the cliffs, twittering speedy chorales. In nymph-fishing the object is to allow the imitation to tumble freely near bottom. Therefore, I've added two split shot to the ten-foot leader, which will take the flies down to the rocks. Of course, if the water is deep, the resultant and hoped-for action is sometimes invisible. This is the case today, and I can only keep a careful eye on the end of my flyline. Any sudden twitch or dart downward can mean that the split shot has bounced over a rock or that a fish has taken the fly.

On the third drift the flyline darts, I lift the rod, and a steady throbbing pressure indicates that *Salmo* has taken one of my nymphs. The trout makes one run downstream, no more than a feet, before shaking the hook, which, because I release most of my fish, is barbless.

I cast upstream and within the first ten feet of drift hook a cutthroat that runs the length of the pool, flashes near the surface twenty yards from me, then sulks on the bottom. Walking downstream, I recover line, pleased with the heaviness of the fish. Two more runs tire it, and as I crank the leader into the guides and reach with my landing net, I feel the sinking emptiness that comes when one's expectations aren't met by reality.

The fish that struggles in the net is *Prosopium williamsoni*, the mountain whitefish, or as a friend who is a fishing guide sarcastically calls it, "the prince of the river." Widely distributed in the western United States and native to the headwaters of the Missouri River basin, the whitefish has a tubular body lacking elegance of line. It also has a short head, an overhanging snout, a blunt and suckerlike mouth, and a uniformly whitish-green color highlighted by a single pink blush on its gill plates. A careful look reveals this mark isn't pigmentation, but gills showing through the transparent gill cover.

The whitefish takes almost every fly that a trout will, fights well, and grows larger than most of its riverine neighbors. In fact, the specimen in my hand is twenty inches long. On most streams in the United States a twenty-inch trout is greeted with hosannas by all except the most incurably blasé. Yet I place the fish back in the river with no more than a disappointed sigh.

Perhaps if *Prosopium*, which means "small mask," had a nose job or visited the Ralph Lauren Shop of the piscatorial world and got some pastels to liven up the drab business-white it wears, anglers would like it more. Alas, even when you can catch many of them, they never seem to satisfy.

This callous fact is brought home with ever more certainty as I work through the pool and take whitefish after whitefish. I stop counting after one dozen. Yet I can't bring myself to leave. The perfume of the rose petals, the cavorting of the swallows, the gentle wind blowing the willows—all seem to demand a trout, to infuse an angler's harmony into the scene.

No trout touches my fly. Soon I begin to think that perhaps the Gros Ventre—whose name means "big, inflated, gross belly" in the French of the trappers—is telling me something. Maybe I can become a master of whitefishing and write a book called *Poisson Blanc*.

Finally I give up, abandon the pool, and walk downriver, hoping to leave the princes of the river behind. Descending to the shore again, I walk in ankle-deep water and scout the rapids and pools where the river falls in an S-shaped bend.

Passing a large rock, I start and jump back a step. At my feet is a writhing, two-foot-long snake. Its ugly, misshapen head sprouts four green eyes and two pectoral fins.

I lean forward and see that I haven't discovered a new four-eyed monster to which will be appended a *kerasoti*, but a copper-colored snake, jaws agape around the nearly swallowed torso of a mottled sculpin.

The sculpin, which resembles a catfish, has thick, rubbery lips and a wide, flattened head with eyes on top. Its ventral fins stick from the corners of the snake's jaws, and the snake's eyes, distorted backward as it tries to swallow the fish, peer at me with a cold, malignant light. It probably thinks I'm going to steal its dinner.

Sculpins live under stones and logs, yet they are fairly spry little fish and I'm surprised that the snake, sliding along looking for a meal, was able to catch it. Perhaps the sculpin was snoozing when the garter snake came upon it.

Yet this one-inch-wide snake attempting to eat a two-inch-wide fish—both bug-eyed, straining, gagging, and gulping—turns this ordinary act of survival into a scene so voracious, gluttonous, and disgusting as to be almost pornographic.

I am unable to avert my eyes. I want to see more and follow the snake downstream, where, trying to elude me, it wedges itself between two rocks. I reach down and grasp it behind its head, and in three heaving belches it vomits up the intact sculpin, whose dorsal fin is now somewhat frayed.

The fish falls on a flat rock, takes a spasmodic gasp, and lies still. Suddenly feeling that I've interfered with an event in which I had no business, I put the snake back in the river and innocently expect it to return to its prey. But it swims off five cautious feet and watches me. Red ants now begin to march from the willows next to the rock. A few walk over the sculpin and, within seconds, communicate by their hurried motions that dinner has arrived. Hordes come from the shore and swarm over the limp fish.

I retire to the bank and watch. The snake, a smart fellow when all is said and done, keeps its beady little eyes directly on mine and won't move. After fifteen minutes I decide that I want to fish for cutthroats more than I want to see who wins the sculpin. I bid the scene adieu.

As the sky blackens and lightning flickers on the far hillsides, I work the pools downstream and catch whitefish in every one. Soon my standing in the river with an eight-foot rod waving in the air while lightning draws closer seems like a poor idea, so I get out and walk on the bank until a beautiful pool appears around the next bend. A rock juts into its depths, and, hoping that the lightning will pass to the north, I clamber onto the rock and cast. The wind has picked up, rain is hitting the water, and a loop of my flyline catches around the butt of my rod. As I untangle it—in a moment devoid of skill—I get a strike. Releasing the line from the butt, I set the hook and feel a vehemence that I haven't felt in any of the other strikes I've received all afternoon. The fish runs off fifty feet of line into the center of the river, broaches, and by its pink sides and flash of orange I know that, at last, I've hooked a native.

I follow downstream as it takes line from the reel, leaps, cartwheels, and slugs it out for all it's worth. Of course, it doesn't know I'm going to release it.

Perhaps I won't even get it to net. The two-weight rod isn't a winch, and the 5X tippet is closer to sewing thread than fishing line, which is why, if you land a big fish on this ultralight tackle, you get to wear an imaginary campaign ribbon on your chest for the next few weeks.

The campaign ribbon is growing with every minute that the fight continues. Each run indicates that this isn't a twelve-incher, or even a fifteen-incher. Once, as I get the trout close and see its olive back glimmer two yards from me, it appears husky and perhaps twenty inches long. It could weigh three pounds. Then it dashes from sight, taking another forty feet of line.

Wind spits leaves across the current. Thunder rolls down the valley. The surface of the stream is alive with pelting drops. Amid the storm, for just a second or two, I suddenly imagine keeping the trout, and broiling it with all the pomp it deserves. I could serve it on a tray, for some friends to whom I've promised a fish dinner, along with the chardonnay that lies on the cool bottom shelf of one of the kitchen cabinets. And I suddenly hear my internal voice say, "Please . . . let me land this fish."

It takes another few minutes to work the tiring trout to the net, where, its broad tail over the rim, it lunges heroically and the fly— that tiny black imitation of *Limnephilus*—flies freely into the rain. No line breakage, no poor technique, only a quirk of fate—and fishing with a barbless hook—lets the fish escape.

As the rain tapers to a close and the thunder disappears to the east, I continue to cast, but I can't raise a strike, not even from a whitefish. Since the storm and the fight seemed to have been set by Wagner, I decide not to close the day with endless Beckett. Hooking the fly into the rod butt, I begin walking upstream on a game trail.

As I break into a clearing, I spy a tawny shoulder on its far edge and two tiny, spotted fawns leaping in the wet grass. No more than a few days old, they take springing leaps as their little white flags dart like the wings of swifts. The mother whitetail, sensing that a still form has appeared in the clearing, raises her head and watches me while her twins jump about her and even nuzzle her belly for milk. Then, with the solemnity of a queen, she walks into the forest.

Angling back to the river, I aim for the spot where the snake vomited its prey upon a rock. Recollecting the start with which I first witnessed the four-eyed monster, I also can't help but wonder if a fishing vest full of carefully tied flies, a 1½-ounce graphite rod, and a funeral of dill and chardonnay make the end any better for a trout than for a sculpin.

The stone where the fish lay lies perfectly bare—no sign of prey or snake or ants. Could those Lilliputian hordes have dragged the Gulliver off? Did the snake return for its rightful catch? Or, by some miracle, could the sculpin have resuscitated itself and flopped back into the river?

No answer presents itself, though the pools below the cliffs lie damasked by rose petals torn by the wind.

PRIVATE WATERS: ROLLING YOUR OWN FARM POND

• • •

VANCE BOURJAILY

THE MOST EXCITING FISH I EVER BROUGHT OUT OF THE WATER TOOK ME two years to catch.

I finally got it on a lusterless, old, machine-tied, Japanese white streamer fly, using a workaday eight-foot fly rod, the maker's name of which has long since worn away. It was equipped with one of those small-boy, skeleton fly reels, without click or drag, a frayed silk line that didn't float anymore, and, for leader, about twenty inches of undifferentiated monofilament snipped off the end of the supply on an abandoned spin-cast reel.

My cast, if that's the word, was a fifteen-footer. I let the old fly sink away, started to retrieve slowly, overhand, and the fish appeared, drifting upward toward the lure, opening its mouth just under the surface, sucking in, and hooking itself.

There were a couple of bullfrogs watching. They didn't move. It was three o'clock of a hot afternoon.

My fish, as I eased it in, was seven, well, six, inches long. It fought with all the ferocity of a ladyfinger being slid out from among the whipped cream and strawberries of a charlotte russe. It looked up at me from the shallow water at my feet, goggling at, I think, the sheer incomprehensibility of what was happening.

I looked back, grinning in absolute joy. I knelt, wet my left hand, took the little thing off the hook, and sent it swimming away with a whispered word of benediction. Then I whooped like a drunk cowboy, dropped the rod, jumped up in the air, turned, and ran all the way down to our farmhouse, half a mile away, to tell the family:

"They survived. We've got a walleye population."

This was in the fourth of the five ponds we've built and stocked with fish on our Iowa farm, and if the fishing memories, some a little more conventionally dramatic, mostly belong to spring and summer evenings, the story of each pond would start with winter dreaming.

◆   ◆   ◆

The first was conceived on a February afternoon, and not by me. I would have to admit, as a matter of fact, that I found it inconceivable, to begin with.

It came into the conversation as my wife and I were being shown the land by a real estate man, but the seller was along, too. The seller was anxious. In his view the place was hilly and farmed out. It had a muddy creek flowing through the best field, a branch of the same creek flowing through another. It had a lot of timberland he hadn't been able to afford to clear, some places that were too steep to fence off, and even several patches inaccessible except on foot. I'm not sure if he realized that some of these drawbacks were assets in our eyes; he kept pointing out commercial virtues he thought we might miss.

"Had corn right here, three good, hundred-bushel years," he was saying as we climbed toward the highest land on the farm. "You could put it in beans now and get a heck of a crop."

I wasn't much of a farmer, but even I knew, looking at the eroded soil, that those hillsides needed to be put in pasture and would be, even so, a long time healing . And that a crop of soybeans would only loosen the dirt more and turn the ruts and washes into gullies. I replied with an unfriendly grunt, and the man changed the subject.

"Me and my brother was going to build a big pond here," he said. "Raise catfish. Now pond-raised catfish, that's the new thing. Sell 'em to restaurants and supermarkets, they'll take all they can get."

"Weren't you telling me the creeks flood all over the bottom fields in the spring?" I asked.

"Well, not every spring. And like I say, when the water goes down, that silt's left with a world of fertilizer in it. Washes off the other fellow's field, right onto yours."

"How could you dam one of those creeks to make a pond? It would cost a million dollars."

"Couldn't do her for a million," he agreed.

"Then where were you and your brother going to hold the water for your catfish?" I asked. "Or were those cornfield catfish?"

"Right here, like I told you." He was pointing across about as dry-looking a gulch as I'd ever seen. Furthermore, it was a gulch full of trees, some of them quite large. The gulch was about ninety feet across and twenty deep, and it cut back between the hill we were standing on and the next hill over, its floor sloping up between them for a hundred yards or so until it split into two smaller gulches and disappeared into deep woods.

Before I could ask my man what sort of fool he took me for, he told me, "Why, you just can't understand at all, can you?" He slowed his speech and separated each word distinctly. "Now, this here we are looking into, it is a main waterway. This here drains about forty acres up above. What you have to do is clear the sides and bottom. Then you block it off with a clay dam, right across, from one sidehill to the other. See? You drop in a tube for the overflow, and you got her."

"Sure," I said. "And what do you do for water? Haul it up in buckets?"

"Didn't I just get done telling you?"

"Are you trying to say there's springs, or what?"

"Runoff. Runoff." He shook his head at my dimness. "Melt of snow and fall of rain. Drainin' down through the grassy roots, and all the weedy waterways, and down between the trees in the timbers. . . ."

I swear I could smell it, when he said that, all that lovely soft rainwater, sifting through leaf mold and around wildflower stems, dripping off limbs and seed heads, gathering, and I almost missed the wonderful thing he said next:

"Believe you could get cost-sharing."

That was when I learned that the state and especially the federal governments are more than casually interested in having farm ponds built, and that the Department of Agriculture may, if certain requirements can be met, help pay for the building. Equally important, the department will send along government engineers, my favorite public servants, to look at locations and do survey and design.

Nor is it inconsistent with my present purpose to add that, although getting its citizens to go fishing is not the government's goal—its interest is in the soil conservation that results from water control—nevertheless, it will good-naturedly send along some fish when things get ready.

By our first summer on the farm, we had our application in for help. The engineers had come out and agreed, to my slight chagrin, that the seller's spot was a fine one for a two-acre pond. We were approved; we solicited bids; we picked a contractor.

Daniel Keith Yoder was and is the contractor's name; he has built four of our five ponds, and I celebrate him here as Michelangelo of the bulldozer. Daniel Keith has an eye for dirt, for where to dig it, how to shape it, finish it, and dress the job. His work delights not only his customers but even the engineers whose designs he accomplishes. Other contractors they grumble at; Daniel Keith is their pet. It was after I had watched him through our first project that I began to hear myself, sworn enemy of all machines with blades, say, "Perhaps, after all, man was born to move dirt."

It began sadly, though, and there were unexpected sorrows down the road. Argue, if you wish, that they make the joys keener; still, I recall my hackberry tree.

Most of what had to be cleared from the pond site was brush, box elder, willow, cottonwood, and aspen—nice things, but fast-growing, and plenty more like them were around the farm. There were, on the other hand, half a dozen decent white oaks and a fine black cherry; but those I could take out with a chain saw and would be glad to have the lumber. There were some straight young hickories, hardly more than poles, which I didn't like to lose, and there was the hackberry. It was the biggest one of its kind on the farm, a beautifully shaped shade tree of no great value as lumber, a relative of the dying elms but immune to the beetles that were killing them, a corky-barked, silvery, big tree.

"Anything you don't want to salvage, we'll grub out and push into a pile. You can burn it or not," Daniel Keith said.

"Or leave it for a rabbit house," said my friend Tom, who was thinking of getting a beagle.

Daniel Keith walked off, to set engineer flags around the projected waterline.

"It's that hackberry, Tom," I said. "It must be a hundred years old."

"You never get anything without giving up something else," Tom said, but I'm pretty sure his mind was sorting through the half-dozen Orvis bamboo rods he owns, as his eyes followed Daniel Keith's journey around the waterline. I decided Tom was watching for places with room for a decent back cast. Thinking so cheered me up, anyway.

Our chief entertainment that August was walking up to watch Daniel Keith on his dozer, directing, as he drove it, the work of two other such machines and a couple of big scrapers that moved most of the dirt.

Once the clearing was done, they rolled back and piled all the topsoil, to use for dressing later. Then, just past the line which the dam was to follow and down at what would be the base, Daniel Keith began, to my astonishment, to dig. What he dug was a trench, eight feet deep and ten feet wide, straight across the bottom of the gulch. This was to be packed with the best clay they could find, he explained, so that water couldn't work through the ground under the dam.

On the day he was to start packing the trench, my wife and I were walking up to watch when we heard the motors stop. All of them.

"That's ominous," Tina said, and we hurried. At the site, we saw that Daniel Keith was off his machine and down inside the trench. He looked up, saw us, and waited till we had slid down to a place just above him.

"Sand," he said, in about the same tone of voice one might use in saying *scorpion* or *rattlesnake*. Sometime in the recent geological past, there'd been a watercourse down there, with a sandy bottom, just the sort of thing the trench was supposed to intercept, but deeper, more extensive. "We'll need to get a dragline now," Daniel Keith said, "and see can he get through the sand, dig it out. It'll cost you. If he can't get it all, we'll have to give up on this pond. The other thing we can do, now, is save the cost. Just fill in and go away, not take the chance. It's up to you."

I'm not sure I said anything.

"Depends on how much a fellow wants a pond, I guess," said Daniel Keith sympathetically.

I looked over at the pile where my hackberry tree lay on its side, roots and all, with brush and young hickories piled against it. There was no thought involved. I just felt like a fellow who wanted a pond pretty much, but I glanced at Tina next. She seemed to be the same kind of fellow, because she nodded without any hesitation at all.

"Let's get that dragline, Daniel Keith," I said, and he grinned, and I'm happy to report that it all worked out. The added cost wasn't more than a couple of hundred dollars. Daniel Keith supposed I knew—but I didn't until later, or I wouldn't have been so firm and cool—that it could more easily have been a couple of thousand.

That first pond, in those uninflated days, cost $2,500. The government paid a little over half.

What we had, when the machines rumbled off, was a deep, raw, two-and-a-half-acre basin, steepest and deepest where the dam blocked off the lower end. I think it was twenty-one feet down, from the brave little flags that marked the someday-waterline, and the question now was *how soon?* In late September we had a half-day's rain. I hurried up to the pond as soon as it ended and saw that the sides of the basin were scarred from little rivulets of water now collected at the bottom in a lot of mud and perhaps a fifty-gallon puddle. At 326,000 gallons of water per acre foot, times 2½ acres, and an average depth of eight feet, we didn't have much more than five million gallons to go. I thought it might take two or three years; it didn't. By the end of April there was water trickling out the overflow tube. By the middle of May it was roaring.

By June, though the pond was a mile away from our creeks, the nearest source of aquatic life, we'd begun to have an environment. Frogs and muskrats had found the pond, an aquatic plant with arrowhead-shaped leaves, and some marsh grass. There were water bugs and dragonflies. A flock of lesser scaup had rested over one night, on their way north. And the next morning I was on my way in the pickup truck, answering a call from the Soil Conservation Service to pick up fish.

These were to be largemouth bass fry. Later I'd get some catfish, but for now it was eight hundred little bass, and I had, in the back, a clean, new, thirty-gallon garbage can, two-thirds full of pond water and held fast with log chains. I went slowly, so as not to lose water, and worried all the way about whether the can was big enough. If I'd had time, I'd have stopped at the hardware store, bought a second can, and gone home for more water. Eight hundred sounded like a lot of fish.

In front of the SCS office when I arrived, and already surrounded by others on the same errand, was a federal-green truck with built-in tanks and the name of a fish hatchery lettered on the door. A couple of men in olive-drab jackets and whipcord pants stood by, one of them with a list. I got out and approached just in time to hear my own name read out:

"Vance Boo—Booj—well, Vance. Is Vance here?"

"Here." I figured I knew whom he meant.

"Eight hundred bass, no bluegills," said the man with the list, and the other one dipped into a tank with a graduated beaker that looked a good deal like my wife's one-pint Pyrex measuring cup. He poured the water out, looked at the graduations, and poured back about half of what seemed to be a seething black mass of tiny organisms. Then he added water back and asked if I had a bucket.

"Is that all of them?" I dipped a bucket of water from my garbage can and handed it up. What he held was three jiggers of fish.

"Probably a few extra," he said. He emptied his beaker into my bucket, and his partner called the next name. I drove slowly back to the farm. I remember pouring three jiggers of fish into five million gallons of water with a sense of total disbelief that I would ever see any of those bass again. But a year later they were five inches long, and we could see them clearly, swimming by in schools of fifteen and twenty. We'd added channel catfish, too, by then, but those we didn't see; they stayed deep.

In their second summer, when the bass were eight and ten inches long, there came an extraordinary day when, wading into the pond to swim, I became aware that there was a cloud of new fry scattering away from my legs. I walked around the edge. There were hatches everywhere.

"They've reproduced," we said, in some awe. "There's a supply of fish now, for food and recreation, that will renew itself as long as the pond is there." We were wrong about that, but meanwhile, and finally, it was time to go fishing.

It was fairly slow that first summer, and the fish were still small. We did so much catching and releasing that my son still won't keep a fish (he eats the ones I catch). On calm evenings they would take surface lures—poppers and flies and things like fly-rod Flatfish—and that same son bought me a gorgeous deer-hair frog for my birthday, having sent off to Orvis for it, which probably did the best of anything we used.

It will not surprise bass fishermen to hear that in the third spring, when the fish were a foot long and more, and the bulls guarding the nests, they would fight anything that came along, never mind how bright, how big, how noisy. They were so easy to catch, in fact, that we stopped fishing for a time—the fish were also full of milt and roe, many of them, and it didn't seem proper to mess up their spawning.

The fishing was nice, now, on summer evenings, particularly from a canoe with one paddling and the other casting in toward shore. That hair frog and other lures of its size would tease the fish out of their feeding stations in the undercut places along the bank, and though they certainly weren't as wary as trout, it took a nice presentation to get one. Nor could we count on them; "How about fish for supper?" became a clear signal to Tina to defrost some hamburger.

It was fun. It was soothing. We built a second pond, the same size, this one without cost-sharing. We left the timber standing in the upper end of the second one, something the engineers wouldn't have sanctioned, in order to create snags as the trees died naturally. This pond became the one in which snapping turtles congregated and wood ducks nested. It produced, after a couple of years and having been stocked from the first pond, larger bass—I couldn't understand why the snags would have that effect and didn't learn how little they had to do with it until a really big fish came out of that second pond.

◆   ◆   ◆

Now I am, of course, like anyone with a strong preference for the fly rod, totally indifferent to how large a fish I catch by comparison with other fishermen. So when a fifteen-year-old called Fred, fishing deep in midsummer with a hideous plastic worm, caught a four-and-a-half-pounder—still our homeplace record, and a sizable largemouth for Iowa waters—I naturally felt no resentment beyond wanting to break the kid's thumbs. It really was a heck of a fish, and I have to admit that a good many lavender plastic worms got bumped along the bottom in the deep parts in the week that followed, and that some other pretty fair-sized bass came up. But it wasn't until I went back to my fly rod that I caught the explanation for why this pond had bigger fish. I was using the hair frog, and what I got first was a remarkably hard strike from what looked, as it swirled, like an eight- or ten-inch bass. I managed to hook it. I'd filed the barb off my hook and so brought the fish in rather quickly, expecting it to do some tail-dancing. Instead, it plunged and fought all the way and when I got it to hand, wasn't a bass at all. It wasn't a catfish, either, the only other species we'd stocked. Instead, it was the fattest, brightest, healthiest-looking young bluegill I've ever seen.

How it got into the pond—along with quite a few more like it, as we soon learned—is anybody's guess. The most persuasive explanation I've heard is that they came airmail. It's said that fish eggs stick to the legs of waterfowl, sometimes, and are transported that way from pond to pond. Whatever the explanation, it's confirmation of the current attitude of fishery technicians: Put in a bluegill population for forage fish, they say, if you want large bass. So it was my intention, as winter approached, to get the bluegills established in the first pond as well, just as soon as spring arrived.

Spring never came for our bass and bluegills, or for our generally forgotten catfish, either. We went off traveling that winter, not that our presence on the farm would have prevented what happened. It's called winterkill. The ponds froze, as they always do, but the weather was more severe than usual, the ice thicker, the snow heavier and longer lasting. As I understand it, the plants in a pond generally continue growing in the winter. Enough light filters down through the ice to keep the photosynthesis going. Growing plants consume carbon dioxide and excrete oxygen; that keeps the fish alive. But if light is totally blocked off, the process reverses. The plants die, the oxygen is consumed by decay, the carbon dioxide excreted. The fish smother.

We returned from our journey in March, as the thaw was starting, and on the first day back I visited both ponds. There were dead catfish, two and three feet long, all around the margins of the ice, and hundreds of raccoon tracks. The coons were cleaning up the carcasses as fast as they could, contesting for them with a good number of crows.

I was sad, of course, and yet we wouldn't miss the catfish; we'd stopped fishing for them, because the pond-raised kind were muddy-tasting, and seen them only when, occasionally, one would hit some sort of bass lure—they liked one called a Johnson Silver Minnow. In any case, whatever hope I'd had that the bass might have survived disappeared in the next few days. It took the bass bodies, for some reason, a little longer than the catfish to start floating to the surface.

I asked around, looking for consolation and found people willing to declare that the winterkill phenomenon was exceptional, unlikely to happen again. Impatient to restore our pleasure, one that friends and neighbors enjoyed as much as we did, I restocked with catchables—foot-long bass from a commercial hatchery, one hundred of them, I think, at a dollar each. I saved two years that way because the new fish reproduced the following spring. We had a pleasant summer of fishing. It was a picnic summer. The bass were just large enough to fillet—we'd make a fire; heat butter in a skillet; shake the fillets, a minute after catching, in a bag of seasoned flour; and sauté them. Ah, they were good.

My friend Tom tried all his bamboo rods in turn that summer at the ponds. The kid, Fred, came back, seventeen now, and couldn't catch anything bigger than anyone else could. My daughter was old enough to learn to cast with ultralight spinning gear and caught her first fish. Not to mention her second, third, fourth. . . . I got a deer-hair crayfish for my birthday this time. Winter came, the second after the winterkill, and I learned that we were in a cycle of hard winters. We lost our fish again.

We had built, meanwhile, a really large pond—an eight-acre affair—at the west end of our farm, in connection with selling off some of the land up there. Because of its size, this pond is winterproof, and we had stocked it, like the very first, with government-donated bass and catfish fry. After the second winterkill, I went to the big west pond, just before spawning time, and caught mature, gravid bass to restock with. They took. They reproduced. After another summer's wait, we had fishing again in the original ponds. I learned about a device that might prevent winterkill and began to yearn—windmill-driven propellers is what they are, floated in rubber rings. They are said to keep an area of water open, thus admitting light and oxygen. They cost, well, not as much as a fishing vacation in Argentina, but, for me anyway, close: they cost $350 each, and I now had three ponds to worry about, the first, the second, and a new one, the most beautiful of all. We had felt flush and built the woods pond just a year before, along with still another—a half-acre, very deep pond with steep sides—near the buildings. A swimming pond. This swimming pond, in which few plants grow, had no fish, either, and so was not a worry. But in the new woods pond, and contrary to all reasonable advice, I'd stocked walleyed pike. Not a pond fish, they said.

It was a deep, well-shaded pond, about an acre, and the prettiest of all. Wood ducks loved it, and so did we. Stubbornly, I bought 250 little walleyes; I knew they wouldn't reproduce, but I thought that, with luck, they might survive. I got them in during August 1978, a year that must be specified because the winter of 1978–79 was the worst in the Midwest since 1935.

And I was out of money and had not been able to spend $1,000 for floating, windmill-driven propellers, one for each of the three fishing ponds.

As that winter got worse and worse, as the ice thickened and the snow deepened, I thought a lot about fish. I thought about them as creatures for which I'd created certain worlds, in which I had put them to grow. I did not think of them as having minds or feelings, but as a form of life I'd fostered which would now, individual by individual, die—not in pain, I thought, or despair, but as victims, nevertheless, of a kind of wantonness, and the wanton was myself. I assumed, as Tina and I brought our flocks and herds through the bitter weather, my third fish kill and did not suppose I would want to restock a fourth time—not until the windmills could be bought, anyway, and perhaps I was too discouraged by now even to believe in windmills.

There came the spring of '79, and yes, coon tracks around the ponds. And yes, I found a small, dead walleye by the woods pond one morning, and after that stopped looking. I didn't want to see dead fish again. Let the coons and the crows have them. Bye, fish.

But we still loved our ponds. If fish couldn't survive in this cycle of hard winters, nevertheless, the ponds were beautiful; the waterfowl and deer and all the other wildlife used them. Windmills might be afforded sometime, or some new technology come along. The snapping turtles had delicious meat in them, and we all loved frog legs.

It was August 1979. About frogs: I don't think of gathering them as a sport, only a harvesting operation. Gigging them at night has no appeal for me. What I've settled on for frogging is a .22 rifle with long-rifle cartridges. These knock a frog out instantly and completely, if they hit at all. So I was slipping along the bank of the second pond, rifle in hand, looking carefully for the next OK bullfrog, when, glancing into shallow water, I saw fish. I took another step and checked myself. Fish? I crouched and looked back, and there they were. Bass. Survivors. Reproducers. That was my first yell of the day. I may even have done a little dance. The next yell, I've described. It came after I'd run back, put the frogs in the refrigerator, swapped the rifle for my nondescript bugging rod, and run to the woods pond. That was the day I caught the little walleye and learned that most of them, too, seemed to have survived. And now I am waiting for another summer, fairly certain that the walleyes have come through the winter passing as I write.

Even before summer, though, there are instructions to follow:

"For two years," said the hatchery man who brought my walleyes, "they'll do fine on larvae and tadpoles. The third year, you ought to add some forage fish. . . ."

And so my fishing fantasy is much in mind, as the ground thaws. It has no trout in it, or muskies or landlocked salmon, no tuna, marlin, swordfish. It takes place in just a few weeks, now, in a small pond to which I may have access—Knowling's or Zach's or perhaps a certain quarry. The fish, of course, are bluegills, fifteen or twenty pairs, mature, ready to spawn. I'll get them, keep them alive, put them in, and some for the bass ponds, too. Then in August, it will be another white streamer fly, a hushed moment, and, as the fantasy goes, another walleye, a year older than the last. Even so it will not be eating size. It will be, I think, what walleye fishermen call a "hammer handle"—twelve to fourteen inches long, two inches thick, and full of bones. Next summer? Maybe there'll be one or two to eat, and the summer after that . . . and, of course, bass to catch, all along. The catfish in the big west pond must be monstrous now. Windmills to shop for. And a new winter dream. I wrote about a fifth pond, small and deep, near the buildings, which we use for swimming. It's unusually clear for a farm pond, because of the steep sides, and the water, twenty-eight feet down, must be really cold. No one is going to encourage me to carry out this plan, and it will take another $500, which I may or may not ever feel I can cut loose, but before I'm done with pond-making, I've got to try trout again. Once, long ago, I answered an ad for "farm pond adapted trout fingerlings," bought a couple of hundred, put them in a pond, never saw one again. But I don't think the problem was temperature so much as oxygen.

So: What I think of now, more often than I ought, is a device called a GenAIRator, made by some people in Wisconsin, which is designed to aerate lakes and ponds. It consists of an electric air pump which you're supposed to fasten to a tree or post on the shore. It feeds air through plastic pipe to a venturi tube, down at the bottom of the pond. The function of the venturi is to send a stream of air bubbling up to the surface, and I assume that this will both give oxygen and, as that cold bottom layer of water is raised up, lower the temperature at the surface.

I don't know for certain that this will enable me to raise trout. I don't know if the windmills would work. I don't know, for that matter, that my walleyes will go on living through hot Augusts as they grow large, or that my bass won't winter-kill again. But fish are like other crops, it seems to me by now. You fix up an environment, you plant, cultivate, protect as best you can, and with luck—and a white streamer, or a deer-hair frog, or even a lavender plastic worm—you harvest. For food, sometimes. For fun, more often. For the feeling of putting into the world a good thing that wasn't there before.

THE PAGEANT OF THE SEASONS

• • •

JOHN WALLER HILLS

Mountains have never had the same attraction for me as plains or river valleys. These have a more enduring claim than the bolder appeal of rocks and snow. There is something about our downs, and still more about the prairie country of Saskatchewan or Wyoming, of Uruguay or Paraguay, which enters into my bones. Their broad, rolling surfaces, wind-swept and sun-soaked, under a wide sky, with an horizon which is always the same and always different, bring me down nearer to natural life and primitive ages than does the wildest and grandest of mountain scenery. And next after plains, and indeed in company with them, come river valleys. I never feel truly at home unless I am conscious of the valley in which I happen to be. For choice, I like to be able to see across it. If you are put down in the midlands of England or in other indeterminate country of that sort, can you say what valley you are in, without looking at a map? Very rarely can you: The country seems, to one who reckons by valleys, to be without articulation or form. You should always be able to tell at a glance where you are. Whether you are in Wensleydale, Swaledale, or Nidderdale should always be plain to you, and you should know instinctively without thinking whether the valley you are in is that of the Eden, the Irthing, or the Caldew. You should always be able to say, That stream which I step across drains into the Test, and that high down which I see divides the Test from the Itchen. Indeed valleys are not only objects of natural beauty, but necessities, if you are to keep in tune with your surroundings. And there is another point. It is not only that the valley itself is pleasing, but the running water of the river gives it heart and life as a fire gives life to a room: and therefore you have both the attraction of moving water and also of its surrounding scenery. And further, if you follow the river and not the rail or the road, you will find that in its twists and its turns it is always showing you the distant view under another aspect, and you get a totally different idea of the country from that gained by one who scours the straight highway only. If also you go right down to the level of the water, as you do if you either fish or go in a boat, you step into a different plane of life. You see much that is hidden from him who only walks the banks—the habits of birds and their nests and flowers which before were unnoticed. You see all this life, not from above, but on an equality, as though you formed part of it. All these attributes are the peculiar advantages of river valleys. And they have the further merit that in no other part of the earth can the changes of the seasons be observed better.

Hampshire combines both plains and rivers, and her downs and her trout streams can be seen in combination. The fisherman's season begins on 1st April. If the spring be such as that of 1924, there is very little change from winter. The broad meadows are still grey. The woods are bare of leaves. The row of beech trees at the top of the chalk cliff does not show a tinge of green, and you have to look close to see the buds on the hawthorn trees at its base. The reeds and sedges bordering the river, bleached by the winter rains, have a faded appearance, and the water, by contrast, looks dark and gloomy. The river runs full and fast and weedless, swirling down all its broad expanse. There are no flowers, for the kingcup, which ought to be in bloom everywhere, hardly shows its glossy leaves as yet, and even the blackthorn does not yet whiten the hedges. Nor have the spring birds arrived. True, snipe are drumming; lapwings, in search of nesting sites, are wheeling and crying; redshanks, wariest of birds, are so silent that they may have started laying; and pairs of sandpipers are resting on their way north: but there are no sedge or reed warblers, and neither chiffchaff nor willow wren are to be heard. However, by every hatch or bridge is a couple of those birds which are almost, I think, my favourites, grey wagtails. Why they are called grey I cannot imagine. Apart from their backs, which are bluish rather than grey, it is the brilliant sulphur yellow of their underparts which gives them their character, and anything less like so sober a word as *grey* cannot be imagined when you see these bright and glowing creatures either poised in the air or tripping delicately over a weed patch. A bird of the north and the west, yet they breed freely in Hampshire, and there were certainly six pairs at Mottisfont. And there are not many days on which you do not see the flashing blue of the kingfisher.

As the year runs on, and evenings grow longer and lighter and the sun gains in power, the valley wakes up. The first abundant flower of the Test is the kingcup. No plant possesses a better sense of arrangement, and its patches of gold are spread over the flat meadows more skillfully than the most cunning gardener could have planted them, with a luxuriant wastefulness as though to tell everyone that spring has really come. The grass, too, of these meadows begins to look less grey, and the band of hungry horses finds somewhat more to eat. And, when once the movement starts, everything comes with a rush. The willows grow green, and the fine black poplars which stud the valley show their bluish leaves. Weeds of all colours choke the river, and sedges begin to shoot up. This time, mid or late April, is one of the most attractive of the year. Trees are bursting into leaf, all their leaves are different in colour, and you do not get that somewhat heavy monotony which a wooded country presents in summer. And there is an air of expectancy and new birth over the landscape. The full glory of flowering bushes and trees has not come yet, and the climax has not been reached: But, as it is always better to anticipate than to possess, no season makes a deeper appeal to the imagination. It is a time of leaf more than of flower. The different tones of the different trees are seen at once and together. And remember that the green of leaves is never seen so well as by water, particularly by running water, for light is reflected at all angles off the glancing surface, making them delicate and translucent. Already, too, the spring birds will have come. The chiffchaff's double call tells you that winter has really gone, the falling cadence of the willow wren strikes on the ear like dropping water, while the grasshopper warbler is trilling that endearing and reellike note of his which ought to make him the patronbird of anglers.

The next stage is when the flowering trees come out. Hawthorns love the chalk and never do better than in Hampshire, gardens are gay with laburnum and lilac, and chestnuts blossom in the woods. In the meadows the kingcup is dying, but its place is taken by cowslips and dark orchis. There is no more beautiful combination of colour, and the yellow and the purple make an admirable contrast. And one by one the summer birds arrive. Yellow wagtails, yellow as canaries, trot on the bank; reeds and sedges are full of warblers; blackcaps are singing and flycatchers busy on the fence posts. The climax of the year has come, bringing the wild rose, the yellow iris, and the mayfly. The iris is another great Hampshire flower and is everywhere in masses, arranged as though nature had gardened it. And the river now has its summer appearance. Patches of the white cups of the water crowfoot lie on the surface, many a hooked trout takes refuge in one of those thick jungles which fishermen call celery beds, the water grows crystalline, its surface flecked with wind-blown petals and pollen of the grass, trout come suddenly into sight, iron blues sail down in droves, and islands of dead weed form round the piers of bridges. The grass in the hayfields is growing long, large daisies appear in it, moths fly at night, and the hedges are starred with wild roses. The evening rise begins, red sedge flies blunder on to the surface, and you can fish till ten o'clock. Then June passes, birds have hatched their young, and family parties of linnets and goldfinches splash themselves at the shallow edge of the gravelly ford.

As the year runs on, and the hay is cut, the valley loses individuality. It remains beautiful, but less distinctive. There are no flowering trees, and the only bush is the guelder rose, not enough by itself, though graceful. I never see its ivory flowers without thinking of chalk streams. There is a pause in nature, until the late summer flowers come. And they do come, in quantities, and at no other time are the banks so gay. Clusters of mimulus with its melted gold, thick spires of purple loosestrife, the homely comfrey, and a few tall columns of mullein make a brilliant garden: Ditches are full of meadowsweet and the air is heavy with its scent: Patches of yellow ragwort cover the bottom of the down, and willow herb in the clearing of the wood is so thick that it looks like a pink mist. Some of these flowers last all through the hot days of July and August, until the turn of the year. Then we slip into autumn, catch perhaps a few fish in September, linger as long as we can, and finally say good-bye to the valley until next April.

But, before you go, do not forget to pay a tribute to the loveliest of all Test flowers, the loveliest and the rarest, the balsam. It is unmistakable, with its olive-dark leaves and its red and orange blossoms, looking remote and exotic, more in keeping with an equatorial forest than our keen and strenuous air. It is not in full bloom till September. It is a wayward creature, because in some years it disappears entirely and in others it is difficult to find. But when it is plentiful it is one of the great sights afforded by English flowers. There are few places in these islands where it grows at all, and there can be still fewer where it blossoms so luxuriantly as on the Test.

But, you may ask, what is there here distinctive of Hampshire? Spring comes everywhere, cowslips grow in many meadows, all rivers have running water, and sedge warblers are not found only on the Test. What is it that gives chalk streams their particular character? The answer to that question is not easy. It depends on atmosphere and tone and contour and association and other imponderable factors. But certain qualities can be distinguished. The bold yet smooth outlines of the down make an agreeable background. Occasionally, too, the side of a hill has been broken into, either by nature or man, and the result is fine cliffs of dazzling chalk. Downs also have their individual beauties. The short, sweet grass, with its wealth of flowers, gives them a special character all through the seasons. And the chalk soil which produces this vegetation gives to the air a limpidity and nimbleness which you do not get on the heavy clays of which much of the south of England is composed. But these light soils have this disadvantage, that they become dry in hot summers. Rain soaks through them, it does not remain to feed the surface, and the down turns a dull, faded yellow. But where you have rivers running through the chalk you avoid this drawback, for they keep the meadows as luxuriant as in spring. And chalk rivers have a pleasing habit peculiar to themselves, of splitting themselves up into many channels, some deep and slow, others shallow and rapid, as though anxious to spread their gift of water over as wide an area as possible. And this natural feature has been increased by the work of man, who by his system of irrigation has carried the boon far and wide. Therefore when the rest of the world grows dry and dusty, Hampshire valleys keep green and cool, there is movement of water everywhere during the somewhat stagnant period of late summer, and the river meadows have features which other fields lack. Fed by the winter water, they have thick crops in April, whilst other fields are still bare. Unfortunately, at Mottisfont the old irrigation system is falling into disuse, and many tracts which are still ridged and channelled for the purpose are no longer flooded. But above Mottisfont, between it and Stockbridge, there are still many fine expanses. Here the sheep are penned down in April, and when they have nibbled the field bare and brown, water is run in again and hay is cut in June.

Hampshire is wooded country, and the combination of wood and stream increases the attractions of each. In the level parts all forest trees grow, and grow well: but the down has its own attributes, juniper bushes, beeches, and yews. All these, like the hawthorn, are chalk lovers. In early spring, when the long line of beeches is a vivid green, the black yews stand out against them solid and heavy: and grass never looks so fresh as in some quiet hollow of the down which is studded with dark junipers. All these features, wood and water, downland and meadow, forest and flowers, are found in the valley of the Test: Some characteristics are peculiar to it, but many are common to all southern England. It is their mixture, their blending, the proportion of each to the whole, which give the valley its enduring beauty.

A
FLY-FISHERMAN'S
PEACE

* * *

GEOFFREY NORMAN

WHEN I FIRST STARTED FISHING FOR TROUT, I LIVED *EXACTLY* 226 MILES
from the nearest worthwhile river. Those were the days of unlimited
oil and neglected speed limits, so on Friday afternoon, it was nothing
for me to beat the Chicago–Gary traffic, fairly skim over the interstate, and arrive at the river less than four hours after leaving my
office. My hands would be trembling as I tied on the first fly in the
dying evening light. Salvation, to my mind, would have been to live
on the banks of a trout stream. Then you could find peace.

And, as they say, it came to pass. But that was ten years later,
when I was certainly older and marginally wiser. My wife and I had
decided on the house before we knew about the stream. It was not that
I loved fishing less, just that I loved other things more. We were one
year married, in a family way, and moving to the country.

I learned quickly that the stream was there. But it was November
and had already snowed once or twice in Vermont. Trout season was
long over. My first New England winter was ahead of me, and I had
much on my mind.

We survived—enjoyed it, actually—and spring came without
much fanfare. The stream remained in the background of my thoughts
until one fine, cool afternoon early in May when I looked down
toward the tree line and saw a vague cloud dancing on the air, like
animated smoke. It took me a while to realize that the cloud was made
up of mayflies. Moments later I was down at the stream, standing on
a rock, watching as the mayflies continued to hatch and as the trout
fed on them. I lived on the narrow, rocky, clear headwaters of the
river, and it was easy to see the fish in the transparent water. One,
especially, held just behind a large rock, and when a newly hatched
mayfly came drifting down the chute of broken water on either side of
the rock, this fish would rise with a strong push of its tail and take the

helpless insect in an efficient gulp, then resume its station, watching for the next victim.

It was hypnotic, and I watched until the hatch ended and the fish stopped feeding. I realized, when it was all over, that it had never occurred to me to run up to the house and get my rod.

This, I think, is the chief joy of living with a trout stream on one flank of your property: this calm, this lack of urgency about fishing. I might feel differently if I lived downstream, on bigger water holding bigger fish with whom intimacy might not be possible. But I don't think so.

Actually, when I want to fish seriously, I don't do it in my own back yard. I drive downstream or to another river—one that is within an hour's drive. But I do occasionally fish the waters at the end of my meadow, especially in the middle of the summer when the fish are taking grasshoppers. I can walk the stream without waders and flip either an imitation or an actual grasshopper out ahead of me and let it drift down over what I know is good holding water. Often I see the fish, by the flash of its side, just as it begins to make its move. I learned how to spot that flash by watching trout feed during that first mayfly hatch some ten years ago.

So, in a way, this stretch of small water is my own laboratory. I go there to observe the fish and the things they eat and also things that eat them, which is an important factor in trout behavior. I have examined nymphs, leeches, sculpins, and crayfish and think I know a little more now about these important prey in the trout's world. I have also watched what happens when a kingfisher flies over a piece of holding water and am conscious, now, of just how keen fish are to overhead danger. I've watched as a trout fed virtually continuously on submerged nymphs while the surface of the stream was covered with mayfly duns. I had read about this phenomenon in books but never quite believed it until I witnessed it on that water I know so intimately. It caused me to examine my total commitment to the dry fly.

I never imagined the existence of those satisfactions, back when I was driving five hundred miles in a weekend to appease my appetite for trout fishing. In my mind, then, to live on a trout stream would be simply an opportunity to fish to exhaustion. Mercifully, it did not work out that way. Living where I do, I have learned that the actual river, the ceaselessly shifting water, and the network of life it sustains had a bigger part all along.

When you live on a river, you don't have to devour it; you can take it in small bites. You are never full; never hungry. That *is* a kind of peace.

JUST A SPRING CREEK

◆ ◆ ◆

CHARLES F. WATERMAN

ONLY A REALLY NOSY TROUT FISHERMAN WOULD NOTICE IT AT ALL, EVEN though part of it runs beside the highway like an irrigation ditch.

It goes as a valley stream is supposed to go, urgently but not very fast, and the riffles tinkle poetically. The grass is tall about it now for the cattle have been fenced out all these years. It isn't very deep, and after the first year or two we stopped using our waders and fished with hip boots, but we stayed off the banks as much as possible. We learned to approach the water stooped a little and walking softly like the duck-poachers who are there every fall, making furtive sneaks past the NO TRESPASSING signs. Trout in shallow meadow streams are attuned to ground vibrations, especially when there are no cattle to keep them at ease.

A friend of ours bought that section of creek and then didn't have much chance to fish it since he lived a long way off, and we began to feel that it was our spring creek almost from the start. He had the fence built and the willows began to grow along with the grass, and the water ran a little deeper as the clumps of vegetation in it became bigger. More trout began to appear, coming up from the river, I suppose. At first there were quite a few fishermen who ignored the signs and walked in from the highway, but the fish were too tough for them and in two or three years they were leaving hardly any boot tracks at all. Take away most of the things that shake banks and splash around the edges and resident trout become suspicious—maybe paranoid.

A foot-long fish was a prize in that water, and my wife, who specializes in persnickety trout with delicate appetites, tied on a number 20 thing she had built the night before, squinting a little, and said with emphasis, "There—is—no—such—thing—as—a—*little*—trout —in—water—like—this!" Of course it is relative, but it is hard to convince a casual fisherman that a fifteen-inch brown trout can be as much of a prize as a twenty-pound steelhead. Debie's leader was fifteen feet long and it tapered to 6X. Her wispy rod was a bamboo made long before, and I shuddered to notice that the guides were wearing badly and that the finish was showing its age. Such revered tools are "re-finished" in dustless laboratories by uncompromising artists who couldn't even guess at the current minimum wage.

I calmed myself by reasoning that other women might want such things as mink stoles or sports cars, and I decided not to suggest that Debie get a nifty little graphite rod for spring creeks. Graphite, she had said, was for rivers and lakes. Cane was for places like "our" creek.

We found ourselves fishing only to rising fish almost from the beginning. There was an occasional trout to be had fishing blind, but that was not the object of the game. There were places where the risers showed regularly, often in tight little pods, but never with much fuss. There seemed to be a variety of hatches—mayfly and caddis—but we never learned to predict them accurately, and we soon learned that our fish weren't very selective as to pattern but were connoisseurs of presentation and approach. Actually, they were so touchy that slipping up on a riser was a little like crossing a practice minefield.

A guest confessed that the risers he had been working on had been put down, but some others had started up ahead. He thought he might have better luck with them. Debie and I exchanged knowing glances in the knowledge that the ones up ahead were the same fish he had scared. No wonder his fishing kept getting more and more difficult.

Actually, a single fish was likely to be easier than a pod of risers. Unless they were going so good that they competed, it was tougher to sneak up on a bunch than on a single. And always cast to the nearest fish first!

When we fished on summer evenings, there would be little groups of sandhill cranes not too far overhead, changing course just a little when they saw us and making their musical ratchet calls that continued when they had landed at their roosting area, but after all these years I still haven't seen the spot. It's not too far from the creek, but there is a patch of timber hiding it. Now and then a flock of Canada geese would come up the valley with mountains as a background. Generally there were the contrails of jet airliners overhead, but I am a little vague as to where they lead. I should check a map and compass for that.

The trout rises are generally silent, dimples that may not give away the size of their makers, and sometimes they are so delicate they are hard to make out where the current is seamed. For several years there was nearly always a rising fish between a watercress island and an undercut sod bank with grass sweepers. It was an almost impossible slot for a dragless dry fly, but on each visit I approached it with determination and crafty schemes. Lay the leader across the upper part of the little island with some slack. Or try to sneak directly below the fish and use a short line. I would snag a number 18 Elk Hair Caddis in the sweepers, or it would drag as my slack leader gave out, making a wake that was so magnified by my concentration that to me it resembled the swimming muskrats that sometimes ended a rising program. Generally the fish left at the first attempt. Brown trout.

Through the years I caught the trout by the watercress island two or three times and he was never very big—maybe a foot long. But even when I hooked and lost him, I was satisfied. Landing him took luck, but I told myself that hooking him took a little something else, and I felt very superior about it. I smugly told myself that it was "'technical fishing."

The creek has been a nesting place for mallards and teal. A bluewing hen going through her broken-wing demonstration in the middle of a shallow spring creek can cause trout to leave their feeding stations and slide temporarily into the waving tendrils of submerged plants or into sod-bank undercuts. A mallard hen, carried away by her own histrionics, can be a squawking, splashing catastrophe. She is not satisfied to see a frustrated wader reel in and slink away from her nesting site. Bedazzled by her success, she must lead him around the bend, and often she will come back for a curtain call just as he has begun to stalk rising fish who have not seen or heard her.

Our trout accept muskrats as part of their scene, pausing only briefly when one crosses their feeding area. By the time of the muskrat's urgent, late-fall preparations, our spring creek has generally gone dead as far as fishing is concerned, but on streams with late-fall fishing the crusty rats will come close and make what must be derogatory comments in cartoon muskrat talk.

The hatches were hard to catalog, but sometimes there were unexplained patterns. One year there did seem to be a scheduled rise in a bend, slightly deeper than the rest of the creek. I believe it was around two in the afternoon, on several successive trips, and since the place took careful wading, I got there early one day and stalked the spot although I saw no fish move. I stood stupidly and stared at the place in the bend where the action was supposed to take place and glared at the sliding water for sight of the tiny blue dun I anticipated. The *Elodea* waved silently but visibility was good, and I could see that all the water about me was troutless. Zero hour approached and I was glad none of my friends could view my fruitless stakeout.

The "spot" was fifty feet upstream, and as I watched it I seemed to feel rather than see something move in the water at my elbow. There, ignoring me, were eleven trout going upstream. They varied in size but were all "good" fish, and they passed within five feet of my boots. They must have come a long way since there was no suitable holding water below me for a quarter mile or more. Within three minutes there was a tentative swirl where fish had risen regularly for years. Two or three naturals floated by me and I cast at the usual spot. The second upstream cast was just right, a little slack giving me a short drift, and a trout took deliberately, showing his snout above water. I set the hook, he jumped high, and the other fish were gone. Triumph.

We'd wade carefully across the gravel and then into the silted, muddy places, and now and then a hidden trout would be flushed from his hiding and dart away, sometimes alarmingly big for a small creek. Fifteen inches long? Still larger? Occasionally there would be an incredibly bulky shadow, usually racing downstream but occasionally disappearing in a bit of undercut bank.

Sometimes the really big trout, browns or rainbows, would rise along with foot-long fish or even smaller, and although they could sip a dry fly or an emerger as gently as lesser feeders, they would usually give themselves away if you watched for a few minutes. The big trout would hurry just a little too much and cause a telltale, outsize bulge, or he would push his nose just a little too far up and make a *glug* to give himself away. I had fished the creek a dozen times before I hooked one of the big ones, and it didn't last long.

I was using a larger "stranger" that did not match the tiny hatch, and the fish revealed himself as a businesslike vee that came out from an undercut sod bank, evidently having seen something he thought merited his attention. He took and I managed to set the hook without breaking my 6X tippet, but the drama was brief. He lunged across some water growth and rushed downstream past me, breaking off in a floundering half-jump thirty feet downstream. Brown trout. I had seen him plainly. He hadn't wanted the tiny things lesser fish had been rising to steadily.

And after that we hooked the big ones several times, probably losing the largest of all, but twice we came up with nineteen-inchers that did not get away—one rainbow and one brown. I do not know how many times we caught the same fish more than once, but the nature of our creek was such that certain spots were likely to hold the larger ones. Sometimes the ones we hooked were feeding in pods with lesser fish, and sometimes they were loners, rising over their own chosen swatch of water and left alone by lesser residents.

There were some feeding patterns that delighted us, making us feel highly erudite in our analysis. There was the brook trout business. The Eastern brook trout were not plentiful, but there were occasions when we hooked a fish from a feeding group and caused nearly all of the rest to move upstream—or we might throw some sort of tangled cast, or slap a fly on the water through clumsy enthusiasm. At any rate, a single fish would frequently resume feeding almost immediately after the rest had gone—and it would be a brook trout, proving to us that the brook trout sustains his reputation of not being particularly thoughty.

There was the ghostly midsummer winnowing sound that I did not recognize for a long while—and finally I found it was made by my old friend the Wilson's snipe performing his mating rituals high in the air. We had found numerous nesting snipe along the creek, and fish-and-game biologists had designated it as one of the best snipe sites of the area.

White-tailed deer appeared from time to time in a brushy spot in a bend of the creek, and they bedded in the heavy grass, leaving narrow trails through it. Now and then there would be a hen pheasant who would take off noisily as I tried to walk softly toward the creek, usually coming from under my feet and jangling my already taut nerves.

All of this went on for all of those years, and the creek looked better each season. We plotted like children against individual fish or groups of fish, and as far as I know, we never killed a trout, even accidentally. Each fall, sometime in September, the fishing would fade, and if we came back during duck season, there would be no sign of trout. We assumed, of course, that they had gone "back to the river," for lack of a better explanation, even though the creek's temperatures stayed moderate.

Then there was a drought that lasted for several years, and although the spring seemed to run about the same as usual, there seemed to be few fish, even after the drought was broken. Two years ago I visited the creek and admired the water growth, but I saw no rises except one that went steadily almost under a fence at the border of the property. It was a little number 20 Royal Wulff that I threw to the fish, and a big rainbow jumped to show his brilliant colors, but I broke him off.

Last year the trout were gone.

A HOME
BY THE
RIVER

◆ ◆ ◆

W. D. WETHERELL

THERE'S A PIECE OF LAND FOR SALE ON THE RIVER, SIX ACRES OF meadow, pine and oak rising gently from the south bank. Through the middle runs a stream no bigger than a person's stride, a stream bridged by weathered planks that creak as they sag. An old woods road runs up to the open field at the hill's crest. There are wild blackberries growing along the edges of this road, blueberries further up in the sun. A spring on top provides water. The view east is of hills and farms and the sunrise.

I walked up to it yesterday in the middle of a summer rain. The small, hand-lettered FOR SALE sign had been nailed to a tree on the far side of the river since May, and though I had been tempted several times, it was only now that I had gotten around to crossing over.

It's good land. If you poke around abandoned hill farms as much as I do, you come to have a sense of whether the land you're walking on was once cherished or once cursed. Shadows that never disappear, even in winter; ground that is rockier than most Vermont ground; stone walls that seem hastily thrown together, as if hurled there by the farmer in his frustration at tilling such soil . . . these are all tokens of land that has been detested, to be avoided no matter how cheaply it may be had. No sunlight for those solar panels you plan so hopefully to install; no soil for the tomatoes your wife wants to plant; a well that dries up every June—land that broke people in the 1780s can break people in the 1980s, in subtle, persistent ways.

My parcel (and how ready I was to call it mine!) had traces of a gentle hand. Someone had taken pains in cutting the road, looping it in gradual curves that understood the contours of the hill. In clearing the meadow, they had spared many of the trees—some of the oaks I was walking under were probably as old as any in Vermont. The stone wall that ran along the western boundary was skillfully arranged, not merely dumped; someone had matched flat rock to flat rock, round one to round one, and it was a masterpiece of its kind. The land, having once been loved, could be loved again.

I found a stump to sit on under a hemlock that held back some of the rain. Our house, I quickly decided, should go in the center of the meadow facing the river. The oaks would provide shade in the summer, but by fall their leaves would be gone and there would be sunlight to warm the bay window in our study. I could write there. We could have a library on the side, with built-in shelves for our books, cedar cabinets for our rods. The bedroom would be upstairs where the last sound we'd hear at night would be the voice of the river. A guest room would go nicely above the garage. A guest room with a large picture window facing east so all our friends could enjoy the view we had come to love.

There would be fishing, of course—fishing that required no advance planning or long drive, but came as easily as a whim on a warm summer's night. The water there is not the best trout water on the river, but its broad and easy air would wear well over the years. There are no deep pools or fast runs. You get the feeling there are only small trout there, not monsters, and it frees you from the burden of catching them. It would be a fine stretch of river on which to teach a child to fish.

I dreamed, in short, of a home that would be worthy of the river that ran by it. There are dozens of homes in this valley; many are weathered farmhouses that blend into their setting as only New England homes can, yet they all turn their backs on the river, and not a single one has been built deliberately to enjoy it.

Wondering about this, I began thinking not only of the land I was walking on and the home my dreams erected, but of the valley and its future. Was it wrong in the 1980s to put all your love into a place of unspoiled earth? Wrong to think that the work and worry and hope that went into it would ever be requited by anything except pollution and development and noise? More to the point: Did anyone cherish this river besides me? Even to pose the question like that was an egotistical conceit, but I was considering the river's future now, adding up its allies, and it was a question worth asking.

The farmers cherish it in their sober, undemonstrative way. I hear them speak sadly whenever a good piece of farmland is gone back to trees or sold to summer people, and the river is why their own land continues productive when all the hill farms have been abandoned. You can catch them staring off toward it in their rare respites from work; after a lifetime of toil, it must come to seem a brotherly presence in the year's slow turn.

Anyone else beside them? Do the fishermen who come here cherish it? I don't think so, not as they should. The people from town fish it in spring and at no other time, and I've followed enough of them through the pools to know they are the ones dumping bottles and cans. The fly-fishermen I meet are almost inevitably out-of-staters, and though they may value the river for its productivity, their interest is of necessity only brief and intermittent.

The river is not famous. There are no summer resorts along its banks, no major ski areas or tourist attractions. Sometimes I think that it is this very obscurity that saves the river, makes it worth loving. Other times, I know I'm wrong, realize that the only thing that will save the valley from the development that will one day come isn't neglect, but the concerted efforts of people who love it as I do, people who I fear are simply not there. Conservationists have banded together to save portions of the Beaverkill and the wild sections of the St. John, but what of all the smaller, more obscure rivers in between? How many of these vanish with hardly a whimper, undefended and unloved?

Vermonters are easy marks for developers. Their insistence on being able to do what they please with their land makes them reject zoning out of hand; their distrust of anything abstract makes them suspicious of regional planning and imposed controls. Times are bad here now—there are people in this valley who live in cold trailers throughout the winter. In the face of their poverty, meeting their eyes, it would be hard to argue against the construction of a new highway or large factory, yet either would doom them just as surely as it would doom the river. Development brings in skilled workers from Massachusetts with whom they can't compete; better highways bring in commuters with money, drive up the land to prices young families can't afford.

The trend has already started. The six acres I was walking across would have sold for two or three thousand dollars as recently as five years ago, but with the condos and second homes inching closer, it was probably priced at eleven thousand or twelve. I wondered if we could afford that with a house. I began to think of mortgage payments, insurance, building permits, taxes. I thought of those things, then I thought of the income the kind of fiction worth writing brings in. My dream house, so easily created, just as easily disappeared.

If it weren't for reality, none of us would have any problems. Still, it costs nothing to dream, and it's a time-honored way of spending a rainy afternoon. I walked slowly back down the road from the meadow, doing my best to rid my thoughts of the future and concentrate on the here and now. The rain, so gentle at first, had changed just as gradually as my mood and fell now with a cool and determined hardness, rattling the trees as loudly as hail.

The wind, switching directions, blew from the north. There was the smell of damply packed earth, the sound of a distant chain saw. A leaf fell ahead of me on the road, then a second, then a third, and as easily and gracefully as that it was fall.

In a hurry now, I turned my collar against the rain and climbed down through another man's land to my car.

THE MARQUESAS: FEBRUARY 29, 1988

• • •

JOHN N. COLE

THE MARQUESAS KEYS ARE A WONDERFUL MYSTERY. SOME KEY WEST historians will tell you the ring of small islands about twenty-five miles west of Key West is the only atoll in the North Atlantic. I have never been to the islands of the Pacific, but I have seen enough aerial photographs of atolls to know that they mark the graves of long-ago volcanos or mountains that sank beneath the sea. A lagoon shimmers at the center of a round, geologic crown of rock and coral: all that's left of the rim of an ancient volcanic peak.

The Marquesas, the popular argument goes, are the remnants of just such a prehistoric drama, a geologic anomaly that rose from the primeval sea far from its brethren in what is now Mexico. Other folks have other thoughts about the unique formation that marks the end of the necklace of keys and hummocks draped along the meeting ground of the Atlantic and the Gulf from Key West to the Tortugas. Some reason that the ring of coral sand and marl was formed in an earthquake. "Mexico is not that far off," they say, "and earthquakes have been happening there for centuries."

Knowing nothing of geology, and less about the genesis of the Marquesas, I can believe the theory I like best. And there is one. Jeffrey tells me there are informed Keys mariners who believe the Marquesas are the child of a meteor—some giant fragment of infinity that plummeted from outer space, or perhaps from another universe. So far removed in time that its fiery flight went unmarked by any being, the visitor from the unknown hurled itself into the warm salt seas of the shoals that rise on the western rim of the Boca Grande Channel. Blazing, hissing, smashing into its final grave, the meteor's calamity left its own mile-wide mark on the sea floor, an almost perfectly round depression wreathed by a circle of islands and hummocks forced from the center of the meteor's impact just as mud squeezes from around a boot sole pressed into a puddle.

Tended by a millennium of solitude, the raw material pushed from the sea bottom acquired its dry-land biota. First the tiny plants that are children of windblown seeds, then the mangroves, propagated by currents and seabird droppings. And finally the maturing greenery that is south Florida's horticultural signature: impenetrable tangles of mangrove roots, scrub pine, saw grass, and dozens more species and subspecies of green, growing vegetation that defies human perambulation and appears consummately designed to protect every anonymous marl hillock from the kind of heedless human exploration that's so often memorialized by the extinction of the very places that once held mystery in their grasp.

Bulldozers, of course, can make an instant mockery of mangroves. In moments, lowered blades eradicate the work of eons, sparing nothing, not even the only salt-sea memento of a dying meteor's final flight. That could have happened, probably would have happened, if the Marquesas and their sister keys to the north had not been protected by the Department of the Interior, which has recently stamped NATIONAL WILDLIFE REFUGE across every map of the watery territory that stretches from Fort Taylor at the end of Key West's Southard Street to Fort Jefferson in the Tortugas. I am no fan of the federal bureaucracy, but each time I look west from any Key West vantage point, and every time I navigate those azure waters in any sort of craft, I write a silent note of gratitude to Nat Reed and everyone else in Interior's Washington labyrinth who engineered the decisions and agreements that have become such an effective shield for what is, I'm certain, the globe's largest submerged national park and wildlife refuge. There is, on Woman Key's northeast corner, witness to what might have happened if Interior had not acted. Not that David Wolkowsky built himself an ugly retreat; he did not. His elevated, wood-framed, and wood-sheathed house at the edge of a crescent of pure white beach is a graceful and sensitively sited structure: the only one between Key West and the Marquesas, built before the territory was taken out of public circulation. But each time I pass it, it shouts to me of a future these keys might have known.

We will not hear its voice today. We are, Jean and I and Jeffrey, aboard his *Waterlight* on a course through the Lakes, the interlocked stretch of shoal channels on the north side of the line of keys that follow the reef from Key West to Boca Grande Key at the northern rim of Boca Grande Channel. David's house faces south, and besides, we are a mile or more north of Woman Key racing across turtle-grass flats in water so clear and so smooth I can see individual blades of grass waving in the current.

How lucky I am. When I made this date with Jeffrey a week ago, there was no way of knowing what our weather would be. Like February everywhere, the month in Key West arrives with surprises. One dawn will open the curtains on a dark melodrama acted by rolling clouds stuffed with rain and thunder. Others torment the sea and land with winds like those that pushed Jeffrey and me into the lee of Archer Key just three days ago. I have been remembering that day and more as I waited for this one.

Because this one was memorable even before it arrived. I had Jean's promise that she would come with me to the Marquesas, the scene of adventures that come to a fisherman only if he is blessed by the fates—adventures that are as vivid in my history as any I have lived. Each has been narrated to Jean in detail, each has been retold to others as Jean listened, wondering I'm sure how many times a tale can survive retelling. This two-week visit to Key West would not go by, I promised myself, without a trip to the Marquesas with Jean.

But only if the weather is right: That was an addendum to my pledge. Jean is not a complainer; she would have made the trip in any weather Jeffrey considered navigable. But I know she is a creature of the land, not a spirit of the sea. She endures every discomfort in the service of her garden; she will politely refuse almost every invitation that involves leaving port.

But given this day's splendor, even an earth mother is exhilarated by the sea. We are afloat on a shimmering mirror of a cloudless sky. At thirty knots, the *Waterlight* glides like raw silk pulled across a polished table. Today, earth's reassuring firmness reaches to encompass a sea as smooth as a meadow in May. Jean's soul rests content.

Over the decades of my wage-earning work as a journalist, I would, in times of particular drudgery, push away from my desk and confide to my coworkers that I was on the brink of abandoning not only my job but my home community and my entire life's routine. Asked what I would do and where I would go, I would say with considerable conviction that I would start over on some island in the Caribbean set at the center of the finest fishing waters on the planet. "I will," I told my listeners, "spend my days in a small boat afloat on a crystal sea where fish flash bright greetings under a tropic sun."

"Yes, that sounds fine," those skeptics would reply, "but how long do you think you can do that before you get bored?"

And my answer was always the same. "I'll try it for twenty-five years, and then take a second look."

Each time I told that ritualized tale, I saw myself at the center of a shoal-water universe, alone with my fish and my fishing. Soon the fancy became a dream, a dream I began to want desperately to come alive.

And today, I tell myself, it has. And today, I tell myself, I know what I said is true: I can do this for the rest of my life, however long or short it may be, and be truly happy doing it. And happiest when Jean and Jeffrey are with me.

When we reach Boca Grande Key and make the turn that starts us across Boca Grande Channel, I am now and at last positively certain of this day's mercies and splendors. The region's entrance to the Gulf of Mexico from the Straits of Florida and the southern Atlantic, this channel is like so many places where two headstrong waters meet. Even on windless days, the surface surges with restless tides and currents ebbing and flowing across Boca Grande Channel's four miles. Pushing two seas together in such relatively narrow confines and in such relatively shoal water is a process sure to encounter resistance. With no room to run, the two seas meet here in an endless turbulence that roils even windless waters. And when gales do blow, this is not an easy place to be. Odd-shaped swells approach from nowhere, rolling against wind and tide; even the most seaworthy boat and experienced helmsman cannot avoid a pounding. I have made the crossing several times with Jeffrey when the best I could do was hold on, grit my teeth, and pray that we would soon reach a lee shore.

And while I prayed, I tried not to remember that the world's-record hammerhead shark was taken from these very waters, a great and terrifying fish almost twenty feet long weighing more than a ton. There are others down there in the depths, I am certain, as massive as the meteor that's buried somewhere beneath the bottom of the Marquesas lagoon.

Today the channel is so wonderfully benign that, as we cross, I inform Jean of its hammerhead distinction. That's how certain I am of this day's good fortune.

Given my Marquesas history, I should be more restrained. On other fine days, other orchid mornings, I have cruised this same course across a well-mannered channel, my hopes flying like a banner in the dawn. Yet those very days kept a secret from me, a shock they delivered just as I began to believe I held paradise in my grasp.

Ten months ago four of us crossed Boca Grande on an early-May morning as soft as a newborn kitten. Jeffrey, my brother-in-law John Graves, his wife, my sister Jane, and myself. Jeffrey seldom carries more than two fishermen; as he does so often, he gave me his blessing and made room. In return, I promised that John and Jane would do the fishing; it was, after all, their charter.

We were looking for tarpon, and Jeffrey brought us to the right place. The reefs, islands, hummocks, and dunes that define the Marquesas lagoon are not a perfect circle. The curving half-circle of land on the northeast quadrant is the largest single land mass: a single, sheltering arm that protects the lagoon from the northeast winds that prevail. To the southwest, its counterpart land arc is a series of small, and even smaller, islands and hummocks. Both Gulf and Atlantic tides and currents sweep along the channels between these independent mangrove masses. Like arteries, the channels feed the shallow lagoon, circulating nourishing sea water across the mile-wide flats. Of these channels, the entrance to the largest is on the due-south curve of the Marquesas circle. Here where its entrance waters are almost ten feet deep is one of the places where migrating tarpon move on their journey from the dark depths of the ocean to their shoal spawning grounds off the southern coast of Mexico.

Certainly not I, nor any of the fishing people I have spoken with, can come up with a dependable reason why tens of thousands of these huge and graceful silver fish should choose to navigate this single, small channel on their thousand-mile voyage to their mating and nursery destinations.

Look at the chart. A few miles southwest of the Marquesas, just beyond the Quicksand Shoals, there is a channel ten miles wide and more than a hundred feet deep that reaches all the way to the Dry Tortugas. Why haven't the tarpon made that their central passage? There they could find invisibility in the depths; here at the Marquesas, their wonderfully prehistoric, deep-sided, armor-scaled, massive shapes glide like shimmering projectiles across the white sand of the channel mouth in water so stunningly clear I have, I swear, seen my reflection in a tarpon's dark globe of an eye as the fish soared under our bow.

I think John Graves is a year or so older than I. Because I've never asked, I do not know. I can, however, vouch for his gristle. A Marine lieutenant who fought and lost an eye in World War II, he is a Texas man in every sense of the weight that heaviest of states implies. His parents and grandparents are the same, and John has written some of the finest, and it is so acknowledged, Texas history, Texas prose, and Texas anecdote that can be found in any library of contemporary history and literature. Unlike me, he is a scholar, albeit one who lives on a two-bit ranch he made for himself in a tiny town called Glen Rose a few miles southwest of Forth Worth.

Because he is a scholar, and because he has, in the latter years of his active outdoor life, taken on fly-fishing as his mission, he was especially enchanted by the prospect of casting one of his hand-tied flies to the largest and most spectacular fighting fish a fly-caster can find. A husky, weathered man who looks like the rancher he also is, John makes his own fly rods on Sage blanks, mounting each guide and applying each coat of lacquer with as much patience as he gives to the individual well-being of the cattle and the goats that are so superbly cared for in Glen Rose.

I have always been fond of John, primarily because we got off to a fine start. Before he married my sister Jane some thirty-five years ago, she was a New York City debutante, a properly educated young lady whose college years had cost the family a bundle. She knew a great many old-money sons and daughters, and, I'm certain, Helen, our mother, harbored high hopes that Jane would, in Helen's words, "marry well." Honestly defined, the phrase meant marrying old money.

Well, in Texas, John Graves might be considered old money, but Texas is a young state, and I'm certain my mother never had in mind a man who wore blue jeans to restaurants and hopped in his pickup truck with cow flop on his stable boots. Nor did she think that the best Jane could do would be to hook up with a man who planned on building his own house, limestone block by limestone block, in a far corner of a state famous for its far corners. "But nobody knows him!" Helen often said; or "Who does he know?" John, as it turned out, had many close and distinguished friends when he met Jane, but, as Helen said, "They're no one we know, dear."

So I was anxious to see how the first encounters would develop when John arrived in New York for the wedding. He was, I had been advised, not a party man. Indeed, the odds were high, a mutual friend advised me, that John Graves would not appear at any of the various receptions and dinners that preceded the ceremony. But he did, and he won. He somehow made it clear by his demeanor and actions that while he obviously believed the city social scene to be something less than bullshit, he would, nevertheless, do what was proper and courteous on Jane's behalf.

He appeared at the gatherings, but he kept himself at a polite Texas remove. Helen had nothing to criticize and everything to be worried about. Her only daughter was quite clearly marrying a man who knew himself and his values well enough to be certain of his standards. John Graves could not and would not be easily moved away from those standards toward others, no matter how important those others might seem to his new mother-in-law.

I was, I must say, delighted. I still am. I think of those cocktail parties almost every time John and I meet.

Which we have done infrequently. Jean and I have visited the "ranch" in Glen Rose twice, and Jane has come east frequently. But

John has not. His visit to Key West was the first time since he married Jane that I saw him outside of Texas. And it was the tarpon, not I, that brought him.

In the early morning of the second day of our three-day charter with Jeffrey, a tarpon took John Graves's brown Cockroach fly and slammed across the flats ripping more than two hundred feet of backing off the reel on the number 9 Sage fly rod John had made for himself in the shed alongside his barn in Glen Rose. Two hours later in the high May sun that had, by then, heated the humid air to close to ninety degrees, the fish was still on, and it was in better shape than John. At least, watching the sweat roll from his brow, I thought so. The tarpon could still jump; John could hardly move. Looking at his steely-gray hair along the nape of his seasoned neck, watching the hard-knuckled and calloused hands kink and curl from the cramps that came from holding the rod for 120 minutes or more, seeing him blink his one good eye to clear the sweat from his vision, I realized that this was a fight the fish might win.

But John Graves hadn't changed in thirty-five years. Just as stubborn, just as ornery, and just as proud as he had always been, he hung in there. Three hours and ten minutes after the tarpon first ate the fly, Jeffrey released him. Although the ninety-pound fish was weary, it did not need as much caring as many tarpon Jeffrey has revived and released.

"That's a lovely rod, John," said Jeffrey, after the tarpon had vanished in the channel, "but I think it's a little light for this kind of fishing."

"Jeffrey," sighed John as he slumped to a seat, "you're right."

Cruising slowly through the channel from north to south, Jeffrey shut down the Yamaha when we reached the Marquesas' south shore and anchored in eight feet of water above a large patch of pale marl. The bowl-shaped depression gleamed under the one-o'clock sun, a ladle of transparent tropical sea unmarred by vegetation, a coral dish as delicately vacant as a porcelain soup tureen polished and waiting on a mahogany sideboard. Jeffrey lowered his small mushroom anchor carefully, and the *Waterlight* swung in the current on a surface as still as cut glass. In the windless torpor, each of our spirits slumped along with John. Released from the stretch of the tensions that had tugged for three hours, we were quite ready to do nothing but sit there, accepting the sun's potent presence while we regrouped for the afternoon.

"We'll have some lunch," Jeffrey said, opening his ice chest. "If a tarpon or two does cruise across this white spot, we'll see it coming. One of you should be ready to cast."

No one moved, so I took my rod from its brackets and laid it along the broad gunwale, Cockroach fly at the ready.

"Be sure you drink plenty of fluids," Jeffrey advised as he passed around ice water, beers, and jugs of Gatorade, "especially you, John Graves. In this sun, you can get dehydrated more quickly than you think."

Sitting on the casting deck, my legs draped over the bow so my toes just touched the water's surface, I joined the general silence as each of us foraged on our tunafish-salad sandwiches. In the flooding tide, the *Waterlight* swung on her mooring so her bow faced seaward; my view as I gulped my Gatorade reached to the southern horizon across an ocean as peaceful and green as a croquet lawn. Not a riffle stirred in the unusual afternoon calm, no short seas had been left by any long-gone gale, not even a vestige of a swell nudged the tranquil surface to announce its parent storm a thousand miles at sea.

Over my years of fishing, I have become conditioned to scanning every sea for signals. Some flags raised from below are as dramatic and unmistakable as the black, new-moon crescent of a swordfish dorsal. Others appear more frequently: white puffs of feeding bluefish as they break water; raindrop patterns of tiny baitfish pursuing an invisible purpose; or the spreading V of a fish wake as some unidentifiable shape swims just beneath the surface. Since my first days on the water, I have been a lucky fish spotter; I have become accustomed to having others doubt my reports simply because they have not seen what my eyes recorded. Knowing this, I was careful not to overstate my case on that somnolent afternoon at anchor. But about a half-mile offshore, something unusual was happening. Of that, I was convinced.

Along the horizon a spreading banner of darker blue flowed like indigo spilled across a lime-green canvas. Some massive, submerged turbulence roiled the flawless surface, altered its refraction, and changed its hue.

"See that, Jeffrey," I called. "Is that a bunch of fish out there, or is it a breeze about to take hold?"

"I don't know," he answered, making it clear by his tone even he could not solve a mystery so distant, so ill-defined.

I kept my eyes on the spreading strangeness. When a tarpon leapt free of the sea, a silver missile fired from a submerged ship, and hung there against the sky at least six feet above the horizon line, I gasped and shouted, my voice charged and the words tumbling even as the fish turned on its side in the air and crashed in a welter of white water.

"It's a tarpon, a big tarpon. Did you see it, Jeffrey, did you?"

By the time my question took shape and Jeffrey was framing his response, the query was rendered academic. From the dark pasture at least six tarpon leaped, and then six more and then others until an incredible tapestry was woven for us by countless giant silver fish. Like a surging school of bluefish or herring grown to monstrous dimensions, tarpon churned, jumped, rolled, pushed water, and leapt again and again, wanting, it seemed, to take wing, to depart the very sea they swam in.

"Sharks! Hammerheads!" Jeffrey yelled. "It's sharks chasing a big school of tarpon. They're driving them like sheep."

In our silence, watching, knowing even then that we were witness to a natural cataclysm few humans will ever see, we could hear a sound—a ripping, as if a vast cotton sheet was being torn from edge to edge. It was the sound of the sea's rending, the hiss of panic as hundreds of tarpon swam at their ultimate and desperate speed. As we watched and listened, the sound acquired new tones, more depth, until it became close to a roar, more like a waterfall's cascade than fabric pulled asunder.

Thrashing, pounding their tails convulsively in the hysteria of their flight, the school of thousands of great tarpon flailed the still surface so violently that the liquid rumble filled the air around us with an awesome echo of distant, rolling thunder. Driven closer to us by still-unseen sharks, the silver and indigo mass began changing color under its dapple of white water that marked each breaking fish. A copper-burnt-orange rose began blooming at the center of the violence, spreading its somber petals until they, too, were a piece of the whole.

"That's blood," Jeffrey said. "Those fish are being torn to pieces."

A new sound made its entrance, one I knew immediately, one every boatman knows: the sibilance of a breaking sea, a wave on the approach. But here? Here in a dead calm.

The wave rolled toward us with surprising speed. Perfectly formed, gleaming in the shimmering sunlight, it crested at almost two feet, lifted the *Waterlight* as it surged under and past us, and crumpled into white water as it stumbled against the shallows of the flats. It was a wave born of apocalypse, a creation of fear, a signal of massacre and futile flight, an echo of the final energies expended by slaughtered tarpon and their relentless butchers.

Herding their silver sheep, the sharks pressed toward the Marquesas shoals, knowing their work would be quicker once the tarpon were forced against the flats.

A dark dorsal, curved and blunt, cut the water as I watched and understood I was seeing a shark, not a tarpon. I was stunned by its speed. Peering from pulpits off Montauk, I have watched many sharks move out of harm's way. There was always a certain languor to their departure, as if they understood the immensity of the depths at their disposal. And I have watched sharks cruising the flats and witnessed their strikes at hooked and wounded fish. But even then, these predators moved with deliberate speed, certain of their ultimate success.

This hammerhead was a projectile. A rooster tail of white water flared from its dorsal as emphatically as it would from a high-speed outboard. The massive shadow shape beneath raced across the bleached flats like a shaft of dark light. I could not absorb the concept; the notion that a submerged creature that large could move so quickly stunned me. There could, I knew, be no defense, no evasion of such startling speed. A new standard of wild behavior had been set. I watched and knew I would judge the flight of every other fish by the mark that shark etched in my memory.

Once pushed against the land, the tarpon scattered, followed by their pursuers. There was no longer a concentration of doom. Only the faltering copper rose still bloomed offshore to affirm the spectacle each of us knew had been ours alone, and would always be. We could, we knew, return to this place, to these Marquesas each May day for the rest of our lives, and never witness such a spectacle again.

Nevertheless, I sought verification. "Have you ever seen anything like that?" I asked Jeffrey.

"No," he said, shaking his head, "no, never."

Sitting quietly, more weary now than we were before we anchored for lunch, we waited for our adrenalin rush to subside. It seemed almost surreal to be so taut in what is thought to be a torpid climate.

Within a half-hour, however, we had revived and chattered easily about the spectacle, John's long battle, and the tarpon's migratory mysteries.

Jane, I noticed, seemed restless.

"Can I slip overboard for a swim?" she asked Jeffrey, and then explained, "All those fluids you made sure we drank are beginning to get to me. I'll just hang on to the boat and do what I have to do, okay?"

"Sure, fine. Do what you need to, Jane. We'll make sure you get back aboard."

Jane stood, her mouth set firmly in that line of determination I know so well, sweat beading on her forehead above her large, brown eyes. I watched to see just how she would, in her late middle age, trim though she might be, negotiate her entrance to the waters of this Marquesas lagoon.

"John," she said to me, in a tone I also know well, "you don't have to watch my every move. Isn't there something else you can do?"

As I turned toward the bow, Jeffrey said, "You might want to wait a minute or two, Jane, before you go over. Look there, about six o'clock, coming toward the stern."

Following the line set by Jeffrey's extended arm, we each looked toward the eastern edge of our coral-dish anchorage. There, outlined in dark and dramatic silhouette against the white sand, was the distinctive profile of a large hammerhead moving directly toward the *Waterlight*. This fish was in no hurry. Quite the opposite. Apparently assured of its complete command of any situation, the shark took possession of the small lagoon. With sinuous, lazy motions as fluid as the currents it moved through, the hammerhead continued its sensual and silent advance until it was directly under our boat.

"God, isn't it beautiful," Jeffrey said in a half-whisper.

I judged the shark to be a foot longer than our flats skiff, which made it at least an eighteen-foot hammerhead, by far the most magnificent and terrifying I have ever seen. Its nearness was even more exceptional. In the sun's glare, I could see each of its luminous, green eyes at each end of the odd airfoil protuberances that extended from its snout. An oddity familiar to saltwater fishermen, the hammerhead's profile had sometimes seemed clumsy to me, a kind of genetic flaw, a handicap. But looking down at that fish less than four feet from us in water as clear as if it were distilled, the hammerhead's most distinctive feature seemed more awesome than awkward, fitting, not freakish.

Hesitating a moment in the darkness of the *Waterlight*'s shadow, the shark appeared to be deliberating its immediate choices. None of us made a sound. Then, with a subtle movement of its sweeping tail, the hammerhead glided across the lagoon onto the flats where we could see its dorsal above water and then back into the channel farther west where it vanished in the darker, deeper unknowns.

Jane spoke first. "Jeffrey," she asked, "have you got a can or a bucket or something I can use?"

◆   ◆   ◆

During the next two days that John and Jane visited with us, staying in the small apartment built above a storage shed in the backyard of our rented home on South Street, I talked with John several times about our days on the water, sharks, and fly-fishing. I learned that he was almost totally committed to the fly rod, using it even when angling for the small bass and perch in the creek running through his ranch and in his dug stock pond called in Texas style a "tank."

Typically, he had thought a great deal about that commitment. And, typically, he had assembled a scholar's library of information on every aspect of the skill. He had learned to make his own rods, tie his own flies, and research his own ichthyological data, and had even begun thinking about how he would convert a plain, empty boat hull into a flats skiff. He is a fellow who goes all the way with his avocations.

I was ready to listen to his ideas. "It's an infirmity without a cure, fly-fishing," he said at one point. "But it's also a pretty deep field of study, bottomless really, which I guess is why it attracts a lot of bookish types, including ex-professors like me. The first symptom is a desire to cast a fly nicely like somebody you've seen somewhere, maybe on a trout river in the Rockies. To lay the line out straight to a reasonable distance, and have the fly land where you want it to. And that may be the easiest part of the whole damned business."

"Ah, yes," I said with some bitterness. "Very easy indeed."

"Then you start throwing flies at fish," said John, "which arouses your curiosity about the kinds of water different species prefer, and what they like to eat. Which in turn, unless you're careful, leads you into trying to imitate what they eat with hair and fur and feathers and tinsel and thread."

"Fly-tying," I said.

"By then there is no escape, and all the rest of it follows. Building rods that will help you cast better, you hope. Messing with boats. Learning about knots and splices and tapered lines and leaders, not to mention all the kinds of fish there are to read about and try to catch, one species after another. All of it follows the simple, fatal fact that you once admired the motions of some lunatic sloshing around in cold river water and waving a thin pole in the air."

"You're sorry you got involved, then?"

"Hell, no, I'm not," John said. "What I'm sorry about is that it took me this long to get around to trying it in salt water. Except that it's great to be hitting a whole new realm of the sport. You know something? At our age, there is no earthly way you and I are going to live long enough to learn all there is to know about this kind of fly-fishing. Isn't that a pretty thought?"

"I may have had some prettier ones from time to time," I answered. "What about other kinds of fishing?"

"Fishing's fishing," said my brother-in-law. "I don't mind throwing a baited hook at catfish when I want one to eat. Sometimes I'll switch to spinning gear if the wind gets to blowing a gale. But it's not the same; it's not as good."

"After watching you and Jeffrey fly-fish, I'm inclined to agree with that," I said. "But I still don't know why the other ways aren't as good."

"Well, they're fine unless you're a diseased fly man, I guess. I don't know why I believe fly-fishing is better, not really. It's got something to do with grace, I think—with handling rather simple tools that feel good and get to working like a part of you, so that using fly tackle is an active and satisfying thing even when you don't catch anything. It's cleaner, too, somehow, and single fly hooks with the barbs mashed down are a hell of a lot easier than trebles on fish that break off, or the ones you bring in and release. I don't often keep them anymore, do you?"

"No, not often," I said, thinking that my answer didn't matter much at that point. It had been a while since I'd brought a fish near enough to have to make a decision. "I believe most of what you say, John, except that I don't find fly-casting to be nearly as easy as you seem to think it is. And I've got a bunch of good spinning rods and reels."

"Keep on using them," John said, and then grinned. "But if you'll learn how to throw a fly right, I bet you'll be giving that spinning gear to Roger. Get some books and videos and practice casting on the grass or somewhere. Did you ever see that casting tape of Lefty Kreh's?"

"Yeah, I've seen it," I said, telling him the same lie I'd told elsewhere. Watching me fly-cast on the Upsalquitch, in Alaska, on the Leirasveit or the Kennebec, a half-dozen other fly-fishermen had asked the same question. Evidently, all I had to do was pick up a rod to indicate I was seriously lacking in instruction. Shit, I told myself now, I don't need to watch a television tape to learn how to cast a fly. But I knew it could help, and that made me even more angry with myself.

"Well, it's a good piece of teaching," he said. "I wouldn't nudge at you about this except that I know you've got the bug. Practice, damn it; decent casting doesn't amount to much. Practice every day. It'll just come to you at some point and you'll wonder why it ever seemed hard. Grace, Brother John, grace will come to you from on high. Amen."

"Amen, Brother John," I said.

◆   ◆   ◆

Jane and John left early the next morning. That afternoon, I took my big tarpon fly rod down to the White Street pier and practiced. *Hey, give it a shot,* I told myself. *Who knows, you might even catch a tarpon.*

A month later, I was still trying and had just one chance left. Knowing Jean and I were due to leave for Maine late that June, I arranged a final trip to the Marquesas with Jeffrey. Roger came with us on a majestic morning just three days before the summer solstice—

long days that arrived in the small hours and lasted until even the most continental visitors had finished their alfresco dinners on the Bagatelle's veranda.

We were up at four, bumping each other in the cramped kitchen, making certain we had packed proper lunches. Since he left high school, Roger has not spent many nights sleeping. Which does not mean he is alert at dawn. On the contrary, his nocturnal ramblings along Key West's restless streets and his silent and determined alcohol intake set him up for sunup surliness. But fishing dulls his churl, and knowing he could rest for an hour once we set our course from Garrison Bight gave him hope.

Like a marionette whose strings go slack, he rolled with the *Waterlight*'s turns, eyes closed, blond-haired head nodding like a sunflower in a breeze. His gentle face with its button nose and boy's mouth looked, as always, angelic in repose—an altar boy at rest. Which is, I suppose, why an altar boy's disguise has so often been used by scoundrels.

I wanted to nudge the slim figure, give him no peace, make him able to receive the glorious messages that dawn was sending us. Even as Jeffrey peered west through the dark, sweeping the sea for the few modest markers that line the all-but-invisible trail, I could look off our stern and watch the dawn's pale tints dilute the darkness on the eastern horizon. Soon enough light had spilled to silhouette morning wings as herons, gulls, and cormorants began their early errands. Alone in my world of sound, speed, and genuine solitude, I wanted, as I always do on that journey through the water wilderness, to take someone's hand, to share the glories we alone were being given.

But Roger was not about to be that person. His concentration on recuperation was absolute, and he did not stir until Jeffrey throttled down and began to use his quiet electric motors to move us along the Marquesas' southern shore where tarpon sometimes gather early on a new day. I made Roger fish first. My perversity sprang partially from my knowledge of the weight of his beer-battered head and my feeling that there were indeed tarpon to be had. I wanted to see Roger react to a strike that stripped two hundred feet of backing off his spinning reel.

In twenty minutes, Jeffrey had put us alongside a school. The fish were daisy-chaining in a casual circle, quite unaware of their visitors. Roger, however, was overly aware of the lumbering, coppery shoulders that emerged from an ocean that had yet to become blue with daylight. In the windless dawn, the sibilant hiss of the fish sounded soft on the morning as the tarpon exhaled air from their flotation bladders. Even their sliding silver emergence and entry to and from the sea could be heard, that most fragile sound of those ultrasmooth, silver-scaled torsos sliding along the warm salt surface.

"Cast now!" Jeffrey said, his crisp voice cutting the paralysis Roger and I shared as we watched the splendid pageant just off our bow.

Raising his rod, Roger's arm pivoted in the school's general direction, but no plug hit the water.

"Shit," Roger said, flipping the bail that he had forgotten and casting again.

"Reel slowly," Jeffrey called from the stern.

Roger stopped reeling and the red-and-white plug wobbled to the surface, followed by a wide-open tarpon mouth as large and as dark as a black bushel basket. "Oh, God," Roger said, then yanked hard. Soaring free of the surface, the plug whipped empty air above Roger's head, snapped back, wrapping line around the rod tip on its rebound. Reaching for the tip, Roger tried to untangle the mess of monofilament, then put the rod on the deck when he realized the complexity of his problem. As he worked, frowning and fumbling, tarpon circled like porpoises for a few more moments and then vanished as gentle ripples radiated from the scene of their dawn frolic.

Gentle Jeffrey said nothing. Unlike so many professional fishing guides, who, I suppose, sometimes feel demeaned by their for-hire status, he never tries to even the score by criticizing an inept fisherman. He does just the opposite: He tries harder to make sure that fisherman is successful.

Poling the *Waterlight* along the south shore, past the entrance to the deepest channel, Jeffrey let his skiff drift into the same coral serving dish we had anchored in four weeks before. I had not forgotten the hammerhead, nor the venue of its visit.

"We'll try it here a few minutes, Roger," Jeffrey said. "Be ready to cast when I tell you. These fish will be traveling, not daisy-chaining."

Sighing with remorse at his earlier showing, Roger stood at attention on the bow casting platform. Believing that I had given him a fair opportunity to hook up, I picked up my fly rod and stood at the stern quarter, just in case. Jeffrey stayed in the bow, ready to instruct if and when he saw a fish turn Roger's way.

Incredibly, as I stared off to the northern sky, my eyes caught the movement of three shapes heading toward us off the flats, not from the deeper water as Jeffrey anticipated.

They came closer, moving steadily, but not quickly. The composure of their procession told me that they had not seen our boat, or, if they had, they judged it no threat.

On they came. I began shaking. My knees, as they always do when I see large fish, deserted their structural purpose. I had trouble staying upright. Even if I had wanted to, which I did not, I could hardly have gotten a word past my tight windpipe.

The tarpon, because that is what they definitely were, never swerved or hesitated. They were, I could tell, going to glide just a few feet from where I stood.

I began swinging my rod in its casting arc, stripping line as I did. Any idiot could cast far enough to reach these fish, I told myself. For Christ's sake, they were practically under our stern.

There were three of them. The two in front were smaller. The single fish, a few lengths back, looked immense. I cast in their general direction.

My fly flopped on the water. By the time it sank to the tarpons' depth, the two lead fish had already moved too far toward the bow. But that third fish found a Cockroach sinking slowly just in front of its mouth. Opening its maw, the tarpon inhaled my fly. I saw it vanish.

When I did, I yanked hard. The fish kept swimming, and that's what saved me. It was the tarpon's progress, not my strike, that did the deed. Before the fish recognized the fly for what it was, its own forward motion snapped the hook against the corner of its jaws.

"Hey!" I yelled. "Hey!"

Spinning, Jeffrey turned toward the stern, saw what was happening, saw the fish dash under the bow and saw the bend in my rod.

Then each of us watched open-mouthed as the tarpon jumped clear less than twenty feet off the bow, crashing back in an awkward, sideways tumble that sounded like a cellar door thrown overboard.

Then that fish took off.

"It's a big fish, a big fish, John!" Jeffrey yelled from the brink of his composure.

"Get up here in the bow," he called as he cleared a path. Holding my rod so its tip pointed at the sky, I edged forward, stepped up onto the platform. The fish made it easier than it might have been. Its run appeared endless, unswerving, and fast. Line disappeared from the Fin-Nor fly-casting reel a generous soul had given me, and I began to be certain the backing would vanish entirely. Nothing I could do could stop the fish, not with a twelve-pound-test tippet tied between the shock leader and my fly line. There was no surge, no struggle. Line left me as if the other end was fast to a heavily loaded trailer truck cruising a throughway downgrade at seventy miles an hour.

Just when I was certain that tarpon's first run was also my last, the fish jumped. I could not comprehend the distance. At first, I thought it was some other fish, not mine. Far to the west, on the way to the

Tortugas, the tarpon leapt free and clear, hung there, and crashed back.

The line went slack.

"He's off," I said.

"No. No," Jeffrey said. "He's headed straight back this way. Reel, John. Reel as fast as you can."

I tried. I turned the crank as fast as my hand and wrist would respond to my brain's message. I could not catch up to the fish. Slack line curved on the water's surface.

"Reel! Reel!" Jeffrey yelled.

I did, desperately. Then, pressure, wonderful pressure. The encounter continued. I could feel the fish; it could feel me. Once again, we were joined. What I'd said to my father was right: Fishing should come first.

"Fly line coming in," Jeffrey called.

I had retrieved all the backing. My aching arm told me it had been a job.

Just as the fly line began to build on the reel, the tarpon turned and began another run: the same truck on the same throughway.

This time, it hit a wall. The reel stopped turning, the rod bent sharply, too sharply. I watched, knowing disaster had been born in that instant of silence. The rod snapped back in my hand like a tree branch bent and released. This time each of us knew the fish was free.

"What happened?" Jeffrey asked.

Looking at the reel, I knew. When the fish had turned and run toward me, and when I was reeling in as fast as I possibly could, the slack in the line had looped back on itself. I had, in fact, wrapped a free-floating loop of backing around the reel. On its next run, the tarpon had gone as far as that loop. Wrapped around the line, it became an instant brake, a stop as effective as any knot. The tippet, as it was designed to do, broke under the pressure. My tarpon was free. My giant tarpon, gone.

"A big fish," Jeffrey said. "A very big fish.'

"Hey," I said, "it took my fly. I cast to it by myself and it took my fly. That's the first tarpon that's ever done that."

Nine months ago that happened, and I can still see that fish leaping against the sky, almost as far off as the Tortugas.

We are fishing inside the lagoon today, in barracuda country. When February's northeast winds chill the deeper waters of the channels, barracuda congregate in the thin water of the Marquesas flats favoring circles of pale sand free of turtle grass and seaweed. From his perch on the poling platform above the stern, Jeffrey looks for their motionless cigar shapes; these fish take the sun as studiously as a Manhattan broker on his first day alongside a Miami Beach hotel pool.

"Fish at twelve o'clock," Jeffrey calls. "He's out of casting range, but let me know when you can see him."

Staring, peering straight ahead, I see the barracuda's shadow profile suspended above the golden sand. "I see him." I raise my rod and begin false casting, the lime-green tassel whipping back and forth.

"Cast now," Jeffrey tells me, and I do.

The line collapses on the surface as if it spilled from an overhead slop jar. The fly is nowhere near the fish.

"Pick it up and cast again," Jeffrey says. "He's still right there."

I yank too hard on my retrieve. The fly pops from the surface headed straight for me. I duck as it wraps itself around the rod. By now, the *Waterlight*'s easy momentum has brought the boat too close and the barracuda glides off.

Jeffrey says nothing, keeps poling, keeps looking.

Half an hour later, after a discouraging series of flawed and fruitless casts, I think I detect a note of weary resignation in Jeffrey's words, encouraging though they may be. He has, after all, put me within casting range of a half-dozen sturdy barracuda, all of whom are still at large and at ease.

"Fish at ten o'clock," he calls, "moving toward eleven." I see the fish, and I cast. The fly lands almost where I want it to go, but I begin stripping line, trying to retrieve it as fast as possible so I can try the cast a second time.

"He sees the fly," Jeffrey calls. "He's after it. Here he comes. Keep stripping. Strip as fast as you can."

Now I can see the push of water racing behind my fly as the barracuda gets up to speed. Then I see the fish. It is less than twenty feet from our bow and racing.

I keep stripping. I watch as the barracuda opens its mouth and eats my fly. I expect the fish to strike the boat. It turns and runs a few feet, then jumps. The sun flashes on its sides of mottled silver.

"Look at that jump," yells Jeffrey. "Get him on the reel, John. Get him on the reel."

As the fish runs across the flats, I keep tension on the fly line with my left hand. In moments, the slack is taken.

"You got him on the reel. Good boy," Jeffrey yells.

The fish makes several jumps, at least three fine runs, and then I have it beside the boat: my first barracuda on a fly. Jeffrey leans over the gunwale and cautiously removes the hook. After a motionless moment, the barracuda waves its tail gently and moves off at a measured pace across the flats.

Jeffrey walks forward and shakes my hand. "Congratulations, Cap," he says. "That was a good fish, about fifteen pounds."

Jean is smiling as I put down my rod and slide onto the seat beside her.

"How about some lunch?" asks Jeffrey. Not waiting for our answer, he opens a cooler and passes around sandwiches and cold juice. Staked off, the *Waterlight* is the only boat inside the Marquesas lagoon, we are the only human souls in sight. Because I know this is a wilderness preserve and because Key West is more than twenty miles east, I feel privileged, lucky to be in this wild and distant place on such a sparkling adventure on such a fine, sun-drenched day.

"There," I say to Jean as I remember John Graves's words, "I've caught a barracuda on a fly. Next will come a tarpon, then a bonefish, and then a permit. Isn't that a wonderful agenda to have in front of me. It took me sixty-five years to get this far. I'm going to have a shitload of fun traveling the rest of the way."

And we hold hands.

A RIVER'S TALE

• • •

JUSTIN ASKINS

THE NEVERSINK GORGE IS THE HIDDEN JEWEL OF THE CATSKILLS. WILD
and stark, its banks brilliant with rhododendron, the Neversink River
sweeps and tumbles here for four boulder-choked miles. A little over
an hour and a half from New York City, the gorge has been protected
for more than one hundred years as a private conservancy and remains
as primitive as a Western wilderness. This river is also my home water.

It was not always so. Ten years ago, knowing little about the
Catskill rivers and even less about fly-fishing, I bought a small house
outside Monticello, New York. A spinning rig had introduced me to
the public sections of the Beaverkill and Willowemoc, but the lure of
solitude drew me farther and farther from the heavily used waters. I
knew nothing of the Neversink until I bought some Geological Survey
maps that showed a virtually untouched river area not ten miles from
my house. My interest piqued, I began to wander the fringe, working
my way down from Bridgeville, where Route 17 crosses.

One January morning I drove to the outskirts, loaded my pack,
and began walking down a snow-covered road. In a few minutes I was
in a stand of enormous hemlocks, listening to chickadees and an icy
mountain stream. The effect of those first steps was immediate and
electrical: The spell of the Neversink's wildness was upon me.

Soon some members of the local hunting and fishing club gave
me permission to explore the area, and I took full advantage, returning
often and looking longingly at that winterbound river. Then the club
allowed me to join as a fishing member, and opening day became my
obsession.

Several times I had tried to teach myself fly-casting, but the
results were meager, my helpless flailing quick to frighten anything in
the water. I was always looking around to make sure no one could see

what I was doing, fearful that I would be turned in to the casting police and arrested for disorderly conduct.

Once I had access to fishing in the gorge, however, my secretiveness changed. Even on weekends, when members of the other clubs that rented from Benjamin Wechsler came up, few fishermen appeared. During the week, it was rare to see anyone near my favorite haunts—the series of pools near Hackeldam and at the large pool above Denton Falls. I could cast with abandon, and my technique improved rapidly.

I knew very little of the Neversink that first year, but those two places opened me to further intimacy. Hackeldam was a particularly effective tutor. It offered deep, undisturbed stretches and chuting rapids, with everything in between. I learned that hair-wing flies like the Royal Wulff and Elk-hair Caddis would stay up in the fast currents, and how to keep them up for as long as possible. Soon, I could trick brookies with a 7X tippet in the quiet pools and hook browns in the broken water. My concentration was intense, although a kingfisher's rattle or the hoarse call of a scarlet tanager might bring me back to a different world, of the rose-purples of wild geranium and fringed polygala, the soft whites of wood anenome and painted trillium.

Slowly I became more comfortable with the river. Sometimes I would look off to what remained of the Hackeldam bridge, built around 1800 by a Dutchman named Hackel. A settlement had grown up here, including a small concern manufacturing barrel staves and grain scoops. The power came from a dam Hackel had built on Wolf Lake Brook.

Other days, my mind would drift further back to when the Leni-Lenape had hunted through the gorge. The Neversink was traditional Delaware territory (probably for the Port Jervis band of Minisinks), and I delighted at how little disturbed the gorge remained from when Indians walked its banks.

That summer, I discovered the comforts of the Campground Pool above Denton Falls. There I would sit at a rickety picnic table laboring on my doctoral dissertation—appropriately, on Melville's landscapes—and watch for rising fish. I must have missed many, but when I noticed, I grabbed my rod, raced through the bluets and forget-me-nots, and began working an active trout. A phoebe had built its nest in the ledge across the river, and if I put down the brown with my ineptitude, I would often watch the small gray bird shooting and dipping along the far bank.

By autumn, I grew restless for new water, eager for fresh terrain, and I began to push farther into the gorge. Perhaps it was the sight of a bald eagle up from the Mongaup Valley, perhaps it was Ben

Wechsler's advice to try the canyon area, where the best fishing reputedly was. I'm not sure. But I felt an irresistible urge to explore.

One mid-October afternoon, with autumn bringing a richness of dark crimson, lemon yellow, and tawny orange to the mixed hardwoods, I crossed the river just above Denton Falls and began moving deeper into the gorge. Asters, fleabanes, and goldenrods covered the banks, with the occasional bright red of a cardinal flower breaking the whites, lavenders, and yellows of the other blooms.

I came first to a long, wide pool where the Neversink slows not far below Denton Falls. In that spacious and gentle water I've watched many rising trout, and I've been able to take a few if I approached warily and my fly was right.

Chimney Pool came next, where the Neversink turns sharply, rushing hard against a steep rock wall, a spot I have always taken as the beginning of the gorge. It was here one afternoon that Nick Lyons brought up an enormous brown on a grasshopper bounced off the far wall. I have had little luck with Chimney, but I know there's at least one big fish in its protecting waters.

Below Chimney I found my favorite place on the river, a stretch where I've pulled in a number of hefty browns. Scores of boulders push the river together here, and it twists and turns quickly, leaving dozens of small, tricky pockets. It's exhausting to wade, but its productivity can be sensational. I went back regularly, that first October, and one afternoon I brought up ten fish in a little over two hours.

The last trout that day taught me never to underestimate the escape strategy of a big brown. I had positioned myself behind a shielding boulder, looking to a tiny, calm oval that simply had to harbor something large. I was using a number 12 Light Cahill because it was easy to see, but each time I dropped the fly into that opening, the fierce current tore it instantly away. I moved closer. The water pulled at my waders. Leaning forward with little balance, I finally kept the fly there long enough for a powerful fish to shoot up and savage the Cahill. In the rushing water he seemed enormous, over three pounds for sure, and I had to let him run or lose him on my 6X tippet. Soon he was a hundred feet away. Now I had to work my way down through the turbulence, all the time keeping sufficient strain on the fish. For ten minutes, I struggled toward him, finally getting to a boulder just above. But the rest had helped the fish, and off he shot, plunging through three more pools before he held again. I knew I was going to lose him, but I went after that brown anyway and unexpectedly reached him once more. He must have sensed my closeness for he darted under two nestled boulders and stopped.

Now what to do? I couldn't pull him back, nor could I reach far enough under to catch him by the gills. I pondered the possibilities and decided to try scaring him back into the open by getting on the other side of the submerged stones and reaching under. As I did, I felt a strong tail push against my hand, and off he charged to the next pool. Amazingly, the trout was still on.

A few more minutes of wading brought us together again, and this time, whether tired or bored, the big brown let me slide my net around him. I let him rest for a couple of minutes, then released him back to his native currents. An osprey had been watching my adventure, no doubt disdainful of such a ludicrous performance.

My life grew hectic after that October lull—too full of dissertations, gray cities, and a broken heart—and it wasn't until springtime that I reentered the canyon. The rhododendron season was half-finished, sheep laurel past, mountain laurel just beginning, great laurel still a month distant. I followed a deer trail through oaks and beeches to Dated Rock Pool. I've seen pictures of giant browns taken out of this bottomless water, but I've never come up with the correct technique to fish it. A sinking line with a big streamer might do, but that technique seems more suited to Western rivers like the Umpqua or Rogue. It was near here that two fishermen met one afternoon: Ray Bergman going south from Bridgeville, Larry Koller moving north from Oakland Valley. A record of their conversation would have been a remarkable testimony to the Neversink's magic.

By that second summer I had fished every pool in the gorge, working Cat Ledge Pool and Long Eddy, High Falls and Round Eddy. Exploring the deeply shaded tributaries had become my passion. Wolf Lake Brook, the recently named Hewitt Brook, Eden Brook—all had small but fine and feisty trout in them. Larry Koller wrote about one spot on Eden Brook:

> It was a picture pool with the water pouring in from a yard-high fall, churning itself among fat, mossy boulders, then flattening out its glide against a low ledge, then swinging around and around in a whirlpool eddy. The pool was deep, its bed a mass of black boulders; the sunlight barely flickered through the heavy overhead arch of hemlock and beech, leaving most of the hole in deep, mysterious shadow. An ideal spot for trout, I had always thought. . . .

Koller was correct, for a day later a youngster pulled a three-pound brown out of that water. According to Wechsler, much of *Taking Larger Trout* grew out of Koller's experiences in the gorge, and the culminating incident of my second summer would fit in Koller's volume.

A number of people from my hunting and fishing club were staying over at the Campground Pool as part of their annual Fourth of July celebration. Trout activity all day was nil, the water temperature soaring into the eighties. Even the late afternoon was dead, though occasionally one of us would cast a few times with no success. Hope had disappeared in the early twilight—thoughts turning to the misty coolness of the next morning—when I spotted a delicate rise about midway through the pool. That spot is usually reserved for a chub, but on a dull day even a chub can be fun, so I pulled my waders on.

"Going chubbing?" someone called, laughing.

"Why not?" I answered with a grin.

Nobody paid attention to me as I began casting above the fish, letting my big Adams drift down to the chub. But this fish wouldn't touch the Adams. *Picky chub,* I thought. After a few more well-placed casts brought nothing, I tied on a 7X tippet, changed to a number 20 Adams, and a dozen times sent it drifting into the ring of the rise. Finally, something tipped up; I gave a slight pull and knew it was no chub I had. Whatever it was simply moved off, steadily, powerfully, then anchored near the bottom. I was astonished that my two-pound tippet had held. *Now what?* Gingerly I tensed the line. But whatever it was didn't move; my rod just bent a little toward it. *It can't be a bass—too stationary. Have I hooked a giant catfish? Impossible. This acts like a big brown.*

The people on shore began to take notice, none sure of what I had, but all aware of it. Again I increased the strain on the line, but the fish remained immobile. Twilight had edged into night, and my audience began giving advice:

"Put a little more pressure on."

"Get the rod up higher."

I picked the rod up just a bit, anxious that my great fish not be lost, but no, it was still on, and I was bringing it closer. Suddenly, it came to the surface, rolled, and we saw a broad, bright trout. It was by far the biggest brown I had ever hooked, and now I had to see it in my net.

For another ten minutes I kept working it closer, knowing the tiny hook could pull out at any moment. Then I saw the fish again, not five feet off, struggling near the surface. Exquisite tension, then the net slipped under it and I was looking at an eighteen-inch brown, its spots red, its flanks silver and orange.

I have since released many fish from that net. Some were larger, but none more memorable. For that evening signified the end of a crucial part of my fly-fishing education. After that, the members of the club fully accepted me, and I felt the river and its gorge had accepted me, too. Walking back along the rutted dirt road that evening, I realized that I could now sense where a brown or brookie might be holding, where a Blackburnian warbler might be found, or a black-throated green, where dwarf ginseng or foamflower might bloom. I had become part of the gorge.

Now, whenever I am away from the gorge and feel the cool steel of the world at my throat, I have only to let myself drift back into those fiery October leaves, to remember that Fourth of July trout in my net, to feel very much at home.

THE SAME RIVER TWICE

• • •

DAVID QUAMMEN

I'VE BEEN READING HERACLITUS THIS WEEK, SO NATURALLY MY BRAIN IS full of river water.

Heraclitus, you'll recall, was the Greek philosopher of the sixth century B.C. who gets credit for having said: "You cannot step twice into the same river." Heraclitus was a loner, according to the sketchy accounts of him, and rather a crank. He lived in the town of Ephesus, near the coast of Asia Minor opposite mainland Greece, not far from a great river that in those days was called the Meander. He never founded a philosophic school, as Plato and Pythagoras did. He didn't want followers. He simply wrote his one book and deposited the scroll in a certain sacred building, the temple of Artemis, where the general public couldn't get hold of it. The book itself was eventually lost, and all that survives of it today are about a hundred fragments, which have come down secondhand in the works of other ancient writers. So his ideas are known only by hearsay. He seems to have said a lot of interesting things, some of them cryptic, some of them downright ornery, but his river comment is the one for which Heraclitus is widely remembered. The full translation is: "You cannot step twice into the same river, for other waters are continually flowing on." To most people it comes across as a nice resonant metaphor, a bit of philosophic poetry. To me it is that and more.

Once, for a stretch of years, I lived in a very small town on the bank of a famous Montana river. It was famous mainly for its trout, this river, and for its clear water and its abundance of chemical nutrients, and for the seasonal blizzards of emerging insects that made it one of the most rewarding pieces of habitat in North America, arguably in the world, if you happened to be a trout or a fly-fisherman. I happened to be a fly-fisherman.

One species of insect in particular—one "hatch," to use the slightly misleading term that fishermen apply to these impressive entomological events, when a few billion members of some mayfly or stonefly or caddis-fly species all emerge simultaneously into adulthood and take flight over a river—one insect hatch in particular gave this river an unmatched renown. The species was *Pteronarcys californica*, a monstrous but benign stonefly that grew more than two inches long and carried a pinkish-orange underbelly for which it had gotten the common name *salmonfly*. These insects, during their three years of development as aquatic larvae, could survive only in a river that was cold, pure, fast-flowing, rich in dissolved oxygen, and covered across its bed with boulders the size of bowling balls, among which the larvae would live and graze. The famous river offered all those conditions extravagantly, and so *P. californica* flourished there, like nowhere else. Trout flourished in turn.

When the clouds of *P. californica* took flight, and mated in air, and then began dropping back onto the water, the fish fed upon them voraciously, recklessly. Wary old brown trout the size of a person's thigh, granddaddy animals that would never otherwise condescend to feed by daylight upon floating insects, came up off the bottom for this banquet. Each gulp of *P. californica* was a major nutritional windfall. The trout filled their bellies and their mouths and still continued gorging. Consequently the so-called salmonfly so-called hatch on this river, occurring annually during two weeks in June, triggered by small changes in water temperature, became a wild and garish national festival in the fly-fishing year. Stockbrokers in New York, corporate lawyers in San Francisco, federal judges and star-quality surgeons and foundation presidents—the sort of folk who own antique bamboo fly rods and field jackets of Irish tweed—planned their vacations around this event. They packed their gear and then waited for the telephone signal from a guide in a shop on Main Street of the little town where I lived.

The signal would say: *It's started.* Or, in more detail: *Yeah, the hatch is on. Passed through town yesterday. Bugs everywhere. By now the head end of it must be halfway to Varney Bridge. Get here as soon as you can.* They got there. Cabdrivers and schoolteachers came too. People who couldn't afford to hire a guide and be chauffeured comfortably in a Mackenzie boat, or who didn't want to, arrived with dinghies and johnboats lashed to the roofs of old yellow buses. And if the weather held, and you got yourself to the right stretch of river at the right time, it could indeed be very damn good fishing.

But that wasn't why I lived in the town. Truth be known, when *P. californica* filled the sky and a flotilla of boats filled the river, I usually headed in the opposite direction. I didn't care for the crowds. It was almost as bad as the Fourth of July rodeo, when the town suddenly became clogged with college kids from a nearby city, and Main Street was ankle-deep in beer cans on the morning of the fifth, and I would find people I didn't know sleeping it off in my front yard, under the scraggly elm. The salmonfly hatch was like that, only with stockbrokers and flying hooks. Besides, there were other places and other ways to catch a fish. I would take my rod and my waders and disappear to a small spring creek that ran through a stock ranch on the bottomland east of the river.

It was private property. There was no room for guided boats on this little creek, and there was no room for tweed. Instead of tweed there were sheep—usually about thirty head, bleating in halfhearted annoyance but shuffling out of my way as I hiked from the barn out to the water. There was an old swayback horse named Buck, a buckskin; also a younger one, a hot white-stockinged mare that had once been a queen of the barrel-racing circuit and hadn't forgotten her previous station in life. There was a graveyard of rusty car bodies, a string of them, DeSotos and Fords from the Truman years, dumped into the spring creek along one bend to hold the bank in place and save the sheep pasture from turning into an island. Locally this sort of thing is referred to as the "Detroit riprap" mode of soil conservation; after a while, the derelict cars come to seem a harmonious part of the scenery. There was also an old two-story ranch house of stucco, with yellow trim. Inside lived a man and a woman, married then.

Now we have come to the reason I did live in that town. Actually there wasn't one reason but three: the spring creek, the man, and the woman. At the time, for a stretch of years, those were three of the closest friends I'd ever had.

This spring creek was not one of the most eminent Montana spring creeks, not Nelson Spring Creek and not Armstrong, not the sort of place where you could plunk down twenty-five dollars per rod per day for the privilege of casting your fly over large, savvy trout along an exclusive and well-manicured section of water. On this creek you fished free or not at all. I fished free, because I knew the two people inside the house and, through them, the wonderful surly old rancher who owned the place.

They lived there themselves, those two, in large part because of the creek. The male half of the partnership was at that time a raving and insatiable fly-fisherman, like me, for whom the luxury of having this particular spring creek just a three-minute stroll from his back door was worth any number of professional and personal sacrifices. He had found a place he loved dearly, and he wanted to stay. During previous incarnations he had been a wire-service reporter in Africa, a bar owner in Chicago, a magazine editor in New York, a reform-school guard in Idaho, and a timber-faller in the winter woods of Montana. He had decided to quit the last before he cut off a leg with his chain saw, or worse; he was later kind enough to offer me his saw and his expert coaching and then to dissuade me deftly from making use of either, during the period when I was so desperate and foolhardy as to consider trying to earn a living that way. All we both wanted, really, was to write novels and fly-fish for trout. We fished the spring creek, together and individually, more than a hundred days each year. We memorized that water. The female half of the partnership, on the other hand, was a vegetarian by principle who lived chiefly on grape-fruit and considered that anyone who tormented innocent fish—either for food or, worse, for the sport of catching them and then gently releasing them, as we did—showed the most inexcusable symptoms of arrested development and demented adolescent cruelty, but she tol-erated us. All she wanted was to write novels and read Jane Austen and ride the hot mare. None of us had any money.

None of us was being published. Nothing happened in that town between October and May. The man and I played chess. We endan-gered our lives hilariously cutting and hauling firewood. We skied into the backcountry carrying tents and cast-iron skillets and bottles of wine, then argued drunkenly over whether it was proper to litter the woods with eggshells, if the magpies and crows did it too. We watched Willie Stargell win a World Series. Sometimes on cold, clear days we put on wool gloves with no fingertips and went out to fish. Meanwhile the woman sequestered herself in a rickety backyard shed, with a small woodstove and a cot and a manual typewriter, surrounded by black widow spiders that she chose to view as pets. Or the three of us stood in their kitchen, until late hours on winter nights, while the woman peeled and ate uncountable grapefruits and the man and I drank whiskey, and we screamed at each other about literature.

The spring creek ran cool in summer. It ran warm in winter. This is what spring creeks do; this is their special felicity. It steamed and it rippled with fluid life when the main river was frozen over solid. Anchor ice never formed on the rocks of its riffles, killing insect larvae where they lived, and frazil ice never made the water slushy—as occurred on the main river. During spring runoff this creek didn't flood; therefore the bottom wasn't scoured and disrupted, and the eggs of the rainbow trout, which spawned around that time, weren't swept out of the nests and buried lethally in silt. The creek did go brown with turbidity during runoff, from the discharge of several small tributaries that carried meltwater out of the mountains through an erosional zone, but the color would clear again soon.

Insects continued hatching on this creek through the coldest months of the winter. In October and November, large brown trout came upstream from the main river and scooped out their spawning nests on a bend that curved around the sheep pasture, just downstream from the car bodies. In August, grasshoppers blundered onto the water from the brushy banks, and fish exploded out of nowhere to take them. Occasionally I or the other fellow would cast a tiny fly and pull in a grayling, that gorgeous and delicate cousin of trout, an Arctic species left behind by the last glaciation, that fared poorly in the warm summer temperatures of sun-heated meltwater rivers. In this creek a grayling could be comfortable, because most of the water came from deep underground. That water ran cool in summer, relatively, and warm in winter, relatively—relative in each case to the surrounding air temperature, as well as the temperature of the main river. In absolute terms the creek's temperature tended to be stable year-round, holding steady in a hospitable middle range close to the constant temperature of the groundwater from which it was fed. This is what spring creeks, by definition, do. The scientific jargon for such a balanced condition is *stenothermal*: temperatures in a narrow range. The ecological result is a stable habitat and a twelve-month growing season. Free from extremes of cold or heat, free from flooding, free from ice and heavy siltation and scouring, the particular spring creek in question seemed always to me a thing of sublime and succoring constancy. In that regard it was no different from other spring creeks; but it was the one I knew and cared about.

The stretch of years came to an end. The marriage came to an end. There were reasons, but the reasons were private and are certainly none of our business here. Books were pulled down off shelves and sorted into two piles. Fine oaken furniture, too heavy to be hauled into uncertain futures, was sold off for the price of a sad song. The white-stockinged mare was sold also, to a family with a couple of young barrel-racers, and the herd of trap-lame and half-feral cats was divided up. The man and the woman left town individually, in separate trucks, at separate times, each headed back toward New York City. I helped load the second truck, the man's, but my voice wasn't functioning well on that occasion. I was afflicted with a charley horse of the throat. It had all been hard to witness, not simply because a marriage had ended but even more so because, in my unsolicited judgment, a great love affair had. This partnership of theirs had been a vivid and imposing thing.

Or maybe it was hard because two love affairs had ended—if you count mine with the pair of them. I should say here that a friendship remains between me and each of them. Friendship with such folk is a lot. But it's not the same.

Now I live in the city from which college students flock off to the Fourth of July rodeo in that little town, where they raise hell for a day and litter Main Street with beer cans and then sleep it off under the scraggly elm in what is now someone else's front yard—the compensation being that July fourth is quieter up here. It is only an hour's drive. Not too long ago I was down there myself.

I parked, as always, in the yard by the burn barrel outside the stucco house. The house was empty; I avoided it. With my waders and my fly rod I walked out to the spring creek. Of course it was all a mistake.

I stepped into the creek and began fishing my way upstream, casting a grasshopper imitation into patches of shade along the overhung banks. There were a few strikes. There was a fish caught and released. But after less than an hour I quit. I climbed out of the water. I left. I had imagined that a spring creek was a thing of sublime and succoring constancy. I was wrong. Heraclitus was right.

SOMETHING MORE

• • •

DAVID SEYBOLD

IN THE FALL THE LOCALS WOULD QUIT THE LAKE AND HEAD UP INTO THE
surrounding hills and hunt the grouse that lived on the fringes of
abandoned apple orchards. They said the lake was too hard to fish in
the fall and that only fools went out and chased the brook trout and
landlocked salmon. They said this because after Labor Day it was
fly-fishing only, and they were not fly-fishermen.

It was only partially true, though, about the lake's being difficult
to fish. There were always plenty of brook trout to be caught that
didn't require much effort. They were in their prespawning period
then, and they traveled in vulnerable schools around the lake. They
would be on the surface, feeding on red and black flying ants and very
small midges, and almost any small dry fly or nymph would catch
them.

But the landlocked salmon were another story. Even the few
fly-fishermen who did fish the lake in the fall left them alone. The
salmon were always shy and elusive and simply too difficult and frustrating to think seriously about pursuing. They would be on the surface, feeding on the same ants and midges as the trout, and their dorsal
fins and thick backs would show so plainly that unknowing fly-
fishermen refused to believe they couldn't catch them. They would see
the salmon on the surface and cast until their arms were weary without
getting so much as a look-see refusal. Or they would hear a salmon's
showy rise as it opted for an unwary trout and put on a streamer and
troll until either their arms wore out from paddling or the motor ran
out of gasoline.

There was, however, a man to whom this matrix of pursuit and
failure did not apply. His name was Andrew Tawney and the lake's
salmon were his passion. He had devoted his angling life to the lake
and to fishing for its salmon, which in time he came to know as well

as a human can know something that is ultimately beyond any mortal's ken. And to pursue the salmon in the fall was his greatest passion of all, for then they were extremely selective and shy, more so than at any other time of the year.

Andrew Tawney was an English teacher in a regional high school who during the fall considered his job an interruption to his fishing. He always tried to conceal his feelings, though, for he was a responsible man, the sort who would not allow his private life to interfere with his job. Yet during the whole of September, the last month of the fishing season, it was not hard to tell he had other things on his mind. He taught his classes by rote and politely avoided after-school conferences with teachers and students. And when the bell rang signaling the end of the day, he would slip out the door and get in his International Scout and drive directly to the lake. He kept his fly rod and a change of clothes in the Scout and a green, sixteen-foot Old Town canoe strapped down on the roof. Barring irksome parking-lot encounters with students and peers, he could drive to the lake in twelve minutes and be on the water by three-twenty. (Yes, he had actually timed it, for every minute mattered.)

The few fly-fishermen who fished the lake knew Andrew very well. They knew his passion for the salmon and admired and envied his ability to catch them. In their time, each had tried to catch the salmon, but none ever did. They would make halfhearted attempts, but eventually they would give up and satisfy themselves with the schooling brook trout while occasionally looking at Andrew, who would be out in the middle of the lake. He would be standing in his canoe and holding a fly rod and staring at the water, his figure silent and intent. Hour after hour, day after day, they would see Andrew staring and staring. When they saw him casting, though, they would stop their own fishing and watch him, for it meant Andrew had spotted a salmon. If the salmon took his fly, his rod would bend sharply at the tip and the line would stretch out, and they would wait for the salmon to leap. When it did, they would shake their heads in awe of both Andrew and the salmon and wait to see how big it was. Then, after Andrew had released the fish, they would go back to their own fishing and try to imagine what it would be like to catch a salmon that way.

It always bothered Andrew when the other fly-fishermen would talk to him about the salmon he caught. They made it sound so extraordinary, as though he were the only one who could ever catch them. He would tell them that what he did was not so difficult that they couldn't catch salmon themselves. Andrew would patiently explain to them how he caught the salmon, but when one of them would try, he'd become frustrated and quit and return to the trout. Andrew would watch and remember his own frustration with the salmon and how he had overcome it by thinking of the salmon as rare jewels that could be his if he persisted in figuring out the combination to the safe they were in. But the simple truth was the others lacked Andrew's determination, and in the end they always reasoned there were too few days left in the season to be wasting time casting to fish that couldn't be caught.

In a sense, it was true that anyone who could handle a fly rod and canoe had the potential to catch the salmon. But in a larger sense, much of what Andrew did went beyond the average fly-fisherman's ability. Being able to cast accurately with a minimum of false-casting, and knowing how to handle three- to six-pound salmon on 4X and 5X tippets and size 18 and 20 flies, accounted for only a few of the needed skills. Keen eyesight, constant observation, unfailing concentration and patience, and the reflexes of a grouse hunter were also required. Even then an angler would still have to be able to paddle fast and hard with one hand while standing, and hold and cast a cocked fly rod with the other hand. If a fly-fisherman could do these things well, and with confidence, and if conditions were right—if the lake was perfectly flat and without so much as a whisper of wind, and if the ants or midges were in the surface film—he stood a fair chance of hooking a few and maybe catching one salmon every afternoon. And then there was the *sense* of knowing and understanding the salmon that went beyond any physical ability. For Andrew it was a knowledge that had become seminal, instinctual.

◆   ◆   ◆

After a few years of being the only angler to consistently pursue and catch the salmon, Andrew began to see the salmon through different eyes. No longer did he regard them as rare and precious jewels. His pursuit of the salmon had become less joyful and more obligatory, as though he were morally bound to catch them. He would stand in his canoe and stare at the water while waiting for a salmon to show on the surface and think: *Suppose I didn't catch the salmon? What then? Would no one catch them?* It was a maddening supposition, for what had become his most compelling reason to catch them was the thought of the salmon feeding on the surface without *anyone* catching them. *And didn't someone have to catch them?*

Then one fall there appeared on the lake a fly-fisherman no one knew. He was younger than the others, even younger than Andrew, who at thirty-four was the youngest of them all. At first he was like the other fly-fishermen and seemed content to fish for the trout. He did cast standing up, though, which none of the others would dare to do. Andrew watched him and saw that he could pick his line off the water and shoot it back out without a lot of false-casting. As a result, the man caught a lot of brook trout, more than the others.

By the end of his first week on the lake, the man had become bored with the trout and decided to venture out into the middle, where he had seen Andrew catching salmon almost every day. Andrew watched him paddle out and saw his excitement when he first spotted a salmon on the surface. He nearly tipped his canoe over from rushing his casts. But even though the man never caught one, he still persisted and did not return to the trout. Between casts, he would sit down and change flies or paddle around until he saw another salmon. Then he would do the same thing all over again.

Andrew watched the man for two weeks and saw how he would slap his hand against his thigh and inveigh against himself in a loud voice whenever he lined a salmon. Through all his failure, though, the man persisted, and Andrew thought his efforts, however futile, were noble, even exemplary. Then, when Andrew heard him scream over another missed salmon and saw him raise his fists in utter and complete frustration, he quietly paddled over.

"How's it going?" Andrew asked, knowing full well that the man was on the verge of reducing his rod to kindling.

"Like a bad job," the man said with a weak smile. "How do you do it?"

"From years of doing exactly what you're doing," Andrew said with a sly smile.

"Well, I doubt I can last much longer. Believe it or not, I actually *dream* of catching them," he said, shaking his head.

"Oh, I believe you, all right," said Andrew in a sincere voice.

They introduced themselves and shook hands across their canoes. His name was Jim Cooper and he had just moved to town from the Cape. He had a friendly face and a pleasant smile, and his eyes were bright and inquisitive. He talked easily and enthusiastically about the salmon and himself, as if he and Andrew had always known each other. He said that he'd done a lot of still-water fly-fishing on the Cape, mostly for browns and rainbows in small ponds, but had never been in the company of salmon. "Which probably doesn't come as any surprise to you," he said with a sheepish grin.

"What do you have on there?" Andrew asked, meaning what kind of fly was he using.

Jim lifted the tip of his fly rod until the leader was out of the water.

"Now, a small Adams. But I've tried everything I own."

"Got any red or black ants? Or gray nymphs?" Andrew asked.

"No. But I wish I did. I've never seen so many ants. They're all over the place. I've got to tie some."

Andrew took a fly box from his vest and opened it. He took out two size 20 red and black ants and two size 18 gray nymphs.

"Try these. Put the fly on as a dropper about a foot above the nymph."

"Hey, thanks a lot," Jim said.

They sat in the middle of the lake and Andrew answered Jim's questions about the salmon while each held the gunwale of the other's canoe. Jim said that the rainbows he had caught on the Cape behaved a lot like the salmon—only the salmon seemed to move a lot faster and spooked easier.

"Your leaders can't be shorter than twelve feet and your tippets can't be much stouter than four-X or five-X," Andrew said.

Then Andrew told him that he didn't have to make long casts like the ones he'd seen him making.

"The thing to do is spot a fish and get as close as you can, so you can watch him very carefully and see exactly how he's feeding and where he's going. If he stays in the same area, he's feeding in a cluster of ants and you usually have time to paddle within casting distance."

Jim listened while he changed tippets and tied on the flies that Andrew had given him.

"Paddle without taking your eyes off him," Andrew continued, "and when you're within fifty feet take one or two easy strokes and then put the paddle down without banging the canoe. You should glide to within thirty feet of him and have at least that much of your line already out on the bottom of the canoe. If you can see his dorsal, and most of the time you will, throw as gently as you can to within a foot or so of it and then twitch the flies. Never throw behind him or too close to either side or you'll line him and put him down for good. If you know what direction he's moving in, throw a few feet in front of him."

When Jim finished tying on the flies, he looked at Andrew and was amazed at how his eyes never left the water. The whole time Andrew was talking he scanned the water searching for feeding salmon. Jim had never met a fisherman as intense as Andrew, or as willing to tell everything he knew.

"When the salmon takes your fly, don't rear back on your rod or you'll pull your fly out of his mouth. They're sipping more than chomping, so let him take a few inches of line before you lift up. Remember to always keep your rod tip low and moving in the same direction as the fish. When the fish feels the hook and the line, he'll do one of two things, depending on his size. If he's small, he's liable to do anything and everything at once, like a smallmouth. If he's big, though, he'll take the fly straight away, then down and at an angle. Then he'll come up and jump and sometimes race at you so you'll think he's going to run right into the canoe. You have to strip in like mad to keep up with him, unless you play your salmon off the reel, in which case you should be ready to strip line off, because when he's close to the canoe, he'll suddenly jump and turn and run."

Jim was trying to keep everything Andrew was saying straight in his mind. So far nothing seemed too much out of the ordinary except the bit about letting the salmon take the line before setting the hook. That would be tough to do. Not only did it go against everything he had ever learned about fly-fishing, it also went against instinct.

"Fish," said Andrew in a low voice. "Just up ahead a hundred feet. Get ready. You take him."

Andrew pushed Jim's canoe away and back-paddled a few yards so Jim had room to cast. Jim stood up and saw the salmon. It was on the surface and feeding in the film. He couldn't see the salmon's dorsal fin, but he could see its back moving and bulging the water.

"Move up just a bit and to one side," Andrew said. "He's coming straight on. Get your line out. Come on, come on. Get it out!" Andrew was trying very hard to control his excitement but knew he was not succeeding.

Jim false-cast until he had forty feet of line out. Then he stripped in and waited for the salmon to get closer. Andrew was standing in his canoe, staring at the salmon and waiting for the exact moment to tell Jim to cast. He was telling Jim to do the same things he told himself to do whenever he saw a salmon, only he was saying them out loud, as though he were coaching a player from the sidelines.

When Andrew saw the salmon's dorsal fin, he said to Jim in a voice that was intense and demanding, "Now. Do it now. Jesus, hit him!"

Jim let go and the flies landed a few feet in front of the salmon. He quickly stripped in the slack line, pointed his rod-tip low to the water, and twitched the flies. The salmon made a rush for the flies, and Jim, whose nerves were doing handsprings, pulled back and up on the rod too soon. The salmon veered off with the suddenness of a hummingbird and went down, leaving Jim standing with his mouth open and his mind racing to remember what the salmon had looked like.

"Holy shit," Jim breathed. He looked at where the salmon had been, felt himself shaking, and turned to Andrew, whose face was flushed but smiling.

"Not bad," Andrew said in a reassuring voice. "Your cast was there. Had you waited an extra second, there'd be a salmon at the end of your line right now."

Andrew paddled over and told Jim how sometimes a salmon will make a rush for the flies, veer off at the last instant and go down, then reappear on the surface a few seconds later. That's why it was so important never to take your eyes off a salmon, even when you missed it, because there was always the chance it would resurface. When it did, you paddled like hell without ever taking your eyes off it. Then, when you were ahead of it, you set up shop all over again. He also told Jim that the chances of catching a salmon by casting over it were too slim to even think about. He said you were always better off paddling like a demon so you could cast in front of it.

Jim's mind was buzzing from the encounter with the salmon, though, and Andrew's words scattered in the air like fall leaves in a north wind. He had never seen anything quite like it. To be able to see the salmon so close to him and then cast to it and watch as it made a sudden rush at the flies was beyond anything he had ever experienced with a fly rod. When he turned to Andrew, he found he couldn't speak. In that instant, Andrew saw in Jim's eyes a look of profound awe, as if he had just witnessed a miracle. It was, Andrew knew, the look of a person who wanted very much to catch the salmon.

In the days that followed, Andrew saw Jim on the lake every afternoon. He was usually already on the water by the time Andrew arrived, and he would be standing in his canoe with his rod in one hand and the paddle in the other. Occasionally, they would raft-up and Andrew would answer Jim's questions about the salmon. And the day that Jim finally hooked and landed a salmon, his only one that fall, Andrew and the other fly-fishermen watched until they saw it leap. Then they cheered as Jim shouted, "Salmon! Salmon!"

When Andrew and Jim saw each other on the lake the following spring, they shook hands and smiled and talked for a long time while motorboats trolled around them. Jim said he couldn't wait for fall and that he had tied ants and nymphs all winter. When Jim said he had dreamt of the salmon all winter and that he had actually felt himself catching them in his dreams, Andrew saw a strange look in his eyes.

The fall came and the salmon moved up from the depths to sip the ants and midges that were caught in the film. Jim was out there, intensely searching the water for the slightest interruption that would mean a salmon was on the move. Andrew, however, did not join Jim because he, too, had dreamt that winter. But Andrew's dreams were not of catching the salmon, they were dreams of seeing himself standing in his canoe, casting and paddling and staring frantically for feeding salmon. The harder he stared, though, the more frantic he became, for he could no longer see the salmon and knew he had to or he wouldn't be able to catch them. And he had to catch them. He had to.

So Jim paddled out into the middle of the lake and fished for the salmon while Andrew paddled close to shore and fished for the brook trout. For the first time in years, Andrew was content and secretly relieved not to be standing and staring and searching for feeding salmon. He became conscious of the lake and everything contiguous to it once again. There had always been something more to being on the lake that went beyond fishing for the salmon, and the time had come to rediscover what that something was.

◆   ◆   ◆

Andrew Tawney never fished for the lake's salmon again. For reasons he could feel more than articulate, he had become content to paddle along the shoreline with the other fishermen and cast to the vulnerable schools of brook trout. It was enough to be on water he knew so well, to feel the canoe glide through reflections of autumn hardwoods, and feel the crisp air against his skin and deep in his lungs. For all his life it would be enough to see the late-afternoon sunlight bathe the surrounding hillsides in soft gold, to see and hear great vees of Canada geese passing high overhead, to smell pungent woodsmoke from hearth fires drifting over the lake, to catch brook trout whose colors were the equal of garish sunsets and lurid swamp maples, and it was enough to know that the salmon were still on the surface and feeding in the film with their twisting dorsal fins and their backs making the water bulge . . . and that another angler was pursuing them.

The other fly-fishermen never asked Andrew why he had quit the salmon. They seemed to understand that Andrew had come to a point in his life when he needed something more from his fishing but that he couldn't seek it because on his mind were the salmon that had to be caught. But then Jim arrived and Andrew was free of his burden. And when Andrew and the other fishermen saw Jim out in the middle with a salmon on his line, they would stop their own fishing and wait to see the salmon leap. When it did, they would shake their heads in awe of Jim and the salmon. Then they would go back to their own fishing and wonder what it would be like to catch a salmon that way. Andrew, of course, never had to wonder. He knew what it was like, and even though it sometimes made him shudder, it always made him smile.

THE
VICAR'S POOL

◆   ◆   ◆

J. P. WHEELDON

IT WAS SIMPLY A DELIGHTFUL OLD GARDEN. A GARDEN WHICH, EVEN ON
the very hottest days, was always full of cool rippling shadows. It was
enclosed from the road, a dusty, drouthy, chalk-white road, facing a
wide, gorse-dotted common, by a very ancient red brick wall. It would
be difficult to say how old it was; but by using the word *red* I do not
wish it to be understood that it was a glaring colour, painful to the eye,
like the outside of a modern stucco-fronted villa, but rather a deep,
full-toned hue, causing one to think, half involuntarily, of very old
wine, or the faded maroon curtains enveloping some ancient four-
poster, standing, of course, silent and grim in the haunted chamber of
an ancient mansion. As one approached the vicar's house across the
beautiful, yet noisy common—noisy with the merry shouts and whoop-
ings of troops of village lads, county players in embryo—and the
setting sun, dying in golden glory, mellowed and softened the old wall
in his warm embrace, the resemblance to the colour of very old wine
was rendered even still more perfect. In the distance it glowed with a
deep purply hue, but as one neared it, one soon found that it was a
mass of different colour, for there were browns of every varied tinge,
umbers, and chocolate red amongst the brickwork, with here and
there a brighter speck. From the graceful contrast with clumps of gay
snapdragon, or fragrant, sweet-smelling "Johnny gillivers," as the
country folks called wall-flowers. Then, in every little interstice in the
broken, crumbling brickwork, beauteous little creeping plants, with
tiny, purplish, star-like flowers, and whose name I know not, flourished exceedingly, in some places covering the crumbling old barrier
with a delicate tracery of little leaves. And so, what with tiny, yet
fierce, grey and white spiders springing from dark and dismal caverns,
whose entrance gates were masked with tender, flaky lichens, in vain
pursuit, I am glad to say, of certain lovely crimson and gold-draped

flies, which were wont to haunt the little holes, for ever popping in and out, I used to think then, as I do now sometimes, when I let loose fancy's rein, that there is nothing one comes across in the course of a country ramble very much more pleasant to look upon then a venerably old, storm-battered, decayed, and crumbling wall, beautified by all the mellow tints which Age loves to carry on his palette.

As I have said already, the road skirting the gorse-dotted common, with its close, crisp grass, where sheep waxed fat, and snowy-plumaged geese, escorted by sundry staid, respectable grey ganders of grave and solemn type, prospered, was hot and dusty with chalky soil. By reason of many years' successive service this was ground to a fine and impalpable powder.

When an east wind was blowing, facing that road was terrible, for then the stinging blast raised such a cloud that waggoners emerged therefrom with their clothes literally powdered over as with a dusting of flour, while lounging, footsore tramps, with weary eyes and travel-stained faces, looked the very picture of misery. But with a wind sighing from the genial, balmy south, and be it said that the inner side of the wall, with its load of blushing peaches and blood-red nectarines, faced that quarter, and so broke the gentle gale, the road lay hot and still, and then entrance into the vicar's garden was like an entry into Paradise.

One was suddenly confronted with a big wooden gate, its timbers pierced and drilled with a multitude of tiny holes, and whereon village Lubins had written many an amorous verse to Chloe. It was just large enough to admit of the exit and entry of a little low chaise, the dear old vicar's only carriage, drawn by a stupidly obstinate, hog-maned, and self-willed grey pony. As one turned the tarnished brass handle of the lock and, opening the door, entered the garden, leaving the glaring road behind, one's senses were absorbed, charmed, and delighted with a long vista of deep green, cool shade. Overhead there was a perfect network of tangled, twisted, and arching boughs, the product of a line of tall elms, which had stood there for generations. Flanking the boles of these ancient trees on either side was a stiff, prim hedge of holy and yew. It was scrupulously trimmed, and to the eye always looked excessively neat, spruce, and orderly. Under foot was a broad and solid path, where trailing ivies, deep in hue and eke of tenderest green, grew round the boles of the elms, with here and there, amidst a gleam of sunlight, which somehow looked garish and out of place amid the still, shadow-flecked solitudes, a clump of primroses, may be, with starry flowers, or else a scattered group of wild hyacinths, with drooping stems and pale blue bells. While the sun glared down fiercely overhead, this delightful pathway was always chequered with shifting shadows, which came and went, and came again, as though the rustling leaves overhead were playing at bo-peep.

There was something cool and refreshing about the very whispering of the moving foliage, stirred as it might be by a gentle southern wind, and on summer evenings more than one nightingale, in company with many a mellow-throated blackbird and answering thrush, a veritable "charm of birds," filled the sweet-smelling garden with a flood of melody. At the end of this pathway one came to a crossing carriage sweep, a rustic jessamine-shaded porch, gay with starry snow-white flowers. This was the entrance to just such a very old house as one sees but rarely in these days. Never, unless it is set deep in the heart of some far-off country side where railways are not, and where the present and hurried feverish rush after wealth has happily not penetrated. Luxuriant and thickly grown beds of orange-eyed and purple pansies lay glowing in the sun under the low, broad-silled windows, with their cool white draperies of lace. A stately magnolia, filling the air with its fragrant yet somewhat oppressive perfume, half covered the low white front of the vicarage, already partly shaded by the foliage of a magnificent mulberry. Then there was a wide sweep of velvet lawn, studded here and there with quaintly cropped box and stunted yew bushes. A curious old stone sun-dial here cast its shadow also. I remember it had some monkish, old-time legend inscribed on its front in strange-shaped, spider-legged letters, but what it was I have forgotten.

This lawn, with its velvety, smooth turf, was the gardener's special pride and boast, and not a leaf or worm cast was ever allowed to disturb the uniformity of its surface. It was broken, however, by oddly shaped beds of flowers, most scrupulously kept, and arranged with an eye to colour and effect. In its centre was a small, yet deep, fish-pond, half covered with lilies, its somewhat formal sides relieved by clumps of rushes; and in this were a few gold-fish, and some ponderous carp and eels. Here I was very fond of sitting, in the long shadow cast by the mulberry, and feeding the big fish with pieces of bread. I well remember how nearly I forfeited the vicar's good opinion by hooking a big carp one sunny day, and playing him hard on a bent pin. On this lawn, on glorious heat-laden days—such days then as one hardly ever sees now—or else on the quaint old garden-seat built round the bole of the mulberry, there was invariably to be seen a gorgeous peacock, whose harsh, strident voice seemed to spoil the delicious quiet and harmony of the place. So much for cultivated primness and effect. All else in the vicar's garden was wildly luxuriant. Wide-stretching beds of odorless violets, seemingly never tended in the least degree, hemmed in rows of early pease, hoed and carefully trained in the way they should go. Tall white lilies, whose cups at early morning held store of sparkling dewdrops; great blush-pink and carmine-hued roses, the flowers so large and heavy that after refreshing summer rainfalls they were bowed nearly to the ground with their own weight; delicate-tinted moss-buds and straggling clumps of sweet pease grew confusedly together, while clusters of sweet williams, cheek by jowl with giant rhubarb plants, jostled proud crimson peonies which flanked sea-kale and asparagus beds. Then the walks were green and mossy, the box-edgings trimmed neatly in one place, while they straggled in another; and, at the foot of the old wall I have spoken of, with its store of peaches and nectarines, there grew a very wilderness of violets, through which, and even crushing the flowers, paths had to be trodden in the rich, loamy earth up to the root of each tree.

But on the farther side of the garden, and beyond where the little turreted clock of the stable showed just above a tall yew hedge, there was a little narrow pathway, a closely-cropped hedge confining it on either hand. This led down to the loveliest trout stream in the world, crossed by a bridge formed of half a dozen planks and a single white-washed hand-rail; the whole supported by stout wooden piles driven deep into the yellow, gravelly bed of the stream. An immense willow-tree stretched its wide-spreading arms half over the stream, making it look even still more deep and shadowy, one end of the hand-rail being nailed to the great wide-girthed trunk. It was my happy privilege in those days to have and to hold full permission to fish in this stream, and many and many a lusty trout have I deluded from under that old willow. The bank just at this place was hard, dry, loamy clay, and year after year a pair of beautiful kingfishers, which the vicar would on no account have disturbed, built a nest in a hole under the projecting roots. On the farther side of the bridge, and where it joined the pollard-dotted meadowside, the water ran shallow, rippling and dimpling with many tiny curls over not many inches of gravel.

On these shallows there were baby trout in galore, which used to gather, like little shoals of minnows, in the gentle eddies and stills close to where beds of watercress, with its dark-green leaves, made rich contrast to clusters of turquoise-hued forget-me-nots, which grew thickly down to the water's edge. There they rapidly pushed their way in the world, undisturbed by the rush of pricky-finned perch from the darkly eddying waters, or of long-snouted, keen-fanged pike from the shelter of trailing weeds. Their chief enemies, I think, were the king-fishers aforesaid; for although now and again I have seen a big trout, on foraging thoughts intent, come out of the deeps with a rush and roll of the waters and try to force his way on to the shallows, he always had to turn back again on account of the little depth. When at last the dear white-haired vicar was convinced that his favourite birds harried the youngsters and badly thinned their ranks, he sent Jabez Groom, coachman and gardener on his small estate—and not without a deal of grumbling on the score of anticipated "rheumatiz"—into the water one summer's day, to drive some stout posts down into the gravel. Then he stretched some very fine wire network across, bending the edges down until they just touched the water. Thus the birds were settled, and although I doubt not they had many a toothsome troutling in their larder at odd times, the "home colony," at least, were protected, and so grew day by day, until at last they took to finding homes for themselves.

Under the willow was the deepest hole of all, and many a goodly trout therein found comfortable, shady lodgings. There was one fish in particular, which the divine and I had watched upon numerous occasions, when he was feeding upon the countless minnows incessantly wriggling, like a little black and olive-green cloud, close in under the loamy bank. This trout had a white patch or mark upon his side, looking like the trace of a bruise against the sides of a hatch-hole, or mayhap the effects of a blow. He was a three-pounder if he weighed an ounce, and now and again the vicar tried his hand over him. In his youth he had been an admirable fly-fisher, but with the frosts of seventy winters powdering his head, he found, as he said, that the possession of old bones, in the process of plashing along by the side of sedgy watercourses, did not agree. Thus, about all that he did do, in those days which I recollect so well, was to stand on the bridge at the farther side of the stream, on warm summer evenings, and throw a fly with a beautiful underhanded cast, which I tried over and over again in vain to imitate, right under the boughs of the willow, and into the deep swirly hole sheltered by its roots. He was exceedingly fond of fishing with a sunk fly, and when his lure had been swept full in the throat of the eddy, he would joggle gently at the point of the rod, so as to produce a counterfeit presentment, nearly as might be, of the struggles of a drowning insect. At the slightest twist of the line, or jar through the supple rod, the dear old boy was death upon a trout, and, in spite of all the gallant upward leaps, the lithe, bounding body, flashing like a lusty bar of gold, flushed with rose hues in the light of the summer evening, he had him out and tumbling and rolling in midstream, from whence he would presently be tumbled into my landing-net.

One night—I recollect it as well as if it were only yesterday—he and I stood upon the little bridge. It was in the thick of the May-fly season, and hundreds of the dainty gauze-winged insects were dancing up and down, up and down, over the tops of the feathery rustling sedges. The sun was just sinking in a blood-red and orange-streaked sky, and the boughs and whispering leaves of the willow looked dark overhead against a sea of pale apple-green and faintest azure. The rich, lush meadows, where lazy sleepy-eyed cattle stood knee-deep in the fat pastures, yellow with millions of buttercups, and flooded with pale golden glory from the dying sun, lay bathed in a soft, misty, Cuyp-like haze of light. There was no motion anywhere, save for the dancing insects, the quick sweep and dash of a little knot of swifts and swallows, the swoop of a spotted flycatcher from the arm of a tree, and the ever-shifting swirl of the hurrying waters. There was no noise, except the murmurous ripple and plash of the stream; now and again the *plop* of a rising fish, the plunge of a water-rat, the shrill twitter and scream of the circling birds, and the low mutterings and grumblings of a far-off angry bull.

Every now and again there was a plunge, followed by a rolling eddy of the dark waters in the hole under the tree. I doubt not that many a score of dead and dying drakes were there washing back and forth in the swirling water. At last, after seeing the big trout come up boldly and suck down fly after fly, my good old friend could stand it no longer and sent me into the house for his rod and fly-book. Then he put up a beautiful cork-bodied fly and after well soaking his cast, sent it with a gentle flick right on to the overhanging roots of the old tree.

"Ah me, that's very bad!" said he, with a kindly, humorous smile, doubtless thinking that the fly was fast. But raising the point of the rod very gently, it dropped beautifully, and in an instant the big trout had it. He was probably cruising at that very moment under the bank. Anyhow, the steel was in him, and in the very next second's space, with a tremendous dash and upward fling into the sun-lit air, the bright drops falling in a twinkling shower from his bent and bow-like body, he was down again and pulling like a mad trout twenty yards below us. With never a thought of old bones then, the dear old warrior, with only thin dinner shoes on, plashed through the wet and sedgy ground, forever ejaculating such phrases as "Holy Father! Got him at last! May He forgive me for using His name. Hold up, you great beast! Ah me, he's in the weeds!—Saints above us, he isn't! Prayers and praises! What a ponderous trout! Devil take him for a pigheaded thing!" And so on, until after a glorious fight, the perspiration streaming down the dear old fellow's head the while, he got him to the side, thoroughly done up, and grappled him. Then he actually crouched down, the tails of his old-fashioned coat dabbling in the stream, while water was oozing up from amongst the aquatic weeds all round his thin shoes, so that he might weight his prize in his withered, leaden-veined hands and say over and over again, the light of victory brightening his dim blue eyes, "Eh me, what a beauty! What a beauty he is, to be sure! And Lord forgive me for swearing."

That night I got three lovely trout out of the same hole—trout which so astonished the vicar—who hinted vaguely at worms or some other abomination—that in the morning, when I strolled down to look at the scene of my conquest and fight my battles o'er again, I saw the lid of a cigar-box nailed to the tree. On it was pasted half a sheet of note-paper, and written thereon, in queer, shaky characters was this not-to-be-denied moral to all trout-fishers—

> A trout killed with fly is a jewel of price,
> But a trout poached with worm is like throwing cogged dice.

Under this I scribbled in pencil—

> Worms I hate, and never use 'em;
> And, kindly friends, I ne'er abuse 'em.

When I came back after a long walk down stream to the "Vicar's Pool," a dearly loved, drowsy haunt of mine in those well-remembered days, I found yet another addition to the literature of the cigar-box lid. It was perfectly simple in its expression, and, I may add, uncommonly welcome. "Come in to lunch, you rascal," stared me in the face; and when I entered the cool room, with its few choice water-colours on the walls, its jars of sweet flowers, and flooring covered with Indian matting, my dear old friend was there to welcome me; and as he poured me out a bumper of cooled, not iced, claret, he said, "There, my boy; that's some of my old '32. Drink it, you vagabond, who can find in his heart to beat an old fisherman, and bless your lucky stars, for there is no better claret in England."

The pool was a very deep hole of some extent, although somewhat uneven in its depth, which lay just below a ford for horses and cattle. Across this ford there were many flat boulders placed, whose smooth surface, when the stream was not flooded, afforded foothold for many a comely country lassie, with short skirts and shapely limbs, tripping to market with butter and eggs, as well as to sturdy labourers passing back and forth to the little village. On the further side there stood three or four great gnarled willows, and in the deep, swift water of the hole there abided a store of perfectly awful trout, the very patriarchs and forefathers of the stream. Just below the pool the stream made a sudden sweep and was lost amongst the drooping foliage of a thick copse of oaks and firs, tenanted by plenty of rabbits and pheasants. Under these old willows the water was eight to ten feet deep, and just beneath the projecting crooked roots, covered with a fringe of silky water-weed, one grand old fellow—a six-pounder to my certain knowledge—had made his home. After fording the shallows, I used to creep, silent and still as death itself, on hands and knees, and gradually getting my head between the tree-trunks, and over the banks, peer down into the smiling lucid depths below. Right under my nose lay the great fish, his smooth brown head just peeping out from the edge of the roots. I could see every roll of his lustrous eye, every gentle fanning wave of his chocolate-spotted fins; and oh, how I longed to get the grip of my fingers fast across that deep, smooth, silvery body, flushed as it was with glints of shifting ruby-tinted gold, and dotted with spots blacker than the blackest and handsomest gipsy-like eyes I ever saw! I vowed that glorious fish should be mine, but how to get him I knew not. I never saw him feed, although now and then, at early morning, I heard heavy plunges in the thickest part of the swift run, which I shrewdly guessed were made by my friend of the tree-roots.

One day, after thinking over the matter deeply, I started out, armed with a trusty pliable rod with upright rings, and about sixty yards of fine, yet stout, silk on the reel. I had made up my mind that I would catch one of the biggest stone loach I could find lying among the pebbly stones and boulders on the shallows and try to float it down to him in his hole. Many an one was unearthed, and many glided away like grey mottled shadows, just as I was in the act of putting my hand upon them. Nothing was ever left but a tiny cloud of shifting sand, which drifted for a few inches in the clear water, and then subsided. At last I got one fat fellow between two flat stones, and holding one hand scooped up under the upper end of his hiding-place, I touched the little fish with the fingers of my other hand, and he instantly wriggled into my submerged palm. That closed, and he was my prisoner. Ten minutes afterwards he was lip-hooked to a perch-hook at the end of a length of gut, and I was guiding the line over the shallows and into the deep waters of the hole. Whereabouts he was I never knew for certain. Somewhere a long way down I knew, and also in the right direction. Presently, and with strangely thrilling suddenness, making my heart leap eagerly, I felt a mighty tug, and the next instant I had a great fish plunging and leaping furiously at the end of my frail line. My first thoughts were of the tree roots, and as he time after time dashed for their shelter, at each fierce rush I butted him savagely and kept him clear. At last he yielded, after a short though tremendous tussle, and plashing through the shallows, I got into the open meadows. Another brief interval of battle, and then I saw that lustrous brown head and silver-spotted body lying on the smooth green sward bordering the pool. When my beautiful prize, held lightly down upon the grass, had fluttered his fins for the last time, I crossed the stepping-stones and peered down under the tree.

There was no trout there then; and so I carried him home to the vicarage, greatly rejoicing, and yet not without a qualm of regret as to the manner of his capture.

I laid him on the table in the cool room on some freshly pulled rushes, and presently the vicar, in a chintz dressing-gown, a quill pen behind his ear and another held crosswise in his thin, colourless lips, a velvet skull-cap covering his snowy hair, came in hurriedly to look at my fish. He gave me a quick, keen glance, and then—

"A beautiful trout indeed!" said he presently, with a deep and long-drawn sigh. "A very beautiful fish! Fly, I presume?"

"No, sir; stone loach."

"Indeed! Stone loach, eh? Hum, ha—stone loach, eh? Well, not so bad as worm, not so bad as a dirty worm, but quite bad enough. However, have a glass of ale, boy, and stop to dinner and tell me all about it."

DANCING
ON THE
SPINE OF TIME

◆ ◆ ◆

HARRY MIDDLETON

IT IS AUTUMN AND THE NIGHT IS CLEAR AND COLD. A GREAT DOME OF stars stretches across the sky as though pulled down tight to be close to the worn, dark ridges of the Great Smoky Mountains. The stars give the night sky a pale white glow, like light reflected off melting candle wax.

It was a good day along the creek. Just before noon, the sky turned black as wet coal and it snowed hard for hours, a great whirl-wind of snow, and still I fished. Snow piled up on the backs of dark, smooth stones. The sudden cold, the unexpected turn of weather, stirred me as much as it did the trout. I had almost forgotten how much fun it is to fish the high country in a good snowstorm.

I have lit the stove, put a pot of chili on. Staring up at the great sprawl of the mountain night, my back snug against a broad maple, I realize again that what I see is like the reflection from a rearview mirror. We see the universe not so much as it is, but as it was. The light I see in the blue-black mountain night, even of the stars closest to the earth, is old light, light that is already more than four years old by the time I see its faint glimmer, old news. Yet, to me, to my eye and senses, it is immediate and urgent, the topography of the present moment, which is forever a wild dance. Meanwhile, beyond my view, if not beyond my imagination, beyond this brilliant mountain night illuminated by spent starlight, the universe continues to reel from its inception, the original Big Bang. It moves, expands like a blind worm probing through dark soil, alive only so long as it moves.

It is all touch and go, whether it is the insect larvae snug beneath the flat-backed stones at the bottom of the creek or distant galaxies adrift in the dark belly of space. It is all dilemma and no final answers, thank the gods.

Taking into account all the earth's creatures, plant and animal, the housefly would represent the average size of life on this tiny blue planet. In makeup, the earth is mostly granite, and granite, in turn, is mostly oxygen. For those who wish to take notice, the most common forms of visible life are mites, algae, sedges, copepods, and springtails. Pull back the worn, haggard skin of the Appalachian Mountains and you could count more than 120 distinctive seams of coal representing more than 120 ancient, fallen, rotted forests.

It's all touch and go. Touch and go.

◆   ◆   ◆

Almost all the leaves are off the trees. They scuttle about the ground, rattle in the cold wind: the year's excess spent, exhausted. Up higher, up above five thousand feet, there is still the bold color of the evergreens, the great dying fir and spruce forests of the Canadian Zone, but here, midway up the ridgeline of the mountains, winter is a study in the latitude of grays and browns.

From the stony brow above my campsite, out on the rippled lip of the ridge, I can clearly see the lights of Bryson City down in the valley. The lights look like flecks of mica shining in some fold of wet, dark soil.

Tomorrow, even if the trout rise, I will have to pack up, move on, hike back down the mountainside and head home, back to the hills of Alabama. I lack Horace Kephart's wild courage, his resolute happy madness, or both. Something compelled him to walk away from one life, including a successful career as one of the nation's most respected and learned librarians, a wife and a family, and a host of attendant obligations, and into another world and life altogether in these mountains. He never looked back.

While the chili cools down, I look down into the valley and see the lights of the houses and know I must go in the morning. There is a mortgage to pay off, a car with a worrisome cough and balding tires, the usual heap of bills to pay. The radio in my study doesn't work. I need to fix it so that at night I can turn the dial to hear how humanity is doing. There is the squirrel in the attic that I haven't been able to evacuate. I've tried everything, even a bucketful of mothballs. I need to get back, put on my headlamp, lay out the sleeping bag on the roof, and wait the squirrel out to find out how it comes and goes.

I need to get home—for a time, anyway. I have two sons. Both expect to go to the college of their choice. There is a cat that depends on me, too, and a month's worth of laundry to do, and a lawn my neighbors expect me to mow, keep tidy and well-groomed. There are taxes to pay and moral commitments to keep and work piling up on my desk.

And so on and so on.

These mountains are fickle and change with each slant of light. The world I see in one range of pale violet is another world entirely in the first pools of morning's pale blues. Things don't end, they fade, dissolve, disappear, and reappear as something altogether different. Even the mountains come and go, affirming the wild rhythm of possibilities and tendencies rather than certainty.

Tomorrow at sunrise I will break camp, walk along the rushing waters of the creek, down the mountainside toward town. I left my car at the Deep Creek campground. When I get to the campground, I will look back up the mountains as I always do, see them rising up out of the morning's thick blue fog. Sometimes they remind me of lifeboats, there for anyone who needs to feel a strong press of wind and solitude and solace against his skin.

◆　◆　◆

The mountains never let me down. High among the clouds, the spectacular and the ordinary, the common and the exquisite, all take shape in the same light and disappear in the same unremarkable shadows. Ten steps on a narrow mountain trail, and the heavy scales of urban life begin to fall away like so much dead skin and I become, almost unconsciously, the honest sum of my parts: a trout angler at loose ends, fishing from first light till last, filling my creel with so much more than trout.

This need for altitude, for cold mountain streams and the possibility of trout, is, I admit, getting more and more impulsive, harder to predict, harder to control. More and more, it surfaces without warning, leaving me happily bewildered and dazzled. One instant I'm putting an edge on a hoe, and the next I am an empty sensorium, greedy for a trout stream's endless flood of stimuli, yearning for mountains laced with fall color, desperate for a hollow's rich smells, eager for the sight of a trout flashing just below the surface of the water. Suddenly, I relax, take on a fly rod's supple character. Every nerve seems a boisterous interpreter of what it feels. The message to the brain is plain, simple: Time is not hard, not flat, not a one-way dimension. Rather, it is fluid, as dynamic and chaotic as a wild mountain river. I want to use it up as fully and completely as it uses me up; feed on it the way it feeds on me, mercilessly.

In the mountains, experience is as rich in vital nutrition as chili and sourdough bread. Sometimes I have lived for days on the energy generated by experience. It is filling and satisfying and lingers on in every cell. A scientist who keeps track of such things says that each second of our lives we are bombarded by at least one hundred thousand random impulses of sensory information. A holocaust of electrical information. Against such an onslaught, I am like a man who has just lost his sight and fumbles about desperately trying to channel understanding—the world—through one less sense. I pick and choose and keep my choices rich. Let mountains dig at my senses, scrape them clean, wash them in some cold mountain river, and hang them in a mountain wind to dry.

Wading in a fine stream, I often reduce myself to a cell within its waters, nondescript flotsam riding wildly on the current of time as it spreads without fanfare down through shadow-filled, rocky valleys and finally onto the wide, flat, sunlit sprawl of the Piedmont. I let such moments carry me for as long as they can and as far away as they can from that which seems to be doing me so little good—office politics and intrigue, crowds, bad plumbing, polluted water and grimy air, traffic gridlock, the increasingly dreary task of simply making a living instead of living a life. Up in the mountains, I let all this go for a time and let myself drift toward what I like and enjoy rather than what others believe I need. Be it for an hour or a day or a week, when I am in the high country, I give up and give in, glide with the slants of light, dream in cool shadows, cast my line after a good fish.

Once on the mountain highway, once the road rises out of these foothills and serpentines about the scalloped slopes of the mountains, things change, sensations change, priorities change. I change. I gather about me only what seems necessary, fundamental; I delight in what is basic—a cool wind, fast water, the smell of sweet earth, a fat trout in deep, clear water. There is an economy and an urgency to life in the mountains, an immediacy that defies exactness, the fixed, the defined, whatever is confined by rules. In spite of all this, there is daylight and dark and everything from joy and exhaustion to fear coloring the light, giving it shape and substance. You take what is given, even the fear—the fear that the next time you climb this way it will all be gone; the mountain will be slag, trees clear-cut, coves developed, valleys bulldozed and seeded with resorts, streams dammed—all of it tragically transmogrified into the bleary, concrete, shopping-mall sameness I fled from, left down in the netherworld of the civilized lowlands.

The fear is here and real and I fight it with the fly rod, which lets me cast beyond the obvious. Using the fly rod demands a discipline that insists that while on the stream great blocks of life, of time in motion, be ignored, cut out. My mind now acts in much the same way, casting only to what seems interesting and promising while keeping the rest of the world at the door, pressed against the window, looking in. The fly rod's discipline encourages me to deal with the small, with currents and eddies and seeps, rather than the enormity of tidal waves. The idea is to concentrate on living rather than merely surviving. The brain is clever and full of such defenses, yet for all its splendor and evolutionary magnificence, it leaves me, in some ways, less than the trout, which knows its world so thoroughly, so completely, seeing and feeling always the whole, while I feast on scraps of rising sun and setting moon, collops of fissured stone, endless slivers of changing light. When I cast to a trout, there is always that feeling, just below the skin, that I might somehow reach beyond it, beyond the given, and feel on my line the full weight of things—the weight of mountain and river laced into flesh and bone of the struggling trout.

THE GIFT
OF CREEKS

◆ ◆ ◆

PETER STEINHART

For years, the vision waved at me from behind a dimly lit window in the back of my mind. In the vision, my son, then five or six years old, stands beside a mountain creek, fishing rod in hand, eyes narrowed in concentration on the line that floats on the sun-dappled water. The rush of streamwater down a long sheet of granite is in our ears, the scent of pine on the wind, the warmth of mountain sunshine on our backs. I cannot see him clearly, only his eyes and the sunlight dazzling off his curly, blond hair. But it does not matter, for I am him and he is me. And we are in the most wonderful of places.

◆ ◆ ◆

I am a fisher of creeks. Perhaps I am not really an angler of fishes. I own a couple of old bamboo fly rods, newer graphite, a four-piece glass rod I carry backpacking or on airplanes. Winter nights may find me hunched over a fly-tying vise. But on those nights the reveries in my mind are never of fish. I know there are small brook trout with bright orange bellies and rainbows with pale pink sides. But in my winter reveries I never see them. I see the splash as one strikes my fly. I feel the tug on the line. It pulls at something in my heart. I see the sunlight dancing on the water, hear the quiet laughter of snowmelt tumbling over rocks, feel the warmth of mountain sun on my back. I never see the fish reeled in. I have no photographs of creek leviathans. I have memories, instead, of places—of favorite riffles, of quiet sparkling pools, of mountain meadows threaded by purling brooks, of eddy-carved bowls in sun-whitened granite.

I keep a lot of these creeks. My grandfather had ten acres of apricot orchard along a creek that wound out of the Coast Range mountains in California. Its banks were shaded with cottonwoods and redwood trees and a thick tangle of blackberry and wild grape vine. On hot summer days, its sun-freckled glades were cool and filled with the song of hermit thrushes and California quail. My grandfather stretched chicken wire across the creek at both ends of the orchard and had a man come out to pour buckets full of fingerling brook trout into it. He put a fishing rod in my hand, and for two summers I fished over the creek's shallow gravel bars and log-dam eddies.

Perhaps thirty years later, in the California desert, while hummingbirds darted from cactus blossoms, a storm cloud brooded over a distant mountain ridge. In the sun-dried silence, I heard the babble of rushing water. I followed the sound a half mile, over dusty hillsides and down scabrous ravines to an unexpected ribbon of clear, cold, rushing water. It leapt from rock to rock and filled little pools in the sand. The discovery seemed biblical, a benediction. It filled me with joy. I followed the creek until it disappeared into the desert sands.

I suspect these remembered creeks map my place in the world. The day-to-day setting is increasingly ruled into roadstripe and telephone line, right of way and property line, a crosshatching that gives one the citified sense that nothing belongs to one and one belongs to nothing. In the city, you look out your door and sense that as the earth tilts away from your feet, it quickly forgets your shadow. Those remembered creeks are arteries pumping life back into the known world. They restore my youthful sense of belonging.

◆   ◆   ◆

The place in my vision was one of those known places. It was high on the headwaters of a Sierra Nevada river under a clear blue California sky.

The stream tumbled down a broad apron of granite, singing brightly all the way, kicking up little comets of spray, smoothing the glacially polished granite. It spilled into a broad pool where the rock had refused to back away from ice and water. Where it rushed into the pool, ten- and twelve-inch rainbows loafed, rising slowly to the surface to pick off the drowned mosquitoes and mayflies that floated down. The water curved tamely through the shade of pines and around a big white sandbar before it rushed down a jumble of boulders and into the lodgepole forest below. I knew the pool well. When I was seven, my father stood me at its edge and taught me to cast. I broke many hooks on the rocks behind me. I lifted many rainbows out of the pool, my seven-year-old heart thumping, the wriggling, silvery fish slapping on the smooth granite at my feet.

The memory of that pool, I suspect, purled through my father's mind as well. He had fished that creek as a boy with his father. He returned to it with me. I wonder if on winter nights thirty years before, by a living-room fire, the same vision had bubbled up again and again through his mind as it bubbled now through mine.

It was clearly an invitation from the creek to bring my son. Creeks belong to childhood. Or maybe childhood belongs to creeks.

A creek is the world young. It reaches up to the mountains and the abode of gods, the source of rain and creation. It leads down to rivers grown heavy with sophistication and sediment, to waters too murky and complex to open to our hearts. Creeks are happy pathways of sun and starlight, dazzling up to the sky, laughing at the freshness of the world, careless of tomorrow and the salty anonymity of age and oceans.

Creeks are one of the ways the earth draws us out of our youthful skins and into the wider world. They are full of strange lives: sand-flecked caddis worms under the rocks, sudden gossamer clouds of may-flies in the afternoon, salamanders wriggling back to winter water, minnows darting like slivers of inspiration into the dimness of creek fate. There are crayfish to jig, water striders defying the principles of fluidity. It's one of the great experiences of otherness, one of the ways we move from the life inside us to the life outside and see that it is alone.

A creek's exuberance may pluck one's imagination and bear it away like a drifting leaf. We may trundle along after it, delighted by its liquid babble, dazzled by the leap and sparkle of sunlight, enchanted by the swirl and eddy and song. The word creek once suggested such beguilement. It probably derives from the word crack, a cleft in the surface of things, through which we are likely to fall. Poets of the seventeenth century talked of fate's appearing in "every creek and turning of your lives." To follow a creek as it disappears around a bend is to seek new acquaintance with life.

And to follow a creek is often to recover one's own youth. In high mountain meadows, I'll trace the course of brooks that gnaw into the lime-green grass and deep glacial dust, marveling at the sparkle of quartz and mica and the silvery quickness of fingerling trout. It is the first thing I do when I arrive in the mountains. I plunge upstream, pursued by the haste of city work and the muttering of freeway tension. I may jog up a creek for an hour, unraveling the mystery of its liquid braid, emptying my mind of tasks. And when I stop and turn downstream again, I feel cleansed and restored. Something has liquefied the crust of caution and washed away my citified cares. I have new eyes and an open heart.

The mechanics of all this remain a mystery to me. I think sometimes that creeks are the way the earth recognizes itself in us, recognizes in the branching of capillary and vein, neuron and thought, the dendritic pattern of rill and river, ravine and canyon. Maybe it sees in the return of blood and sweat, generation after generation, an echo of the return of water through snowfall, runoff, the salty dotage of the seas, and the rebirth of rain clouds rising off the oceans and heading back to the summits. Maybe there's a conversation that rings between the water of the creek and the water of human protoplasm. Maybe what we hear in creek murmur is the rumor of confided ancestry. It's all beyond me. But I find creeksong exceptionally reassuring.

I knew that part of this vision was the desire to make a gift of that assurance. The real gifts we give our children are the senses of mastery and belonging and comfort. They are the hardest things in life to grasp, elusive as the flight of bats, fragile as the wings of butterflies. They are easily lost or crushed in our citified existence. They cannot be put away in boxes or hoarded on the shelf like clothing or electric trains. They have to live on in the soul, to be carried and chipped and battered and used throughout life, or they die. They become part of one's eyes and heart, and therefore precious.

So, one summer day, my son, then seven, and I hiked fourteen miles to camp beside a blue Sierra lake. And the next morning we hiked five more miles, following the river as it leapt over rocks in fine waterfalls, spilled down sheets of slick granite, and played with sunlight and the scent of pines. We climbed higher, up to where the forest thinned and we could look up at solitary juniper trees growing out of the bare gray rock of mountain ridges. We crossed side streams and tributaries. And all the while, the river uncoiled into strands of creek and rediscovered its own youth. And at last we came to the pool.

My son unfurled his line and cast it out over the water. It settled with barely a ripple at the head of the pool. The Black Gnat at the end of the leader bobbled on the water. And as the first rainbow rose darkly in the water and struck at the fly, that leap of joy shot up his line and straight to my heart.

◆   ◆   ◆

I still carry the vision of him, his blond hair catching the sunlight, a fish slapping at the bare granite at his feet. He dances triumphantly, shifting from one foot to the other, rocking back and forth, smiling broadly as he lifts the fish off the ground. The golden light of endless days is in his eyes, the silvery fish wriggling on his upheld leader. I am him and he is me and the creek flows through us both. Which of us is caught? Which is the captor? Which the giver?

SMACK-DAB IN THE MIDDLE OF THE ROCK

◆ ◆ ◆

PAUL QUINNETT

IT'S NOT EASY TO WRITE ABOUT YOUR HOME WATERS. I'M NOT SURE why. Maybe words alone won't do it justice. The word *favorite*, for example, is too puny to do the work. *Chosen, preferred, ideal*—none of these is strong enough, either. What is strong enough? Read my will.

Of course there was some consternation about my desire to have my ashes spread over Rock Lake during a June mayfly hatch. But those who love me know there'll be hell to pay if I don't get my way on this. I made the decision a long time ago, and, although I was probably a little drunk at the time, it still stands. Cold sober I feel the same way. No eternity in a pine box for me; just toss me, as the Ames Brothers used to sing, "smack-dab in the middle."

To get an idea of what Rock means to me, you have to understand that all my life I've been shading life's major decisions toward the perfect fishing spot: where I went to college, where I went to graduate school, the profession I chose (psychology—a job you can do most anywhere because, as it turns out, there are troubled people everywhere), and where, finally, I found a job, built a house, and raised a family. That place: eastern Washington, southwest of Spokane.

There are fifty lakes within fifty miles of my house, and you cannot step off the front porch and walk ten miles in any direction without ending up neck deep in good trout water. And this is to say nothing of northern Idaho's nearby crown jewels of Priest, Pend Orielle, and Coeur d'Alene lakes, and all the rivers and streams between. If this is not God's private fishing hole, we at least share the same ZIP code.

I can't remember my first trip to Rock Lake. It was probably in 1965, and, since I had only a couple of fishing pals in graduate school at Washington State University, I probably went there with Larry

Grand, an Italian mycology major from Penn State who lived next door to Ann and me in the graduate-student warrens. (I say *warrens* because of the sheer volume of pregnancies, newborns, and toddlers around the place and the apparent primary activity of the breeding adults.)

Rock had two things going for it: It was open year-round, and it was close to WSU—*close* meaning it only took four or five dollars' worth of gas to get there and back. Larry and I could shoot up there for a Saturday afternoon in the dead of winter and it was like, well, getting away from all the bullshit they specialize in shoveling around institutions of higher learning. Too poor to own a boat or a fly rod or waders, or even decent cold-weather gear, we would hike the three miles down the railroad tracks to the inlet stream, build a fire to keep warm, and sling egg-baited hooks and slip sinkers out into the murky waters. Then we'd sit and talk and wait and watch the rod tips.

And, hell yes, we'd catch trout; big rainbows mostly, some a couple of pounds. They were strong fish, hell-fighters, jumpers, and line-peelers. A couple of those silver-flash, run-and-dash bruisers, and, well, all the crow you had to eat in graduate school tasted just a little better. Usually flat broke and meat hungry, we took everything home to eat. But sometimes we'd kill one on the spot, clean it, and broil it right at our warming fire. Ha!

Rock is a strange lake. After twenty-five years, I'm still learning about it. A few people fish it, but mostly they stay away in droves. And for lots of good reasons: too far from the city, poor boat launch, only one access, too dangerous when the wind comes up, too many reefs, too many stories of drownings and lost lower units and sinking boats and fishermen never heard from again, and Indian ghost stories, and, of course, the Rock Lake Monster. Since no one lives on the lake and there are no resorts, little fishing news leaks out, and what does get out is often bad: "Never got a strike, but then we got blown off the son of a bitch before we got started." You can go to Rock in the middle of a summer week and be the only fisherman on the lake. And we're talking about the largest natural lake in eastern Washington—nine miles long, three-quarters of a mile wide, and in some places, more than 270 feet deep.

Around most of the lake are lava cliffs, cliffs made from the second-largest series of lava flows in the world. Some of them rise three hundred feet above the lake and, with only narrow ledges to separate the flows, continue straight down into the water. Your sonar can read four feet deep off the bow of a twelve-foot pram and two hundred feet off the stern. Standing in a boat casting flies to a submerged ledge, you can look straight up a three-hundred-foot slab of lava to see, maybe, a turkey buzzard lofting on the thermals along the rim. Arches, pressure ridges, year-round waterfalls, nooks, crannies, caves, screes of broken stone the size of Volkswagens piling into the water between the cliffs, and at the head of the lake a narrow plain between the canyon walls where the Indians camped for centuries. In such eye-pulling splendor it's hard to keep your attention fixed on fishing. Puzzled, I researched how such a lake came to be.

Carved out by the great glacial Lake Missoula floods over some 800,000 years, Rock Lake is one of the deeper depressions in what are called the Channeled Scablands, a roughly 15,000-square-mile basin of scoured and grooved and channeled basalt almost completely surrounded by mountains and nearly encircled by three rivers—the Columbia, the Spokane, and the Snake. The scope of the work that was done when the ice dams of glaciers blocking the Clark Fork Valley began to melt and the great lake repeatedly cut though the dam and rushed south is impossible to imagine. (Consider that Lake Missoula was some 3,000 square miles big and contained 500 cubic miles of water—half the contents of present-day Lake Michigan.) The last flood some 20,000 years ago ran 800 feet deep, at an estimated 9.5 cubic miles of water per hour (or ten times the flow of all of the rivers of the world combined), for two to four weeks—plucking away loose bedrock, moving lava blocks thirty feet across like pebbles, and stripping away 150 feet of soil as it cut the deep channels that make up the Grand Coulee to the west and the Rock Lake chain to the east.

Rock is too much trouble for most people. Few signs point the way. It took me several years to learn about a road here and a road there, and to meet the right farmers, so I could even get close to the lake at other than the south-end access. Narrow, dangerous, and locked, only two roads lead down through the cliffs to the water. So you have to boat the lake and that spooks people, or should. You can be one hundred yards from shore, zipping along at top speed, and then, biinnng! you hit a basalt reef not six inches under the surface. A cautious driver, I still ruin at least a prop a year.

The wind is the worst. We've a steady sou'easterly that blows five to fifteen on good days and that, if you work it right, can set your boat on a perfect down-lake drift along the shorelines. But spring and fall bring the heavies, and with Rock lying south to north, a thirty-mile-per-hour wind will set up whitecaps from one end to the other, and you don't want to be out there in anything marginally seaworthy or less than fourteen feet long, although I've risked my life a number of times (and bailed a lot of water) in twelve-footers. And if you do get caught out, there are only three or four places where you can make a safe landing along some twenty-odd miles of cliff and rock shoreline. The chance of a rescue by another fisherman? Slim to none.

There's a little private graveyard on Lyle Stevens's property (the only beach on the lake) to mark the loss of four young men who disappeared in Rock years ago—a graveyard I gave considerable thought the day I got caught seven miles down-lake and the wind kicked up to fifty-five miles an hour. We made it in a sixteen-foot Lund, but it was a white-knuckle deal, especially after I popped off one of the prop blades on a reef. To save myself the disappointment of driving to the lake to find it too windy and too risky to launch and fish, I keep a wind chime hanging outside my writing-desk window; if it's tinkling, it's too windy for Rock.

So why go there?

For the history. For the raw, almost untouched beauty of the place and to see, each time, the basalt cliffs, the scattered, old-growth, crowned-out ponderosas tucked away from the logger's saw in impossible draws and canyons, the yellow and red and blue lichens flourishing among the stone columns. To hear the rock wrens and maybe see turkey buzzards and raptors and kingfishers and magpies and goldfinches and water thrushes and the thousands of swallows that return each year to nest in the cliffs and feed on the insect hatches. And to smell the sweet white syringa in full June bloom where it grows near the water side by side with the wild roses.

There are mule deer in the mornings. You can see them come down the thin trails to water or to lie up under the shade of bluffs on a hot August day. And raccoon and beaver and coyote and marmot and gray squirrels and mink and, once in a while, a rattlesnake swimming.

And, of course, I go there for the fish. The wonderful fish. But it isn't easy fishing, or at least it isn't easy until you've put in your time.

What sort of fish? Ah, that's part of the mystique of this home water. The native sucker was in the lake when the pioneers arrived in the 1860s. Then came plants of largemouth bass, crappie, carp, and perch, although few are ever caught. You find pumpkinseed sunfish in the few weed beds, but again, few are caught. The main fare: brown and rainbow trout. A few thousand are stocked each year by the game department, but the majority of the fishery is sustained by its own reproduction. There are just a few spawning areas in the lake itself, most of the spawn taking place in the vast stretches of Rock Creek, which feeds the lake and exits south into the scablands.

"How big is he?"

"Nine pounds."

"I say eleven to twelve."

"Fifteen if he's an inch!"

This is brown-trout talk among the few Rock fishermen. With plenty of forage, no lack of room to grow, and damn little pressure, the browns grow big. Estimates of the size possibilities of fish in the lake can get a little weird—especially when you mark on your sonar a fish that's as long as a baseball bat. Or longer. But then you have to remember that, at some time or another, all of the big waters in Washington have been illegally stocked with sturgeon from the Snake and Columbia rivers system. So, when you get cleaned off while you are using something like a plug or spoon or big gob of night crawlers, there are at least four possibilities: a huge brown, a thirty-pound carp, a 250-pound sturgeon, or the R.L. Monster.

The best Rock Lakers I know have broken off legitimate browns above seven or eight pounds. I mean, two-witness browns. I've broken off a few that looked that big and have netted a number of five-pounders. Although I've often forsaken the fly rod and tried trolling huge plugs on the surface in the spring and fished deep with down-riggers in the summer, and gone back on the surface in the fall and winter, and fished well into the night, I've never hooked the Ghost, the one my money says will go fifteen pounds.

You see them that big, though. Once my father and I were fly-fishing size 12 Pale Sulphur Duns and taking numbers of small browns along the shoreline when, while Dad was stripping in an eight-incher and as I was leaning over to net it for him, a brown with the head and maw of a gator lunged out of the murky depths and took trout, fly, and leader in one bite.

Because of the farm runoff carried down-canyon by Rock, Black, and Pine creeks, the lake stays a milky-green color much of the year, only clearing well in the late fall. But by June there's enough visibility for the trout to begin rising. And rise they do—steadily most of the day for sulphur mayflies, and in the late afternoon for midges. If the farmers don't spray too heavily up above, there is wonderful hopper fishing from July until the first frost.

The hopper fishing is the best, especially for the browns. Because of the towering cliffs there is always—somewhere on the lake, no matter the position of the sun—shaded water. In the heat of the day and as the hoppers misfire or get blown out over the cliffs, they helicopter down and land *kerplunk!* in the water. Then they start swimming for shore. And guess who's waiting for them in the shadows.

If you're there, too, working a Joe's Hopper or a big Muddler or whatever pattern you like, you will have action, guaranteed. And I mean with the chance of a big brown. But a few seasons back we had a major infestation of grasshoppers, and they bombed the hell out of the fields on top with pesticides. Since then, the hopper fishing has slowed, although you can still take the occasional cruising brown on a big bushy fly—maybe just from its memory of the good old days.

◆   ◆   ◆

Rock is always good to a guy like me. I enjoy the eating side of fishing as much as the catching side, and the lake provides both. In half a lifetime on the same water, you learn where the meat markets are. I've just enough crappie holes to be able, most any time of day in most any month, to pull into a submerged tree, flip out a jig and bobber, and start reeling in the specks. Not a lot of them, but always some. Because there's so much predation going on and no single species overpopulates, the crappies run to sandwich size (two fillets to a fishwich). We take enough for dinner, no more, then get back to the trout or bass and generally keep neither of these.

There are more things to know, more drop-offs and bars, and sunken trees and bays where the crappies congregate and the bass nest in the first warm days of spring, and why, as summer gets going, you should carry an ant pattern, because, once, you remember finding a huge school of trout slurping and sucking and dining on downed ants caught in a wind-formed feeding lane behind a rocky point and took fifteen of them in fifteen casts.

It's funny how the brain works, how it makes permanent certain visual memories. I can go to home waters, cast to the corner of a rocky cove, and remember, with perfect clarity, a trout I took from the exact same spot maybe fifteen or twenty years ago. I can't remember who was with me or how old I was or what was happening in my life then, but I can remember the trout, the color of it, the heft of it, the sex of it, the fly it took. It's better than a camera because, with the remembering, there is a tightening in the throat you don't always get from film. And one hopes, if there's a dance after this one, you'll get to keep these best-held memories.

But the fish are only a part of home waters. The other parts are people, the people you've taken there in a kind of this-is-mine pride, or the friends you've burned sunlight with on the broad waters, and the kids you've raised there. Yes, raised there. People think children are raised in homes; not so, children are raised in families. And where a family fishes together, so it comes together. Maybe you've fished a thousand waters, but if asked where of all those places you'd most want to be together again for one last fishing trip, the answer will be obvious. Why? Because that's where the bulk of the treasure is stored.

I've fished a lot of different waters and plan to fish a lot more, but there is always one place where, to paraphrase Robert Frost, when you have to catch a fish, they have to let you catch one. I guess Rock is it for me—at least it's where my spirit keeps returning.

The other night as I lay in bed awaiting blessed sleep, I found myself trudging along in the snow over the abandoned Burlington–Northern railroad tracks that lead to the head of the lake and that, in the dead of winter years ago, Larry Grand and I used to hike to get to Rock's inlet stream for a day's trout fishing. In my coming dream it is dark, but the distant gray of dawn makes shadows possible. I am walking quickly, anxious to get to the fishing. I am as I came into the world: alone. I am eager, but content. I am going home. Remember: "smack-dab in the middle."

THE COTTAGE
BY THE
ITCHEN

• • •

VISCOUNT GREY OF FALLODON

THE COTTAGE THAT I PUT UP BY THE ITCHEN IN 1890 WAS INTENDED
only as a fishing cottage; a place in which to get food, sleep, and
shelter when I was not fishing. It became a sanctuary. The peace and
beauty of the spot made it a sacred place. The cottage belongs to
angling memories, but the fishing became a small part of the happiness
that was associated with it. For thirty-three years the chosen spot
remained a place of refuge and delight, not in the fishing season only.
For the last four years, indeed, I had been unable to fish with a dry fly,
and the original purpose for which the cottage had been put there
ceased to be. Great changes, however, had been taking place and were
inseparable from a new epoch. For the first fifteen years there was little
change and had been little change for many years before this time. I
had seen the old mill at the village not far away replaced by a new
building, and the dull, monotonous sound of a turbine had replaced
the lively splashing of a water-wheel; but otherwise things remained as
they were. The cottage was invisible from any road; it was approached
by an old lime avenue, long disused, and the track down this was not
suited for any wheels but those of a farm cart. There was a little
wayside station on a single railway line close by; but the quickest route
from London was to go by a fast train to Winchester, and thence drive
to a distance between four and five miles to the nearest point to the
cottage that was accessible by wheels. This was a drive of at least half
an hour in a one-horse fly. Presently taxi-cabs took the place of the
horse conveyance and reduced the time of the drive to a quarter of an
hour. Was this an advantage? On balance it was not. For escape from
London meant that hurry, noise, and bustle had been left behind: I
had entered into leisure, where saving of time was no object, and often
I would walk from Winchester to enjoy the country. There was a
footpath way on each side of the river. By one of these one entered the

cottage without, except for the momentary crossing of one road and of three secluded lanes, having had touch or sight of a road. There were thirty-three stiles on this path. It happened not infrequently that I could not get to Winchester till the latest train arriving there some time after eleven o'clock. The walk then lasted well into the midnight hour. In the dusk or dark it was easier to walk by the road than by the path. There was much charm in this midnight walk. Traffic had ceased, cottage lights had been put out, the inmates were all at rest or asleep. Now and then one heard in passing the song of a nightingale or a sedge-warbler, but in the main there was silence. It was pleasant after the hardness of London streets and pavements to feel the soft dust about my feet. On a still summer night there were sweet and delicate scents in the air, breathed forth from leaves and herbs and grass, and from the earth itself. It was as if one's own very being was soothed and in some way refined by the stillness, the gentleness, and the sweetness of it all.

Then came the age of motors and tarred roads. Few people, I imagine, seek the smell of tar for its own sake. To me there is nothing unclean or nauseous in it, but it is a coarse, rough smell. The sweet and delicate scents of the night were obliterated by it, as if, overpowered and repelled, they had sunk back into the leaves and earth from which they had ventured into air. The strong smell of the tar seemed to disturb even the stillness of the night: The soft dust was no more, and the road was hard as a paved street. Not all, but much, of the charm of the night walk was gone.

There were other changes too; small houses of the villa type were built along the road that was nearest to the cottage. Doubtless there are more of them now, for the cottage was accidentally destroyed by fire in January 1923, and I have not seen the place for some years. The sense of change was in the air. It may be that change is for the good:

> The old order changeth, yielding place to new,
> And God fulfils himself in many ways,
> Lest one good custom should corrupt the world.

It is not for us, who cannot foresee the future, who perhaps cannot rightly understand the present, to childe or to repine too much. Only it is impossible for us, who in our youth gave our affections to things that are passed or passing away, to transfer our affections to new things in which a new generation finds delight.

The beauty, however, of chalk-stream valleys still remains wonderful. The river still waters meadows that are unspoilt and unchanged, and its clear purity is guarded and protected.

Still glides the stream and shall for ever glide,
The form remains, the function never dies.

Thus, as the angler looks back, he thinks less of individual captures
and days than of the scenes in which he fished. The luxuriance of
water meadows, animated by insect and bird and trout life, tender
with the green and gay with the blossoms of early spring; the nobleness
and volumes of great salmon rivers; the exhilaration of looking at any
salmon pool, great or small; the rich brownness of Highland water; the
wild openness of the treeless, trackless spaces which he has traversed
in an explorer's spirit of adventure to search likely water for sea trout;
now on one, now on another of these scenes an angler's mind will
dwell, as he thinks of fishing. Special days and successes he will no
doubt recall, but always with the remembrance and the mind's vision
of the scenes and the world in which he fished. For, indeed, this does
seem a separate world, a world of beauty and enjoyment.

The time must come to all of us, who live long, when memory is
more important than prospect. An angler who has reached this stage
and reviews the pleasure of life will be grateful and glad that he has
been an angler, for he will look back upon days radiant with happiness, peaks and peaks of enjoyment that are not less bright because
they are lit in memory by the light of a setting sun.

SEASONS
NOW AND THEN

• • •

RUSSELL CHATHAM

THE GUALALA HOTEL IS ONE OF THOSE UNINSTITUTIONALIZED LAND-
marks that still remain to remind us of a time when California belonged to the Spanish and Russians or, later, the Swiss, who came to
live and farm so peacefully. Not that these people had anything in
particular to do with the hotel, but when you see the rather chaste
two-story building washed in warm afternoon light, you are reminded,
if abstractly, of an Andrew Wyeth painting, or if you were born here
before about 1940, of all the places and people out of your childhood.

Gualala is a tiny town lying on the northern California coast
about halfway between Jenner, at the mouth of the Russian River, and
Fort Bragg. Pronounced with a silent G, the name appears vaguely
Spanish though it was the Russians who used this territory. Some
historians believe the word is the Spanish version of *Valhalla*, while
others maintain it comes from the Pomo *walali*, "Where the waters
meet."

It works either way. The Gualala River lagoon stretches for nearly
a mile before breaking through its sandbar to the ocean, and the two
flirt with each other much of the way, especially when the sea is
rough. And the countryside here is abundant, the river and ocean
yielding rich harvests of fish and shellfish, the forest full of game. No
hero fallen in battle could contrive to have his soul rest in a more
generous hall.

To those of native distinction, the word *California* is pronounced
slowly in the mind, as if speaking with a modest Italian or Spanish
accent, to dignify the word and make it somehow expressive of an
ambience having nothing whatsoever to do with suburban sprawl,
freeways, bizarre population densities, and the positively lethal disre-
gard for history Southern Californians pioneered.

You can still see some of the underpainting in places like the

Salinas Valley, where the farms don't seem to change much. The old people were uncomplicated and, along with their crops, cultivated attitudes of decency. Many ranchers and farmers grew rich, became millionaires in some cases, but few considered it a matter of consequence. When the time came, as it did to so many, that unfair taxation forced the sale of land to developers, they did not gleefully take the money and run. They despaired for loss of the soil.

The coast north of San Francisco remained largely provincial until about ten years ago, when the Flower Children decided they would rather live in the country. They showed by example that if you could manage the right blend of welfare benefits, food stamps, Medi-Cal, unemployment insurance, subsistence gardening, checks from home, and Volkswagens, the last thing on earth you needed was a job opening close at hand. You could lie back in the sun out there in the middle of nowhere and pick your nose until hell wouldn't have it.

Until that time, Gualala was an isolated north-coast community. And it has been, in fact, the last in the region to knuckle under the pressure of the times, the first being Mendocino City, north of there, where vacationing art teachers seized control years ago.

My family began going to Gualala before the Depression for the steelhead fishing. It took at least two days to get there from San Francisco, over dirt roads that became impassable in wet weather. If you went at all, you took your fishing pretty seriously and planned on staying a while.

Those were not years when Leisure Time lay heavily on people's hands. Backpacking and camping were for eccentrics, jogging would have been inconceivable, and hang gliding hadn't been invented.

One December, my father, uncle, an old gent named Walt Mullen, and my father's roommate at Stanford, Pinky Mahoney, made an expedition to Gualala to fish and hunt.

My father loathed fishing, especially where it involved a boat. His view of it maintained that the seat of a rowboat was harder than a landlord's heart and had only one purpose: to make you suffer in the region of your rear end. My father's opinion of the Gualala River as a fishing stream derived from a day early on when he caught a logger's boot in the lagoon after trolling for it for five hours.

So he talked everyone into going hunting. They would take a handcar up the logging tracks and shoot some quail. The first covey they found, everyone but Pinky had shots and missed. Pinky allowed that no one seemed able to hit his hat. My father wondered aloud if Pinky would like to throw out his hat and settle the matter. No, instead they'd do this: My father would throw his hat in the air and

Pinky would shoot at it, then Pinky would throw his hat and it would be my father's turn.

Pinky was from a distinguished Boston family. His 20-gauge was an elegant Parker double. His hat was made in England. My father admired Pinky for his candor, generally, but never failed to raise his British eyebrows over the fact that Pinky wrote a master's thesis severely critical of Boswell's *Life of Johnson.*

My father put a stone inside his sweat-stained Dobbs and gave it a toss. Pinky missed with both barrels.

"Your turn, Pinky."

As Pinky removed his wool cap, Walt and my uncle slipped off their safeties behind his back and stood waiting. When the hat sailed out over a blackberry bush, six loads blew it into infinity.

They took me to Gualala shortly after 1950. It was a little like leading the boy caught smoking to a whole box of cigars and demanding he exhaust his interest. Perhaps not quite that, but my parents were alarmed at the obsessive hold fishing had on me. I would have dashed through a forest fire in a flammable sweater if I thought there might be a trout on the other side.

They opted for the join-'em approach, and the next thing I knew my uncle was buying me a Pflueger Supreme casting reel and a nine-foot, two-handed bamboo rod. That winter when the weather broke, school was out of the question. We were going to go steelhead fishing at Gualala.

We fished with bait, fresh roe, which we tied into "berries," small balls wrapped in moliene, a material not unlike nylon stocking. In the lobby of the Gualala Hotel, tables were set up so you could tie your bait. This was the main function of the lobby, except when a few old-timers played pinochle in the afternoons while everyone else was out fishing.

What you did was to tumble your bait through the places where steelhead were apt to be lying. You cast slightly upstream, then followed with your rod tip as the current took the berry around below you. Whenever there would be a pause in this drift, you would strike, because often the steelhead would take very gently, then let go.

You were always hanging up on the bottom, forever fixing a new rig. Someone was always talking about someone else he knew who had gone a whole season without catching a fish. As my bait swung around again and again, I wondered if that was going to be me.

Some of the real veterans claimed they pretty much knew the difference between a fish and the bottom, so naturally, they snagged up less often. I was on the bottom constantly. In that icy canyon, my hands would get so cold I couldn't work a swivel or tie a knot, so I would retreat to the beach and kneel down, where I would try to warm my hands before rerigging.

"What are you doing?" my uncle would ask with impatience. "Praying? Get your line in the water. How do you expect to catch anything kneeling on the beach?"

Then, back at the hotel in the evening at the bar, he'd tell everyone with mock concern, "He prays all day for a hit, but he never fishes. Spends more time on his knees than one of the Apostles."

My uncle was so good he could cast his bait and sliding sinker into a teacup at thirty yards. He used an old eleven-foot Leonard rod with a hardwood handle he'd made himself and a classic J. A. Coxe free-spool reel. He knew where the fish would be and he could feel pickups when there was almost nothing to feel. Once, he found a school of fish near a cut bank. He was getting a pickup on every cast, hooking a fish on every fourth or fifth. He called and had me cast in there, but I couldn't feel a thing.

"You're not casting far enough," he said. "Make it about three inches more."

I'd try, and even when the cast was right, I couldn't feel the pickup. He'd stand there and watch my line and he'd see a pickup I couldn't even feel.

When fishing was really tough and he was one of the few on the river to have hooked anything, he'd let me play and land it, then up at the hotel when the men asked how it went, he'd say, "The kid got one."

◆   ◆   ◆

I want to go back strongly enough not to care what a number of intervening years may have wrought. Few things in memory stand out quite so clearly as seasons in Gualala. Youthful enthusiasm distorted the proportion, but even in the light of later perspective, those times are rich. You know you have tasted the best there is, and somehow even if there are only leavings, they will still have a touch of that flavor.

This winter of 1975–76 is disastrous on the coast. Hardly a drop of rain has fallen on California. It is the driest year on record. In February, when there should be six inches of bright-green grass everywhere, there is only dust.

The streams remain at summer level. On the California coast, where there is no such thing as snowfall, precipitation is largely rain, which comes during the winter months. In the six months from May to October, only one or two percent of the annual runoff finds its way to the sea.

The Gualala River, then, like all the others, is practically dry when I see it in late February. A few fish make it over the shallow riffles at night, but the main schools hold in the big pools waiting for rain. All winter long there have been reports of masses of fish in the lower pools: Thompson, Minors, Mill Bend, the lagoon. The water is crystal clear, the fish very touchy. You have to fly-fish using long, light leaders and small flies to hook anything.

Word spreads through the angling community so that these pools are elbow to elbow with fishermen. The news reaches my uncle and he decides to go up for a look. He hasn't been to Gualala for at least fifteen years, maybe longer. He gave it up when the fishing slid down-hill to practicably nothing in the late fifties and the crowds became intolerable. He hasn't seen anything.

"How can they do it?" he asks when I see him. "The whole fun of going fishing at the Gualala was you could get a pool to yourself. There must be twenty or thirty fly-fishermen in every hole, all casting into the same spot."

Today, among these younger Californians, the notion of having a pool to yourself is as foreign as a ride in a Model T Ford along the coast from Jenner on a dirt road, having to stop every few miles to open gates.

It is about two o'clock one afternoon as I cross the bridge at Gualala and decide to look first at the Thompson Hole. The old river road is now paved, the turnoff, unfamiliar. A sign says COUNTRY ROAD 501, CAMPING, and there is an arrow.

The camping turns out to be at the Thompson Hole where there is another sign, this one rather enormous: "Gualala River Redwood Park. 4.50 per day per car, 90.00 per month payable in advance. Up to four persons. Each additional person 25 cents per day, 7.00 per month. Checkout hour twelve noon. Day rate 1.00 per car. We re-serve the right to refuse admittance to anyone."

You think about the old boy who used to spend the whole win-ter under the dark, damp redwoods at Thompson's in a leaky canvas tent. No one could understand why he didn't die of pneumonia, because it was always wet inside. All he cared about was catching steelhead. Every so often someone would bring him a bag of gro-ceries and a handful of candles. Today he would probably be refused admittance.

Actually, when you think about it, it gets cold enough in there to freeze the balls off a brass monkey, and only a masochist would want to camp in that dungeon when, for another four bits, you can get a comfortable room with maid service over at the hotel.

The road to the river, which has always been no more than two ruts you take your chances with, is now asphalt. Where it comes back out of the campground there is a sign in red letters warning you WRONG WAY. All the redwood trees are wired for lights.

At Thompson's, nine people are fishing, five fly-casters and four bait-fishermen. One of the fly-fishermen evidently snapped his fly off on the beach earlier and is now fishing without one. I wonder why he doesn't notice this while I do, since he is approximately fifty yards closer to where his casts are landing than I am.

The fishermen are directing their attention at the deepest part of the pool where, under normal conditions, you would never find a steelhead. But in this low water the fish are piled in there so thickly, if you climb the bank, you can see them as a dark mass, changing shape once in a while like a huge amoeba.

The lower end of the pool, where the steelhead usually lie, is all but dry. The old redwood stump in midstream, which has been there as long as anyone can remember, is wholly visible. Ordinarily, only the tip of it shows when the river is at fishable levels during the winter.

One of the verities of fishing the Thompson Hole is that if you are the first one in the morning to roll your bait past the log, you'll have a fish. It is very strange now to be able to see the bottom all around it.

I wade across, not getting my knees wet, to the top end of Minors Bend. It is fine bait water, where the current flows against the other bank. Snags and windfalls give it a fishy appeal. Sometimes you can catch spawned-out fish on flies here if the water's not too high, but it's always a good bait spot. No one is fishing it.

Down at the deepest part of the bend, three men are fly-casting from small prams. Two others are wading near the boats. On the cliff across the stream, ten or twelve people are bait-fishing.

One of the men in the boats turns out to be Bill Schaadt, whom I've not seen for several years. We are happy over this accidental meeting, and Bill excitedly describes how the fishing has been and how it is today. The steelhead are schooled up just off the old alder, milling somewhat, biting spasmodically.

I think of the day here at Minors about twenty-five years ago when the late Claude Kreider, then a popular outdoor journalist, came down and saw Bill fly-fishing and, taking out his spinning rod, announced that it was too muddy for flies. That day, Schaadt landed thirty-three fish, one of which was nearly twenty pounds, at the time the largest steelhead in the world ever caught by fly-fishing.

In waders, it is almost too long a cast to reach the fish. I watch the other fishermen and am embarrassed for them, for their lack of fly-casting ability, their dull expressions, the obvious fact they do not truly see or understand the essential life of the river around them.

I can feel all too precisely how many feet, even inches short, a certain cast is, or when a subtle surge in the current snakes it away from the fish. And it takes several line changes to find the one which sinks exactly right so the fly is down among the fish, yet never on the bottom.

When I was still learning to fly-cast, I would have been ashamed to be seen handling my tackle as poorly as these men fishing near me. Perhaps it's no more than Calvinistic intolerance, but it still seems a lack of pride is a sad thing. These fellows cast sloppy lines yards short of where they must be and routinely retrieve as if just throwing it out there is enough of an act of faith to justify a reward. It is quite easy to imagine them going a whole season without ever catching anything.

Bill and I fish in silence for an hour. I look up at him, shake my head. He shrugs.

"Where are all the regulars?" I ask.

Bill is stern but matter-of-fact. "They're dead."

◆   ◆   ◆

In the lobby of the hotel are some of the old photographs, even though the hotel has changed hands and the bar is remodeled. There is no pretense in these familiar pictures; they are clearly not intended for public entertainment and, in their simplicity, defy the falseness of brochure aesthetics. They not only record tangible evidence of good fishing, but a lack of hysteria as well. There is a curious quietude registered on the faces of these men as they squint into the winter sun.

I remember Johnny Verges, Hank Adler, Lou Villa, Allan Curtiss, Fred MacMurray, Neil Gordon, Joe Panic, Gunderson. Where are these men now? A few dead, but not all. Do they still come here to drift their baits through the pools and rapids? If so, do they stay at the Gualala Hotel?

My room is on the second floor, Number 3. Merve Suitor used to stay in . . . was it 8? Merve was always here. He came in on Monday, went home again on Friday, all season long. Everyone wondered how he managed, but he did. He woke early in the morning, three-thirty or four, and read until it was time to go to breakfast at six.

He'd get out on the stream with everyone else as soon as it got light, even if he did grumble about it. But as soon as the sun came up, he'd find someone on the beach to talk to. He'd sit up there all day periodically yelling, "A good man'll get 'em" or "What would the experts do?" or "Chatham, you'll never make a pimple on a real fisherman's arse."

Joe Panic owned the hotel at the time, and he often made a lot of noise behind the bar. Just after Fred MacMurray married June Haver, they came up to go steelhead fishing. After toughing it out on the river one cold day, June came into the bar, took her waders off, and asked Panic to please rub her ice-cold feet.

"Aw, gee, why don't ya get one a these married guys to do it?"

One night, in a playful mood, while Fred was talking about fishing with some of the others, she plugged in the jukebox and started trying to find someone to dance with. I was probably about a sophomore in high school at the time, and when she got around to me I was frozen with fear. For some time after that, my name was preceded by the nickname "No-dance."

Fly-fishing was considered pretty exotic back during the early fifties. But there were some who stuck with it all the time: Curtiss, Schaadt, Joe Paul, Frank Allan, Carl Ludeman, Jim Golden, and a few others.

Now nearly everyone fly-fishes and you seldom, if ever, see any of the old-time bait-fishermen. It is evidently hip to be a fly-fisherman. Young anglers on the stream have the most stylish tackle. Many sport badges or arm patches declaring their affiliation with clubs or organizations. There is no doubt that, by and large, they aren't as bigoted or opinionated or as secretive as their earlier counterparts. And, if you can trust what you see, not nearly as knowledgeable either.

Things change. We got used to the new highway bridge even though it ruins the solitude of Mill Bend, not to mention the Racetrack Riffle, which it spans. Now, when you start up the hill into town, a large billboard welcomes you to Gualala. Among other services, you learn you now have two choices if you want to get your hair done: the Gualala Beauty Salon or Shurl's Curls. There are the inevitable real estate offices, two huge service stations, and a brand-new post office–bank complex that looks as if it just landed.

A bright new green-and-yellow Volkswagen bus pulls slowly to a stop in front of the hotel. A shiny canoe rests on the roof of the bus. A California Couple get out and look with interest at the quaint building. He has a perfectly trimmed beard, her hair is long and light. They are dressed in denim. They will probably have dinner at the hotel and would perhaps think it amusing to take a room for the night.

Meals at the hotel used to be potluck, family style, always hearty. The same dining room is now a popular restaurant on the coast. On weekends you can barely squeeze in, and the barroom sometimes looks like a dress rehearsal for "Soul Train."

On the second floor at the east end of the hall is a window covered by a gauzy curtain. Through it you see a vertical cross section of typical coast landscape. Below, the green, uneven yard, fish house, moss-covered shed, pines, then the stark white Baptist Church, dark-green cypress, and more pines against a sky bleak with the present threat of rain.

Yes, it will rain, and never was it so needed. But you can't help responding like a steelhead fisherman and curse the weather.

You walk down the hall to the front of the building and look out at the ocean. The sandbar is dense with sea gulls and the surf is enormous, crashing over into the lagoon. Breakers explode against headlands to the south. When you look that way you think of the Sea Ranch, a vast new second-home and retirement community which sprawls for ten miles below Gualala.

You have been aware that there is hardly a bit of funkiness or eccentricity left. People used to do things on the coast like decorate their barn or yard with abalone shells. These days tourists would see that and start screaming ecology because a lifetime collection of abalone shells looks like a lot. Even more than that, most objections would be on grounds of taste.

Many point to the Sea Ranch as an example of clean, tasteful planning and architecture. Instead, is it possible that the Sea Ranch is not in good taste at all, but is rather sinister? For starters, they have cut off public access to the ocean for ten miles.

In another, more important sense, the whole development is self-conscious and self-indulgent. It is truly a realtor's dream of take-and-take-more come true. You sell the large, expensive homes on the hill to the wealthy on the basis that the lower slopes will remain "open space."

Then, when you run out of hill, you start working your way down until you've filled all the land with homes, diminishing in size and price as the elevation drops.

Architecturally, this may be the final moment of the Bauhaus, of that Aryan insistence that you remain in step. All the buildings are alike: bleached cedar, tinted glass, triangles, trapezoids. Modular units.

The old barns and other buildings weren't designed by architects imposing their conformist notions on the countryside. The old buildings had a sense of modesty, of legitimate purpose, and they did not insult the landscape.

Even the Sea Ranch logo, hatched by some graphic designer and looking oddly pre-Columbian, is harsh and entirely out of place. Over and over again it pokes out from behind the bushes to tell you not to trespass.

◆   ◆   ◆

Two things are no longer there which were a real part of fishing at Gualala: the mill with its rumbling and smell of smoke, and the sound of diesel logging trucks coming down out of the canyon.

Funny thing is, we all screamed because logging ruined the river and there seemed to be no stopping it. And now that it's gone, it's somehow worse because you have only this rather spineless situation left where everything is manicured and complete directions are posted.

Where you park, or rather where you are now told to park at Thompson's, there is a sign on one of the trees that says TO BEACH AND RIVER AREA. This is in case someone is not able to recognize a river or a beach even though they are both only ten yards away.

Fishing in the canyon, there is a sense of loss without the logging trucks. Yes, you will have to adjust, but you think that maybe a nice muddy, rutted gravel road plus the downright recklessness of those old drivers might have alarmed some of these denim dandies in their Malibu Classics enough so they would never venture as far as Thompson's, or ever come peering through the trees to find the crossing to the Donkey Hole.

You try to hold the bitterness at bay, but it creeps in anyway. You wonder if you are merely expressing some sort of class prejudice, but what you finally come down to is that there are just too goddamn many people.

◆   ◆   ◆

There is an hour of light left. The day before, the lagoon had been boiling with fish. You wonder if they might move up to Mill Bend on the tide. They would be bluebacks mostly, smaller, late-run fish.

The wind is up, blowing in from the south. With it there will be rain. The sky is leaden. In a few days the season will close, and each year it is the same. One day you may stand here and fish, the next you may not.

You always regret not being able to fish in March, one of the most interesting months. You think how nice it would be if there were a special catch-and-release season. After all, the closure is to protect fish heading back downstream to the sea. Secretly you know that most people wouldn't bother to fish if they had to release everything.

The steelhead are here, rolling and splashing everywhere. The wind is fierce, and that, plus the gloom of evening, will, you hope, offset the clear, shallow water. It is nearly dark when the take comes and it is a surprise, as they all are. In that moment you know, yet do not understand, why you spoiled so many years fishing for these things.

You want to say it has to do with intercepting a migratory cycle, that it puts you in touch with certain seasonal mysteries, is at least a partial definition of the cosmos, life itself.

But this has all been said before by thoughtful men, and it is true, only no matter what is said it's never enough, never really *it*. Or perhaps it's too much, because we are in that region of the senses, of the heart, where experience defies translation, ridicules explanation.

You have gone to some good deal of trouble to be here, not only currently, but through years of asking, searching, trying. Now you're banking one of the jackpots. These cliffs are dark and exquisite, the cypress so expressive they seem to be reaching, gesturing. It is as if they were imploring you to love them.

The stumps lying in the water go so far back beyond memory that they become almost like characters in a book or play. Each time you look, they are themselves and something else; memories layered thickly in the back of the brain.

Coming up tight on the steelhead is like confirming the answers to a thousand impossible questions, being admitted into secret chambers of knowledge. It is only in the moments after that you face the fact you have done nothing extraordinary.

It rains all night and you can hear the wind pushing at the window and soughing through the forest. At six you go down for breakfast. You remember those times when you came in here and the fishermen were talking, eating, and you came away from the table with some notion where everyone would be on the river. If you excused yourself early, they knew you fully intended to be the first one through the lower end of Thompson's by the log. They wouldn't leap from their chairs and try to head you off; they also knew overeagerness was a function of youth.

This morning in the old dining room there are a couple of construction workers, yourself, and two or three other fishermen. You are already in your waders, and one of them asks if you think the river has come up during the night. You shrug.

It's still raining, so you decide it best to go down to the highway bridge and check the stream. In the first light of dawn you can already tell, by looking over toward Mill Bend, that the river's too light. When you get to the bridge, the water is light brown. The sign that says NO FISHING FROM BRIDGE looks strangely alone in the gray light. You wonder what kind of moron would ever fish off this bridge anyway.

You drive to Thompson's, where you can determine how much the river has risen and how the flow has increased. You feel there might be a chance as the fish move over the riffle from Minors and stop here for a few moments.

At Thompson's you see the same fishermen as the day before. They are standing tentatively on the bank right where they were fishing yesterday. One of the fly-fishermen nods and says with authority, "Better have your fast-sinking line on today."

You realize, not without a mixture of alarm and pity, that he fully intends to fish the precise piece of water as he had the previous week when the steelhead were forced to hold there by conditions. Now, that stretch is a raging chute barren of fish; even those swimming quickly through will do so near the shallow side where the current is less severe.

No one is paying any attention to the lower end, the only possible place you could hope to fish. As you watch, several wakes come over the riffle.

You reflect that the old boys would have that spot sewed up tighter than a surgeon finishing an appendectomy, but here it is wide open. Casually, you wade in, watching the lip as several more fish ease over. A steelhead boils right in front of you, then another. Across the river, the tip of the log is visible.

It's a long shot, with visibility in the water of less than three inches, but you tie on a large black fly and cover the rollers with short casts. In a moment of luck you have a take, but manage to hold onto it for less than half a minute.

The current grows stronger as rain keeps falling. Debris is floating past. The log is now underwater, and you only know it's there by the trailing wake of disturbed current. The fishing is over.

You stroll to the car and put away your tackle, then walk over through the redwoods to where you can see the huge tree that slopes into the water at the head of the pool. That too, like all the others, has been there since anyone can remember.

As if looking for something even more primordial, you watch the cliffs, covered with bright yellow moss, then the river where it bulges against them. The redwood log is young compared with the cliff. How long ago had it come to rest there? Had the sun ever shone on that moss, even in the summertime?

The canyon is so deep here that with the darkened sky, it is like being in a cathedral. The light is dull, and you keep coming back to the mossy cliff, which seems illuminated.

For me, this is a gallery of spirits, though now they are less real than ever before. I look at the river steadily for perhaps a full minute, and my mind expands that sixty seconds into a century, a millennium. In my limited way of sensing things, I feel this will go on forever.

WILD DOGS COULDN'T DRAG ME AWAY

◆ ◆ ◆

MICHAEL LEVY

WHEN YOU FISH ON A DEADLINE IN THE POPULAR PRESS, IT'S HARD TO pick a favorite stream. Harder still (if it's a good one) to keep its name out of the newspaper.

That's unfair, but there it is.

Any local newspaper's fishing writer knows that his favorite stream won't stay appealing long if he "tells all" to his avid readers.

There are other bothers attendant on becoming a fishing writer, too, not least among them the need to fish for a lot of species in a lot of places using a lot of methods—none of which you would choose if you fished for yourself. Fishing should be something to do on a free afternoon, to get your mind off deadlines and phone calls and the Byzantine internal struggles of your company's middle management. Bankers, car salesmen, teachers, and machinists who like fly-fishing can just head out to the stream and be done with it. But fishing writers can't.

When I fish, it's usually to learn how to cast spinners for muskel-lunge or flip pork rind for bass or belly-boat for walleye using weight-forward worm-rigs so I can write about it. Now, this is not a bad job. And I am not complaining, mind you, but it neither allows for much fly-fishing nor does it leave one much time to cultivate a special relationship to one stream or body of water.

However, Wiscoy Creek—though I know it only in spots and know those spots far from well and have gone as long as two seasons between visits—the Wiscoy is the nearest thing I have to home water. My infrequent visits are escapes from workaday angling, for I sneak there to fish for my soul and no one else's edification. And when I do find a few hours to fish the Wiscoy, I am returning to my earliest fishing, too; for, unlike most people, I started angling with a fly rod.

Since I'd like to end my angling days fly-fishing, I try to make

time to fish without notebooks—practicing casting and untangling
back casts, losing flies, mismatching the hatches, and (once in a great
while) getting it all right or getting lucky and hooking a fourteen-inch
fish.

On those rare and special days that I can fish for fun rather than
profit, the Wiscoy is reasonably close, reasonably productive, and now
relatively uncrowded, thanks to New York's Great Lakes Fisheries
Program and its year-round angling for behemoth salmonids.

It was more crowded twenty-one years ago when I first met this
little stream on Opening Day.

The very date of Opening Day probably has some cosmic signifi-
cance. In the Empire State, trout fishing (nowadays called "inland"
trout fishing to differentiate it from the Great Lakes stuff) begins on
April Fools' Day. But my story begins a couple months earlier, just
after I moved to Buffalo from Princeton, New Jersey. Or maybe it
begins a little earlier yet, when I began my career as a scrivener and,
incidentally, as a fisherman.

My Jersey doctor had suggested that I needed to get outdoors and
forget the office at least one day a week if I planned to beat the ennui
and chronic fatigue that plagued me, an early victim of what is now
called "job-related stress."

"How about golf?" he asked.

"Played it in high school," I replied. "Hated it. Besides, the way
I played, I got apoplectic about the third or fourth hole. How about
fly-fishing?"

"Why'd you say that?" Doc asked.

"I saw Bing Crosby fishing for salmon on the Spey on TV last
weekend and it looked pretty interesting."

Doc's face lit up. He was a Montanan, he said as he ripped a page
from his prescription pad. "I grew up fly-fishing, it's just the thing you
need," he muttered as he scribbled.

Here is what he wrote:

*1 fly rod, 7½ to 8½ feet long, glass okay, bamboo better. Get 7
wt-forward line, forget the GBH stuff.* [The weight system of line
numbers had just started replacing the old letter designations for
different line diameters and tapers.] *Get leaders about same length
as rod, tapered down to about 5X—store clerk knows. Flies—dries:
bivisible, Royal Coachman, gray or white Wulff, size 12 to 16. Couple
of streamers like dark Edson Tiger. Get a few MUDDLER MIN-
NOWS!*

Together with fairly frequent applications of aspirin (for the rheu-
matics that have kicked in during the last few years) this remains one

of the finest prescriptions for health, if not happiness, ever written. It was even fairly legible, as prescriptions go.

So I began fly-fishing in 1967, trying to learn out of books; obtaining and later *giving away to a kid* what I think now must have been a "collectible" bamboo fly rod; eventually buying a seven-foot, six-weight rod that was not as short as the then-current fads, but short enough so that the guys who fished "midge" and "flea" rods on Stony Brook on Opening Day or the Ken Lockwood Gorge later on in the season would not laugh me off the water.

Now, of course, these same fellows are using the latest fashion in sticks: nine-foot graphite rods to fish two-weight lines. I still use my original glass rod and still catch fish with it.

All this is by way of explaining that I knew no other fish but trout and no other method than fly-fishing when I moved to Buffalo to take a job at the *Buffalo News* on February 1, 1969. This date is important, for it is in February that most northern trouters start feeling forlorn, anxious, and in need of solace.

After my new colleagues had shown me where the coats were hung, explained where the coffeepot was situated in the back shop, and told me what time lunch break was, I asked if there were any other trout fishermen around.

"Frankie Lewandowski," these nonanglers said, pointing out a jockey-sized guy who mostly worked in the composing room. Frankie was America's oldest copyboy and the most avid early-season trout fisherman I have ever met.

Two months after being introduced, at eleven P.M. on March 31, he was gently tapping his horn button to beep discreetly in my darkened driveway. It was snowing and the thermometer hovered at twenty-two degrees Fahrenheit. But it *was* Opening Day, by God, or would be, once midnight had rung.

Mercifully, there was no breeze. Not so mercifully, the thermos fell from my pocket as I tossed hip boots into the backseat and I heard that most dire of Opening Day sounds, the tinkle of glass.

"I always used to do that, too," Frankie said. "Why doncha get a steel bottle?"

"Any place open now?" I asked.

"Nah, but we'll find a place later—and I brought plenty of tea. Which you'll need.

"See," Frankie went on, "I want to get to my spot early so we can start right in, once fishing is legal at twelve oh one." Frankie—like most anglers reared on put-and-take fishing—was a great believer on being there firstest with the mostest.

And we were: there where the Wiscoy cuts through meadowland

near the crossroads at Bliss, just north (or perhaps it is west) of the little bridge—more or less at the beginning of the creek's public angling access.

"You know, in New Jersey we don't fish until April fifteenth," I said. "It's farther south, too, so it's a lot more comfortable. . . ."

"Well, it's a lot nicer here in May, too," Frankie replied, "but c'mon—it's Opening Day!"

We pulled scarves tight around throats and crunched through knee-high snow to reach the stream. We rigged short leaders with split shot and bare hooks and began the 1969 trout season in the deep, crisp, almost mythic dark of a subarctic midnight: tossing salted minnows upstream to let them dead-drift down and across.

At 12:05, Frankie had his first trout of the season, a good one, too, perhaps eighteen inches long.

At 12:20, I heard a thumping sound coming from around my knees and risked using a flashlight to see what it was. The sound came from miniature ice floes, as it happened. I was hearing them hit my waders, but not feeling them.

I quit fishing, taking solace in Frankie's Chevy (which had a good heater), his tea (he carried an extra thermos), and his blackberry brandy (which, I learned on subsequent trips, was a major reason Frankie fished at all).

But on this miserably cold and uncomfortable day, which saw Frankie limit out and then catch and release maybe six more fish, and me bat zero, I did get to see a lot of the Wiscoy. The stream apparently rises in two places, according to the map: Lake Willette to the south and a spring on the north branch (a brook trout headwater). They meet in the hamlet of Bliss to work east and south in a meandering line perhaps ten miles through farmland and lea, lazing through long, slow, cut-bank loops past indifferent Holsteins and through a mile-long "artificials only" stretch with a three-fish daily limit.

At Pike there's a little dam at the fairgrounds, then a ten-mile stretch that's fishable most of the way. The stream enters a valley and slows to a crawl, then flows out of a small-scale power dam to enter a small gorge and tumble over rocky runs. After that the Wiscoy eventually joins the Genesee River.

For generations, along with its sister, the East Koy, and nearby streams like Ischua Creek, the Wiscoy typified state-managed, put-and-take "trout" streams. Each spring, New York State would put, and hordes of anglers who fished those water then would take, until the "hatchery product" (not to be confused with real stream-bred trout) petered out, usually by June.

When New York began planting Pacific salmon in Lake Erie and

Lake Ontario in 1965, the new "Great Lakes regulations" allowed year-round trout fishing in the lakes and their tributaries up to the first impassable barrier. State hatchery managers, granted a new, state-of-the-art facility on the Salmon River, went into a breeding frenzy to increase geometrically the numbers of brown and rainbow trout and various strains of steelhead and plant them in the Great Lakes along with uncountable millions of coho and chinook salmon. More recently, New York has started restoring Atlantic salmon and even is trying huge *Seeforellen*—a kind of European monster brown trout of the sea-run variety—in the Great Lakes.

All this has lured trophy hunters away from these mere inland trickles. The meat hunters left, too, for if you are going to catch stockers to eat, why look for a stringer of tiddlers when one seven-pound rainbow will feed your whole family, and the neighbors' kids as well?

Just about that same time, Trout Unlimited started up in the Buffalo area and the local chapter adopted the Wiscoy. Working with state fisheries biologists, TU's sweat equity over the last fifteen years has turned the Wiscoy into:

1. A wild-trout stream with naturally reproducing trout; no more stocking is done there.

2. An improved venue for the fly-fishermen, with fast runs and stabilized banks, and gravel spawning beds.

3. A stream well-known in outdoor columns primarily for item one (above)—which means that even fewer meat fishermen come here than otherwise might.

So, although there are no secrets on or about this stream, it is still possible to go almost anywhere along its whole length and to make, with a modicum of privacy, the kind of horrible mistakes a beginning fly-caster will make. It remains a stream where I can hide my duffer's clumsiness in anonymity; where I can try to regain my touch with my instrument of choice; where I can lay aside spinning, casting, and all the other gear I use for published forays after bass, walleye, muskie, walleye, panfish, Great Lakes salmon, and more walleye that readers hereabouts demand.

On the Wiscoy, one can find a little peace, solace, and even, sometimes, solitude.

Meet another angler here and he or she will likely be casting flies, or at least using delicate spinning gear. The occasional grizzled dairy farmer taking an afternoon off with a can of worms and a cigar will suggest that you fish the pool he rests by, or tell you to wade past his pole (which will, of course, be supported in a Y-shaped stick), since he's "just fooling around, anyways."

The Wiscoy never had shoulder-to-shoulder fishing on Opening Day the way Princeton's Stony Brook has, for example (the Wiscoy— and Opening Day here—is a helluva lot colder!), but the Wiscoy did see far more anglers when it was a put-and-take stream than it does these days. And back then a lot of them were bait-fishermen who were far more aggressive than today's fooling-around farmer.

But there are always exceptions to what we fly-fishing snobs think of as the bait-fishing "norm."

Like the man with the Luger, who taught me how to roll worms and catch trout with ultralight tackle.

This was in the early days, mind you, back before there was this Great Lakes stuff, back when I still fished only for myself and not for copy; back before Buffalonians started to fish so adamantly for bass and walleye.

I was doing some streamer-fishing at the Boy Scout camp, about midway between the village of Pike and the Wiscoy's melding with the Genesee. It was early May and the leaves were only just a lacy fringe, imparting an aura of expectation to the new-green tree branches. Skunk cabbage was in bloom, though, and some May apple, too. The creek here is crossed by a foot bridge—or was, seventeen years ago. Upstream of the fairly speedy riffle at the bridge lay a series of deeper, slower pools.

I was standing on the bank of one of them, doing textbook drills with a small white streamer (cast upstream, dead-drift through the pool, and retrieve the two-inch minnow imitation in one-inch jerks) when a pleasant-looking fellow in his late thirties came walking upstream carrying a stubby four-foot rod fitted with the tiniest spinning reel I had ever seen.

He wore canvas pants and hip boots and a fisherman's vest.

And a shoulder holster from which the butt of a World War II-vintage 9mm Luger protruded.

We stopped to smoke and chat (smoking was still legal and quite a social thing to do in those bygone days), and he explained that he was worming his way upstream.

On or about Opening Day anywhere in this cold north country, worms work a lot better than flies. In fact, up till then, about the only time I ever actually *caught* any of these elusive fish was on worms. And the only limit of trout I ever took fell to earthworms. (The trout were needed for a ritual Opening Day feast. They were delicious.)

But pinching enough split shot on the leader to get the worms down deep, where they need to be early in the season, messed up the casting. Fly-casting without the split shot messed up the presentation. So by the time I met the man with the Luger, I had switched to fishing nymphs and streamers—thus restoring my fly-fisherman's purity, even though the switch to artificials meant far fewer fish caught.

I more or less explained all this as I admired the spin-fisherman's stringer.

"The trick with worms," said my pistol-packing acquaintance, "is to use no weight at all, which is why I use this ultralight rod and two-pound-test line.

"And you have to toss your worm in real easy," he cautioned. "No splash. Then, let it roll through the pool as naturally as possible, like it was washed in by the rain."

The Luger was optional worming gear. He carried it for the wild dogs, he said.

It seems that feral dogs do roam some stretches of the Wiscoy, and my worming mentor had been menaced by a pack of six of them a year earlier. He had to fend them off with his fishing rod as he crept his way backward the half-mile out to the road and his car. That scared him thoroughly enough that he went through the six-month process required of upstate New York residents to get a pistol permit.

"I bought the Luger because my buddy let me have it pretty cheap," he said, "but I guess a twenty-two-caliber target pistol would be enough—if you knew how to shoot." He carried the pistol whenever he fished this creek, he said, adding that he was surprised I had not met up with the wild dogs.

Since that encounter, I have met other anglers toting pistols on the Wiscoy. And not one of them looked, spoke, or acted like Rambo types. Some of them even carried fly rods.

Out-of-staters please note: You can't get a license to carry side-arms in this state, so I leave to your imagination the danger of feral dogs to the unarmed. It's just one more thing you'll have to factor into your calculations—if you decide you'd like to come fish my stream.

It is true reports like these that help keep one's home water quiet and uncrowded.

DRIFTING DOWN
THE RIVER
OF MY MIND

• • •

LIONEL ATWILL

THERE IS A RIVER IN MY MIND THAT FLOWS FROM THE HEADWATERS OF a dream. It's a twisty stream, full of matted greenery, a river that cuts through corridors of looming, ominous trees. The water is a touch off-color, the shade and opacity of old iced tea. The current is swift enough to move a boat but slow enough not to threaten. Birds fly overhead and wade the shallows. Turtles and snakes sun on the banks. And in the primordial ooze that divides the water from solid land, evil things lurk, things unknown, things best left that way.

This is the river to which I've escaped a hundred times or more. It is an imaginary stream, a place in my mind where I can hide when life's not quite right, where worries and transgressions cannot follow. As a kid—through college, in fact—I'd go there several times a week. Blue books didn't know the way, nor did irregular Latin verbs or square roots or the periodic table of the elements or the blue-stained organs of biology-lab frogs. Later, in the army, I traveled those waters during hygiene lectures, in the middle of hurry-up-and-waits, and at two in the morning on an ambush of some no-name trail in a no-name paddy in that no-name little war. Even now, as an adult, I still find solace there, whenever I can get away.

Anyone who has ever fished or floated or simply stood, alone, and stared at moving water has a similar river in his or her mind, I suppose. Rivers are hypnotic, mysterious things; they're life's generic metaphor—life could do a lot worse. It's fitting that a river should flow through that corner of the mind where we sometimes hide.

I'm not sure why my river has always been a slow, turbid waterway—a small Amazon—for the rivers I grew up on were always fast and cold and rocky, Yankee trout waters, not semitropical, mud-brown streams, slower than day-old grits.

Maybe it's because I've always known too much about trout

streams; there isn't enough room for mystery on water I've fished all my life. Maybe it's because you can't float a rocky, rampaging river with the same casualness and ease that you can a lazy, turbid stream. Whatever the reason, I've always enjoyed that slow, brown water of my mind.

It first appeared without texture or detail. There was indistinct greenery on the shore. There was the occasional rise of a fish and sometimes a mysterious swirl of something bigger than one might catch on hook and line. Beyond that, the details blurred. But as I've traveled and seen waters here and there, I've filled in bits and pieces, like coloring in the outlines of a paint-by-the-numbers scene, until now that secret river is as rich and full of life as any waterway on earth.

I've put in some Spanish moss from Georgia, some flooded timber from an oxbow in South Carolina, a blue heron and a sextet of anhingas from the Everglades. Bits and pieces have come from else-where, but much of my river has been colored by a small stream in central Florida, a river so similar in texture and feel to the water that had cruised my mind for so many years that, when I first saw it, I thought for sure that I must have plied its bends and backwaters in some other life.

That river is the Oklawaha. The very sound of its name takes me there now.

No one would ever describe the Oklawaha as a tumbling caul-dron, a tumultuous river of awe. The Oklawaha oozes along in its own soothing style. There are private pockets of water off the main river, pools framed in water hyacinth, and numerous side channels screwing through the flooded timber, which tries, but fails, to contain the stream. Collectively, these backwaters and elbows create a web of water that is larger than the sum of its parts.

I first saw the Oklawaha by accident. I'd set out for a day of fishing on the larger and more powerful St. Johns, shipping out in a rented fiberglass kicker with a twenty-horse outboard and a trolling motor on the bow. Such a boat didn't belong on the St. Johns, I soon realized. Not that it was physically too small for the river; no, it simply was intimidated by the razzle-dazzle of a thousand weekend bass boats, party barges, and multiengined cruisers. So when I putted past the confluence of the Oklawaha, I turned and found a river more in scale with my mode of travel.

The first quarter-mile of the river drew the occasional big boat, but upstream, where the channel narrowed and set to twisting like a corkscrew, the slick, powerful cruisers and hot bass boats were at a disadvantage. My kicker came into her own, and soon I had the river to myself.

I came on a side channel, which I followed. After an hour of slow motoring, the trees from both shores were scratching my gunwales, so I turned the boat, cut the engine, and began to drift with the current.

It was then it struck me how familiar this river was, how it matched that river of my mind, that hideaway to which I'd fled over the years. There was isolation here but not loneliness. There was peace and calm amidst the raucous cries of birds and the *sploosh* of rolling gar and jumping fish. There was even that hint of danger, which materialized in the form of a ten-foot alligator that launched from the bank and swam under my boat, setting up a wave that has grown larger and more dangerous with each telling.

I spent the rest of the day drifting down the Oklawaha. I fished haphazardly, which to my way of thinking is often the best way to fish. I started small, tying on a popping bug, a Sneaky Pete. I like Petes. I like their Day-Glo colors and their startled, cartoon eyes. Petes look as if they know that their sole purpose in life is to be swallowed by large mouths filled with pin-sharp teeth.

A bluegill took my first cast, an adolescent bass my third. Encouraged by this ascending scale of fish, I took off the Pete and affixed a big, feathery fly done up in purple and black. It looked like something one might pick off the floor of a 1950s burlesque house, the flotsam of an entertainer named Belle or Ruby or Baby Jane.

I worked that teaser along the edge of the weeds. I'd cast and let it sink just below the surface and wait and wait and wait as my bass-fishing southern friends had taught me to do. Then I'd twitch it an inch so the feathers rippled through the water, and I'd wait and wait some more. On most casts, nothing happened. On one, an ugly snake rippled out of the weeds, and I pulled the fly in as fast as I could strip. On three or four, the bottom dropped out and bass sucked down the fly with a violence people who spend little time on the water would never ascribe to a fish.

I landed two, I recall, small bass of a couple of pounds, not worthy of a raised eyebrow on the St. Johns but honest heroes in the crannies of the Oklawaha. (There are bigger fish—far bigger—I discovered, in those backwaters, but bigger fish rarely fall to a haphazard fisherman, at least not to this one.)

The rest of my time on the water that mystical day I simply lazed in the sun, taking in the details of the river: a limpkin stalking apple snails (can a snail be stalked?); an eight-inch alligator floating motionless in a soup of *Elodea*, patiently waiting for something small and edible to swim by (or for sufficient time to pass so that it might grow, uneaten, to the size of that ten-footer, thereby rendering everything in this water, including me, "small and edible"); a cottonmouth swimming cross channel with that don't-mess-with-me look for which his species is justly famous; and tens if not hundreds of tipsy turtles balancing precariously on rocks, logs, and even other turtles, their legs extended, like ladies drying their fingernail polish in the hot Florida sun.

It's good to have such a river on which to float and fish away the day, to turn to when life gets fast and hot; it's even better when that river's always with you, when it flows forever through the passages of your mind.

LIME CREEK

◆ ◆ ◆

STEVEN J. MEYERS

LIME CREEK IS BOTH A PLACE AND AN EMBLEM. FOR ME IT IS A DISTIL-
lation of the character of a region I know as home and within which
I live. It is neither far away, nor separate from me. We live here,
together.

The creek is not particularly long or broad. Its main stem travels
roughly twelve miles from its headwaters (a few miles southwest of
Silverton, deep in the San Juan Mountains of southwestern Colorado)
to its terminus at the confluence with Cascade Creek. Its width ranges
from a few feet at its beginnings to twenty-five feet or so at its widest
shallow riffles. Yet of all the streams I have sat beside, walked along,
or waded through, I find it the most powerful in experience and
memory.

It begins in the glacial cirques of high peaks and never leaves the
mountains, but the terrain and climate zones it travels through are
quite varied. It can be a calm meander through a lush mountain
meadow or a tumultuous roaring torrent through a narrow, rock-walled
gorge. Its banks can be stark with the limited but beautiful life of the
tundra, or they can be verdant with the complexity of a mountain
forest nourished by rich, moist soil. In short, Lime Creek is everything
a mountain stream should be.

In the San Juans there are more remote streams that are just as
varied and beautiful. There are less accessible streams that lend cre-
dence to the illusion that a personally discovered stream belongs to
you and you alone. A highway follows the course of the Lime Creek
valley, and a dirt road meanders beside the stream where the deep
gorges give way to gentler terrain. In an area so dominated by wilderness, it must seem strange that this relatively accessible creek should
become an emblem of place.

To ignore the presence of man here would be naive, but there is wilderness here, too—land that shows little evidence that man exists. The San Juans, like many other wild places, straddle the border between wilderness and human habitation. Lime Creek, wild yet well explored, is a manifestation of this truth. It is not my private stream, no matter how compelling the illusion may be. The creek helps me to remember that even apparently undiscovered, remote streams do not become mine alone upon discovery.

Beyond Lime Creek's varied terrain and habitat, beyond its existence as a wild yet known place, Lime Creek embraces all that the San Juans are for me because it is a place where I have spent a great deal of time. I have waded the streambed, walked the woods, and climbed many of the peaks surrounding the valley. From here the creek leaves the mountains to join the ever-increasing flows that eventually become the Pacific Ocean. Here in the San Juans, however, it is a headwater, a source—a good place for the discovery of one's own roots and meaning. I have been in Lime Creek long enough now to have seen a child born while I hiked its woods, to have seen a loved one die while I fished its waters. I have seen a generation pass and another begin to flower. I know the creek will outlast me and my memory. I know there will come a time when all human impact on the creek will be gone. For now, however, we share a place in nature.

◆   ◆   ◆

Lime Creek, as you may guess, is a superb trout stream. If you suspect that I spend a great deal of time fishing Lime Creek, you are right. And as much as I love the Lime Creek valley and as much as I love fly-fishing, wedding the two loves was as natural for me as love itself.

Tellers of fishing stories are always making up phony names for their favorite streams to protect them from discovery, or downplaying the quality of fishing to keep others away. Some people will probably be furious with me for revealing the whereabouts of such great fishing, just as friends have chided me for singing the praises of the San Juans in other books and articles. I plead the happy insanity of a man in love with a place. In addition, I must confess that I have not lost all faith in my fellow man. Somehow I am not yet fearful that either the San Juans or Lime Creek will be overrun with hordes of insensitive, noisy, beer-can-slinging invaders. I hope I'm not wrong. It doesn't seem to me that the subtleties of Lime Creek would attract or hold for long anyone who would destroy it, and the experience of these subtleties might greatly enrich the lives of those who get to know the valley. Who am I to keep all this to myself?

The trout in Lime Creek come from many different populations.

Most are wild. Some are stocked. The stocked trout are at a distinct disadvantage in the creek's fast water and difficult conditions. Few, it seems, make it through too many winters. Most succumb to baited hooks, lures, or flies, or fail to reproduce and die without progeny. The few stocked fish who do survive long enough to reproduce have the genetic moxie to ensure that the wild populations that result from their breeding success will continue to make it and continue to adapt to their surroundings. They will, in effect, become truly wild.

The wild fish whose ancestral roots began in a fish hatchery inhabit the lower stretches of the creek. Here, there are a few brown trout, which were brought to this country from their native Europe. There are a great many brook trout, which were originally found in the streams and lakes of eastern North America. Although most are small, some achieve monumental proportions for mountain stream brookies (nine to ten inches) and a brilliance of color and scrappiness when hooked that inspires admiration. Wild populations of rainbow trout, which are native to the West Coast of North America, also inhabit the stream. These acrobatic leapers would seem to be the favorites of anglers. They grow larger than brookies, fight splendidly, and are not quite so hard to catch as brown trout, which quickly become wary after exposure to angling. Finally there are the true natives of Lime Creek: cutthroat trout. These trout, threatened throughout their range by interbreeding with introduced trout, environmental degradation, and the hard knocks of trout life, appear to be thriving in the upper reaches of Lime Creek. They are protected from genetic disaster by the physical barriers of a topography that keeps away stocked fish and introduced wild populations, protected from anglers by the relatively rough country, and, so far at least, protected from environmental degradation by the pristine and natural environment through which Lime Creek's headwaters flow. If there is one fish that represents the angling soul of the San Juans, it has to be the Lime Creek cutthroat.

I would be lying if I were to say that fishing for cutthroat trout can be done without mixed emotions. I have done it for a great variety of reasons. One was simply to get food, although I no longer keep cut-throats, preferring to fish for food among the less precious and rare species. Another reason has been to reassure myself that they remain in the watershed. Each year, after the long winter, I find myself consumed with the fear that they might have been wiped out in the bitter cold. I am unable to relax until a good day of fishing near treeline has reassured me that the population remains alive and well. So far, each spring this has proven to be the case. Still, I would have to be fairly insensitive or uncaring to think that the act of putting a hook, even a barbless one, in the lip of a trout is a matter of no consequence, that involves no responsibility. A choice to act in this way can be made in ignorance. Many fishermen, I think, fish in such an envelope of arrogance. Many more grapple with the conflict between their passion for fishing and their legitimate love of their quarry, and in so doing find resolution for issues that transcend the mere act of fishing.

To resolve the conflict in a place like the Lime Creek valley, with a fish as noble as the Lime Creek cutthroat, makes the resolution somehow more profound and the lessons learned perhaps more significant than what could be achieved in the midst of civilization or on a trout stream unlike this one. This stream has likely changed little since the retreat of the glaciers at the end of the last ice age. It has seen and been seen by nomadic hunter–gatherers. Today it is a place that can provide continuity between us and those who hunted here long ago. It can also help us understand the biological inheritance they bequeathed to us.

When I fish the creek, I often become lost in the concentration required to find, stalk, and induce a trout to take a fly. There is water to read and wade safely. There are trout to locate and somehow not frighten. A decision must be made about what insect might appeal to the fish and what fly might successfully imitate it. Finally there is the cast, and if all goes well, the rise, the setting of the hook, the playing and releasing, or the solemn matter of killing the fish so that it can be eaten later.

Sometimes the concentration becomes so intense that hours pass with little notice of anything beyond the watery world of the creek. I have been startled out of this mental isolation by many things. Water ouzels have flashed past me, landing midstream on rocks where they peep their distinctive call and dip their tails in characteristic fashion. Once an eagle buzzed me in a way that made me wonder if he had decided only at the last minute that I might prove too heavy to carry off as dinner. Sometimes the light has changed dramatically, suddenly glowing a brilliant red on the summits of surrounding mountains as twilight gathered, and I have been left staring in midstream, my line trailing uselessly in the current, struck dumb by the awesome beauty of mountain light. More times than I care to remember my concentration has been broken by the sudden discovery that I have stepped into a hole deeper than my waders or over my head, and I have sputtered, wallowed, and floundered to shore, having gone quickly from the bliss of reverie to the violent shaking and panting that come after an unexpected fall into frigid water. Never, however, has any event startled me as much as the protestations of a pine marten that assaulted me verbally from streamside when he came upon me standing in midstream, lost in concentration.

The marten had come to the stream for whatever reason martens come to streams. He certainly had not come to see me. I first became aware of him when I heard a hideous hissing. Looking in the direction of the noise, I saw him jumping up and down in a large flat rock, baring his pointed teeth in a ferocious display. Clearly he was angry. After a few minutes of this he ran off into the streamside willows, but returned minutes later to resume his display. His anger was obviously directed at me and his behavior exhibited no fear. He seemed to view me as a rival. He wanted me out of his territory. What we had here was a battle for turf. Without thinking, I bared my teeth, stared him in the eye, and began hissing and jumping myself. After a few seconds of this he ran off and did not return.

After his departure I sat on his streamside rock and wondered, *What the hell kind of behavior was that from a supposedly intelligent being? What had happened to reverie and compassion and empathy? Why had I acted so strangely? What right had I to interfere with this natural being trying to protect his territory?* Thank God no one had seen me! How would I ever have explained that display? More important, how would I ever explain it to myself?

How do I explain that I fish for and sometimes kill creatures I profess to love, living things that fill me with wonder and affection? Questions like this often lead people toward vegetarianism. I have a friend who says she does not eat anything that would try to run away. Are vegetables fair game because they cannot run? Do they die any less than animals when we cook and eat them?

Any creature that eats to stay alive must live from the death of others, whether they be plant or animal. That someone else does the killing for us in most cases does not relieve us of responsibility. If we view this killing as murder, we must either sanction murder or commit suicide through malnutrition. Few of us choose death and few of us sanction murder. Where is the resolution of this conflict?

The resolution lies, I think, in the realization that life and death are natural events. One creature's death as food for another involves a gift that, if not willingly given, should at the very least be gratefully received. If there is no gratitude for this gift, then life is indeed cruel and brutal. If, however, the acceptance of this gift is seen as a celebration of life, if one realizes that ultimately one's own death will feed the earth and sustain life—if only as fertilizer—then there is a wholeness to the cycle. A sense of belonging to the natural world and an acceptance of death, our own and that of other beings, that can never be achieved in denial.

When I fish and do not kill, I sharpen my skills and my insight. I believe that prehistoric hunters occasionally did the same. The fish I catch and release are, hopefully, less likely to be caught in the future. When I fish and kill, I do so with gratitude. I thank the fish for its flesh and I try to kill it quickly and with as little suffering as possible. This behavior was foreign to me before I fished Lime Creek.

A large part of my learning about food, and the roles of the hunter and the hunted, was crystalized in my encounter with the marten and in my strangely instinctive response to his display. The marten challenged me in a battle for territory. Lost in my hunt, having no time to think, I responded as a hunter and answered his challenge. On that day and in that battle, the challenger backed down. I know that it will not always be so.

◆　◆　◆

Lime Creek defines a valley that lies in the mountainous northeastern part of a larger region known as the Four Corners. Named after the spot where four states join, the region includes the southwestern mountains and semiarid basin of Colorado, the canyon country of southeastern Utah, and the mountain, mesa, and desert country of northwestern New Mexico and northeastern Arizona. This is an immense and wild region with incredibly diverse topography. It is also a region of incredible mineral and energy wealth. Four Corners is not just the name of the region, it is also the name of a coal-fired electric generating plant, one in a series of such plants that is reputed to be among the biggest emitters of sulfur dioxide in the world. Lime Creek, the aspen wood I so love to walk, and the sky that illuminates them, all lie in the path of those emissions. A sky that Edward Abbey once called the last great clean-air reservoir in the United States is now threatened by the energy needs of the Southwest. Just as the beauty of the great cathedrals of Europe is slowly eroding from sulfur dioxide pollution and associated acid rain, so is this forest, which is the embodiment of their source and inspiration.

Once, as I stood in midstream fishing the lovely, flat glide of water that flows through the aspen wood, I looked at the deep blue sky and the light in the aspen wood and wondered. How long will it be before my cathedral is lost to the excesses and deceptions of economic development, excesses and deceptions whose source lies partly in the desire for a better life, but more often in the exploitation of that hope by those whose only motivation is the dark selfishness of greed? How

long before we realize that the energy waste and opulence that char-
acterize our lives can be supported only temporarily, even by the vast
reserves of coal that lie beneath the land of the West? What will be
left when the sky above Lime Creek has been stolen?

◆   ◆   ◆

Remember how I described Lime Creek as being wild, yet civilized? I held this in mind as I eyed my bulging pack one autumn
evening. A road would take me right to the edge of the stream. I
would cross the creek, walk as far as was comfortable, and make camp.
If the pack got too heavy, I'd just park it and set up camp. Forget about
the pounds, let the trip take care of itself. And it did.

I drove in and parked where the road runs next to the creek at the
valley floor. Shouldering my load, I began to hike upstream through
an aspen glade that had partly turned but remained mostly green. As
I walked, the pack became heavier (nothing unexpected here), and I
soon decided that there was no need to carry it a long distance. After
less than a mile I came to a pool that I had often fished, but not very
successfully. If I were to cross the stream here and pitch camp in the
glade by the pool, I thought, I might be able to watch it for a while
and figure it out. This reasoning, aided by the weight of my pack, led
me to do just that.

After my load had been put down and my camp assembled, I
worked my way upstream. I fished from about noon until four, working
a little over a mile of water, fishing fast and not terribly well. I caught
eight fish, missed countless others, and startled more than I care to
mention from their holds beside and under rocks.

This is often the case when I get to the stream after an absence.
There is a rhythm to the woods, to fishing, that is very different from
that of work in town. It takes a while to slow down and find it again.
Toward the end of the afternoon, however, the pace of the woods
began to take hold of me. I remembered that I was in no hurry to get
anywhere. My camp was waiting for me a short hike downstream. I
had no clock and no evening appointments. I began to relax.

The last pool I fished had also caused me trouble in the past.
Above it, the canyon narrows and becomes a rock-walled gorge. In the
pool itself sheer walls contain the flow. Wading upstream is difficult,
since the pool is deep and has a swift current. At the head of the pool
the gorge makes an abrupt bend of nearly ninety degrees, and the walls
of the canyon narrow from the sixty-foot width at the tail of the pool
to perhaps twenty feet. Fifty feet beyond they widen again and open
into steep, grass-covered slopes. The foot of the rapid at the head of
the pool lies beyond the bend, beyond the narrow walls. It is unreach-

able by wading and holds the best fish on this stretch of stream. Rarely have I fished it. More rare still are the times I have fished it well.

On this day, after four hours in the water getting the feel of the streambed, finding confidence in my footing and allowing my internal clock to slow down, I decided to try it once again. Usually I would work out as far as possible in the current, then try to cast a long line up through the narrow gorge and into the wider pool beyond (a tactic that often resulted in bad casts and scattered fish). This time I clung to the narrow walls and worked my way into the mouth of the upper pool by climbing along the walls of the deep gorge. When I reached the neck between the upper and lower pools, I found a ledge from which I could make a comfortable cast of about forty feet into the water at the head of the upper pool. I was surprised to see fish rising there.

My first cast took a very nice ten-inch rainbow, my second a twelve-incher. These I thanked for their meat and killed for dinner. With the trout tucked safely away in my vest, I inched my way back down the wall and made it safely out of the gorge. With dinner secured and a wonderful afternoon behind me, I walked downstream to camp.

Dinner was a celebration of the day. I fried the fish in butter and seasoning and ate them along with spaghetti and bread sticks beside the pool where I had chosen to set up camp. I watched the currents and the fish that came to feed on the evening hatch of mayflies. We ate together. In the past, with only an afternoon or evening to fish, I had spent little time watching this pool. More often than not I had waded in, cast a line, and waded through on my way upstream. I had taken a number of small brook trout here and once, several years ago, a good-sized rainbow from the turbulent water at the head of the pool, but I had never taken a good fish from the deep water in the center, an area I knew had to hold at least one large fish. As I watched this evening, I saw a large fish that seemed to hug the wall of rock near the center of the pool. His feeding was leisurely and unhurried. He took insects with a slowness and deliberateness that indicated a sense of security. Few fishermen, I thought, had placed a fly there, or a spinner or worm, and few predators could surprise him there. It was a short trip from the wall to cover in the undercut rock below.

The fish and I enjoyed our respective meals and retired when evening came. Just before sleep came upon me, I remember looking out of my tent and up at the face of Twilight Peak towering above the canyon. It was bathed in the red light of alpenglow, a beautiful sight.

Morning broke with clear skies and unbelievably cold air. My breath was visible, and the walls of my tent were covered with frost. Sometimes mornings like this inspire me to rethink getting up. On

lazy mornings I might prepare and consume hot tea and oatmeal from
the comfort of my sleeping bag on the ground outside the front door
of the tent. After a few more cups of tea, the sun might hit the tent,
the temperature would rise, and so would I. Unfortunately, on this trip
I was camped at the bottom of a deep canyon, so no light would hit
the tent until very late, perhaps ten o'clock. The indirect light of the
fall morning was lovely, however cold, and the white trunks of the
aspen were glowing in the soft morning light. I had come to photograph as well as to fish, and this light was made for the black-and-
white film I was carrying. After a few hours the sun rose above the
shoulder of Twilight, and the light, though beautiful, became too
harsh for the pictures I had in mind. I sat beside the stream to rest,
empty my mind, and enjoy the first rays of the sun.

The morning I spent photographing along the stream and in the
dense groves of aspen that bordered the creek near where I had
camped. My mood was quiet and my pace slow. Photographing is
something like fishing. If you arrive in the woods with your adrenaline
pumping and rush about madly exposing film, little that is good
emerges. After time passes and you assume a less frantic pace, images
start to come. The previous day and the night in the woods had
already slowed me down, and I was seeing a great deal.

Later I broke camp, but before wading across the pool with my
pack and moving on, I decided to search the water to see if there was
any sign of the large fish I had spotted the previous evening. After a
few minutes I saw a disturbance that might simply have been the
water's flow broken by an irregularity in the rock wall at the edge of
the pool, but having seen a good fish there the evening before, the
disturbance took on new meaning. My first cast to the spot was about
a foot short, but my second was dead-on, and a massive head slowly
came out of the water to inhale my fly. When I struck, the fish dove
for his home. I was able to force him out into the pool, where he raced
about frantically, leaping, tail-walking, trying to escape. Several minutes later, I was supporting with both hands a fourteen-inch, fat-
bellied, brilliantly colored rainbow trout, moving him gently back and
forth in the shallow water at the tail of the pool. When released, he
went straight for the undercut ledge of the rock wall. The pool had
yielded what was, for Lime Creek, a very large trout, and also one of
its secrets.

My hike back to the car through a sunlit autumn aspen wood was
slow and filled with thoughts. Any fisherman understands the joy of
finally seeing a large fish in a pool where for years he had suspected
one, and the added joy of solving the problem of how to land it. Any
photographer appreciates the pleasure of a morning spent deep in the

woods with glowing light and the white bark of aspen. Any hiker knows the joy of a day, a night, and a morning out in the woods, self-contained and happy. There had been all of this, and more: a crashing tree, a bounding deer, water ouzels moving upstream with me as I fished, ground squirrels and chipmunks chattering to me from streamside, a splendid wood, a glorious stream, narrow gorges, and open riffles.

◆   ◆   ◆

The winter snow now lies deep upon the waters of Lime Creek, in the forested valley, on the high, windswept slopes above treeline. It began falling toward the end of October.

It stopped snowing for several months after the initial storms and began again in earnest in January. Now, beneath many feet of powder, insulated from the bitter cold of nights at high altitude, the trout hold, sluggish in the icy water. Immature caddis flies and mayflies bide their time beneath the rocks and mud of the streambed. Seeds fallen from pods and flowers during the autumn nestle in the decaying warmth of the forest detritus, awaiting their time to blossom. Ptarmigan burrow into the snow, their black beaks and eyes giving them away in the sea of white despite their efforts at concealment, waiting for the rocks and their mottled-brown plumage to reappear. Ermine lope through the snow leaving tracks like legged snakes, narrow furrows with paw prints. Spring will come.

Marmots have long since ceased to be active and, along with the bears, have holed up for the winter, somewhat like the people of Silverton. Frost collects inside our windows, and on cold nights inside our doors and walls as well, while woodstoves burn. Spring will come again.

Soon the days will be noticeably longer and warmer. The sound of birds chirping will fill the morning with song. One day soon the water of Lime Creek will reappear, the insects will hatch, the trout will feed, the flowers will bloom. The pine marten will argue with me. The eagle will swoop over me. I will stumble and fall again in the icy waters, and I will dry again in the warm sun, laughing. Life will go on in Lime Creek—as it always has.

MAKING TIME

◆ ◆ ◆

THOMAS R. PERO

IF WE HAD THE TIME, I WOULD FIRST ASK IF YOU HAD EVER CAUGHT A brown trout in March. You would likely answer no, not that you can remember. So I would invite you to come fish the Deschutes River on a clear, crisp morning in late winter.

We would park in a grove of fragrant juniper. We would look out across dry, rolling hills of sage and bitterbrush at a series of brilliant, snow-sprayed mountains in the shimmering distance. The high desert air would feel sharp and thin in our lungs. One more sip of coffee and we would be making our way with assembled fly rods down steep rimrock to a rushing river, brimming with a strong green flow through weathered cattails.

We would stand alert, perched like neoprene-wrapped herons in knee-deep ice water, waiting for tiny, dark-brown stoneflies to begin bouncing off the water's surface. And strain our ears, listening, as well, for an ever-so-perceptible *plop*, signaling a rising trout.

At last a hungry brown trout, whose ancestors came from Europe to this Western desert stream some nine decades past, would mistake your bit of floating fluff and hook for a meal. After an admirable struggle, you would hold all seventeen inches of this yellowish, leopard-spotted fish upright in the cold current. You would let it go with the winter sunshine strong on our faces.

◆ ◆ ◆

If we had the time, we would play hooky on a fine spring day in early June. We would bring a picnic. We would drive into the Cascade Mountains, through dark lava frozen by centuries and through thick, green stands of lodgepole pine. We would hike in hip boots and short sleeves across an alpine meadow. We would stop and notice the unfurling flowers of a bright-red Indian paintbrush; we would be startled as a mallard hen flushed at our feet from her clutch of ivory eggs.

We would follow the clear, sparkling beginnings of the Deschutes—here more accurately a creek—upstream. We would pause at each miniature bend, taking turns drifting carefully baited hooks or artificial nymphs through inviting pools. The trout, mostly palm-sized brookies with a scattering of rainbows, all wild, would not seem to discriminate. Provided a natural drift, these little wild fish would eagerly take whatever we offer.

Come evening we would slip my canoe into the mirror-calm of nearby Hosmer Lake and paddle through the tule reeds to a chorus of splashing coots and scaup. Casting wet flies and stripping them back rapidly, you would touch your first silvery Atlantic salmon—from the only home of the species in the West.

We would marvel at ospreys, circling and diving with precision for the cruising salmon, and watch as the imposing panorama of Bachelor Butte reflects a rosy glow in the chill of fading light.

◆   ◆   ◆

If we had the time, come July or August, we would make a summer pilgrimage south from central Oregon to where, in the wonderful poetry of my angling friend Peter Coyne, the North Umpqua lies like ladled silver.

We would rise early each morning beside Zane Grey's old river to try for an Umpqua steelhead: an elusive, quicksilver shadow as long as your arm. This mysterious ocean wanderer has no real business taking your glittering fly and usually does not. For a steelhead returns to the emerald pools of its birth, struggling up churning whitewater rapids, to spawn, not to eat.

Yet we would chance the odds. We would spend our luck casting endlessly under towering Douglas firs. We would wade treacherously swift runs paved with slippery ledges, ever hopeful that one summer-run steelhead—just one—in an improbable burst of energy will cash in your generous hours of patience for precious minutes of exhilaration.

◆   ◆   ◆

If we had the time, we would reserve as much as possible for September and October, for the glorious days of fall fishing.

Would we launch our boat in search of a well-fattened rainbow cruising the channels of Crane Prairie Reservoir, under a Kodachrome sky with a confectioner's dusting of fresh now on South Sister?

Or would we wander up a tiny tributary to Wickiup Reservoir, placing our rods aside, calling a truce, and crawling on our stomachs to watch lusty brown trout build spawning redds of clean gravel?

Probably we would be most happy doing it all.

Then we would take a final drift-boat ride down the lower Deschutes, to where this river of rapids joins the broad Columbia, hundreds of miles from its emergence from snowmelt-charged Cascade Mountain springs.

We would finish the dinner dishes in our sandy campsite among the alders. The canyon walls would appear cold blue from reflected moonlight. A coyote would whine, somewhere in back; then another bark sharply, out in the sagebrush.

I would pour you three fingers of amber whisky. We would toast—to the river, to the fish, to being alive on a night such as this. From crackling flames would emerge tomorrow's dancing steelhead, swimming now through the starry night.

THE CLEVELAND WRECKING YARD

♦   ♦   ♦

RICHARD BRAUTIGAN

UNTIL RECENTLY MY KNOWLEDGE ABOUT THE CLEVELAND WRECKING Yard had come from a couple of friends who'd bought things there. One of them bought a huge window: the frame, glass, and everything for just a few dollars. It was a fine-looking window.

Then he chopped a hole in the side of his house up on Potrero Hill and put the window in. Now he has a panoramic view of the San Francisco County Hospital.

He can practically look right down into the wards and see old magazines eroded like the Grand Canyon from endless readings. He can practically hear the patients thinking about breakfast: *I hate milk*, and thinking about dinner: *I hate peas*, and then he can watch the hospital slowly drown at night, hopelessly entangled in huge bunches of brick seaweed.

He bought that window at the Cleveland Wrecking Yard.

My other friend bought an iron roof at the Cleveland Wrecking Yard and took the roof down to Big Sur in an old station wagon and then he carried the iron roof on his back up the side of a mountain. He carried up half the roof on his back. It was no picnic. Then he bought a mule, George, from Pleasanton. George carried up the other half of the roof.

The mule didn't like what was happening at all. He lost a lot of weight because of the ticks, and the smell of the wildcats up on the plateau made him too nervous to graze there. My friend said jokingly that George had lost around two hundred pounds. The good wine country around Pleasanton in the Livermore Valley probably had looked a lot better to George than the wild side of the Santa Lucia Mountains.

My friend's place was a shack right beside a huge fireplace where there had once been a great mansion during the 1920s, built by a famous movie actor. The mansion was built before there was even a road down at Big Sur. The mansion had been brought over the mountains on the backs of mules, strung out like ants, bringing visions of the good life to the poison oak, the ticks, and the salmon.

The mansion was on a promontory, high over the Pacific. Money could see farther in the 1920s, and one could look out and see whales and the Hawaiian Islands and the Kuomintang in China.

The mansion burned down years ago.

The actor died.

His mules were made into soap.

His mistresses became bird nests of wrinkles.

Now only the fireplace remains as a sort of Carthaginian homage to Hollywood.

I was down there a few weeks ago to see my friend's roof. I wouldn't have passed up the chance for a million dollars, as they say. The roof looked like a colander to me. If that roof and the rain were running against each other at Bay Meadows, I'd bet on the rain and plan to spend my winnings at the World's Fair in Seattle.

My own experience with the Cleveland Wrecking Yard began two days ago when I heard about a used trout stream they had on sale out at the Yard. So I caught the Number 15 bus on Columbus Avenue and went out there for the first time.

There were two Negro boys sitting behind me on the bus. They were talking about Chubby Checker and the Twist. They thought that Chubby Checker was only fifteen years old because he didn't have a mustache. Then they talked about some other guy who did the twist forty-four hours in a row until he saw George Washington crossing the Delaware.

"Man, that's what I call twisting," one of the kids said.

"I don't think I could twist no forty-four hours in a row," the other kid said. "That's a lot of twisting."

I got off the bus right next to an abandoned Time Gasoline filling station and an abandoned fifty-cent self-service car wash. There was a long field one one side of the filling station. The field had once been covered with a housing project during the war, put there for the shipyard workers.

On the other side of the Time filling station was the Cleveland Wrecking Yard. I walked down there to have a look at the used trout stream. The Cleveland Wrecking Yard has a very long front window filled with signs and merchandise.

There was a sign in the window advertising a laundry marking machine for $65.00. The original cost of the machine was $175.00. Quite a saving.

There was another sign advertising new and used two and three ton hoists. I wondered how many hoists it would take to move a trout stream.

There was another sign that said:

THE FAMILY GIFT CENTER
GIFT SUGGESTIONS FOR THE ENTIRE FAMILY

The window was filled with hundreds of items for the entire family. *Daddy, do you know what I want for Christmas? What, son? A bathroom. Mommy, do you know what I want for Christmas? What, Patricia? Some roofing material.*

There were jungle hammocks in the window for distant relatives and dollar-ten-cent gallons of earth-brown enamel paint for other loved ones.

There was also a big sign that said:

USED TROUT STREAM FOR SALE.
MUST BE SEEN TO BE APPRECIATED.

I went inside and looked at some ship's lanterns that were for sale next to the door. Then a salesman came up to me and said in a pleasant voice, "Can I help you?"

"Yes," I said. "I'm curious about the trout stream you have for sale. Can you tell me something about it? How are you selling it?"

"We're selling it by the foot length. You can buy as little as you want or you can buy all we've got left. A man came in here this morning and bought 563 feet. He's going to give it to his niece for a birthday present," the salesman said.

"We're selling the waterfalls separately of course, and the trees and birds, flowers, grass and ferns we're also selling extra. The insects we're giving away free with a minimum purchase of ten feet of stream."

"How much are you selling the stream for?" I asked.

"Six dollars and fifty-cents a foot," he said. "That's for the first hundred feet. After that it's five dollars a foot."

"How much are the birds?" I asked.

"Thirty-five cents apiece," he said. "But of course they're used. We can't guarantee anything."

"How wide is the stream?" I asked. "You said you were selling it by the length, didn't you?"

"Yes," he said. "We're selling it by the length. Its width runs between five and eleven feet. You don't have to pay anything extra for width. It's not a big stream, but it's very pleasant."

"What kinds of animals do you have?" I asked.

"We only have three deer left," he said.

"Oh . . . What about flowers?"

"By the dozen," he said.

"Is the stream clear?" I asked.

"Sir," the salesman said. "I wouldn't want you to think that we would ever sell a murky trout stream here. We always make sure they're running crystal clear before we even think about moving them."

"Where did the stream come from?" I asked.

"Colorado," he said. "We moved it with loving care. We've never damaged a trout stream yet. We treat them all as if they were china."

"You're probably asked this all the time, but how's fishing in the stream?" I asked.

"Very good," he said. "Mostly German browns, but there are a few rainbows."

"What do the trout cost?" I asked.

"They come with the stream," he said. "Of course it's all luck. You never know how many you're going to get or how big they are. But the fishing's very good, you might say it's excellent. Both bait and dry fly," he said smiling.

"Where's the stream at?" I asked. "I'd like to take a look at it."

"It's around in back," he said. "You go straight through that door and then turn right until you're outside. It's stacked in lengths. You can't miss it. The waterfalls are upstairs in the used plumbing department."

"What about the animals?"

"Well, what's left of the animals are straight back from the stream. You'll see a bunch of our trucks parked on a road by the railroad tracks. Turn right on the road and follow it down past the piles of lumber. The animal shed's right at the end of the lot."

"Thanks," I said. "I think I'll look at the waterfalls first. You don't have to come with me. Just tell me how to get there and I'll find my own way."

"All right," he said. "Go up those stairs. You'll see a bunch of doors and windows, turn left and you'll find the used plumbing department. Here's my card if you need any help."

"Okay," I said. "You've been a great help already. Thanks a lot. I'll take a look around."

"Good luck," he said.

I went upstairs and there were thousands of doors there. I'd never seen so many doors before in my life. You could have built an entire city out of those doors. Doorstown. And there were enough windows up there to build a little suburb entirely out of windows. Windowville.

I turned left and went back and saw the faint glow of pearl-colored light. The light got stronger and stronger as I went farther back, and then I was in the used plumbing department, surrounded by hundreds of toilets.

The toilets were stacked on shelves. They were stacked five toilets high. There was a skylight above the toilets that made them glow like the Great Taboo Pearl of the South Sea movies.

Stacked over against the wall were the waterfalls. There were about a dozen of them, ranging from a drop of a few feet to a drop of ten or fifteen feet.

There was one waterfall that was over sixty feet long. There were tags on the pieces of the big falls describing the correct order for putting the falls back together again.

The waterfalls all had price tags on them. They were more expensive than the stream. The waterfalls were selling for $19.00 a foot.

I went into another room where there were piles of sweet-smelling lumber, glowing a soft yellow from a different color skylight above the lumber. In the shadows at the edge of the room under the sloping roof of the building were many sinks and urinals covered with dust, and there was also another waterfall about seventeen feet long, lying there in two lengths and already beginning to gather dust.

I had seen all I wanted of the waterfalls, and now I was very curious about the trout stream, so I followed the salesman's directions and ended up outside the building.

O I had never in my life seen anything like that trout stream. It was stacked in piles of various lengths: ten, fifteen, twenty feet, etc. There was one pile of hundred-foot lengths. There was also a box of scraps. The scraps were in odd sizes ranging from six inches to a couple of feet.

There was a loudspeaker on the side of the building and soft music was coming out. It was a cloudy day and seagulls were circling high overhead.

Behind the stream were big bundles of trees and bushes. They were covered with sheets of patched canvas. You could see the tops and roots sticking out of the ends of the bundles.

I went up close and looked at the lengths of stream. I could see some trout in them. I saw one good fish. I saw some crawdads crawling around the rocks at the bottom.

It looked like a fine stream. I put my hand in the water. It was cold and felt good.

I decided to go around to the side and look at the animals. I saw where the trucks were parked beside the railroad tracks. I followed the road down past the piles of lumber, back to the shed where the animals were.

The salesman had been right. They were practically out of animals. About the only thing they had left in any abundance were mice. There were hundreds of mice.

Beside the shed was a huge wire birdcage, maybe fifty feet high, filled with many kinds of birds. The top of the cage had a piece of canvas over it, so the birds wouldn't get wet when it rained. There were woodpeckers and wild canaries and sparrows.

On my way back to where the trout stream was piled, I found the insects. They were inside a prefabricated steel building that was selling for eighty cents a square foot. There was a sign over the door. It said

INSECTS

A PLACE
AT DAWN

◆　◆　◆

DATUS C. PROPER

OUR NATION'S CAPITAL IS NOT AN OBVIOUS PLACE TO LOOK FOR TROUT fishermen. It steeps in a region of humid air, dry rivers, low altitude, and high confusion. Most of the week, Washington frets about any-thing except fish. Put yourself in this situation, however, and tell me what you would like to do on the weekend. People are the same here. There must be somebody in the town who doesn't want to go fishing— perhaps even several such people, though I have not met them. What is new is that today's young professionals do not start with worms and sunfish, like the rest of us. When they have bought their cathedral-ceilinged townhouses and BMWs, the next thing they want is fly rods. Then they go to fishing schools and start taking up space on my favorite streams.

The change is for the good, I guess. We need the newcomers to vote for running water and care for it. It's just that they care so unanimously, every Saturday. If I wanted a social gathering, I'd go to a party—if there were anybody left in town to give parties.

Shall I tell you of a secret stream which, the biologists say, is underfished? Well, there are still a few hallucinating biologists around, but the underfished stream is halfway between Novosibirsk and Vladi-vostok. It has carp.

There is, however, a secret place in time. The time is when the moon has set and the rising sun is a deep red. My stream will be there, still secret, under the river mists of next summer's dawns.

Company is nice on long, dark trips, so a hard-driving buddy and I teamed up a couple of times last year. Getting there was half the fun. Maybe a little more than half: H.F. makes great conversation. He didn't take all that long to wake up, considering that this was three hours earlier than usual, and Lord knows he has a right to be tired. We spent some time rummaging up his tackle, then drove to the Quik &

Dirty for a breakfast of home-fried cholesterol, which improved his attitude. Strong coffee got the talk flowing, among other things. Coffee is a diuretic. Translation: It requires a stop half an hour down the road. By that time the caffeine was wearing off, so we tanked up again. Made it to the river after just one more stop.

I was only half-right about the yuppies' BMWs. The other half is four-wheel-drive trucks. When we got to the bridge, their 7.2-liter V-8s were already subduing the puddles in the parking pullout. That's when I knew that we were late—your huddled masses yearning to breathe free never show up till the fishing is over. The sun was throwing sharp shadows as I broke a record for the thousand-yard dash in chest waders. Somewhere upstream there had to be a trout working overtime. H.F. was running low on caffeine by now, so he fished near the car, and he said, later, that he'd had a good time, even if the trout failed to appreciate the sacrifices he'd made for them.

Those trips got us out of the town, all right, but they did not get the town out of us. We found a place on a map and lost the dawn.

Having run out of victims, I follow a different rhythm these days. It is Izaak Walton's. Perhaps he started to make sense on the third reading. More likely, I just got old enough to hear his advice: Study to be quiet.

◆   ◆   ◆

Listen to the ghosts. They move before the east begins to turn light on hot summer mornings. The first to appear are those you don't like: ghosts of in-baskets past, present, and future. Whether you like Washington or not—and I don't—you have to admit that people here work hard, then worry about not working more. An old college coach used to say that every hour of sleep before midnight was worth two afterward. I guess he knew that the ghost of work unfinished likes to rouse a fellow in the small hours.

You could put a pillow over your head and return to a sweaty sleep. You could go to work instead of fishing. Alternatively, you could call up a better variety of ghost. I call up the Pennsylvania limestone country, back when there was a cock pheasant crowing in each fallow field. I see spring creeks running full, without foam-plastic cups bobbing around. Vince Marinaro is moving upstream at first light with his cigar laying down a fog. I wish that he would hold still. I will go look for him at a few of the pools he showed me.

This kind of ghost is tuned into the right frequency, unlike my clock radio with its bad news. The distance between bed and car is short, and getting out of town is easy, too: All roads start in the capital, and no one is on them at this hour except me, a raccoon flashing his eyes just up the street, and a fox wafting across the beam of my headlights. Let's not count the puree of parkway opossum; 'possums should never attempt to waft. Except for them, the ghosts are comforting. Like other urban areas, Washington is a wildlife refuge, up to a point. You wouldn't expect grizzly bears. The BMW kids only welcome nature till it tears up the garbage.

I am awake. Not high, but not about to doze off, either. Coffee would make my sun rise early, but what goes up must come down, and I don't want to be down when the fish start rising. The ghosts are enough to keep me awake at the wheel.

There are plenty to look out for in the limestone country. Once it was covered with passenger pigeons, and there were elk, even bisons. When I first got here in the sixties, the buffaloes were gone but there were still so many pheasants, quail, and rabbits that we could hunt any old way and get what we craved for Sunday dinner. Now I slow, roll down the window, and let a humid breeze wash me clean of town. At the same time I breakfast on Proper's Patented Silent Sandwiches. The world is not ready for the recipe, but you can believe that they will sustain me through a day's fishing without lunch, if it comes to that. They will also let me drive, eat, and listen for cackling pheasants at the same time. I do not hear any. The limestone abundance is still there, but these days it seems to be expressed in grackles and starlings, which are surly before sunrise, like young professionals.

On a side road close to Vince's old Spring Run, the rabbits reappear in force. One of them seems to be playing with a gray squirrel or—more likely—discussing who's in charge around here. A woodchuck waddles for his hole when I slow down. He looks like me in waders. These are animals that thrive either on the farms or in suburbia, and the limestone country is now a mixture. Brand-new houses with brand-new trucks are just behind the fog. This used to be a country of properous small farms, nice to live in. More nice people want to live that way now. The old, red-roofed barns are still there, but the farmhouses are rented. The farmers are in Florida.

At this time between night and day, though, the town called York Springs looks about as it used to—the new money wants country, not old towns. There in Bosserman's Grocery, Ma's Kitchen, big old brick houses, little white frame houses built, perhaps, around cores of cabin logs. Just on the other side of the Appalachian Trail there is a spring where I will drink on the way home. It runs from hills where a few American chestnuts still live long enough to produce a sweet harvest. Tourists at the fruit stand are willing to pay more for the stale, glossy-hulled European chestnut; it is what they recognize.

Mist still hangs thick over Marinaro's favorite stretch of the

Spring Run. Good. The tricos-might hatch before dawn on a hot night with clear skies. "Trico" is short for the genus *Tricorythodes,* which is composed of very small mayflies that emerge in very large numbers. This is progress: Before the new sewage plant in Carlisle, the water was too polluted for mayflies or trout. Now the fish gorge from July through September. They eat till their stomachs are stuffed like fat black sausages, and then they eat till the food consumed two hours earlier is forced out their vents. As best I can tell from stomach samples, the trout eat almost nothing but tricos during these months. Of course, if I want to catch trout, I need to arrive before they start feeding. And if I want to catch them without giving away the secret, I need to sneak off before the trucks show up and somebody wants to follow me.

There is another reason for furtiveness: women. They appeared on this stream shortly after the mayflies and the trout. Each woman is accompanied by a man, and each pair is dressed in matching vests, khaki safari shirts, new caps, and shiny black fly rods. This, too, is progress. When women defend trout streams, politicians listen. Besides, the newcomers look nice in neoprene waders.

I do not measure up. The real me is hidden by a sweaty visor, a pair of flip-up sunglasses, a shirt that gave at the office, and army-surplus pants with one pocket converted to a patch. My rod has a kink from the time I glued its ferrule back in place. My image began to worry me when I noticed the girls scooting back toward their boy-friends as I stalked the banks. Then I saw how the hero dressed in a movie called *Revenge of the Nerds.* Everything became clear: I thought I was looking for trout, but the women thought I was looking for revenge.

This will change. Khaki paraphernalia comes on sale in September. I shall stock up, and next summer, ma'am, you will see a new man on the Spring Run. You are a civilizing influence.

Upstream, the spoor of the anglers dwindles quickly. They can't drive here. The bottom is rank with sedges, thistles, and wild snap-dragons; underfoot there are muskrat holes dropping suddenly to four feet of spring water. It is not a comfortable hike, and it's not beautiful, either—not like a brook-trout stream in the woods—but it's wild. A pheasant agrees. I hear the first of the day crowing, down in that jungle somewhere, then a second replying from far upstream. They complete the exorcising of Washington.

I stop to watch two big water snakes who have crawled on a jumble of logs blocking a side current. Last week I was casting to a sizable brown trout near here when a snake grabbed it by the tail. The trout got loose, but not till all three of us argued for a while. Now, while the snakes glare at me and I glare back, there is the faintest

movement at the edge of the scum above the logs. A minute later the
ripple comes again. I cast a little nymph over the logs, let it sink an
inch or so, and a trout takes innocently. It could tangle me, if it knew
what to do, but it does not, and it comes flapping over the logs before
it figures out what happened. It had been taking nymphs like a real
fish, but it is only a stocked rainbow, stubby fins betraying ignoble
birth. I release it downstream from the snakes, perhaps increasing its
life expectancy.

A trico dun drifts downstream, so I take a minute to change my
nymph to a low-floating winged fly. The mayflies will tell me what to
do from now on. This stream is supposed to be difficult to fish, and it
is, for the folks who get here after the rise. But now there are enough
duns to interest the trout and not enough to distract them from my fly.
They feel safe in deep, cool water. Humid air dims the low sun enough
to let me slip up and cast from a comfortable distance. It is a place to
renew my confidence that I am sometimes smarter than a fish—or at
least smarter than a stocked rainbow.

The stocked brown trout are not much more clever. They have
been in the stream over winter, but they come from a strain bred for
peaceful coexistence in the hatchery. Such fish should, I suspect, be
removed from the stream before spawning season, lest they mix their
genes with those of the wild population. The problem is that I would
feel obliged to eat them if I killed them. They do not taste very good.

Still, even decadent trout are worth chasing. But for them I
would never have learned to see the mayflies, which are still beautiful,
wild, and mysterious. How do the trico nymphs emerge from their
shucks? Why are there so few duns on the stream? And then why, a
little later, are there tens of thousands in the air? I see them by
squinting toward the light in the east: little disembodied wings glint-
ing in the air like sunbeams, duns molting for a second time, turning
into adults ready to mate and lay eggs and die. I tie on a spent spinner.
It imitates a falling sunbeam on a tiny hook.

Beneath overhanging clumps of grass, a bubble appears quietly,
floats downstream, repeats: the winking rise of a trout profiting from
death like me. My fly must land in the inches between two clumps and
float under others. It takes many casts. When everything works, the
fish takes, pulls harder than the rest, but comes flashing to the net.
This is a real trout—a stream-bred brown with fins like a butterfly's
wings and a bright rim of sunrise-red on the adipose. Tame trout don't
have that.

Back at the parking spot there is, of all things, a casting school
going on. Lefty Kreh is teaching. I am not making this up. Some of the
students are good, too. Reminds me that I have been meaning to learn

how to cast one of these days. Meanwhile, I try to sneak into the old
moss-colored station wagon. It is moss-colored because there is moss
growing on it. There is no truth, however, to the story that I forgot a
woodcock under the seat; I do not get enough woodcock to forget one.
Perhaps a silent sandwich did sneak off and hide one morning.

Next season, ma'am, you will see me in a new metallic-khaki
four-wheel-drive, capable of fording the worst humidity in the mid-
Atlantic. I'll still be evasive about the fishing, though. It is not a
secret, exactly, but I'd just as soon not spread the word that real trout
are in here. Besides, you might laugh if I tried to explain about an old
place upstream between moon and sun.

THE
CREEK

• • •

TONY DAWSON

MY RELATIVES STILL WHISPER ABOUT ME. THEY SHAKE THEIR HEADS disapprovingly and talk about a willful kid who squandered his childhood chasing rainbows. All right, I plead guilty to the "willful" part, but don't peg me for a dreamer. The rainbows I chased were iridescent—all red, gold, and green—but they also had spots and fins. And unlike their heavenly counterparts, these swimming bands of color gave me a priceless reward, the ability to appreciate nature's simple pleasures.

Why else, after thirty years, can I clearly recall the bluebird days when light diamonds and water striders danced on a Mill Creek riffle? The diamonds were only sun sparkles, and water striders—miniature rowing shells of the insect world—skittered through the light. Six delicate, oarlike legs propelled them easily against the current with a power that amazed me then . . . and does still.

Less pleasant, but equally valued, are memories of stone bruises, bug bites, sunburned thighs, barked shins, and the prickly warm feeling of blood flooding into a cold appendage. Like my relatives, you probably find that strange, and you may be right. On the other hand, I have an explanation. It was all tuition to the School of Piscatorial Pursuit, things to be loved or endured in exchange for basic fishing lessons.

In the late fifties and sixties, growing up in a conservative farming town in eastern Washington State offered some distinct benefits. Relatively insulated from troublesome times—drugs, the sexual revolution, and later, protests over the Vietnam War—kids could enjoy childhood. Best of all, the "great outdoors" and its mysteries lay just outside our small-town city limits.

That proximity encouraged my family to summer at our three-room cabin in the Blue Mountains, a short drive from town. Mule deer and elk wandered nearby ridges; ruffed grouse drummed and dusted near limpid valley streams brimming with rainbow trout and Dolly Varden. Only one stream, Mill Creek, ran near our summer retreat, and, when I was five, my excited parents took me to dangle a worm from a bridge across its course. For this, my first fishing adventure, they created a Rockwellian scene.

We made a "rod and reel" from a willow sapling, some twine, and a safety pin. While my mother distracted me, my father sneaked beneath the bridge to pin a store-bought rainbow to the end of my line. A few tugs later, I hauled in the predressed, skillet-ready prize, safety pin securely closed on its lips. No matter. The moment the trout hit the bridge planking, I was the one that was hooked.

For the next few summers, I hounded my father into occasional fishing excursions back to The Creek—our unofficial name for the only creek around. Though not an angler himself, my father felt a parental responsibility to encourage my interests. Besides, it was a good way to keep me occupied and out of mischief. He even presented me with a corroded, telescoping, steel fly rod and an old, spring-wound automatic fly reel, both rescued from the dark recesses of a neighbor's garage. Mustering all his fishing wisdom, he filled the reel with monofilament line.

Straight from hell, the collapsible "trunk rod" was made to fit handily into the trunk of a car and, believe me, that was its best feature. As for the reel, *if* the mechanism engaged, it retrieved the fine monofilament at lightning speeds. Often, the end result was a hook hanging in the rod tip as broken line whipped around the spool. Crude equipment? Absolutely, but high technology in the eyes of a child.

◆   ◆   ◆

My ninth summer was the beginning of independence. Still armed with the old, steel rod, and wearing the standard summer uniform for grade-schoolers—an old T-shirt and cutoff jeans—I explored alone, stalking native rainbows that finned riffles near the cabin. Though I didn't really notice at the time, that outfit had profound effects on exposed parts of my anatomy. One was "wader's tan," the dark-brown thighs and dead-white calves and shins acquired during long hours of standing in reflective, knee-deep water. Another was the ever-changing road map of scratches resulting from daily encounters with nettles and blackberry bushes. In addition, mosquitoes hovering near quiet water were absolutely merciless.

Another problem was the old, high-top tennis shoes that served as my official wading gear. Only sneakers battered and torn by wear could be sacrificed to such nonstandard duty. Treadless bottoms, missing eyelets, broken laces, and torn gaps between canvas tops and rubber soles were the most common defects. I wore the shoes sockless, to speed water drainage, and sometimes it seemed there was more gravel between my toes than in the creek. Unpadded ankles and bare shins were always black-and-blue from colliding with submerged rocks and logs. Without rod in hand, I suspect I looked more like a needy urchin than a budding fisherman.

It was difficult for a boy to learn the finer points of fishing without instruction. Initially, success came hard and was the result of persistence and the judicious use of natural baits. Early on, I learned that both trout and Dollys would take commercially prepared salmon eggs, but it was far more cost-effective to use the earthworms that could be found under streamside rocks. In the heat of summer, worms disappeared in search of moisture in deep soils. My renewed quest for bait eventually led from stream bank into the stream and to the small aquatic nymphs known locally as periwinkles. I would later come to know them as caddis nymphs, but, at the time, they were simply handy, free, and, once peeled from their odd casings, irresistible to The Creek's native rainbows.

One particularly snag-filled day, Providence introduced me to something closer to real fly-fishing. After losing my last, precious bait hook, I was delivered new terminal gear in the form of a weathered Royal Coachman wet fly snagged in shoreline brush. Its feather wings were split and frayed, and the body herl and floss were nearly unwound. I had never held an artificial fly before and found it mildly fascinating, but, in the pragmatic analysis of a young fishing fanatic, it was just another hook. The rescued fly, decorated with a fat periwinkle, was soon drifting through a nearby pocket of holding water.

The first cast brought a fat, fourteen-inch 'bow flashing across the current from a cross-stream rock shadow. The fish grabbed my beefed-up offering and bolted for its hideaway, firmly setting the hook. I was too stunned to do anything but hang on as the rainbow jumped repeatedly, valiantly fighting the current and my excited, inept maneuverings.

Moments later, I kneeled to examine the gasping fighter as it lay in the shallows, the bedraggled Coachman imbedded in its jaw. The lesson was not lost on my quick, young mind. *This fly-fishing stuff just might amount to something.* After all, the beautiful native was the biggest trout The Creek had ever given me. Still not a True Believer, I continued to fish with bait, but the seed had been planted.

Stronger reinforcement came in midsummer, after the last feathers had been torn from the old Coachman. Grasshoppers were everywhere, and I had discovered the joy of floating unweighted, live hoppers through my favorite riffles. Beautiful, pan-sized rainbows darted after nearly every one. The only problem was catching bait. Once the morning sun got the hoppers moving, cornering one of these winged acrobats took some real effort. After ten or fifteen minutes of chasing around a shoreline meadow, my hands would close on one of the exasperating insects. Then it would spit the brown saliva kids call tobacco juice on my fingers as I carried it to the stream and its fate.

One particularly hot day, I was on my skinned and bleeding knees in the dust—sweating, frustrated, my wet sneakers full of foxtails—when a shadow fell over me. I looked up into the friendly eyes of a silver-haired fisherman who seemed to have stepped from the pages of *Field & Stream.*

He removed a modestly brimmed hat and wiped his shining brow with a plaid shirt sleeve. The hat bore a small pad of sheepskin into which were hooked several artificial flies—one like the Coachman that had produced my biggest trout, and another that vaguely resembled the furious hopper spitting tobacco juice on my thumb.

A small landing net, fashioned from well-finished wood, dangled from a ring on his khaki fishing vest. Across his chest was the leather strap of a wicker creel riding near his right hip. A worn pair of hip boots encased his legs, and a delicate, long rod, its tiny eyelets festooned with a bright lime-green line, rode weightlessly in the crook of his right arm.

"Catch anything?" he asked, trying to treat me as a sporting equal while eyeing the hopper in my hand. "I'll bet the rainbows really like those grasshoppers." Too embarrassed to speak, I nodded and pointed to two fat ten-inchers lying on streamside moss.

"Nice going," he said. Then he smiled and added, "There is a fun way to catch fish without chasing hoppers. Would you like me to show you?" Again, I nodded. Not quite ready to allow my last captive to leap to freedom, I stood to watch him tie the grasshopper fly to the clear leader at the end of the fat, green line.

He walked to the edge of the riffle, and, with an elegant wave of rod, line and fly were airborne. A second flick of his wrist sent the fly to the edge of the current near a rock eddy. Almost instantly, there was the flash of a trout turning toward the offering. A split second before the fish reached the feather and hair hopper, the angler flicked his wrist again, lifting the fly from the water. To say I was impressed would be understatement.

"Here," he said, placing his beautiful rod in my hand. "You try for that fish."

Expecting the weight of my telescoping clunker, I tensed my small arm, but the fiberglass rod was featherlight. It was longer than my trunk rod and felt awkward at first, but I was soon whipping the hopper back and forth on a short line and wasted no time in getting it in the water. It landed ten feet from the trout's lair, but was instantly snatched by another feisty rainbow. The long, flexible rod let me feel the fish in a new, enjoyable way—every vibration and tail pulse transmitted to my hand; it also gave me more control. It was magical.

The fisherman netted the trout, worked the hook from its lip, and gently released it. Then he nipped the fly from the end of his line and laid it in my palm.

"It's a Joe's Hopper," he offered, without my asking. "Works great in midsummer when careless grasshoppers start falling into the creek. Just let it float past any rock that creates a little slack water. Keep it—see what it can do."

With that, he turned and waded the riffle, heading steadily upstream. As he rounded the next bend, he stripped some line and began false casting. Then he was out of sight.

I never met the fly-fisherman again, but I remembered the look of him down to the small patch on the back of one wader. Over winter, money saved from odd jobs permitted me to buy a tolerable double-taper floating line and a basic single-action reel. Considerable whining produced an eight-foot fiberglass rod the color of honey, a Christmas gift offered by resigned parents as much in the spirit of self-defense as holiday cheer. The wicker creel also under the tree was a total surprise.

In time, I became a fly-fisherman. I learned about tapered leaders, nail knots, roll casts, and double hauls. I recognized most popular Western fly patterns on sight and spouted the awkward mixture of numbers and letters describing fly lines the way most kids recited batting averages.

I also became a naturalist. Unconsciously, the cycle of aquatic insects, the dynamics of current flow, and the behavior and biology of the fish, mammals, and birds that frequented The Creek all became part of me. A growing curiosity led me to seek more formal answers to questions about nature. That pointed me toward college and a degree in biological science—training that is the basis for a career observing and interacting with nature.

As an adult, I have finally come to realize that The Creek was my summer companion, playground, teacher, and refuge for nearly a dozen years. That remarkable stream with an unremarkable name taught lessons that have flowed through the rest of my life. Long ago, I left eastern Washington for Alaska, where people literally live for the fishing. But it really doesn't matter where I stand. Whenever and wherever light diamonds play across the riffles, a part of me heads back to The Creek . . . and home.

MY
FISHING
POND

• • •

STEPHEN LEACOCK

IT LIES EMBOWERED IN A LITTLE CUP OF THE HILLS, MY FISHING POND.
I made a last trip to it just as the season ended, when the autumn
leaves of its great trees were turning color and rustling down to rest
upon the still, black water. So steep are the banks, so old and high the
trees, that scarcely a puff of wind ever ruffles the surface of the pond.
All around, it is as if the world were stilled into silence, and time
blended into eternity.

I realized again as I looked at the pond what a beautiful, secluded
spot it was, how natural its appeal to the heart of the angler. You turn
off a country road, go sideways across a meadow and over a hill, and
there it lies—a sheet of still water, with high, high banks, grown with
great trees. Long years ago someone built a sawmill, all gone now, at
the foot of the valley and threw back the water to make a pond,
perhaps a quarter of a mile long. At the widest it must be nearly two
hundred feet—the most skillful fisherman may make a full cast both
ways. At the top end, where it runs narrow among stumps and rushes,
there is no room to cast except with direction and great skill.

Let me say at once, so as to keep no mystery about it, that there
are no fish in my pond. So far as I know there never have been. But
I have never found that to make any difference. Certainly none to the
men I bring there—my chance visitors from the outside world—for an
afternoon of casting.

If there are no fish in the pond, at least they never know it. They
never doubt it; they never ask, and I let it go at that.

It is well-known hereabouts that I do not take anybody and
everybody out to my fishpond. I only care to invite people who can
really fish, who can cast a line—experts, and especially people from a
distance to whom the whole neighborhood is new and attractive, the
pond seen for the first time. If I took out ordinary men, especially men

near home, they would very likely notice that they got no fish. The expert doesn't. He knows trout fishing too well. He knows that even in a really fine pond, such as he sees mine is, there are days when not a trout will rise. He'll explain it to you himself; and, having explained it, he is all the better pleased if he turns out to be right and they don't rise.

Trout, as everyone knows who is an angler, never rise after a rain, nor before one; it is impossible to get them to rise in the heat; and any chill in the air keeps them down. The absolutely right day is a still, cloudy day, but even then there are certain kinds of clouds that prevent a rising of the trout. Indeed, I have only to say to one of my expert friends, "Queer, they didn't bite!" and he's off to a good start with an explanation. There is such a tremendous lot to know about trout fishing that men who are keen on it can discuss theories of fishing by the hour.

Such theories we generally talk over—my guest of the occasion and I—as we make our preparations at the pond. You see, I keep there all the apparatus that goes with fishing—a punt, with lockers in the sides of it, a neat little dock built out of cedar (cedar attracts the trout), and, best of all, a little shelter house, a quaint little place like a pagoda, close beside the water and yet under the trees. Inside is tackle, all sorts of tackle, hanging round the walls in a mixture of carelessness and order.

"Look, old man," I say, "if you like to try a running paternoster, take this one," or, "Have you ever seen these Japanese leads? No, they're not a gut; they're a sort of floss."

"I doubt if I can land one with that," he says.

"Perhaps not," I answer. In fact, I'm sure he couldn't: There isn't any to land.

On pegs in the pagoda hangs a waterproof mackintosh or two, for you never know—you may be caught in a shower just when the trout are starting to rise. Then, of course, a sort of cellarette cupboard with decanters and bottles, and gingersnaps, and perhaps an odd pot of anchovy paste—no one wants to quit good fishing for mere hunger. Nor does any real angler care to begin fishing without taking just a drop (*Just a touch—be careful! Whoa! Whoa!*) of something to keep out the cold, or to wish good luck for the chances of the day.

I always find, when I bring out one of my friends, that these mere preparatives or preparations, these preliminaries of angling, are the best part of it. Often they take half an hour. There is so much to discuss—the question of weights of tackle, the color of the fly to use, and broad general questions of theory, such as whether it matters what kind of hat a man wears. It seems that trout will rise for some hats, and for others not. One of my best guests, who has written a whole book on fly-fishing, is particularly strong on hats and color. "I don't think I'd wear that hat, old man," he says; "much too dark for a day like this." "I wore it all last month," I said. "So you might, but that was August. I wouldn't wear a dark hat in September; and that tie is too dark a blue, old man."

So I knew that that made it all right. I kept the hat on. We had a grand afternoon; we got no fish.

I admit that the lack of fish in my pond requires sometimes a little tact in management. The guest gets a little restless. So I say to him, "You certainly have the knack of casting!"—and he gets so absorbed in casting farther and farther that he forgets the fish. Or I take him toward the upper end and he gets his line caught on bulrush—that might be a bite. Or, if he still keeps restless, I say suddenly, "Hush! Was that a fish jumped?" That will silence any true angler instantly. "You stand in the bow," I whisper, "and I'll paddle gently in that direction." It's the *whispering* that does it. We are still a hundred yards away from any trout that could hear us even if a trout were there. But that makes no difference. Some of the men I take out begin to whisper a mile away from the pond and come home whispering.

You see, after all, what with frogs jumping and catching the line in bulrushes, or pulling up a waterlogged chip nearly to the top, they don't really know—my guests don't—whether they have hooked something or not. Indeed, after a little lapse of time, they think they did: they talk of the "big one they lost"—a thing over which any angler gets sentimental in retrospect. "Do you remember," they say to me months later at our club in the city, "that big trout I lost up on your fishpond last summer?" "Indeed I do," I say. "Did you ever get him later on?" "No, never," I answer. (Neither him nor any other.)

Yet the illusion holds good. And besides, you never can tell: There *might* be trout in the pond. Why not? After all, why shouldn't there be a trout in the pond? You take a pond like that and there ought to be trout in it!

Whenever the sight of the pond bursts on the eyes of a new guest, he stands entranced. "What a wonderful place for trout!" he exclaims. "Isn't it?" I answer. "No wonder you'd get trout in a pond like that." "No wonder at all." "You don't need to stock it at all, I suppose?" "Stock it!" I laugh at the idea. Stock a pond like that! Well, I guess not!

Perhaps one of the best and most alluring touches is fishing out of season—just a day or two after the season has closed. Any fisherman knows how keen is the regret at each expiring season—swallowed up and lost in the glory of the fading autumn. So if a guest turns up just then, I say, "I know it's out of season, but I thought you might care to take a run out to the pond anyway and have a look at it." He can't resist. By the time he's in the pagoda and has a couple of small drinks (*Careful, not too much! Whoa! Whoa!*), he decides there can be no harm in making a cast or two. "I suppose," he says, "you never have any trouble with the inspectors?" "Oh, no," I answer; "they never think of troubling me." And with that we settle down to an afternoon of it. "I'm glad," says the guest at the end, "that they weren't rising. After all, we had just the same fun as if they were."

◆   ◆   ◆

That's it: illusion! How much of life is like that! It's the idea of the thing that counts, not the reality. You don't need fish for fishing, any more than you need partridge for partridge shooting, or gold for gold mining. Just the illusion or expectation.

So I am going back now to the city and to my club, where we shall fish all winter, hooking up big ones, but losing the ones bigger still, hooking two trout at one throw—three at a throw!—and for me, behind it all, the memory of my fishing pond darkening under the falling leaves. . . . At least it has made my friends happy.

RUNOFF

• • •

THOMAS MCGUANE

THE FISHING LIFE IN MONTANA PRODUCES A PARTICULAR APPREHENSION
that affects fishermen like a circadian rhythm: irrational dread of runoff. Early spring is capable of balmy days; and though the water is cold,
the rivers are as benign as brooks in dreams, their pools and channels
bright and perfect. But year-round experience shows that in short
order they will be buried in snowmelt and irrigation waste, and their
babied low-water contours will disappear under the hoggish brown
rush. Once runoff begins, the weather is often wonderful. The cano-
pies of cottonwood open like green umbrellas. But it can be a long wait
before the rivers clear, a wait so long it seems possible to lose track of
the whole idea.

In early spring, it is time to begin when friends say, "I know I
should get out. I just haven't had the time." Here is the chance to
steal a march, to exercise those fish whose memory has been dulled by
the long winter. Crazy experiments can be undertaken at this time,
such as photographing a trout held in your left hand with a camera
held in your right hand. Before-the-runoff is time out of time; it is the
opportunity to steal fishing from an impudent year.

You can tell when you have started early enough when the first
landowner whose permission you ask stares at you with xenophobic
eyes. His first thought is that you are there to pilfer or harm his family.
Let him examine your rod and scrutinize your eyes. The eyes of a
fisherman are not so good; so keep them moving. Spot a bit of natural
history and describe it. Above all, don't say that your dad and your
granddad before you fished this same stretch at their pleasure. The
landowner of today does not like any surprising seniority just now.
He's having hell holding on to the place. Turn and go to your vehicle.
Don't back to it.

A sign of real desperation for me is when I begin to tie my own

262   Thomas McGuane

flies. I once made the simple accommodation that others do this better than I do, that they are meant to fill a fly need in others. They are professional fly-tyers and their monkish solitude is rendered habitable by the knowledge that their creations are helping all-thumbs types like myself drag hogs onto the gravel. But this compact with an invisible support team was something I could no longer honor by March; and I began to fill fly box after fly box with my crude Elk-hair Caddises, Griffith's Gnats, and Gold-ribbed Hare's Ears.

I wandered around the various forks of my home river, separated by many miles of rolling hills: One would be running off, the other clear, depending upon the exact kind of country it drained. I clambered down slick or snowy rocks to dangle my thermometer in the water. But in the spring there was, even on a snowy day, a new quality of light, as if the light had acquired richness that you could feel, that trees, grass, and animals could feel, a nutritious light coming through falling snow. There had come a turning point and now spring was more inexorable than the blizzards. I knew the minute this snow quit there would be someplace I could fish.

The next morning was still and everything was melting. I went to a small river out in the foothills north of where I live. This early in the year when I drive down through a ranch yard or walk across a pasture toward the stream, my heart pounds as it has all my life for a glimpse of moving water. Moving water it the most constant passion I've had; it can be current or it can be tide; but it can't be a lake and it can't be midocean where I have spent some baffled days and weeks more or less scratching my head. The river was in perfect shape, enough water that most of its braided channels were full. There were geese on the banks and they talked at me in a state of high alarm as they lifted and replaced their feet with weird deliberation.

As soon as I got in the river, I felt how very cold the water was. Nevertheless, a few caddises skittered on top of the water. An hour later, some big gray drakes came off like a heavenly message sent on coded insects, a message that there would indeed be dry-fly fishing on earth again. I am always saying, though it's hardly my idea, that the natural state of the universe is cold; but cold-blooded trout and cold-blooded mayflies are signs of the world's retained heat, as is the angler, wading upstream in a cold spring wind in search of delight. Nevertheless, the day had opened a few F-stops at the aperture of sky, a sign and a beginning. I caught one of the mayflies and had a long look: about a number 12, olive, brown, and gray the operative colors, two-part tail. I had something pretty close in my fly box, having rejected the Red Quill and the Quill Gordon as close but no cigar.

A couple of brilliant male mergansers went overhead. They are hard on fish and despised, but their beauty is undisputed. In a short time, they would migrate out of here and I didn't know where they went. They were referred to in Lewis and Clark's journals as the red-headed fishing duck, a better name.

The river combined in a single channel where the volume of water produced a steady riffle of two or three feet of depth. I started where it tailed out and worked my way up to where slick water fell off into the rapids. The mayflies were not in great numbers but they were carried down this slick and over the lip into the riffle. My staring magnified their plight into postcards of Niagara Falls, a bit of sympathetic fancy canceled by the sight of swirls in the first fast water. I cast my fly straight into this activity and instantly hooked a good rainbow. It must have been the long winter's wait or the knowledge that the day could end any minute; but I desperately wanted to land this fish. I backed down out of the fast water while the fish ran and jumped; then I sort of cruised him into the shallows and got a hand on him. He was a brilliant-looking fish, and I thought I could detect distress in his eyes as he looked, gulping, out into midair. I slipped the barbless hook out and eased him back into the shallows. Two sharp angles and he was gone in deep green water.

It started to cloud up and grow blustery. The temperature plummeted. I went back to my truck, stripped off my waders, put up my gear, and started home, past the black old tires hung on the fence posts with messages painted on them about cafés and no hunting. I kept thinking that the sort of sporadic hatch that had begun to occur was perfect for leisurely dry-fly fishing, if the weather had held. By the time I got to the house, it was winter again and I was trying to look up that dun, concluding for all the good it would do me, that it was *Ephemerella compar*. Even as I write this, I visualize a trout scholar in pince-nez rising up out of the Henry's Fork to correct my findings.

When you have stopped work to go fishing and then gotten weathered out, your sense of idleness knows no bounds. You wander around the house and watch the weather from various windows. From my bedroom I could see great gusts of snow, big plumes and curtains marching across the pasture. Did I really catch a rainbow on a dry fly this morning?

◆   ◆   ◆

The next day broke off still and sunny, and spring was sucking that snow up and taking it to Yucatán. I ran into a friend of mine at the post office who had seen a young male gyrfalcon—a gyrfalcon—hunting partridges on my place. In an hour, I was standing with my fly rod in the middle of a bunch of loose horses, looking off a bank into a deep, green-black pool where swam a number of hog rainbows. I had been there before and you couldn't approach the spot except to stand below where the slow-moving pool tailed out rather rapidly. The trouble was you had to stay far enough away from the pool that it was hard to keep your line off the tailwater that produced instantaneous drag. You needed a seven-foot rod to make the cast and a twenty-foot rod to handle the slack. They hadn't built this rod yet. It would have been a two-piece rod with a spring-loaded hinge driven by a cartridge in the handle with a flash suppressor. Many of us had been to this pool to learn why the rainbows had grown to be hogs who would never be dragged onto a gravel bar. They were going to stay where they were with their backs up and their bellies down, eating when they wanted to. I had to try it anyway and floated one up onto the pool. I got a drag-free drift of around three-eighths of an inch and went looking for another spot.

Geese and mallards flew up ahead of me as I waded, circling for altitude in the big bare tops of the cottonwoods. The air was so still and transparent you could hear everything. When the mallards circled over my head, their wingtips touched in a tense flutter and made a popping sound.

In a little back-eddy, caddises were being carried down a line of three feeding fish. I arranged for my fly to be among them, got a drift I couldn't begin to improve on, and a nice brown sucked it down. I moved up the edge of the bar to some more feeding fish. There were geese on the bar who had been ignoring me but now began to watch me and pace around. I noted one of the fish was of good size and it was feeding in a steady rhythm. I made a kind of measuring cast from my knees. The geese were getting more nervous. I made a final cast and it dropped right in the slot and started floating back to the good fish. I looked over to see what the geese were doing. The trout grabbed the fly. I looked back and missed the strike. I delivered an oath. The geese ran awkwardly into graceful flight and banked on around to the north.

This was a wonderful time to find yourself astream. You didn't bump into experts. You didn't bump into anybody. There were times when you could own this place in your thoughts as completely as a Hudson Bay trapper. The strangely human killdeer were all over the place. I considered them human because their breeding activities were accompanied by screaming fights and continuous bickering. When they came in for a landing, their wings set in a quiet glide while their legs ran frantically in midair. The trees in the slower bends were in a state of pickup-sticks destruction from the activity of beavers. A kingfisher flew over my head with a trout hanging from its bill. I came around a bend without alerting three more geese, floating in a back-

water, sound asleep with their heads under their wings. I decided not
to wake them. I ended my day right there. When I drove up out of the
river bottom in my car, I looked back to see a blue heron fishing the
back eddy where I'd caught a trout. On the radio were predictions of
high temperatures coming, and I knew what that low-country meltoff
would mean to my days on the river.

◆　　◆　　◆

Spring was here and it was hot. In one day it shot up to the
eighties. I could feel the purling melt come out from under the snow-
banks. Runoff was going to drop me in midstride.

I drove away from the places that I thought would get the first
dirty water, away from the disturbed ground. It was daybreak and out
on the interstate I found myself in a formation of Montana Pioneers,
driving Model Ts. This piquancy didn't hold me up long, and I soon
made my way to a wonderful little district where various grasses,
burgeoning brush, wildflowers, and blue-green strips of fragrant sage
had all somehow got the news that spring had sprung. The cover was
so deep in places that deer moving through it revealed only their ears,
which flipped up and disappeared. An old pry bar lay lost in the grass,
polished smooth by use. Ranchers never had the help they needed and
they were all masters of prying; these bars had the poetry of any old
tool, old dental instruments, old greasy hammers and screwdrivers
around a man's workshop, especially when the tool owner is not in
immediate evidence, or dead.

The river whispered past this spot in a kind of secretive hurry. I
got in and waded upstream, and sat on a small log jam to tie on a fly.
The logs under me groaned with the movement of current. I was
suddenly so extremely happy, the sight of this water was throwing me
into such a rapturous state of mind, that I began to wonder what it
could mean. I sometimes wondered if there wasn't something misan-
thropic in this passion for solitude.

I put my thermometer into the river, knowing already it was
going to come out in the forties. Taking the temperature of the river
is like taking your own temperature, the drama of the secret darkness
of the interior of your mouth; you wait and wait and wait long enough.
Is it ninety-eight point six or am I right in thinking I don't feel too
good? The water was forty-nine degrees, fairly acceptable for now.

Across from my seat on the log jam was an old cabin. These old
buildings along Montana trout rivers were part of their provenance,
part of what came back to you, like the wooded elevations that shaped
and bent and pushed and pulled each river so that as you tried to
recreate one in your mind that winter, there was always a point you

got lost, always an oxbow or meander where a kind of memory white-out occurred. I was always anxious to return to such a stretch and rescue it from amnesia.

· To reach my pool, I had to wade across the riffle above the log jam and then work my way around a humongous, dead, bloated cow, inflated to a height of five feet at the rib cage. The smell was over-powering, but I needed to get to that pool. There was a mule deer doe back in the trees watching me with her twin yearling fawns. One already was getting little velvet antlers.

For some reason, I was thinking how many angry people, angry faces, you saw in these romantic landscapes. It was as though the dream had backfired in isolation. There were the enraged visages behind pickup truck windshields with rifles in the back window at all seasons of the year. I remembered an old rancher telling me about a rape that had just occurred in Gardiner, and in his eyes was the most extraordinary mixture of lust and rage I had ever seen. He lived off by himself in a beautiful canyon and this was the sort of thing he came up with. A friend of mine from the Midwest looked at the chairs in a restaurant covered with all the local cattle brands and cried out in despair, "Why are these people always tooling everything?" The plea-sures of being seduced by the daily flux of the masses were not avail-able. All the information about the world had failed to produce the feeling of the global village; the information had exaggerated the feeling of isolation. I had in my own heart the usual modicum of loneliness, annoyance, and desire for revenge; but it never seemed to make it to the river. Isolation always held out the opportunity of solitude: The rivers kept coming down from the hills.

Having reached my pool, having forded the vast stench of the cow, I was rewarded with a sparse hatch of sulphur mayflies with mottled gray wings. I caught three nice browns in a row before it shut off. I knew this would happen. A man once told me, when I asked him when you could assume a horse would ground tie and you could go off and leave him, knowing he would be there when you got back: "The horse will tell you." When I asked an old man in Alabama how he knew a dog was staunch enough to break it to stand to shot, he said, "The dog will tell you." There are times for every angler when he catches fish because the fish told him he could; and times when the trout announce they are through for the day.

Two of the most interesting fish of the next little while were fish I couldn't catch. One was on the far side of a current that ran along the side of a log. The trout was making a slow porpoising rise. I managed to reach him and he managed to rise; but drag got the fly at the instant he took and carried the fly away. The next fish I saw, another steady feeder, rose to a Light Cahill. The dinner bell at a nearby ranch house rang sharply; I looked up, the fish struck, and I missed it.

I caught a nice rainbow by accident, which is the river's way of telling you that you've been misreading it. And then thunder and lightning commenced. I got out of the river. Bolting rain foretold the flood. I went up and sat under the trunk lid of my car, quite comfortably, and ate my lunch, setting a Granny Smith apple on the spare tire. The thermos of coffee seemed a boon almost to be compared to the oranges we kept on ice during the hot early weeks of bird season. The rain steadied down and I could watch two or three bends of the river and eat in a state of deep contentment. I didn't know of a better feeling than to be fishing and having enough time; you weren't so pressured that if you got a bad bank you couldn't wait until the good bank turned your way and the riffles were in the right corners. And the meal next to a stream was transforming, too, so that in addition to the magic apple there was the magic peanut-butter-and-jelly sandwich.

The rain stopped and I went down to where an irrigation ditch took out along a riprapped bank. I had a very nice Honduran cigar to smoke while I watched a heron fish the shallows. The air was still. I puffed a great cloud of smoke and it drifted across the little river; I imagined it was the ghost of my grandfather, who loved to fish. The ghost glided past the heron, who ignored him politely.

I just knew something was going on. There was a readiness. The rain had barely withdrawn. The sky looked so heavy you felt if you scratched it you'd drown. This was the storm that would loose the mountain snows, and the glistening fingers of this small river system would turn brown as a farmer's hand. Time, in its most famous configuration, was "running out." It could be the storm that made runoff really get under way, my last day on the stream for a good while. One had broken out of the pattern of home life and work and beaten inertia for the moment: might as well keep going.

I crawled down into a canyon made by the river. It was not far from where I had been fishing and the canyon was not that deep. But I needed both hands to make the descent, to lower myself from projecting roots and points of rock; and I had to throw the rod down in front of me because there was no good way to carry it. I found myself between tall cream-and-gray rock walls. The river flowed straight into dissolved chimneys, rock scours, solution holes, and fanciful stone bridges.

The sky overhead was reduced to a narrow band, and the storm had reformed over that. More killdeer conducted their crazed, weeping, wing-dragging drama around my feet. The storm became ugly and

I looked all around the bottom of the small canyon for a place safe to be. Lightning jumped close overhead with a roaring crack. The rain poured down, periodically lit up by the very close lightning. What little I knew about electricity made me think that bushes were a poor connection; so I burrowed into a thick clump of laurels and became mighty small, studied the laurel: round, serrated leaf, brownish-yellow bark, a kind of silvery brightness from afar. It had become very gloomy. By looking at the dark mouths of the caves in the far canyon wall, I could monitor the heaviness of the rain while the steady rattle on the hood of my parka filled in the blanks. I spotted a lightning-killed tree at about my level on the far side. The river had seemed so cheerful and full of green-blue pools. Now it was all pounded white by rain, and only the darker vees of current indicated that it was anything but standing water.

Then the air pressure could be felt to lift. The dark sky broke wide open in blue. An owl crossed the river, avoiding the return of light. The rain stopped and the surface of the river was miraculously refinished as a trout stream. I looked at the drops of water hanging from my fly rod. I thought of the windows of the trout opening on a new world and how appropriate it would be if one of them could see my fly.

The standing water along roadsides in spring was a wonderful thing. On the way home, I saw a flight of northern shoveler ducks, eccentric creatures in mahogany and green: and off in a pasture stock pond, teal flew and circled like butterflies unable to decide whether to land. I wondered what it was about the edges of things that is so vital, the edges of habitat, the edges of seasons, always in the form of an advent. Spring in Montana was a pandemonium of release. There were certainly more sophisticated ways of taking it in than mine. But going afield with my fishing rod seemed not so intrusive and the ceremony helped, quickened my memory back through an entire life spent fishing. Besides, like "military intelligence" and "airline cuisine," "sophisticated angler" is an oxymoron. And if it weren't, it would be nothing to strive for. Angling is where the child, not the infant, gets to go on living.

It was ten minutes to five. There was absolutely no wind. I could see the corners of a few irrigation dams sticking up out of the ditches. The cottonwoods were in a blush of green. I was ready for high water.

MENUNKETESUCK JUSTICE

• • •

EDWARD R. RICCIUTI

ABOUT SEVENTY-FIVE FEET FROM OUR LIVING ROOM TELEVISION, BEFORE which each autumn I experience the thrill of victory and the agony of defeat while watching Notre Dame on the gridiron, lies a mudhole of a man-made pond, backed by a seasonally flooded oak and maple swamp. We bought our house in the country some twenty years ago *because* of that soggy land, which I have proudly stewarded.

I love those sloshy eight acres, to me an estate, but which a grizzled local farmer once described, to my dismay, as a "city lot." Ruffed grouse haunt the tangled edges. Deer runs lace the sweet pepperbush. Pileated woodpeckers knock at the dead oaks, in which wood ducks sometimes nest. One night this winter I turned on the outside spotlight and saw four raccoons, two opossums, and a whitetail within fifty feet of the house.

The swamp dries up in summer. So did the pond, once. Mostly, though, it just shrinks to a mucky goo, with a foot or two of water pooled in the deepest part—about seven feet below my lawn, which I am trying to naturalize so it need not be mowed.

The pond makes my life enjoyable in myriad ways. It is recognized on an official piece of paper from Town Hall as a firehole, from which the volunteers could fill up their tanker truck in case of conflagration. My home-insurance payments are lower because of it. Maybe that's why almost everybody has a pond. Dick and Dixon down and across the road (it's called Roast Meat Hill Road, but that's another story) have one. On Stevens Road, around the corner, Harry has one, where his cows drink. So, I think, do the Waltons—honestly, that's their name—and Big Tom, west of them. Where Stevens joins the state highway, Larry, at the post-and-beam company, just dug one, which he claims is going to hold trout. I wonder. I saw it today and if it were mine I'd call it Big Muddy.

If disaster ever happens when my pond is low, I hope the tanker pumps can handle mud and dead swamp-maple leaves, not to mention an old snow shovel and some toy soldiers my son tossed into the water ages before he stood more than six feet tall, weighed 220 pounds, bought a motorcycle, and spent his days thinking of ingenious new ways to worry me, nights.

Mostly, I love the pond because amphibians, my favorite creatures, and reptiles, second to my liking, frequent it. Wood frogs, spring peepers, spotted salamanders, green frogs, bullfrogs, leopard frogs, northern water snakes, painted turtles—you name it—live and breed there.

Moments before I began writing this, in late March, I heard the quacking calls of the wood frogs and the sleigh-bell sounds of the peepers, and then walked to pondside and saw the masses of spotted-salamander eggs, each encased by its own capsule of jelly within a greater mass of transparent goo. By the time I finished the writing, the water was churning with bullfrog tadpoles, fresh from wintering over. They enticed Wilbur, my doofy white cat, to jump in. This was his first spring. He learned the hard way, at least, for a cat.

The pond teems with bluegills and largemouths; some of them were brought in as eggs on duck feet, others were stocked after the last time the pond dried up. Some of the bluegills reach a hefty size. Most of the bass are little buggers, but a few grow to a pound or two, not all that bad for a backyard New England mudhole.

Once I caught a big white catfish in the lower Connecticut River, six miles away. I put it in a bucket of water and brought it home. My wife turned up her nose in distaste. That hurt. Her great-grandfather was a lieutenant in the First Alabama Infantry during the Civil War. When I met Chiqui, she lived in Tennessee. I had expected her, with her Southern roots, to react to the catfish with as much relish as I would to a plate of polenta.

I let the catfish go in my pond. He—as a certified male chauvinist, I considered that magnificent fish of masculine gender—prospered. Every so often all summer, I'd see him, gulping air or lying in the shallows waiting for an unwary bullfrog tadpole. Sometimes, I thought he regarded me with a kind of cold-blooded camaraderie.

The next summer, I found him again. I had tossed out a worm to catch a bluegill or little bass. That catfish almost ripped the rod out of my hands. After I brought him to land, I tenderly removed the hook and let him go, affectionately. I thought I saw him wink as he vanished into the murk.

I never saw him again. I know, however, that he survived until

August. That was when those two young buccaneers Jake and Nate arrived. Their full names are Jacob and Nathaniel, and their father claims, with some proof, to be a descendant of Captain Edward Teach, otherwise known as Blackbeard the Pirate. To my mind, his and his children's subsequent actions testified in behalf of his assertion. Father, who has even less competence than I do with rod and reel, had decided to teach the boys to fish. So, I invited Jake and Nate to try for bluegills in my pond. And then I went off to run some errands.

They scored. Big. Really, really big. When I arrived home, my wife told me, "They caught a big catfish." They sure did. They caught my catfish, took it home, and cooked it. My catfish! And they said he tasted like mud.

It was a case of the chickens coming home to roost in the small forms of Jake and Nate, not to mention their father, the one I've always suspected really caught the fish, or more probably, snagged it by accident. He couldn't catch a flounder in a fish market. Jake and Nate had been sent to gain retribution by whatever deities govern the ethics of gentlemanly angling. You see, I had committed an angling abomination some seventeen years before, an abomination visited upon a beautiful fish in the stream that I consider my fly-fishing home waters.

◆　◆　◆

The stream, the Menunketesuck River, is located a quarter mile away from my pond, and just a week ago as I write this, I caught several brown trout and a brookie there, while in the woods a grouse boomed. About ten years ago, at ten A.M. on New Year's Day, with open water remaining in the river, I caught a native brookie, perhaps the first trout taken that year in the state of Connecticut. Last summer, Freddie, at the beer store, told me that he was after a whopper brown in a certain pool south of the new state highway bridge. I ran down there with my spinning rod and caught it on a mealworm. I put it on the bank and kept fishing. Freddie, naturally, hadn't told me about the three yellow-jacket nests next to the pool. A few minutes later, I turned and found Freddie's trout covered with the hungry yellow-and-black insects, and a bunch more homing in on it. They ate the fish. I ate crow.

At any rate, the Menunketesuck is a small stream, maybe thirty feet across at its widest sections, much less along most of its ten or so miles before it reaches Long Island Sound. Woodland borders most of the stream, which as it flows toward the salt water rushes over several moss-encrusted stone dams, some dating to colonial times. A short walk from the west bank one can find the foundation of the house where the missionary Titus Coan, said to be the first to bring good Christian living to Hawaii, was born. The dirt road on the south side of my land bears his name.

Shortly before we moved into our house, the former owner took me down to the river, extolled the fishing there, and showed me the dam. Most of the dams on the river had been breached long ago. But this one remained standing. About five feet over my head, water cascaded over its crest, falling in thin, shimmery sheets past the mossy stone and into a few small pools. There, the river was only about fifteen feet across, although it widened again about fifty yards downstream.

Some weeks later, as spring was moving toward summer and we were living in the house, I took fly rod in hand and headed down the path to the dam. Given my abysmal ineptitude with a fly rod, it was an act of supreme presumptuousness, or perhaps optimism. A professional fly-rodder I know once called me the Dark Prince of Fly-fishing. That was after a colleague, writing in the *Atlantic Salmon Journal*, described me fly-fishing in Yugoslavia as looking and sounding like a "crazed Buddhist monk in a Grade B karate movie." Granted, my skull is shaved and I have engaged in karate. But crazed? Well, maybe when I get excited, which is often.

Still, the setting by the dam was the type that merited the use of a fly rod rather than my customary spinning rig with worms, and it was spring in the country. After moving from suburbia, that first spring in our new country home had been delightful. Fishing rods replaced shotguns on the gun racks in pickup trucks. A great blue heron visited the pond. A grouse walked through the backyard. A pair of red-shouldered hawks courted in the sky overhead and nested at the edge of Clarkson's field, across the dirt road, as they have every year since. And there, in a pool below the dam, lay a handsome rainbow trout, probably stocked by the state upriver, but in view of its fifteen-inch length, not that season. Perfect.

I unlimbered the fly rod—no small task for me—and tied on something or other with fuzzy wings, then dumped it into the water. It hit with a *splat* amidst a swirl of fly line. The trout never even looked. Half an hour later, the fish hadn't moved and I had lost the something-or-other in a tree. I went home.

Undaunted, I returned each morning for the next three days. Each day, I found the trout—and it ignored my indelicate presentations.

It was the morning of the fifth day. And I had a number 10 hook tied where a fly is supposed to be. Wriggling on that hook was an energetic garden worm. I flipped that worm into the froth at the base of the dam. It drifted a few feet until it was in clear, calm water right over the fish's snout.

That night, I ate a rainbow trout with flesh as pink as lox. It was an undeservedly inglorious fate for a fine fish. But justice would eventually be served. I know that in some mysterious way that meal later cost the life of my friend the catfish. And they said he tasted muddy. It served *them* right, too.

LOVE AFFAIR

DENNIS BITTON

IT BEGAN INNOCENTLY ENOUGH, IN MY YOUTH. WE MET, GOT AC-
quainted, and made some fond memories. Later, in my teens, we
became more intimate—I drank a little deeper, got hooked a little
more. Then there was a period of separation of many years. When we
did meet again, it was offhand and distant for a few years, even though
we were now physically close together. Finally, I decided to take the
plunge. I'd get to know her better, no matter what it took. Well, that
was several years ago, and since that initial decision to get better
acquainted, I've made an investment in time, attention, and dedication that only another lover could appreciate. Ours is a relationship of
give-and-take, a relationship I wouldn't trade for anything. And my
charmer is no lady, she's a river. My river.

My river is the South Fork of the Snake River in Idaho's southeastern corner, next to the Wyoming line. I live in Idaho Falls, Idaho,
at the mouth of the canyon where the South Fork leaves the mountains and enters Idaho's vast desert plain. There she's robbed by
irrigation canals of more than half her volume before she joins another famous Idaho stream, the Henry's Fork, to form the Snake
River. Robbed, diverted, and dammed, she never gets to be what she
could be.

Still, in her upper stretches, the South Fork provides some of the
best fishing for cutthroats that can be found anywhere. There are
brown trout here, too, big ones. But it's the cutts that attract the
fly-fisherman. On a good day, a competent fly-fisherman can take forty
cutthroats. And more than half of them will be more than sixteen
inches long. They may well take a simple mayfly pattern like a Light
Cahill, or my favorite, the Renegade dry fly. I prefer a number 14. We
also use another Renegade pattern on the South Fork, the Super
Renegade. A repulsive thing of two-colored chenille, and three

different-colored webby feathers, it's an attractor wet fly. Fished from a drifting McKenzie boat, tight up against brushy and rocky banks, it can produce slow, quiet takes from cutts and violent, thrashing ones from browns.

Admittedly, you will fish twenty days a season to have two perfect days, but the potential is there. That's the important part. The South Fork is alive, and she responds to those who fish her well. Full of native Snake River cutthroat trout, she may well be the only river in the world that has a good supply of both native trout and brown trout within her banks. I'm prejudiced of course, but she deserves the praise.

In the summers she flows at 10,000 cubic feet per second. Often, in the spring, she'll run twice that size, ripping at her banks and rerouting her own flow. During the winter, the Bureau of Reclamation (rhymes with *wreck*) runs her down to 1,000 cfs or less. That exposes her too much, and every year thousands of fish die in her side channels while irrigators dewater her for next year's potato crop.

Still, she's a survivor. I once had a Fish and Game official tell me that his studies of the South Fork, going back forty years, indicated that man had tried everything he could to destroy this river, but that she kept coming back year after year because of her size. She heals her own wounds, despite man's intervention and interference.

The South Fork of the Snake River starts just fifty miles from my home, at the base of Palisades Reservoir in Swan Valley, Idaho. My grandfather's brother had a ranch there. When my father was growing up, his father took him to Swan Valley to visit and fish. When I came along, my father did the same with me. That's how I became so familiar with the South Fork in my youth and teens. It was a family tradition.

In the fifties and sixties, the South Fork was less crowded than she is now. But she didn't necessarily provide better fishing. The South Fork has always had a local meat fishery. Folks came here to kill fish. Only in the mideighties, when the Fish and Game Department felt compelled to put on a slot regulation and limit the wanton killing of cutthroat, did the fish population start to take on some size. The slot regulation was quite simple, actually: Any cutthroat between twelve and sixteen inches had to be released. And barbless hooks had to be used on all portions of the river where the slot was in effect. It was designed to provide surviving spawners. That would protect the cutthroat's future and provide recreation for fishermen.

The impact was dramatic. I remember it well. I was fishing with two of my friends late in July, just a few weeks after the regs had gone into effect in early June. Usually, you'd take a few fish of eight to fourteen inches during such a day's fishing and be satisfied. On this day, after several hours of slow action, we found a side channel where the water was relatively shallow and we could see fish rising to flies on the surface. We agreed to take turns in one nice riffle. One of us stepped into position, made a cast, and immediately had a cutthroat on. He moved down to the tail of the pool and the next guy took the beauty spot. Each of us hooked up about six or seven times, in the same pool with successive fish, and all of the fish were about sixteen inches long, heavy, deep, and very, very feisty. We figured they were churning up the pool so much that each fish would be the last. But it lasted a long time and we took a lot of nice fish.

Experiences like that make lasting impressions. The three of us looked at each other and shook our heads. Collectively, we thought we knew this river well. But the river had far more potential than we'd given her credit for. She'd just given us a glimpse of some spectacular fishing in one side channel, fishing less than fifty feet of running water. The river is almost sixty miles long. In that sixty miles, the number of side channels and high gravel bars in the middle of the river where you could fish for pods of fish, as we did that day, is staggering. The South Fork is a giving river.

But there's more to a love affair with a river than numbers. There's a spirit here. Born, bred, and raised with controversy, strife, and dissension, the South Fork remains serene. Indeed, many of us use the South Fork to reduce stress. Sometimes we fish her two days a week. Some question our judgment.

"How can you fish the same river, day after day?" they challenge. "Don't you get tired of catching all those dumb cutthroat? Don't you want to experience something different? Why don't you fish the Henry's Fork or Silver Creek? They're the famous waters in Idaho."

Well for one thing, no matter how often you fish the South Fork, she's not the same. The river's flows are constantly fluctuating, with daily changes in discharges from Palisades Dam. That, along with the daily changes in temperature, barometric pressure, wind, and sunshine, make her moody. Even if you're with her every day, you can't predict how she'll react to changes. You may know and love her, but you'll never completely understand her, never truly possess her.

Take the fish, for example. Given a large volume of water to move around in, they do just that. One day's glory hole may be the next day's empty pool. And the fish respond to pressure. Years ago, you could catch Snake River cutthroat relatively easily. With an increase in the number of fishermen using the river, that's no longer true. You now face the very real possibility of watching a hundred fish a day move to your fly and reject it. I've seen grown men curse, throw things, almost cry. After twenty to thirty rejections from a dozen fish in just one pool, you begin to wonder if the river isn't really just a tease.

On those days when everything works, though, you know the river is at least a good friend, if not a lover. I had one of those experienced outdoor-writer types visit me one summer. I told him before he got here that he might experience a twenty-to-forty-cutthroat day. He didn't seem impressed. Well, my river delivered for him the day we fished. After the thirtieth fish on a number 16 Elk-hair Caddis, my guest was still enthusiastic, definitely not bored or tired of catching fish, and making plans for a return visit. I was proud—proud that my river had produced for me when I wanted her to, proud that she hadn't ditched me when I needed her.

It's not always that easy. I've had days when I was skunked on the South Fork. She's disappointed me a number of times. She's scared me a few times, too. I sank my boat on her one day. She took just one second to fill my boat to my armpits. And I was standing up at the time! She drowns a few people every year, but lets a lot more of them off the hook, spares them despite their idiotic performances.

I've had days when everybody was catching fish but me. I've had days when I was catching so many fish it actually became embarrassing. I've had days when the fish would hit anything I threw at them, and I've had days when matching the hatch became a science at the doctorate level. They'd hit just one fly, in one size, period. And you always seem to have just one or two of those particular flies with you. The South Fork knows. She always knows.

The South Fork demands respect. You have to give her time. You have to pay attention to her. If you fish her willy-nilly, she'll not respond. If you treat her right, she'll treat you well.

I've had a lot of memorable days on the South Fork of the Snake River. There was the day we drifted up on a cow moose and her calf, browsing in the streamside vegetation. The wind was in our face, and the calf saw us but the mother didn't. We came within twenty feet before she noticed us and hurriedly ushered her calf through the willows, up the bank, and out of sight.

I've watched young bald eagles play tag in the sky, as high as five hundred feet and as few as fifty feet above the South Fork. I've drifted my boat right underneath eagles perched in trees, with young in their nests. I've watched ospreys fold their wings, drop like arrows into the water, and come out with fish—sometimes, big fish. They always swing the fish around to face in the direction they're flying.

I remember taking a good friend fishing and having him hook up with a one-in-a-million, solid-colored cutthroat that looked for all the world like a goldfish. I forgot to take a picture, I was in such a rush to get the fish released safely.

I remember a thirty-inch brown trout that took a number 16 dry fly and came out of the water like a tarpon. I screamed like a nine-year-old boy, it scared me so.

I remember looking out over a piece of water and seeing twenty to thirty rises at once and trying to decide which fish to cast to. I remember working over one fish for hours. I remember staying put in one spot and catching twenty fish without moving twenty feet.

I remember sunsets that would challenge Kodak. I remember a rainstorm that was so heavy and so localized that others on the river wouldn't believe we got that wet standing up.

I remember falling down in the South Fork, too. I remember watching friends and family falling down in the South Fork. I remember when one of my sons realized he was about to fall and voluntarily sat down so that he'd at least know where he was and what he was doing.

I remember days when we caught rainbows, browns, large-spotted cutts, fine-spotted cutts, whitefish, and brook trout. I remember successfully fishing the salmon-fly hatch with Super Renegades that didn't match the hatch at all.

I remember the day when my cousin's rod came up missing in the boat. As best we could figure, he had left a fly dangling over the edge and a fish took the fly and the rod.

I remember the laughter and pure joy that people experience when they visit the South Fork for the first time. I remember introducing some people to their first fish on a fly.

I remember particular fish at particular spots. I remember the nine-and-a-half-pound brown that felt like a train engine on the end of my line. I remember the cutts lying in the snow when we beached them during a day's fishing in October.

I remember days on the river with nobody else around. It was just me, my buddy, and the river. We make quite a trio. With any luck at all, this relationship will last a long time yet.

I love the South Fork of the Snake River. It started the day I made a commitment to her. My wife knows about it, and she approves. My children understand. My friends understand. Even my mother understands. This is one love affair that didn't go wrong.

NIGHT
SHIFT

• • •

STEVEN A. GRIFFIN

A MUCKY, SMELLY, TANGLED TRAIL SNAKES THROUGH A CEDAR SWAMP
from a road-end that is almost big enough to hold two cars. Every
footfall comes with the risk of plunging knee-deep into Michigan
quicksand. Slime drips from waders when the path finally climbs a
little hill and then slides down to the river's edge. The water flows
clear, the bottom is rocky, and the cool river chills rubber-clad, sweat-
soaked feet.

A whitetail doe wades, too. Earlier she had walked through
streamside greenery into the river, where a patch of weedy growth
caught her interest. Now she pokes her head beneath the surface a
quarter-minute at a time. Water runs off her neck and weeds dangle
from her mouth as she straightens and chews her salad as sloppily as a
three-year-old kid forking spaghetti.

Whitetails fear land-borne humans, but not those who walk in
the water. So I wade downstream, ever closer to the deer, until only
forty yards separate the two of us. The doe eats helping after helping,
until finally she walks resentfully into the brush, and I shuffle downstream another hundred yards to a hole that should hold big brown
trout. The river will provide the deer's meal tonight, but not this
fly-rodder's. I just want to work the night shift and won't demand
wages in trout. If there's a fight, the fish will swim away from it,
winner or loser.

Hexagenia limbata, giant Michigan mayflies, may rise from the
river tonight. From eggs laid a year ago hatched wigglers that spent
more than eleven months burrowed into mud, sand, and gravel.
Maybe on this steamy summer night they'll swim to the surface, split
their skin, and take flight. If so, they'll return in a few days to lay
another generation of eggs and then die in the surface film.

Brown trout work both ends of this life-and-death drama. Forget about those browns of lore and literature, delicate nibblers of tiny insects. When these big flies come, the trout emerge from the safe lairs where they spend most of their time. They swim in midriver, gulping down as many hatching or returning flies as they can. They're saps, too, for fake mayflies.

But these gourmand browns are hard to catch, for these big bugs are bugs of the night. The action starts at full dark. Not sundown or dusk or twilight. Dark. Can't-see-the-river-bottom dark. Can't-see-your-fly-line dark. Can't-tell-what's-making-that-noise-in-the-bushes dark. Night-shift fishermen usually arrive early, play small fish with small flies for a couple of hours, and wait for the dark, glancing often above the river in hopes of seeing giant flies aloft. A can of beer fished out of a vest's back pouch quickly grows beads of sweat in the muggy air. The beer disappears as the daylight does, slowly, deliberately.

I once worked in a chair-making factory where discipline followed a prescription. The first time you showed up late, left early, goofed off, or broke a similar, relatively minor rule, your foreman wrote a letter of reprimand and placed it in your file. Second offense, second letter. Third offense, you went on the night shift, joining other troublemakers and the firm's newest workers.

In late afternoon the plant reached full heat, sunlight stored in its concrete walls. Ceiling fans only made sure that everyone was equally oppressed. Welding and painting and sweating filled the hot air with smells. It was a good place to leave when the day's work was done. The night shift's workers flashed outlaw smiles as they milled around the time clock. Among those they passed on their way in were home-bound big bosses and office workers, the "white shoes" who monitored the daytime world.

Radios played better music at night. Lunches packed more seasoning. Intercoms told better jokes. Nighttime supervisors were young, eccentric, or both. And night shift paid a little higher wage. After days, weeks, months, or years, the summons to day shift would come. And some transplanted workers would start figuring how to acquire two warning letters and another spell of night shift.

A trout stream's night shift it just as relaxed as that factory's. At full dark, nobody knows how you're dressed, how you're equipped, or how you cast. Unless you're creeling trout, nobody knows how accurately or honestly you measure a fifteen-inch brown. The big shots who know the Latin names of bugs and how to tie ninety-three knots and which quaint fly shops serve which far-flung famous rivers have gone home. They'll come back tomorrow to polish the image of sport and stream. Meanwhile, they've left you trying to shake life into a balky flashlight; trying to reach a mosquito boring into the middle of your back; trying to find stuff in the devil's fishing vest—yours was neatly organized. But the sun fell and finding anything has become a game of feelies.

You will too often grab your flashlight and cast its light across the river in a fish-alarming search for bugs. On many nights, the flies aren't there. Hot nights, muggy ones, bring the best hatches, and then only for a few days. Finding those few days is the problem. You can pick a date, any date, in late June and early July. Or you can call fly shops for updates. Your odds of hitting the hatch on any particular evening are about the same either way. So you just go when you can.

Tonight the hatch started, then stalled. Other fly-rodders iden-tified smaller, twilight bugs and picked fish-fooling imitations from their fly boxes. I was glad enough to watch deer, to cast the coils out of a neglected fly line, and, when the lights went out, to consider the sounds and smells of this river.

I could name this river, but I might be wrong. One of my best friends first brought me here and made me promise not to disclose the spot. In the years since, I've learned which dirt roads to follow to get here, but I've never overlaid my mental map on a paper one to learn the names of the roads and verify the name of the river. It's more important to know the river than its name. And I know this river when the night turns first black, then gray under a rising moon. I know what it means when the river gurgles louder unseen, and I know the *cherrk* sound of a feeding fish fifteen feet away.

Earlier I had picked a funny-looking, fuzzy bug from the fly box, a fly nowhere near as graceful as the mayflies that occasionally drift downstream. I tied it onto a stout leader. Now I sloppily slap it down on the water. Another *cherrk* and the line draws tight, a fat trout fighting what it thought would be an easy meal. Stream browns don't really fight long, and this one soon swims on a short leader alongside me. I reach to grasp and unhook it and laugh when I find that in the dark it's darted ten feet away. Again the fish comes in; this time it swims away free.

But the handful of *Hex* that brought the trout and me together was another tease. No more flew or floated. No more browns broke the surface film. "Did you ever really hit this hatch right?" one of our group will ask a couple of hours later as we trudge upstream in the black night. "Yah, once or twice," will come the reply with a laugh. "And that was when I didn't expect it." You can watch the calendar and the water temperature and the air temperature and the humidity and stack all the known odds in your favor. And when you catch the big-bug hatch with perfect timing, it comes as a surprise, like most things about night-shift fishing on this midsummer stream.

Beavers slap tails on the midnight water, stalling hearts and jump-starting bladders. Bats circle overhead, challenging rational understanding and nurturing B-movie fear. At least you can see and identify those creatures. The river is populated mostly with sounds, and I know what makes them only as I know the name of the river: because someone who apparently knows more told me. I am surer that some of the other things they tell me are true.

I kicked up a cloud of sand when I stepped from a moss-covered log into the river at dusk. As the sediment wafted downstream, tumbling over a gravel lip into a waist-deep hole, I felt as if I'd farted in church. The hole looked innocent, a place for cheerful water to pause between sprints over gravel or silt. But at dusk it sulks like a predator, waiting for careless prey to wander too close. The friend who first brought me here, who may or may not have told me the river's right name, was that prey a few years ago. Now he cinches a belt around his waders and wanders less. He sent me to this hole. He's happy to watch, as the light fades, for insects flying above a smooth run fifty yards upstream. He watches the surface. And then it's dark, and he listens. A feeding trout's *cherrk* is answered by the splash of deer hair on a fifteen-foot tether. Good cast.

Many fly-rod rules are suspended as the fishing calendar flows through June. The flies are big, the trout are hungry, and the best fishing is at night. Anglers who usually count on finesse now rely upon nerve. Fish a spot, not a stretch. Pick a spot on your home water, a place you know, so that you can find your way back to the car at night's end, even if the flashlight dies. But don't worry about the car now. There's fishing that needs doing, a dark night full of it. Between the slurps of trout come the slaps of beavers, the buzzings of mosquitoes, the swishes of cold water. A shifting boot makes an obscene, muck-sucking sound. Every noise is louder than it should be.

The day has light, the night shift has sound. The trade's a fair one. You risk getting a wet butt, and being scared by stuff you can't see and sure as hell can't identify. You're bitten first by black flies, then by mosquitoes, unless you use pools of insect glop that can eat the coating off a fly line or the epoxy off a rod. You lose sleep and must dodge midnight-highway deer on the drive home. And what do you get in return? Privacy, more than anything. No canoes threaten you. And nobody's watching. Any cast that ends with the fly wet is a good one. One that lands in a tree is okay if you can pull the big bug loose. This river's daylight anglers are image-conscious. They wear fashionable fishing togs and carry brand-name tackle. Their loops are tight, their beards, trimmed. But at night, a twenty-year-old glass rod is fine, even if it bears capital-letter line designations instead of numbers, even if it's balanced with an automatic fly reel.

When it's dark, really dark, nobody sees. Nobody cares. Not the mud, the bugs, or the fish. And certainly not those of us who work the fly-fishing night shift.

IN THE
ENCHANTED

* * *

TED WILLIAMS

EVERY TROUT FISHERMAN I KNOW HAS HIS WOODS. HAVING ONE'S WOODS
is important—like having family or a country. Mine are the Maine
woods. And the excuse I use to get into them—the brook trout—is as
beautiful an excuse as anyone could find.

At night I like to lie by the spring that feeds ice water and trout
fry to Secret Pond and watch for meteors amidst brilliant stars and
planets undefiled by ambient light. Or listen to barred owls conversing
between mountains. Two miles north are the Canadian Pacific railroad tracks—the only link with rural civilization other than thirty-five
miles of jeep road.

Canadian Pacific. Even the name conjures the romance worthy of
these woods. You can hear the train for half an hour until it finally
threads behind Megantic Mountain in Canada, and, as in the song,
you are carried ten thousand miles—then brought back suddenly by
the crack of a beaver, the outburst of peepers, or the demented laughter of a loon.

Sometimes, when you jeep the surrounding valleys by day, you
catch the glint of this and other trout water nestled between granite-
strewn mountains. On the foot trails that lead into it you climb
quickly out of the cuttings into big, wild boreal forest. From the ledge
where an eastern cougar stared coldly up at George Young as he circled
in his float plane, you can gaze out over Canada and back to Maine's
flat middle—and see nothing but forest and lakes. It is beautiful,
curative country and I can never get enough of it. They call it simply
The Enchanted.

It is so named because one dark winter night—while one hundred
loggers, all in the prime of life, were eating supper—His Satanic
Majesty danced and sang on the camp roof. The performer, although
not to be confused with the rock group of the same name whose work

is advertised as "forty minutes of noise," nonetheless crooned arrangements that, apparently, were strikingly similar in tone and composition. It happened when western Maine was still clad in virgin white pine.

My friend the writer—poet Arthur MacDougall, barely out of high school then, stood on a sidewalk in Bingham while John Kelly reproduced as best he could the hideous caterwauling he and the other men had heard, and then recounted how they had searched with lanterns from Dead River landing for miles in all directions and never found a human footprint in the new snow. You, MacDougall, No-Birds, and I may doubt that it was actually the devil, perhaps dismissing the whole episode as the excess of some night-tripping catamount or dog fox. But, as MacDougall writes in the introduction to his *Dud Dean, Maine Guide*, "we weren't there."

And who, you ask, is No-Birds? He is my old Colby College roommate, Robert J. Daviau, a Philadelphia lawyer from Waterville, Maine. He is called No-Birds because that's how many "pa'tridges" he always kills whenever they manage to get into the air before he shoots and usually even when they don't. I'll venture that half the doctors and a third of the paper barons in Kennebec County have been sued by him or his father, Jerome; and whatever they say about the Daviaus, which is plenty, it is never that they failed to do their homework or don't know where to fish for wild squaretails. "It's going to take them quite a while to spoil The Enchanted," No-Birds always says.

Back when Jerome still came into the office, No-Birds used to live in terror that the Old Man would learn that his own flesh and blood had divulged to me the very pond that he, Jerome, had been given by Aimé LeCours and which he, in turn, had lovingly passed on to young No-Birds (after he had fished it out, of course).

It was not that his father disliked me a great deal, No-Birds kindly explained. It was just that my home, at least in the legal sense, was in *Massachusetts*—the void, the nether world, the primal chaos into which the southern border falls away. That made it about sixty times more sinful than telling someone from Maine, a heinous offense in itself. To make matters worse, Jerome knew that the pond had long ago recovered from the pounding he had given it. No-Birds used to plead with me to call it Secret Pond, even when it appeared that only he and I were present. We've renamed the river and the surrounding townships, too.

◆　　◆　　◆

One mid-September Monday, No-Birds and I struck off into The Enchanted in my old blue Bronco on a washed-out jeep trail that soon grew slick in the soft rain. A hard frost had killed most of the deerflies, and the swamp maples had gone scarlet. Big, gangly varying hares trotted across the road and sat, scratching at fleas and cleaning their ears. About thirty miles in, a pileated woodpecker dipped out of a dead spruce, turned, and bobbed along in front of us for fifty feet before veering off into the forest. The warm air was perfumed with balsam and that delicious woods scent of dead leaves and damp earth.

At Secret Pond cutoff, No-Birds slogged out into the middle of the Cold River, directing me across the ford with hand signals and dramatic facial expressions, high-stepping backward toward the far bank as the spirited vehicle crashed and splashed over the smooth boulders, shipping water through the left door and voiding it through the right. The Bronco cavorted up the bank and plowed through thick alders, with the metal canoe banging obscenely against the roof and water gurgling in the exhaust system.

Back on the trail again, I stopped and dismounted. While No-Birds walked back across the river to sweep away our spoor, I cinched down the canoe and, rubbing my head (which had also banged obscenely on the roof), tried to decide what to do about the windshield wipers that were now bent rakishly back over the cabin like cricket antennae.

No-Birds appeared, studied the antennae curiously, and said, "Let's go." He climbed aboard and started knocking his knees together as he always does when impatient or bored. Once—when we had decided to attend Indian Thought class and were listening to the professor explaining, in broken English, the "Noble Eightfold Path"—a girl had turned around and asked No-Birds to please hold still because he was making her "seasick."

I shifted into low range and ground on up the mountain, holding down the brakes to dry them out. All the little brooks that cut across the road were quickening, and hidden under lush sumac and raspberries were jagged rocks and potholes that jarred our teeth and kept the spare tire trading between roof and toolbox. We fishtailed up the higher slopes, slicing the black earth.

"Road's got worse," I grunted.

"Good," declared No-Birds. "River scares off some of 'em but not all of 'em."

"Once it scared you off," I said, recalling the time he, Francis Carter, and Bill Violette had come onto it in flood and driven all the way back to Elmont (population one), walked the tracks down to Tinkumtown (population zero), tried to hike in over Range 7, and gotten lost. No-Birds had ranted about it for a month. I'd asked him how come they hadn't left the truck and just waded across the river.

"Eee Tabernack!" he'd shouted. "It would have taken away your *house!"*

No-Birds' favorite stretch of the Secret Pond road is six miles in, just as you turn off for the final, downhill mile. Here the beavers have engineered things so that about fifty yards of road is under two feet of water. It looks dreadful, but it's all hardpan and there's usually nothing to it. According to No-Birds, it turns back 80 percent of the 20 percent who are foolhardy enough to ford the river.

Even so, No-Birds points out grimly that there are still "traffic jams" on this, his favorite grouse road. "You ought to see the bird hunters up here in October," he laments. "It's *crawling* with 'em. That's how they find the pond. I'll get all the way in here at eight in the morning and there'll be a jeep in front of me. And then one'll come up behind me, and I can't turn around, and they poke along, and I get pissed. . . . *Eee Seebwais."* (If you want to rile up No-Birds, remove the breast meat from a pa'tridge, hang the empty carcass on a forked stick, spread the tail, and prop it up along one of his ground-sluicing roads. Then drive in with him and let him do the shooting.)

We slid down the last few yards of road, sometimes with the brakes locked, No-Birds muttering and spluttering about the perversity of precipitation—how rain adjusts itself precisely to coincide with his golf and fishing and how snow refuses to fall until after he hunts deer. "The luck of Daviau," he solemnly intoned.

But no sooner had he struggled into his waders and slicker than the rain stopped and sunlight, diffusing through the low overcast, turned the forest smoky gold. "I'm keeping them on," he announced defiantly. "If I take 'em off, it's gonna rain again." Then he trudged off down the path with the cooler and tent.

As I fumbled with the canoe straps, I caught little glimmers of Secret Pond through the dark, tall spruce that lined the path. No leaf or blade of grass stirred, and all around was ringing silence broken only by the distant telegraphing of woodpeckers and the occasional lament of a white-throated sparrow.

I had the canoe on the ground and was filling it with fishing gear when No-Birds yelled from the pond. "Williams, c'mere quick, and bring your camera." Expecting a bear or at least a bull moose, I snatched up the metal ammo box and dashed down the path.

It was only the foliage. On the high banks all around the pond, maple, beech, and mountain ash glowed with impossible shades of red and yellow. It was reflected with undiminished brilliance in the still water. And in the middle of it all: the purple top of Secret Pond Mountain. If autumn in Massachusetts is, as is unceasingly reported, "a riot of color," then this was civil war. As I admired it, I also took time to notice that no trout were rising. "Look at that," declared No-Birds with a grand sweep of his arm.

"It probably would have waited," I commented as I chewed the cap off a plastic film canister.

The beast that No-Birds fears most—a leech, neatly trimmed with orange like a fancy bookmark—undulated over a sunken log. I picked it up and flipped it onto his slicker.

◆   ◆   ◆

We piled the rest of the gear into the canoe and slid it down the path to the water. With about two inches of freeboard, I paddled to the spring. No-Birds met me there and reached out to steady the bow while I swung my feet over the gunwale, scattering the trout fry that hung in the spring's shallow outflow. "Hey," he said, "Aimé's boat isn't here."

We unloaded, pitched the tent, and put our rods together. Then we pushed off in the canoe to look for the boat. It is an ancient, square-ended, flat-bottomed affair that Aimé built twenty-five years ago when there was no road, with lumber he'd hauled in from Elmont. Like everything Aimé builds it is indestructible. No-Birds loves to fish from it because it doesn't tip or swing in the wind when he anchors over the spring hole. "I don't relish fishing out of this canoe with you, Williams," he said.

We found Aimé's boat drifting in front of the beaver house, nearly submerged and with both anchors gone. No-Birds did not speak for a full minute. Then, in his controlled courtroom voice, he said, "The Canadians have done this to me." The Canadians—who, according to No-Birds, drive Cadillacs to within a mile and a half of the pond on a "superhighway" that runs in from Megantic—are among the many tests the Lord has devised for him. They keep two aluminum boats chained to a tree on the western shore.

After we bailed Aimé's boat we found, under the seat, a plastic bag filled with sand and tied to a length of squidding line. "Look at that," shouted No-Birds. "That's their anchor! I'm telling you, Williams, there's nothing stupider than a C'nuck, *nothing*. One spring I'm in here with Aimé and we hear this *put-a-put-a-put-a-put-a-put*. You know what they'd done? They'd *carried* an outboard motor in here. *Can you imagine that?* They'd lugged an outboard motor a mile and a half through the puckerbush! And then, when they got done, they lugged it back!"

"Let's go fishing," I said.

But now No-Birds was in full cry. "They worm the piss out of this pond! And don't think they drive through customs to buy a Maine license. And don't think they quit at eight trout. *God*, would I love to take an ax to their boats!"

No-Birds found two new anchor rocks, then poled off toward the spring hole. I drifted along the north shore, under the mountain, flicking out a little Mickey Finn and twitching it back. There still was no sign of feeding activity on top, but salamanders were floating up to sip little somethings from the surface film. Secret Pond is clear, but not sterile-clear. When you kneel and lean over it to drink, and then shade your eyes with your hands while the ripples tickle the tip of your nose, you can see tiny globular creatures sculling around. There are no chubs or dace—only wild brook trout with scarlet, ivory-edged fins and chestnut flanks flecked with ruby and sapphire. No-Birds swears he can distinguish them from all other trout solely by their taste.

I worked the whole fishless shore, constantly distracted by splashing from the spring hole. Every time I looked, No-Birds was kneeling in the bilge, rod high, arm straining out with the landing net. He stripped the fast-sinking line with quick little jerks, his rod tip motionless and six inches under the surface, setting only with the line the way Jerome had always insisted he do it. Presently, his line hand flew from his waist to his ear like an umpire after a clean tag at home plate. Missing the strike, he flung his hat on the seat, then missed another as he bent to pick it up.

"You doing any good?" I asked.

"I got 'em coming," he admitted. "And are they colored up! C'mere. But slow. Don't spook 'em. Just drift in."

He held the gunwale and flipped me the Canadians' anchor line. "Here," he said. "Tie up so's it don't bang."

"Let's see your fish."

"Under the seat."

There were five, all over a pound and in full spawning colors. He had arranged them so that their broad maroon tails were in a perfect line.

"Get in," he said. *"Quietly."*

"Nah, I'm going down to the outlet."

"C'mon, get in, Williams. Don't be foolish."

But I pushed off and continued on my way. It was not all chivalry on my part. No-Birds doesn't throw a bad line, but he is never satisfied with his distance and keeps double-hauling until sometimes the line gets away from him and coils around his shoulders like a corn snake on a rat. And his droppers increase by a factor of three your chances of getting snagged. Once I'd told him that he should be glad for whatever distance he had and just shoot; that, in trying for the moon, he lost everything. And he'd answered: "You know, Williams, you're right.

That's my problem with everything I do—golf, court, sex, *everything.*"

Down by the outlet the deep hole in front of the beaver dam was shaded by a floating carpet of maple leaves. There was fresh beaver activity even though Aimé had trapped out the pond the previous winter, partly because the two Daviaus had convinced each other and him that the beavers spoil the fishing by raising the water level. The only weakness in the theory is that there are always beavers and the pond produces more trout now than it did sixty years ago when there were no beavers within thirty miles and Aimé still fished with worms.

In the middle of the cove, where the water is only three feet deep, a good fish flashed up from the mossy bottom and snatched the Mickey Finn. I set hard, knocking the paddle into the water, and saw him streak under the canoe. Before I could strip in a foot of slack he was in the pool by the dam. I felt the line tighten against my index finger and thrilled at the marvelous power pulsing through the graphite. Then I played him off the reel, trying to work him out of the hole. Twice I had him up over the lip into the shallow water and twice he lunged back. At last he came—with violent head shakes, and I felt him burying into the moss and scrubbing his jaw against the underlying gravel. He surfaced with a headdress of moss, and I knew he was mine, or rather, Aimé's. I led him in, caressed his silken sides until he lay still, then gradually tightened my grip and hoisted him aboard. He was big even for Secret Pond, with flattened sides, a jutting lower jaw, and all the colors of the surrounding hillsides.

That night three juvenile otters frolicked along the shoreline, No-Birds feigning outrage and vowing to report them to Aimé. We sat by the fire, listening to barred owls and watching the sparks and smoke from the dry spruce rise straight up into the infinite northern night.

"They got a lot of this in Massachusetts?" inquired No-Birds with another grand sweep of his arm. He shoveled two more trout onto his plate and took a long pull of spring-chilled beer. Then he said, "You oughta see Fatso eat these fish."

"Which one? Violette or Carter?"

"Well," said No-Birds, pausing reflectively. "I was thinking of Carter, but . . ."

"I've seen it," I said.

"Too bad, though, eatin' 'em like this in the fall when they've lost so much flavor." He belched and sucked his greasy fingers.

We heard the train at midnight—a faint hum that grew louder over the span of about fifteen minutes and then diminished for another fifteen until it was well into Canada and you couldn't tell if you were still hearing or just remembering.

Hours later, it seemed, when the night was even blacker, No-

Birds jabbed me in the ribs with his elbow. In semisleep, I wondered what the hell he was doing crashing around in the woods, then realized he was in the tent with me. "What's that?" he hissed. It sounded as if mature trees were being snapped off at their roots and hurled into the pond.

"His Satanic Majesty, I guess."

Presently, we could hear snorting.

"*Eee B'twais!* It's a goddamned moose. Those whores would just as soon go through a tent as around it. Williams, we're dead!"

The crashing, splashing, and snorting got louder and closer. Now we could feel the ground shaking.

"*Ah-ga-ga-ga-ga-ga-ga,*" declared No-Birds. Then there was just splashing that gradually faded into the night.

After much commentary, No-Birds settled down. I was almost asleep when he said, "Hey, Williams."

"What?"

"If Aimé's been in, he's gonna think it was us did that to his boat."

"Nah, he'll know it was the Canadians."

"Yeah," said No-Birds. "I been thinking about that. I don't think it *was* the Canadians."

"Who, then?"

"Clarence Boudreau. He hates me enough."

No-Birds had a point. I had met the friendly, rheumy-eyed old man here three summers before. He and a companion from Coburn Gore had hiked in from the Canadian side, not to fish trout but to drink whiskey. He'd goggled at my Massachusetts plates, stating in his 78-RPM French Canadian dialect that he had now seen everything. After he had poured me a drink and interrogated me about how I'd found the pond, he'd explained that when he used to be in the paper business one of the Daviaus—it was not exactly clear which one—had either sued him or overcharged him or, possibly, both.

I allowed to No-Birds that if Boudreau had been at Secret Pond, Aimé would probably know about it.

"You bet he will," said No-Birds. "You don't come into The Enchanted country, mister, without Aimé LeCours knowing it."

In the morning I lay on my back inside the tent, looking up at the frost canopy through the thin, wet cloth, and inhaling the wonderful fragrance of woods and water. I could hear red squirrels scuttling around the camp, and somewhere far away a raven croaked. After many years I had finally come to agree with the Daviaus that there is never any point to fishing Secret Pond before the sun is well up. "She turns on at nine o'clock," says No-Birds. "You can set your watch by it."

No-Birds struggled out of his sleeping bag like a hatching mayfly, pulled on his Bean boots, and crawled into the morning. "Blue sky," he conceded grudgingly. Pretty soon he started frying the bacon, something he never permits anyone else to do. I was halfway out the tent when a clanging and banging arose from the western shore. It was the Canadians.

No-Birds flung his hat to the ground and danced upon it. "On a Tuesday," he shrieked. "On a Christly Tuesday!"

For a long time he stood there with his hands on his hips. Then he stalked to the spring, hauled out the plastic bread bag full of trout, dumped them onto the moss and started counting. "Let's get out of here," he said. "All's we need is four more fish. We can get them in Hoss-shoe."

We had no trouble on the way out, except that the road was still wet and we had to winch up the first fifty feet. "It's a beautiful pond," said No-Birds. "But it ain't so beautiful when it's fulla C'nucks."

Aimé wasn't home, so we left a package of trout in the well and turned south on the Old Lake Road to Horseshoe Pond. Before long an ancient, green pickup truck full of firewood rattled past us. "Stop, stop, stop," screamed No-Birds. "That was Aimé." But Aimé had seen us and was already backing up. He strode over with his thick arm extended, bright blue eyes dancing, and wearing a big, semitoothless grin: Aimé LeCours, the total population of the abandoned timber town of Elmont, the Maine legend who has trapped, hunted, fished, guided, and logged The Enchanted exactly twice as long as No-Birds and I have lived. He crushed our hands and pumped the splinters.

"How's fishing?" he asked.

"Horrible," said No-Birds. "We left some trout in the well." He then revealed, in all its lurid detail, the tragedy of the boat.

"I be *demmed,*" said Aimé.

"Has Boudreau been around?" asked No-Birds.

"Sure. But not in dere."

"Must have been those guys from Megantic, then."

"Could be," said Aimé, rubbing his short, steel-gray hair. "But I don't t'ink."

◆   ◆   ◆

After that trip I didn't see No-Birds again until the next summer. Twice in October we had talked on the phone, and twice I had tactfully declined road-hunting invitations. With his family-photo Christmas card came a note telling of his extraordinary good fortune during deer season. First of all, he had killed two deer. "See, Williams, it works," he'd written, referring to his perfect church-attendance record, recently mandated by his wife.

But an even richer blessing had befallen him. He, Aimé, Carter, and Violette had gotten snowed in at Elmont, and one night when the trees were cracking and the snow was swirling, there had come a tapping at the cabin door. They'd thought for sure that His Satanic Majesty had appeared for an encore, but it was only two deer hunters with frost-crusted beards and Dr. Zhivago eyes who had just walked six miles down a mountain because the pond they had camped beside had frozen over and the float plane couldn't land to pick them up. They had pretty much given themselves up for dead and were astonished to find humans in Elmont. So they babbled happily about the pond and the mountain and the ancient trapper's cabin that belonged to any wilderness traveler who came upon it. And the *brook trout.* Here they paused suspiciously, looked around the room, and inquired, "Does anyone here fish for brook tr . . ."

"No," croaked No-Birds, pulling up his chair to pour them each a coffee mug of bourbon.

◆ ◆ ◆

In mid-June I called No-Birds to see if he wanted to go fishing. "Guess what," he said. "I got a new fetish. White-water rafting." It seemed entirely out of character, but then he explained that he was done with it forever and done with listening to Violette. A client— doubtless a disgruntled one—had tipped No-Birds off to huge square- tails stationed between the appalling rapids of the Dead River. On hearing the news, Violette had dropped everything and rushed to the K Mart to purchase, for thirty-five dollars, a rubber raft "reinforced for white water." The following morning they had run sixteen miles of river—the first mile in the raft, the last fifteen in their life jackets.

"We come around this corner," said No-Birds, "and I hear this whining. It gets louder and louder. And I say to Violette, 'Jesus, Billy, I didn't think they were cutting wood in here.' All of a sudden we're sucked in. *White water? Eee Taberwhit!* I thought we were dead. I kept sticking my fingers into the holes in that raft until I ran out of fingers. We lost everything. Our rods. Our flies. *Everything.* How pleasant do you think it was, swimming down to The Forks in April?"

"You been into that new pond yet?"

"Williams," he said, his voice suddenly low and serious, "you won't *believe* this pond. Aimé took me in a couple of weeks ago. No compass. No map. No nothing. He just went. When we got there, I thought there was something wrong with the pond. It was *boiling.*

Bang, bang, bang, Aimé builds this *beautiful* two-man raft. You ever take a good look at the hands on that guy, mister? It takes me half an hour to cut down this dead cedar, and when I float it over to him, he's already got six, and he says, 'T'anks, Bob, but she's too short on one end.' *And did we catch fish!* It's quite a poke in there, though. Six big ones. Up a mountain."

He could not go fishing, he explained, because he had a big case coming up. When I asked him what it was, he said, "You'll love this one, Williams. A guy from Norridgewock threw 'fecal material at an officer of the law.' "

So without clearing it through No-Birds—or even telling him about it—I navigated into the pond myself, although not before also navigating into, and around in, a vast muskeg that nearly disgorged me into Quebec. Warblers rustled through the hardwood ridges, and the lush forest floor was strewn with white moccasin flowers and trilliums. I slept on the ground and discovered in the morning that I'd been about five minutes from the pond. It was a pretty pond, smaller and weedier than Secret, almost on the top of the mountain, and with a few hundred feet of green peak rising from its north end. Tree swallows wheeled and dipped, and trout fed steadily. All around were paper birches bigger than any I had ever seen.

The cabin was better than No-Birds had described it. Bears had raked the logs and torn away the window screens, but the glass was unbroken and the door well-hinged. It had a tin roof, a sink, a wood-stove, and two bunks with foam mattresses and nice wool blankets that must have belonged to the deer hunters. On the pine-board walls were notes and greetings written by trappers, hunters, and fishermen. One was dated November 16, 1928. Twenty feet from the door was a clear, bubbling spring. I didn't waste any time setting up my rod, finding the raft, and going fishing.

I drifted around the pond, dropping tiny Quill Gordons into the paths of cruising trout. If the line landed quietly and I gave them the proper lead, they'd bulge up through the bright surface, waggle their tails, and suck in the fly. They were fine, gaudy fish, more streamlined than those of Secret Pond and entirely free of lice, and they fought splendidly against the thin rod. I caught them all day long, and when the water went from silver to pink, I realized I'd forgotten lunch.

Below me, and fifteen miles to the southwest, a corona enveloped Secret Pond Mountain, and from its summit two dazzling spires of sunlight stretched into the azure sky. Peepers shrilled. Mayflies danced. A bat appeared. I killed three trout, poled ashore, and secured the raft by pushing the black-spruce pole between the logs and hanging from it so that it sank into the mud bottom.

In the morning I inscribed the following message over the sink with the felt-tipped pen from the binder of my fishing journal: "Found pond June 20, 1979." (That part, at least, was true.) "Many, many large fishes here got by us on lures and werms. Raft okay, but someones should makes a bigger one so we all can fish at onetime." And I signed it: "Raymond Poirier, Marcel DuBois, Jacques Lefleur, Guy Laclair, and Maurice Nadeau." I then festooned the raft with bloody tinsel from the gut cavities of the trout I'd cleaned. And into No-Birds' landing net I knitted an immense, green-mottled, rubber-skirted Buzzer Bait that I had purchased for the occasion. On the way out I found the trail Aimé had blazed, and in a wide, muddy place where it crossed a brook, I shuffled around for five minutes, making footprints.

◆   ◆   ◆

Two weeks later I found myself picking lettuce, chives, cucumbers, and tomatoes under a blackening sky in front of the old Elmont blacksmith shop. Now it is Aimé's house. On the other side of the C.P. tracks is No-Birds' fishing–hunting camp, formerly the schoolhouse. In the alder run are the moldering remains of the post office, under the popples the rusty safe from the general store, and, in the dark woods all around, mossy cellar holes. Twenty-five families lived here from the beginning of the century until the Great Depression.

Aimé, who moved in from Megantic at age seventeen, gets quiet when he stops on the footbridge spanning the Cold River and gazes out over the ghost town of Elmont, Maine. His neighbors, as he says, just gradually drifted off. "Dey'd find another place, and dey'd just drift off." But Aimé was tougher and more stubborn. "Dey'll have to take me out feet first," he said then and says now.

It took me ten minutes to carry the vegetables the two hundred feet to the house because of all the wild strawberries in the path. No-Birds was sitting on the porch, knocking his knees together. "C'mon, c'mon, c'mon, let's go," he said. Aimé backed toward us and No-Birds carefully tucked the vegetables into his backpack—an ancient canvas affair that sagged to his lower lumbar.

The first hundred yards of trail had been churned up by the trail bike which Violette had talked No-Birds into buying three weeks earlier so that they could whisk right up the mountain to "Unknown Pond." The grim tale was plainly written beside each blowdown and granite outcropping. No-Birds said that he'd almost been killed by the Christly contraption, that, after their twentieth wipeout, they'd just left it where it had fallen and walked in, that it was now for sale back home in his garage, should I wish to purchase it, and that he was done listening to Violette.

All the way up the mountain Aimé lamented the physical decay of old age. And No-Birds and I responded with our usual sympathetic grunts, jogging so he wouldn't get out of hearing range.

"*Tabernoosh!*" exclaimed No-Birds when a brood of grouse exploded in our faces.

When we came to the muddy flat full of my footprints, I said, "Hey, No-Birds. I thought you told me no one else fished this place."

"That's just Violette and Carter," he muttered. But clearly, the seeds of doubt had been planted.

By now the sky was full of lightning, and the undersides of the birches and sugar maples were turning up in the wind. "I bet it's clear in Waterville," remarked No-Birds. "I coulda been playing golf. I'm telling ya, this country makes its own weather."

As we hauled ourselves to the brow of the hill that overlooks Unknown Pond, No-Birds swept out both arms and said, "Now, Williams, I'm gonna show you something that a Massachusetts man has never seen and never ought to see." The rain began five minutes after we were inside the cabin.

We knew better than to argue with Aimé when he insisted on sleeping on the floor. So No-Birds threw down the foam mattress from his bunk, I threw down my blanket, and, since they would have gone to waste otherwise, Aimé crawled between them. The front moved through about one A.M., and starlight poured into the cabin. At sunup the thermometer on the porch read thirty-eight degrees.

While No-Birds relit the fire, Aimé sat on the mattress studying a small bottle of brandy. "Should we drink it?" he asked. Before I could say yes he said, "No," and tucked it back into his pack.

"How are you holding up, old man?" called No-Birds as he squatted in front of the stove, fanning the smoldering birch bark with his hat.

"*Seebwais,*" announced Aimé. "I'm stiff in all ze wrong places." Then he went off into a long dissertation on his deteriorating health. He still had a few more bad teeth to pull. No, he didn't use pliers too often. Usually just wire. "The worst t'ing," he said, "are dose goddemmed heart hay-tacks. It's like you got stabbed in the chest with a knife. Ai, *Tabernack!* You can't breathe. You can't walk. You can't do notting. You got to put down your pack. . . ."

That's where the brandy comes in, he explained. It has the effect of opening up one's cardiovascular system so one can eventually— after, say, an hour—continue about one's business in the woods. "But for quite a while dere it's purty tough."

I kept waiting for No-Birds to notice the inscription over the sink. It was important for him to find it himself, but I didn't want him to leave us alone in the cabin so that he could accuse us of writing it. Finally, as he was lacing up his boots, I sauntered over to the sink and idly perused the various graffiti on the wall. As No-Birds was moving toward the door with an empty bucket in each hand and his toothbrush clamped between his teeth, I said:

"You know a Raymond Poirier?"

"Nope."

"He was here in June," I said.

"Yah. June nineteen-fifty."

"No. This June."

No-Birds dropped the buckets and flew to the sink.

As Aimé said later, he almost had a heart hay-tack himself. "C'nucks," screamed No-Birds, holding the sides of his head and dancing around the cabin. "Oh my God! C'nucks. C'nucks. C'nucks." Then he ran outside to check the raft.

The rest of the trip was everything I'd expected it to be. And even No-Birds had a good time once he was full of trout and beer, and once I had told him that in spite of *everything,* it would still take them quite a while to spoil The Enchanted.

THE FINEST TROUT IN THE RIVER

◆ ◆ ◆

HARRY PLUNKET GREENE

IT MIGHT NATURALLY BE SUPPOSED THAT IF ONE HAD THE FISHING OF A trout-stream like the Bourne, one would not leave an inch of it unexplored, but it was a fact that up to this time none of the rods had ever taken the trouble to investigate the top quarter-mile of the water. Savage and Sharkey had somehow got it into their heads that there was nothing worth troubling about above the "lagoon" immediately beyond the viaduct, and as they lived close to the top of the fishing, all the rest of us, myself included, had tacitly accepted this as a matter of fact. Nowadays the whole of this region is a vast watercress bed, and anyone looking out of the window of the train, when passing over the viaduct, would never realise that there was, or ever had been, a river there at all; but in those days there were two streams above, as well as below, the bridge, meeting a little way up and stretching as one, for a quarter of a mile to the end of the fishing.

We had all of us come on occasions as far as the hatch below this final stretch, but, in the belief that the water above was a blank, had always turned back when we got there.

On August 31st of this year, the last day of the season, I found myself at this hatch at about six o'clock in the evening. I had got four fish averaging 1¼ lbs., but it had been a bad rising day, cold and windy. At six o'clock it suddenly turned warm and calm, and I was sitting on the hatch smoking a pipe before going home, when I thought that, just for fun, I would walk up to the end of the water. I expected nothing, and had half a mind to leave my rod behind and saunter up with my hands in my pockets. I got over the fence and strolled up on to the bank unconcernedly, and, as I did so, from one weed-patch after another there darted off a series of two-pounders racing upstream like motor-boats. I dropped like a stone, but the damage was done. I just sat there cursing the day I was born and myself, not only for

having lost the chance of a lifetime—for the iron-blues were beginning to come down thick—but for having left this gold-mine undiscovered and untouched for two years—and to-day was the last day of
the season! If there had been any handy way discovered of kicking
oneself physically as well as mentally, I should have been unrecogn-
isable when I got home. Every fish was under the weeds long ago, and
I might just as well pack up my traps and clear out.

There was an old broken-down footbridge about a hundred yards
above me, and I thought that I would go up to it and explore the reach
beyond, more with a view to the possibilities of next year than with
any hope for the present. I got down from the bank and circled round
through the meadow till I got to it, and was just picking my way across
its rotten planks when under my very feet I saw a small nose appear,
followed by a diminutive head and the most enormous shoulder I ever
remember to have seen in a chalk stream. I froze stiff where I stood,
except that my knees were shaking like aspens, for there right under-
neath me was gradually emerging the fish of my life. I do not mean to
say that I have not caught bigger fish before and since, but this was a
veritable star in the dust-heap, a Cinderella stealing out of the kitchen
that we had all despised, and the romance of the thing put him (pace
Cinderella) on a pedestal of fame from which I have never taken him
down.

It was agonising work, for he swam up in the most leisurely way
at a rate of about an inch in every five seconds, while I was straddled
across two rotten planks, either of which might have given way at any
moment, and had to pretend that I was part of the landscape. He was
immediately under me when he first showed up and I could easily have
touched him with my foot. What fish will see and what they will not
see will ever remain a mystery! It was then about half-past six (old
time), the time of day when one's visibility is most clear, and yet he
took not the smallest notice of me. He just strolled up the middle of
the stream contentedly as though he were having a smoke after dinner. I can still feel my joints creaking as I sank slowly to my knees and
got my line out. It fell just right, and he took no more notice of it than
of a water-rat. I tried again and again, lengthening the cast as he
moved up, and at last he rose towards it, examined it carefully and,
horror of horrors!, swam slowly after it downstream through the bridge
under my feet! It would have been laughable if it had not been so
tragic. There was I pulling in the slack like a madman, and leaving it
in wisps round my knees, scared lest he should see my hand move; and
he passed me by without a word and disappeared into the bowels of the
bridge.

I just knelt there and swore, trying to look over my shoulder to see if he had gone down below. There was no sign of him, and the situation was painful in the extreme, for my knees were working through the rotten woodwork, and if I tried to ease myself, I should either bring the bridge down with a crash or anyway evict Cinderellum for good and all.

I bore it as long as I could and was just going to give it up and scramble out anyhow, when I saw that nose slide out again beneath me, and my old friend started off on his journey up-stream once more.

I began on him with a shorter line this time, and he took the fly at the very first cast like a lamb. If he was a lamb as he took it, he was a lion when he had it. Instead of running up-stream, as I hoped and expected he would do, he gave one swish with his tail and bolted down through the bridge, bending the rod double and dragging the point right under. It was done with such lightning speed I had no time to remonstrate. I threw myself flat on my stomach and got the rod side-ways over the bridge, and then the fight began. I was on one side of the bridge, and he was half-way to Southampton on the other. He got farther and farther downstream, going from one patch of weeds to the next, and digging and burrowing his nose into the middle of it, while I just hung on, helplessly waiting for the end. He quieted down after a bit, and finding that he could not rub the annoying thing out of his nose on the south side, he determined to explore the north, and he began to swim up towards me. I must have been a ridiculous sight, spread-eagled on the rotting planks with splinters digging into my legs and ants and spiders crawling down my neck, vainly endeavouring to hold the rod over the side with one hand, to wind in the line with the other, and to watch him over my shoulder all at the same time. Fortunately, I must have been invisible from below, but the moment he got under the bridge he saw the rod and tore past me up-stream with the reel screaming. But now we were on even terms and there was a clear stretch of water ahead, and I was able to play him to a finish. I was really proud of that fight, for, in addition to the cramped style which I was compelled to adopt, it took place in a stream ten feet wide, half-choked with weeds, and I got him on a 000 Iron-blue at the end of a 4X point. He weighed 3¾ lbs. when I got him home, and I have always bitterly regretted that I did not get him set up, for, with the exception of an 11¾-pounder in the hall of Longford Castle, caught in the Avon by one of the family on a "local lure" (the name of which neither fork nor spade would dig from me), he was the most beautiful river-trout in shape, colour and proportion I ever saw.

MOTHER'S
DAY

• • •

MARGOT PAGE

TOM HAS JUST TOLD ME THERE IS A HORNY BULL PRESIDING OVER THE
field. So I have chosen to slip along the barbed-wire fence that sep-
arates me from His Majesty's moody black-and-white harem, who eye
me grumpily from their emerald pasture next to the Battenkill.

I put in upstream, Tom heads down. We have wrestled this sunlit
May afternoon from the demands of parenthood, for it is both a
holiday and a Hendrickson hatch and we want to be together on the
water.

I stride confidently into this venerable New England river; the
spring floodwaters which have ravaged and crumbled the banks have
receded, and the river looks manageably low. Deceptively so. Smooth
and seemingly shallow, the Battenkill is actually a swift and pushy
river and is renowned for its tricks. Immediately, I stagger and brace
against the numbing onslaught, the mossy slate and marble stones
rolling and tipping under my clumsy, oversize wading boots.

But the river permits me, with characteristic prettiness and grace,
to remain upright, and I position myself across from an overhanging
tree branch which Tom has pointed out. The water in which I stand
is achingly clear, a foot and a half deep, and dizzying in its powerful
onrush. On the far bank, the cows form picturesque Vermont back-
drops, like trendy cutouts. Behind me, on the other bank behind a
lattice of trees, a family is having one of the first barbecues of the
season—mouth-watering aromas waft lazily over to me along with
happy yells and garbled conversation. The spring sun burns my
washed-out arms and shoulders red.

I have found a pod of fish underneath the branch, and the fish are
rising greedily, recklessly, steadily. I pull in one after another over a
two-hour period. They are strong fighters. The sun, the tensing of my
leg muscles against the dragging water, the rhythmic casting, the

consistency of the hatch, are mesmerizing. I work off a winter of sloth, I work toward a happy summer, a productive future.

Tom is picking his way upstream in the glaring sunlight. He makes it look so easy; I nearly got swept away when just picking up a foot to change my position. I console myself with delusive thoughts about being such a fairy wraith that I am too light and thin to fight the water.

Pulling out fish after fish, I get back the music I've missed since last summer. I relearn technique, discover my touch, conquer the harmless release. The sun beats, the fish rise, the Vermont landscape burgeons and trembles with lushness, life.

Tom has made his way up to me and watches proudly. He gave me this spot as a Mother's Day present, for that is today's holiday, and I have joyfully made use of his gift. It is only when he stands next to me that trouble erupts.

I have hooked and brought close to me a large fish, the best of the day. I earned this baby with a successful marriage of ability and luck, I think as I carefully play him in the sweeping current. Tom, gracious and generous with the spirit of the holiday, says helpfully, "I'll get him." Before I think to protest, his hand on the line, the swelling current, and the size of this healthy, frisky bugger conspire to snap him off. *Snap.* Gone. Pissed! I say a few bad words. "I'll land my *own* fish," I trumpet. Tom dissolves upstream.

And then my anger passes. Tom had lovingly given me the choice water, the gods had created a Vermont masterpiece of hungry, fat fish, clean water, and brilliant landscape, and a new sun burned us with love and possibility. I have much to be grateful for.

I stagger upstream to Tom with many ridiculous arm gestures and jerky leg contortions to prevent me from falling when wading. The journey seems to take forever. When I reach Tom, I kiss him, say I am sorry, and thank him for the day. We hold hands as we sit on a log on the bank in the late-afternoon light.

TIMELESS RIVER

• • •

JACK SAMSON

IN ITS UPPER REACHES, THE RIO GRANDE IS A TIMELESS RIVER WHERE change has meaning only in terms of the people who have come to it. Unlike the lower stretches where it meanders through desert and flat land and man has built along it, the Big River from southern Colorado down through northern New Mexico is today much as it was when it was formed millions of years ago. Except now there are brown and rainbow trout in it.

Out of the vast mountains of Colorado, fed by heavy rains and a network of tiny feeder streams, the Rio Grande springs from the eastern face of the Continental Divide and then cuts south, slicing New Mexico in half before turning southeast to form the U.S.–Mexico border and finally emptying into the Gulf of Mexico.

I discovered the Rio Grande as a trout stream in the late 1940s when, as a student attending the University of New Mexico on the G.I. Bill, I fished it with tiny, number 18 and 20 dry flies in December, when there was a hatch of tiny snow flies. I caught nice browns and rainbows, but nearly froze doing it.

I can remember most vividly the days in late May and early June on the Rio Grande when the stoneflies hatched. The hatch does not last long—perhaps a few days at a time. If we were lucky, someone would call us in Albuquerque and tell us the hatch was on. The surface of the river at the bottom of the Rio Grande Gorge would be dimpled with the rings of rising trout. The big tan and black flies, an inch and a half to two inches long, would be dipping and skittering across the surface as far as we could see. And the big trout would be rhythmically rising in the long pools—the distinct *slurp* of the rises carrying above the low murmur of the current.

It was a heart-pounding time. It seemed forever before we had the rods rigged and had donned the chest waders with felt-soled shoes. The best of the rise was usually in the late afternoon, when the west side of the river was in the shade. Those few hours flew like minutes. We would forget to stop for anything. By dusk we would be cold, wet, tired, and hungry, and facing a thousand-foot climb out. But there were those huge rainbows and browns that struck so savagely and fought so hard in that strong current. And—sitting in the car at the top of the Pine Tree Trail north of Arroyo Hondo as the sunset was a blaze of red and gold on the horizon—there were the stories to tell and retell of the day. And ahead would be a couple of drinks and a hot meal of Mexican food in the Sagebrush Inn just south of Taos.

The other best time to fish the Big River—besides during the stonefly hatch—was in October. The New Mexico skies are their bluest then and the summer clouds are all but gone. The days are cool, the weather is dry, and the browns are spawning—running up the feeder streams that empty into the Rio Grande. I have seen browns as big as logs lying in the current at the mouths of the Red River and the Rio Hondo. On some of the upper stretches of these rivers, I have seen big browns slithering across sand and gravel bars in water not more than a few inches deep to reach their spawning beds.

I remember a fisherman who may have known more about fishing the Rio Grande than anyone else who ever lived. He is dead now, but his name was Bud Parr. He used to live in a log cabin at Cedar Springs—a cut in the canyon wall to the east of the Gorge. I first met him in 1947 when he would fish the river every day with a steel casting rod and level-winding plug reel. He used to cast big, four- to five-inch-long copper and brass wobbling spoons, letting them drift deep and slow, down and across the current in the big pools. Some of the browns he caught would make one's breath stop. He had half a dozen of their heads nailed to the cabin above the doors. Dried, dusty, and taut in the arid climate, they looked more like the heads of muskies than of trout.

It was easy to fantasize while fishing the Gorge. The Big River rolled and thundered its way from boiling rapids to long, sinuous pools, some of them more than a hundred yards long. The wind moaned through the branches of the occasional ponderosa pine and the piñon or juniper tree. Deer browsed along the banks or sipped from the water's edge. Beaver lived in the mud of the banks, and waterfowl inhabited the Gorge all year. Now and then there would be the paw print of a mountain lion or black bear in the streamside mud. The canyon was infested with raccoons, mink, ground squirrels, marmots, coyotes, and chipmunks. Buzzards circled overhead in the clear air or sailed down the river on the steady air currents. Everywhere the cliffs bore the whitewash markings of nesting great horned owls, red-tailed hawks, or prairie falcons.

On the faces of large basalt rocks all along the bottom of the canyon were petroglyphs chipped into the rock by the Anasazi: the ancient people. Resting in the shade of a boulder when the fishing was slow, we could imagine those ancient ancestors of the Hopi, Zuñi, Navajo, and Apaches, as they came to the river from the deserts, knowing it carried water to raise crops. And these crudely carved and scratched images of their nature gods—the deer, the snake, the beaver, the antelope—still speak in a strong voice to those who will listen.

I fished the great murmuring river all during the late 1950s and early 1960s as my three sons were born in Corrales, a small town just north of Albuquerque. I was a staff writer for the Associated Press, back then, and I also wrote outdoor columns for newspapers and outdoor stories for magazines as a free-lance writer. I went East in 1965 to work in New York and got trapped in the business of making money. Raising three boys required considerable income, and the years seemed to flash by as they grew into young men.

◆　◆　◆

In 1979 I suddenly realized I had not fished the Big River in years. I had fished rivers over much of the world since leaving New Mexico, but had not returned. I was on a business trip for *Field & Stream* (of which I was then editor), returning to New York from California. I had a sudden urge to see the Gorge and to fish the river again. It was July and I decided to get off the plane in Albuquerque and rent a car. I had brought my fishing gear in a separate suitcase—compact, lightweight waders, an eight-foot, four-piece Hardy graphite fly rod, and my fishing vest stuffed with fly boxes, leader material, and other assorted gear.

The river and the Gorge were still timeless. Driving up the Rio Grande Valley from Albuquerque, through Santa Fe and Espanola, there were many signs of change. Much of the traditional adobe architecture, which characterized most of the towns and villages of the valley, had been replaced by fast-food establishments, mobile homes, commercial buildings, stores, and condominiums. Freeways crisscrossed the mesas, replacing the dirt and asphalt roads of years past. But as one left Espanola and entered the small farming community of Velarde to the north, the feeling of permanence returned. There the valley narrows to small adobe farms and mud-walled churches nestling in the green lushness of vegetable farms and river-irrigated orchards. North of that, I entered the mouth of the canyon—rock cliffs climbing steeply to the sky on both sides of the highway that runs alongside the river on the way to Pilar and then Taos to the north. From that point on change ceases.

I parked the car at the top of the rim of the Gorge a few miles down the piñon- and juniper-bordered dirt road west of the highway just above Arroyo Hondo. The sun was a bright, burnished ball in the clear blue of a midafternoon sky as I shouldered the waders and vest for the steep walk down. A piñon jay called as I peered over the edge at the Big River—a twisting ribbon far below.

Half an hour later, the odor of damp mud, wet sedge grass, and the chamiso sage of the riverbed wafted up from the canyon bottom. The west bank was just beginning to darken in the shadow of the west rim far overhead. The water was not clear, but no rain had fallen that day. Like most days in the summer, the water was slightly murky. A sudden rain in the area of Questa or Red River, and the entire river could turn either a brick red or the color of a chocolate milk shake in less than an hour. Then it meant no more fishing for the day. It generally took at least twenty-four hours to clear again—provided no more rain fell. The sky was clear. There was time for at least a few hours of fishing if my luck held.

When the water is clear or slightly murky, the Rio Grande is a fly-fishing river. I waded into the river, feeling the cool of the water on my thighs and the strong pull of the current. The twin flies—a Rio Grande Ring and, rigged above as a dropper, a Badger—were both on number 12 hooks and dressed to fish dry. The secret of fishing the river in the Gorge is to keep both flies moving like living insects, skipping and skittering across the current. I had learned the secret of dry-fly-fishing the Gorge from Clark Funk, a Taos businessman who had grown up fishing the river. One throws the fly across and slightly downstream and allows it to skip across the surface. Most strikes will come from behind rocks protruding from the current or when the twin flies reach the bottom of the swing close to the bank.

A small brown flashed out from behind a rock and took the lower fly. I let it fight to a twisting, darting finish in the shallows below me before unhooking it and releasing it to the water. No sense in taking small fish when there were so many larger ones.

An hour later, a twelve-inch rainbow and a fourteen-inch brown were nestled in the pocket of my fishing vest. I climbed out of the current and, in the shade of a large boulder, cleaned them both before returning them to the pouch. I would have the chef at the Taos Inn cook them up for me that night. The center of the river was now in shadow. The breeze had grown stronger, and a large white cumulus cloud loomed over the Gorge to the north. The sky around it had taken on a leaden look. With luck the river would stay relatively clear for at least another hour.

I had taken the small camera out of my shirt pocket to photograph a petroglyph of a snake on the face of a dark, streamside boulder, when I noticed a splash close to the far bank and behind a big rock. I sat down and stared at the spot. It was several minutes before the splash occurred again—the rise of a large fish. Putting the camera away, I moved down the shore opposite the spot. Just above the rock was a small willow with the white, filmy mass of a tent-caterpillar nest draped in its branches. As I watched, the fish rose again just below it and another fish rose about ten feet below the first one. They had to be eating caterpillars. The far shore was at least forty yards away and the river was running fast and deep between me and the spot. Remembering the big trout of years past, I took off the two-and-a-half-pound tapered leader and replaced it with an eight-pound leader. I took out a yellow Wooly Worm—the closest fly I had to a tent caterpillar—and waded into the river.

The current in the center was strong enough to send me dancing on tiptoes as the water rose close to the top of the chest waders. Getting a foothold below the big rock where the fish had been rising, I glanced at the sweep second hand of my wrist watch and waited for the next rise. When the fish came up, leaving a wake as it took the insect, I began counting. A minute and a half later it rose again. Taking a long breath, I cast the Woolly Worm just above the spot and let it sink. Nothing happened. I let the fly swing in the current and, on the next cast, dropped it several feet above the first spot. The trout took it on the first twitch, and I quickly set the hook.

I almost lost my footing as a huge rainbow shot out of the water, fell back with a splash, and headed downstream. I had more than one hundred yards of twenty-pound Dacron backing on the reel, so I simply raised the rod tip and hoped the big trout would stop before entering the mouth of the next rapids below. The graphite rod bent double under the strain, but turned the big fish in deep water downstream. The fast water was all on the side of the fish, and I thanked the gods that I had switched to the eight-pound-test leader. After twenty minutes of stubborn, underwater battle, the big trout came to the shallows and lay on its side. I slid it up and over a shallow sand bar and grasped it behind the head. I held it up and fastened the hooked jaw to the small pocket scales. The scale read five and a quarter pounds.

I removed the fly and eased the big male fish into the current. Everything was fine. The river and the Gorge had not changed—would never change. My grandchildren could come to this beautiful, remote spot and do what I had just done. Time had not touched this place.

THE APPROACHING STORM

• • •

JEANETTE FOSTER

A FAINT ORANGE LINE ETCHES THE HORIZON AS THE GLOW FROM THE digital clock reads five-thirty A.M. The air surrounding the boat carries the smell of mesquite mixed with salt. A splash breaks the sea's tranquil surface. On cue, a squadron of pelicans, flying in formation, floats just inches above the surface of the water searching for the flash of silver signifying breakfast.

The stars blur, then fade, as the faint light of dawn thickens and brightens as the sun creeps over the horizon.

Herons, gray-suited doormen with skinny legs, perch on the shoreline rocks. In the background, rough-edged mountains glow in the muted morning light. By six o'clock, the pelicans, now well fed, insert themselves among the herons on the rocks and begin to preen. The muted veil covering the terrain lifts. We pull anchor and motor away.

With the bay not twenty minutes behind us, we stop to cast. Within a few minutes my fly reel starts its high-pitched clatter, signaling a hookup. Seconds later, my fishing buddy's reel cries out in harmony. Behind the boat, two dorado explode through the surface, struggling against the taut lines.

Just another typical day on my home waters.

• • •

Fishing is essentially personal. Finding one's home waters is also very personal. Home waters are not necessarily where you live or grew up or even where you caught your first or biggest fish. I live in Hawaii, but what should be my home waters have been defiled by development and depleted by overfishing. I have had to look elsewhere for waters to soothe and relax me and, at the same time, recharge every cell of my being. Finding such a place can't be done with the eyes alone. Waters surrounded by incredible beauty may appeal to the eyes, but not to the heart. Highly productive fishing may appease the ego, but few would call stocked lakes and managed streams home waters.

No, home waters are felt. You instinctively recognize your home water. Fishing becomes an act of Zen meditation. The answer to what equipment to use, what fly line, which fly, appears as part of the dreamlike dance with the water.

◆   ◆   ◆

The passions of Mother Nature—violent earthquakes, torrential rains, and hurricane-force winds—have pummeled my home waters, yet they retain the serenity of a place that has made peace with itself. My home waters are the Sea of Cortez in Mexico. I identify with these waters. When my life fills with tension and upheaval, I retreat to this area, which has weathered great storms and come to a resolution.

I say I go to the Sea of Cortez to fish. But in truth, I go to observe, to be still and watch the barely visible clues the waters reveal. Fishing mirrors life: You select the skills, equipment, and knowledge you think you will need and then cast about, hoping to be successful. Like life, fishing is not about how many or how big the things are you take from it, but the quality of the time spent.

The Sea of Cortez straddles two worlds: the serene past and the encroaching future. Off the coast of Loreto, in the southern third of the Baja California peninsula, lies an area of my home waters that both fuels my soul and breaks my heart.

Two "planned" resorts, just outside Loreto, the oldest city of the Californias, founded in 1697 by missionaries, preview the future for this rural coast. Just three miles from the thatch-roofed Loreto airport, the Nopolo resort rises like an oasis out of the desert. The "master plan" calls for the building of thirteen hotels, a golf course, a marina, and a residential community of five thousand in place by the turn of the century.

Twelve miles south, and an eon away from Loreto, lies Puerto Escondido, another resort–marina planned for the next century. Here, developers propose more hotels and golf courses and a residential community of thousands. I worry about what these developers will do to my home waters, knowing what similar projects have wrought closer to home.

In dramatic contrast, the town of Loreto has no high-tech blue-print extending into the twenty-first century, but remains true to the traditions of the past. The palm-tree-lined main road ends with the mission Nuestra Señora de Loreto, established in 1697, and from which Father Junípero Serra set out in 1769 to found a chain of missions from Mexico to northern California. Dusty roads, faded adobe houses, and overgrown vegetation suggest an older era of a simpler life of work, family, and church.

In keeping with tradition, every day, at noon, when the mission's venerable bells explode into an angelic chorus, shopkeepers lock up, laborers put down their shovels, and children issue forth from the school for siesta.

After siesta, the residents crawl back to life, a life that revolves around the sea. Marine activities radiate from the town's collapsing pier. On any given day, a dozen locals patiently station themselves on the gnarled remains of the old jetty, hand-lining for fish no larger than a child's hand. At the base of the pier, fanning out across the beach, lies Loreto's fishing fleet, dozens of small punts called *pangas* you can rent for seventy dollars a day, which, as a weathered sign proclaims in English, "includes captain/guide."

Off Loreto lies a fleet of islands anchored randomly in the placid waters. Layered with multicolored mineral deposits, the scarred rocks and blunted peaks tell the tale of eons of earthquakes and rising waters. Tucked into the rocks lie anchorages so perfect, they could only have been designed by a divine hand. Boulders strewn across the mountainsides disguise the passageways until a mariner is within yards of the openings. Underwater canyons, which rise swiftly to meet the vertical cliffs and curved bays, provide mooring areas with nearly 360 degrees of protection.

Night comes abruptly to my home waters, when the sun vanishes behind the dusty-rose curtain of central Baja's mountains. Slowly the silver moon rises over the reaching arms of the saguaro cactus on one of the islands.

Fishing begins before dawn. We motor out to the roadstead to stalk the local *panga* fishermen and learn their grounds. These fishermen are the masters of this kingdom. Painted in glowing colors, the skiffs, powered by occasionally cantankerous outboard motors, are piloted by men who have spent their entire lives on the Sea of Cortez and can read its mysteries the way we read the daily newspaper. Where the *pangas* go, you can bet your last peso, the fish will be.

Beneath the sea lies a relatively untouched Garden of Eden. Electric-blue wrasses dart between colorful corals, rock scallops abound, schools of silvery mullet slink along the bottom, a rainbow retinue of tropical fish flit about, and prehistoric-looking cabrilla coast in the muted light.

But the idyllic underwater pageant is misleading. In an abandoned salt-mining village on one of the islands, off which we cast for roosterfish, the shell of the old mill dominates the remains of the formerly prosperous village. Rusty equipment, encrusted now with layers of snow-white pelican and vulture guano, stands out against the colors of the desert. Empty tequila bottles, a dilapidated bed, and faded salt bags litter the solitary street of deserted houses and whisper stories of the lives of the former residents.

Baked by the sun, the scorching, still air hits three-digit temperatures. Languid vultures lounge on the decaying scrap strewn across the desolate landscape. I scan the waters, looking not only for the flashes of color or motion that reveal roosterfish, but for a reason why man has the ability to destroy whatever he touches, and why he so often exercises it.

A few days later, my home waters give me more evidence of the excesses of man in the twentieth century. On another, smaller island, we don't even bother to cast—the decaying carcasses of roosterfish litter what otherwise would have been a picture-perfect sand beach. The smell of rotten fish permeates the air, and carcasses pollute the waters. The weapons of destruction lie drying in the midday sun: two gill nets draped over a fisherman's shack. Few living creatures remain in the once-abundant waters of the bay.

Fishing no longer occupies my thoughts. I worry about my home waters and what the future brings.

It is October, a season of change in the Sea of Cortez. During the summer months, the winds blow dependably from the southeast; in the winter, from the northeast. In October, as we soon discover, they can blow from any direction. Soothing as my home waters generally are, at times they become unpredictable, violently unpredictable, reminding me that the elements control man's destiny and not the other way around.

Under the protection of a steep cliff and secured by a well-set anchor, we retire for the night. Within thirty minutes a forty-mile-an-hour wind whips up from the southwest (our only unprotected side), creating confused seas as the winds churn the waters and hurl them against the cliffs. The fifty-foot sailboat anchored next to us begins to pitch violently from stem to stern.

In the grip of the sudden storm I find the answer I have been looking for: Complaining about the raging storm will accomplish nothing. There is no room for whining, only for action.

Back home, I take the only action I know how to take: I write. I write to fill magazine pages with descriptions of the beauty of my home waters: the leaping of satin-black manta rays, the breaching and blowing of pods of whales and dolphins, the rolling of the azure waves pummeling the ancient rocks and rummaging along the sweeping beaches.

I write about the magic, too: newborn sea lions nursing, marlin exploding from the sea in an aerial display, and early-morning light pouring onto the desert and bringing its colors back to life.

And I write about the heart-stopping feeling when a fish swirls on a fly, when a school of tuna swarms into view, when a roosterfish tugs at the end of a line.

But I have seen the storm of degradation approaching. I hope my writing will not turn out to be just another form of yelling into the teeth of the gale, but an action that will help save my fragile home waters across the sea.

HOME RIVER

. . .

PAUL SCHULLERY

FISHING HAS A REPUTATION AS AN INNOCUOUS, FAIRLY MINDLESS PAS-
time enjoyed most by shiftless people. Perhaps that impression would
be lessened if nonfishers understood more about wild water. Calling
fishing a hobby is like calling brain surgery a job. The average visitor
driving through Yellowstone sees no farther than the surface of the
water. At best the lakes and streams are mirrors reflecting the surrounding scenery. For the alert fisherman, especially the fly-fisherman,
the surface is not a mirror but a window.

Drive through Hayden Valley, along the Yellowstone River. If
you aren't a fisher, you'll see many things, but the river, except where
it is ridden by waterfowl or waded by moose, will rarely enter your
thoughts, much less stimulate your spirit.

It's different if you fish. The surface of the water tells a story: That
hump followed by a series of lessening ripples (if they were larger, they
would be called standing waves) is proof of a rock or a stump submerged below. Those boulders on the far shore break the current,
which moves slower close to them as the rock rubs, catches, and
retards it; fish and smaller creatures press themselves close to such
obstructions to ease the labor of maintaining position in the current.
The quiet eddies behind this logjam are home for schools of minnows
and the occasional dragonfly nymph that will feed on them if it gets a
chance. Soft swirls and rings on the river's surface are made by trout
rising gently to inhale newly hatched mayflies floating on the surface
as their wings dry. This water is a wilderness of its own, full of life we
do not know and beauties we have not imagined. The fisherman is not
unique in appreciating it—any good naturalist finds it absorbing—but
the fisherman has found special ways of becoming involved in it.

◆   ◆   ◆

The Gardner River is a small rocky stream born at about 9,000 feet in the Gallatin Range a few miles southwest of Mammoth. In its entire length of about twenty miles it drops more than 3,500 feet to its mouth at Gardiner, Montana, where it joins the Yellowstone (because of a quirk of events, the town is spelled with an *i* and the river is not). It flows from its headwaters pond at first north, then east, then south-east, and across Swan Lake Flat to its junction with Indian Creek at Indian Creek Campground, where it crosses under its first bridge, the road from Norris to Mammoth. After this brief encounter with civi-lization, it runs east and then north, around what we call the "back" of Bunsen Peak, where it drops into its little-traveled canyon. Far below the vertical basaltic cliffs, the river gurgles along, pouring 150 feet in one jump over Osprey Falls and out across the eastern foot of Bunsen Peak. It passes under another bridge, the Mammoth-to-Tower road, and almost immediately is joined from the southeast by Lava Creek, which has just left its own canyon. The greater flow then follows the west foot of Mt. Everts almost due north until it dumps, rather privately, into the Yellowstone River right at the park boundary in Gardiner.

I caught my first trout from the Gardner. When my brother, a fly-fisherman of long commitment and great learning, heard that I was to move to Yellowstone, he forced into my hands a complete fishing outfit, insisting that I learn to fly-fish and initiating me in a pastime that has at times been more a way of life than a sport. That first time, however, I was so intimidated by all the new devices and techniques that I was busy fiddling with the reel when a hungry little brown trout grabbed the fly I was paying no attention to, and I landed him only after considerable discussion and with relief that I'd chosen such a private spot for my first outing.

It turned out, as I was then just discovering, that fly-fishing is genuinely unlike other types of fishing. The flies—usually small, del-icate imitations of various forms of insect life, made of feathers, hair, and yarn tied to a small hook—have practically no weight. They cannot be cast with a spinning or casting rod like other lures that weigh enough to be thrown and drag the lines along behind them as they go. In fly-fishing, you are casting the weight of the line, instead. Fly lines, the best of which cost thirty dollars, are thicker than other fishing lines, thick enough to be worked back and forth through the air on the same principle as a bullwhip. The fly is attached to a fine monofilament leader on the end of the line and simply goes along for the ride. Fly lines are usually plastic-coated and tapered on the end to improve the smoothness of the cast. It takes some practice to master this kind of casting, but to watch an accomplished caster working

seventy feet of line on an eight-foot rod, to see the line looping and
rolling straight out behind him, then, as he pushes the rod forward, to
see the line roll cleanly out in front of him and settle gently across a
stream, brings to mind more artful motions—ballet, perhaps—than
are normally associated with fishing.

I spent my whole first summer fishing alone, in the privacy of my
own home river, until I could push out a decent trout-fishing cast of
forty feet and could catch Gardner fish with some regularity (it was
only later that I even realized that some people could cast three times
as far with less effort, and learned how much there actually was to
getting good at fly-fishing).

Learning to cast was only the beginning, and the least fun, of
learning to fly-fish. Fly-fishing introduced me to the aquatic world I
mentioned earlier, led me to look under countless rocks in the shallows for squiggly little marvels I never dreamed existed. It led me to
learn to read water: to study a current and its behavior for what it
could tell me about what lay beneath—where the insects, shelter, and
fish might be found. In this it taught me to appreciate running, moving water and the constancy of its workings. For never did I visit this
river without seeing something new, some slight change in the flow or
in the cut of a channel or in the shape of a bank. The changes became
part of the excitement for me, and each spring I eagerly awaited the
passing of the snowmelt runoff, not only so that I could fish but also
to see what new shapes the flow had taken in favorite spots. Over the
years some pools silted in; others deepened. A dislodged log would jam
in a new position, and I would investigate it as the current dug a new
trout shelter beneath it.

Most of this happened very slowly. A tree might be washed from
its place on the bank by a sudden flood, but more often it would be
undermined gradually, as the water loosened the soil, bit by bit, finally
persuading the tree to fall. If rivers were human, they would be very
patient people.

Without fly-fishing I would never have gotten to know the dipper, a chubby, gray bird of the West that is surely the cheeriest friend
a fisherman could hope for. The dipper, or water ouzel, has puzzled
many visitors; a ranger I know was once approached by a concerned
visitor who reported seeing "a little gray bird commit suicide by walking right into a creek." The dipper, song-bird-shaped and a totally
unaquatic-looking creature, lives on aquatic insects and small fish,
chasing them down in the water without the benefit of webbed feet.
Dippers build nests on low, overhanging banks, right at the water, and
spend their days splashing around in the shallows, frequently in very
fast water (I've also seen them in lakes, where they may "fly" along

right under the surface for several yards in pursuit of insects). They get their name not from their habit of taking an occasional "dip" in the water but from an enchanting mannerism. As they jump from rock to rock, or sit surveying a likely current from shore, they do little bobbing knee-bends, one after another. At first it seems like a nervous twitch— something you hope they'll get over—but soon you get used to it, and the dipper's little dance and shuffle become a special part of the day. Usually there is no more than one in sight, or maybe just a quick twittering warble as one flies by, but one winter when most of the river was rimmed with ice, I saw half a dozen at one time, each inspecting a different icy shelf along successive pools, a veritable platoon of bobbing, dipping, "fly"-fishers, attracted to the warm open water of the lower river. I suppose they compete with the trout for food, as they compete with me for trout, but it makes no sense to me to worry about such congenial competition. They and the trout have been living together for a long time, and I don't interfere all that much. Fishing depends a lot on such things as dippers, anyway.

But it depends as well on occasional success at catching fish. Success depends on many things, including skill, but especially luck. However, after you practice a lot you learn that more is involved than mere mechanical proficiency or good fortune, and that at times you expect to catch fish just because, well, you feel that you will.

For example, there are days when I feel especially in touch with the end of the line, when I feel every lift of the current, every tick of the hook on gravel, every tug of vagrant weed. Such a day was an evening in July, the most productive (of fish, anyway) I ever had on the Gardner.

I'd just read a book about "soft-hackle" flies, simple little wet flies without tails or wings: just slim bodies of fur or floss with a turn of partridge feather near the head. The partridge feather was marked with fine black lines that gave each individual barbule of fiber a segmented look; the barbules, in the water, responded to every wisp of current as the fly drifted along below the surface. Together, they flexed and wiggled like the legs on a struggling insect. Or so the author suggested: I don't know what the trout took them for, only that they took them. As more than one naturalist has pointed out, trout, having no hands, must examine curious objects with their mouths, whether they think they are food or are just amusing themselves to pass the time.

According to my stream log, the water this day was "gorgeous and low," and the angler was described as "a trifle low himself," though I don't recall why; the reason is probably better forgotten and surely was while fishing on this golden evening. As the shadow of Terrace Moun-

tain climbed the slope of Everts in front of me, the trout greeted the
flies with embarrassing abandon. Each pool yielded its fish hastily; no
sooner would I make my cast and begin to probe the suspected pockets
and recesses of the opposite bank with the quivering fly when another
rainbow would yank it, and me, from our thoughtful investigations.

By the time I reached the pool I most wanted to fish, I'd already
released eight or ten small trout, up to ten inches, and was planning
to throw away all my flies and replace them with hundreds of these
magical soft hackles. This pool, a larger, broader version of most on
the river, was about sixty feet across, and from where it was formed by
a fast, bouncy riffle to where it broadened and fanned into an ankle-
deep tail it was perhaps one hundred and fifty feet long. Along the east
bank it was three to four feet deep, and the bank itself was undercut.
It was one of the few pools on the river with that ominous darkness
that says "big fish." Five years earlier I'd caught a fifteen-inch brown
here on a grasshopper imitation, the first respectable brown I'd ever
caught.

I squeezed a couple of small split-shot onto the leader about a foot
above the fly (this practice is not recommended in the book I'd been
reading, and many fly-fishers are offended by such a tactic as crass and
unsporting, but I needed to work the fly deeply through this run,
and I am generally unhampered by delicate sensitivities at such times)
and waded into the shallows at the head of the pool. Remembering a
lesson from another book, I pitched the fly slightly upstream of the
pool, letting it sink as it washed from the riffle into the deep quiet
water. I waited until it was moving slowly through the deep water,
then, with a quick upward motion of the rod, I dragged it back to the
surface. This, I'd read, imitated the upward motion of an emerging
caddis fly. The fish must have thought so, and in an hour I doubled my
total take, keeping a thirteen-and-a-half-inch brown for a late dinner.
Unlike most pools on the river, this one occasionally yielded several
fish from the same spot. Never before had it yielded fifteen as it did
this night, but as long as they kept coming, I felt no urge to move on.
Toward dark I set the hook in a less yielding mouth and was met with
firm resistance followed by a quick run that peeled a few yards of line
from my reel. The fish didn't jump, but had the quickness of a rainbow
(I have an unscientific approach to this; it *felt* like a rainbow). After
a few minutes of short zigs and zags, parrying with the fish as I moved
down to the shallow flat at the tail of the pool, I was able to pull it near
enough to see. It was a big rainbow, fifteen or sixteen inches, and still
quite strong. My leader was too light to simply horse the fish ashore,
and I was in for several more minutes of fight when the fish turned into
the current and fled downstream toward the next riffle, one of the few

up here that I was honestly afraid of—a vicious little roller coaster of jagged rocks and slippery footings, nowhere more than three feet deep but a guaranteed soaking for a clumsy wader. I held tight to the line as the fish swung below me and gained weight and speed in the quickening pull of the current. As soon as the line tightened directly downstream of me, he broke off, taking the fly with him into the little rapid. I retrieved an empty line, with no regrets for once, pleased to have made the acquaintance, for the first time in five years, of the king of the pool.

These good-looking pools are usually not so generous. Another one, far downstream along the road to the North Entrance, frustrated me for a year or two. It was formed where a flat riffle broke over a bank and dropped into a hole the river had dug against the road embankment. I couldn't see the bottom of this one, and so I privately christened it the "salmon hole" because several huge fish could have hidden safely in the dark shadows under its broken surface.

I couldn't even figure out how to fish it. Approach from either side was by high banks where I was visible to the fish. As I climbed down to the stream, I'd see smaller fish scatter from the shallows to the hole, presumably alerting whatever big fish lurked there. One evening I started in about a quarter mile above the hole, wading back and forth across the river between the deeper spots and catching just enough small fish to keep my interest up. I arrived at the riffle above the hole just about dusk. My normal approach was the standard approved one for fly-fishermen: I would try to cast up over the pool from below with a large floating fly. This time, however, unorthodoxy struck, and I crept through the weeds to a point near the upper end of the pool. The Gardner's fish aren't too particular about fly pattern; there's usually little need to imitate the prevailing insect activity precisely, so I rarely even think about such things. I had noticed, though, that on previous nights there were a good many large, heavy-bodied crane flies in the air, flying just a few inches above the surface of the water, presumably mating (crane flies are those giant mosquito-like bugs that resemble flying daddy longlegs; their immature forms are usually aquatic, and the adults lay their eggs in quiet water). I couldn't imagine any self-respecting fish not noticing these big guys, and so I rummaged through my fly boxes for a likely imitation. The one I found was a graceful monster fashioned by my brother some years earlier of elk hair on a very long hook. It was well over an inch long altogether. Still crouched in the weeds, I fastened it to my leader, and, somehow avoiding the high sage that waited to grab my backcast, I laid the line clear across the pool to the shallows near the far bank. Immediately the fast water in midpool dragged the line downstream, and the effect on the fly, on me, and on the fish, was electrifying. The fly floated quietly for an instant in the still water, and then, as the faster water hurried the long belly of line downstream, the fly was pulled out across the deeper water, skating hurriedly along on its light hackles and looking just like those big crane flies.

Its first such skating performance was uninterrupted, but not, I was sure, unobserved. With a mild case of the shakes and a quickening pulse, I let the line drift completely down, then, still crouched, I lifted it into a low backcast and again tossed it across the pool.

Again the line bellied and doubled in the fast current. Again the fly rested only a second, then began its quick skittering over the deep water. But it had moved only a couple of yards when a big brown trout shot from the pool near it and took the fly in a smooth downward motion. (Too surprised at that moment to consider this attack, I later realized how rarely it happens; fish usually just stick their heads up to the surface and inhale whatever is floating there, but this fish actually jumped high and clear of the water and took the fly on his way down, as he re-entered the water nose-first. Perhaps prior experience with the crane flies had taught him that they escape if approached from under-neath, or perhaps he just got so excited he missed the fly on his way up and lucked out and got it on the way down.) With a power that surprised me he bulled right up into the very point of the pool directly beneath the fastest water at its head. My leader was light, so I had to play him gently, and I figured on gradually wearing him out as he fought both the current and my line. I hurried to the tail of the pool to keep well below him, but I must have pulled too hard, for he turned and raced past me into a stumbling riffle full of snags and small rocks. I somehow managed to lead him past the worst snags to a grassy bank in the quieter water below, where I foolishly dragged him up onto the shore just as the fly fell from his mouth (again, this happens often in fishing books, but of the thousands of trout I've caught this is the only time it's happened to me). He was a little over fourteen inches, a fine fat resident brown, and a fish I probably shouldn't have removed from the gene pool but did.

The salmon hole is completely gone now, replaced by a shallow, silty run that developed one spring during a violent spate of snowmelt. Its trout seem to have moved at the same time to a new big run that the river created about fifty yards upstream. I fished it recently after a long absence, and in about half an hour had at least fifteen rises to large grasshopper imitations, so I apparently didn't do the gene pool any permanent harm.

◆   ◆   ◆

The brown trout came to North America in the early 1880s from the United Kingdom and Europe. It had reached Yellowstone (and the Gardner) by about 1890, where it quickly helped other nonnative trouts replace the local cutthroat trouts and grayling. One reason this happened is that browns are a lot harder to catch than cutthroats and therefore withstand fishing pressure much better. A preliminary study done in ponds near the park showed the cutthroats are sixteen times as easy to catch as browns (brook trout, known for gullibility, were only nine times as easy to catch as browns). People who have reason to think about such things wonder if cutthroats would be as easy to catch as they are if they, like the browns, had been fished over by savvy anglers since the 1300s. What must such predation do to the genetic makeup of a fish population, having the easiest-caught individuals removed from hundreds of generations?

The question is of special interest in Yellowstone, where in recent years sportfishing has become primarily a matter of fun rather than of meat acquisition. Because there are too many visitors to feed each a wild trout, park regulations and modern sportfishing fashions have combined to promote catch-and-release fishing—fishing for fun, not meat. Under proper lure restrictions, practically all the released fish will live to be caught again and again.

But the browns, as hard as they are to catch that first time, are harder than hell to catch again. I learned that on my home river. A tiny step-across tributary ran past my quarters, bordering the lawn and then dipping into a sage field for maybe fifty yards before swinging behind a neighbor's lawn, where it widened into a small weed-filled pond. The water was partly runoff from that hot springs, so it was mineral rich and supported heavy vegetation and lots of insect life. Brown trout were there, apparently remnants from hatchery ponds that had once sat nearby and had been fed by the creek. The pond was fished only by a couple of neighborhood kids, who rarely caught anything, and the neighborhood osprey, who rarely put anything back. And me, for a few weeks one summer.

There was a narrow channel about three feet wide through the weeds, then the pond itself, about forty feet wide and three feet deep at the most. The whole stretch ran no more than one hundred and twenty feet, the length of one backyard. The trout rose easily to insects in the quiet water of the channel and the pond, and I could see them clearly, holding there within short casting distance. On hot, bright days they all settled into a slightly deeper depression in the middle of the pond. From a hillock that bordered the yard I could see them holding there, in two rows. There seemed to be about fifteen of them.

I started fishing this stretch one evening after work. It was very civilized, standing on the comfortable lawn and dropping a wiggly little wet fly in front of each trout and snaking them out across the weedbeds as soon as they were hooked. I quickly measured each fish, clipped off a portion of the adipose fin (a harmless if insulting operation), and slid them back into the water. The first evening I caught five, measuring four to thirteen inches. The next night I caught five more, four to ten inches, and again clipped them all. The next night, two more. Five nights later, seven more. The afternoon after that I caught five more. The twenty-first fish I caught had a clipped fin; it was the thirteen-incher I'd caught the first day, a couple of weeks earlier. Over the next few weeks I caught a few more with clipped fins, but I'd learned a new respect for the brown trout. As informal as my little study had been, it had shown me what tough teachers the brown trout can be. I preferred easier.

A friend from Iowa, an enthusiastic outdoorsman, visited me one September. Because of an eccentric graduate chairman we had once taught under, we had adopted a formal manner of addressing each other, after our chairman's manner.

"Mr. Palmer, you must learn about fly-fishing. This isn't the Big Muddy, you know. We have trout here, not those disgusting mudfish you're so fond of catching."

"Mr. Schullery, if you can suppress your elitism about the Mississippi, I would like to learn about fly-fishing."

His first lesson was on the Lamar, near Calfee Creek. The upper Lamar contains many quick, unschooled cutthroat trout, easily caught most of the time. When we walked down to the river in front of the patrol cabin, it was late afternoon but the sun was still bright on the water. It would not have looked, to an Iowa angler, like a very promising time to catch a fish.

"You sit down here on this rock, Mr. Palmer. I must find a grasshopper." I kicked through some nearby brush and quickly sorted an inch-long hopper from the leaves.

"Watch this closely, Mr. Palmer. It's important." I tossed the hopper into the stream about six feet from shore. It landed kicking, stirring up little ripples as it was washed along. It had floated only a few feet when it disappeared in a splashy blur of trout mouth, a small explosion of water that left Mr. Palmer wide-eyed. He was hooked. Within a few minutes I had him slapping a few feet of line out over the water, giving these unruly little cutthroats a chance at a bushy dry fly. One after another they poked their noses up under it, inhaled it, mouthed it thoughtfully for a second, then spit it out and sank back to shelter. Each time Mr. Palmer watched the whole rise, take, and rejection with a slack jaw and a slack line, never once trying to hook the fish.

"Mr. Palmer, you have to set the hook when they take the fly. Weren't you paying attention to the lecture?"

"Yes, Mr. Schullery, I understand. I saw you do it." He was earnest in the face of my exasperation.

"Well, then, Mr. Palmer, why didn't you set the damn hook?!"

"I never think of it at the time, Mr. Schullery. It's all so interesting to watch."

A few days later I took him to the upper Gardner. I led him to the bank and rigged up the rod as I continued my instruction.

"Now, Mr. Palmer, you should learn about where trout hold in the current." As I spoke, I worked about thirty-five feet of line into the air, keeping it airborne above me, casting back and forth, ready to deliver. This was one of the few stretches of river I know of where what I was about to do was not the worst kind of reckless arrogance.

"They like water at the edges of the current, Mr. Palmer. See that rock there with the little eddy behind it, where the water is sort of still?" He was attentive, if skeptical, as I dropped a small dry fly into the spot, where it was instantly drowned but not eaten by one of the suicidal brook trout that inhabited this precious run. Mr. Palmer choked quietly as I whipped the fly back with a triumphant "Aha!" Then, as I dried it with some false casts, I remarked casually, "Look for calmer breaks in the current, Mr. Palmer, even if you can't see a rock or anything, like this one up here." I laid the fly onto a little slick in midstream, immediately grabbing it back from another splashy rise. This was not instruction; this was performance. Again and again I brought trout up, hooking a couple, missing most, reveling in the show they and I were putting on. And each time I'd raise a fish, Mr. Palmer, his voice a mixture of envy, respect, and disdain, would mumble, "Mr. Schullery, you bastard," or "This can't be. . . ." I don't know how many fish I showed him in fifteen minutes, but it was many more than I'd imagined I would. The Gardner and its trout performed royally in beginning the education of yet another fly-fisherman.

◆   ◆   ◆

A home river is that rarest of friends, the one who frequently surprises you with new elements of personality without ever seeming a stranger. The revelations are gifts, not shocks. Like Mr. Palmer, I seemed always to be discovering new secrets of the river; they weren't really secrets at all, just places waiting for me to become smart enough to notice them. It might be a new trout lie, hidden under a log and invisible from the trail I usually walked; a beaver dam that must be fished this season because it will be silted shallow by next; a deer bed in the willows behind a favorite pool; a deep pocket I never noticed until I walked the bank opposite the trail. What makes this so precious, like so many other meaningful pastimes, is the anticipation of revelations yet to come, or discoveries not fully understood, such as the dark pool swarming with Diptera that I discovered one day while searching for a drowning victim and never later returned to, off duty. Like the stretches of canyon water I never fished, that pool is a mystery and a promise, probably worth more in anticipation than it will be in actual sport.

Some revelations are bigger. Recently, in an isolated stretch of the upper river, where only brook trout were thought to reside, a pocket of rainbows was found, survivors of some long-forgotten stocking mission of several decades ago. They lived, unknown and unfished, in one short stretch of river, neither expanding their range into better-traveled waters nor shrinking into oblivion. Further study may prove them to be of considerable scientific value. Like the other nonnative trouts in Yellowstone—brook, brown, and lake—they were placed here in the early days of fisheries science, before distinct strains of each species were hopelessly crossed and mixed in the great trout factories of modern hatcheries and in countless rivers where thoughtless and well-intentioned fisheries crews dumped new strains of trout on top of existing native populations. Yellowstone has waters, including my home river, that were stocked before that energetic "management" chaos mutilated our Western trout taxonomy and have not been stocked since; waters that now may give more than sport—they may yield museum-pure strains of trout that we thought we'd lost. It may not be easy for the nonfisherman to comprehend why such knowledge makes the fishing more exciting than it otherwise would be, but it is immensely satisfying to know such a thing. Fishing is a quest for knowledge and wonder as much as a pursuit of fish; it is as much an acquaintance with beavers, dippers, and other fishermen as it is the challenge of catching a trout. My home river does not always give me her fish, but the blessings of her company are always worth the trip.

THE MAN WITHOUT A RIVER

GARY SOUCIE

I'VE TRIED, REALLY TRIED, TO LOVE ONE RIVER MORE DEEPLY THAN ALL the others. But it doesn't take. I fall in and out of love too easily with rivers and streams, a hapless victim of crushes, infatuations, and disappointments. Just when I think "the real thing" has finally come along, some new river will throw her curves at me and make me itch to roam again. It's worse than it is with women (except that I've never wound up intensely disliking a river I used to love). It isn't simply a question of fidelity, though. It is ever so much more complicated than that. In both cases.

Being a two-time loser at marriage, maybe I should have known I'd never develop a deep, abiding relationship with a single body of water. Still, it has surprised me. Having lived my whole fly-fishing life in New York City (I only embraced the sport a decade or so ago), I ought to have become one of those die-hard Catskill purists. But purism doesn't suit me; every one of my fly boxes holds at least one *thing* placed there specifically to put the fear of Rambo into the blue-blooded hearts of purists: molded-plastic "flies" of dubious pedigree, bright-orange Girdle Bugs, and those outrageously gaudy dry flies that you buy six or eight to the dollar in those plastic rotary dispensers. Besides, the Esopus and both branches of the upper Delaware remain mostly baffling to me, and—dare I even admit it?—I've never even fished the holy waters of the Beaverkill. Not once. *Some* fly-fisherman!

I grew up along the banks of the Kankakee River in Illinois, which might be considered my natal home water except that I haven't fished it in more than thirty years and probably know it less well now than rivers I've fished just once or twice more recently. Anyway, I was a plug-caster and bottom-fisherman back then and only used a fly rod once in my youth.

◆   ◆   ◆

Tom Bates and Ron Erzinger and I had gone camping near the mouth of a tributary creek downriver from the town of Kankakee, and Ron had brought along a fly rod. He was only the second person I'd ever seen use a fly rod, the first being my mother's cousin Jim Himes, who never let me use his rod, but who once hooked me in the back with a bass bug.

Before we started fishing, we set up camp and our knife course. That summer we had graduated from mumblety-peg to a game in which we went from tree to marked tree, throwing knives at the next one. If the knife stuck in the target tree, you advanced and got another throw; if you missed, or if the knife fell out, you stayed put and waited your turn for another try. I'm not sure the game had a name; it was just something we had invented to kill time. Once our knife course had been marked, our army-surplus shelter-halves set up, and our fire ring made, we set out to explore the environs.

There were plenty of weedbeds along the river margins that looked just perfect for smallmouth bass, pike, and pickerel. And there were rocky shoals out in the fast current, about as far as we could cast. That looked promising for channel cats on bait. Dinners seemed assured. We might not even have to open the cans of vegetarian burger patties and chicken in stock that we had brought along, just in case. The first afternoon of fishing didn't produce any lunkers, though, so Ron decided to try fly-rod poppers on panfish in the mouth of the creek.

On his second or third cast, Ron had a feisty little bluegill on. Two casts later, it was a red-eyed rock bass. Dinner prospects looked good, and so did fly-fishing. After Ron had given Tom and me a little casting instruction-by-demonstration, we took turns using his fly rod. We didn't catch much—barely enough small bluegills and rock bass for a spartan meal—but it was a lot of fun. It's also the only real fishing memory I have of the trip. The strongest memory I have is of Bates— who was prone to claustrophobia—thrashing and writhing and shouting as if possessed by the D.T.'s, trying to get out of the itchy-wool army-surplus mummy bag he'd zipped up to the chin.

As I recall, when we weren't fly-fishing the mouth of the creek, we spent more time throwing knives at trees than plugs at weedbeds. Why I didn't then decide to take up fly-fishing on my own, I can't remember. My family was so poor, maybe the reason was economic; I know I never owned more than one rod and reel back then, and I even used to shoplift lures and hooks and sinkers when I couldn't afford to buy them. At any rate, I went back to knuckle-busting level-wind reels and casting rods. Maybe if I had lived on a trout river I would have become a convert, but that's only speculation by hindsight, and you can't get much more tenuous than that.

◆   ◆   ◆

My first fly-fishing river—the Thurso, in Caithness in northern Scotland—can hardly be called home water. It was more like a brief fling above one's social station with a foreign peeress. I only fished it three days and never even got a rise out of its salmon. But it, and the trout lochs in the Orkneys, did get me hooked on fly-fishing. And hooked good.

The Scotland trip was typical of my fly-fishing apprenticeship: fishing way over my head in fast company on press junkets to the kinds of places that real fly-fishermen would die for. I even wrangled an assignment from the *Atlantic Salmon Journal*, as hard-core a steely-eyed specialist's magazine as exists anywhere. I had planned to practice fly-casting in Central Park early in the mornings, before going to work, but I was so busy clearing the editorial decks for the trip, I never got in a single practice cast. So I showed up at Kennedy Airport with virginal borrowed equipment and two or three days' fly-fishing experience more than a quarter century earlier. My experienced companions on the trip included George Reiger from *Field & Stream* and Tony Atwill from *Sports Afield* as well as two other writers from the *Chicago Tribune* and *Diversion* magazine.

But God loves and protects fools, and I caught the first brown trout the first morning we spent fishing the Orkneys. Early-season conditions were, as the Scots say, dour, and my fish turned out to be half of that first day's entire take.

Beginner's luck didn't travel with me over to the Scottish "mainland," though. During our briefing, Eddie McCarthy, the Thurso's river superintendent, described the perfect salmon-fishing conditions: overcast skies, just enough wind to ruffle the surface without complicating casting, and an air temperature four degrees warmer than the water temperature. We saw no such conditions in our three days on the Thurso River. The first and last days were hot and sunny; the second day was blustery and almost wintry cold. None of us caught any fish.

No, that's not exactly true: Occasionally a kamikaze brown trout would attack our big, double-hooked flies and manage to hook itself. On the Thurso and other British salmon rivers, you aren't allowed to return trout to the water. Salmon fishermen so despise egg-eating trout, the gillies stuff them down the holes of rabbits or ferrets—I can't remember which—along the streamside paths. (Perhaps at least partly in retaliation, the trout fishermen in the Orkneys say they'd rather fish for carp than salmon.)

Georgeous as these hallowed salmon waters are—and Reiger and I spent our third day fishing Lord Thurso's private beat, as lovely a stretch of stream as I've ever experienced—this combination of snobbery and churlishness rules them out of contention as my home waters, even if ever I were lucky enough to live alongside one of them for a time. As for trout-loch fishing, drifting sideways before the wind in a rowboat and casting long leaders with three wet flies attached is novel and pleasant, but it just doesn't have enough sex appeal to keep me interested very long.

◆　　◆　　◆

Since those halcyon days, I've had the good fortune to fly-fish other distant waters in Yugoslavia, Sweden, Alaska, and northern Canada, as well as wonderful waters nearer by in the Poconos and on Long Island, in Maine and Vermont, in the Florida Keys, in Montana and Missouri. Because I sit on a board at the University of Missouri's School of Journalism, I get out to the Show Me State almost annually. And when I do, I always get down to the Ozark trout streams. In fact, when I was asked to serve on the Science Journalism Center's national board, I agreed on the condition that the annual meetings be held during trout season. That turned out to be an easy request to grant because it is always trout season somewhere in Missouri.

My fly-fishing trips typically begin with a cab ride to the airport, and I've now fished more in Missouri than in New York. I've fished the Current River, the Meramec, the North Fork of the Smith, several different creeks, and private waters. Some of these waters I have fished just once, others, several times. I have floated them in rafts and john boats and canoes, waded them for long or short distances, fished them while steeple-casting from wooded banks. I've caught brown trout, rainbows of several strains, large- and smallmouth bass, and the biggest green sunfish I've ever seen.

Maybe I like fishing Missouri so much because I've seldom been skunked there (only twice, I think, and both times on the Current). But it's more likely because of my fishing companions. Usually I fish with Chuck and Sharon Tryon, the coauthors of *Fly Fishing for Trout in Missouri*, the cofounders of Ozark Mountain Fly Fishers, and two of the finest fishing companions imaginable. Fishing with them is, as Chuck is fond of saying about almost anything from a bright spawning trout to a broken tippet, "outstanding." I also enjoy Ozark fishing with Spence Turner, a fisheries biologist with the state Department of Conservation; the well-known outdoor-humor writer Joel Vance; and

Bob Lindholm, the state's assistant attorney general and a prize-winning photographer. These are good people, and good people are as important to good fishing as good fish.

On one trip I remember particularly well, Joel and Spence and I drove down to Rolla to pick up Chuck and Sharon after a day's canoe-fishing the Current. Atypically, Joel caught the only fish, a nice smallmouth. (In his stories and magazine articles, Joel usually describes himself as a feckless fellow of many thumbs, a humiliating incident or outdoor accident just waiting to happen. This trip began like a Joel Vance article: He had forgotten to bring along a fly reel, but fortunately both Spence and I had spares.) The plan had been to float the North Fork, but the water was already high, and an overnight downpour accompanied by scattered tornadoes settled the issue. On Chuck and Sharon's suggestion, we headed for the Spring Valley Trout Ranch (sort of a salmonid dude ranch) on a private stretch of spring creek in the southernmost Ozarks.

After a short pit stop for coffee and a midmorning snack, it suddenly occurred to Spence that he and Joel and I had left our rods and reels locked up in the cargo bin of his canoe trailer in the Tryons' driveway—a hundred miles back up the road. Going back for them was out of the question. I suggested that we stop at a tackle shop and buy inexpensive replacements. I was reminded in unison that we were in the Missouri Ozarks, not West Yellowstone. But we had our waders with us, and I had my vest, so we pressed on, trusting that the ranch would have rental or loaner equipment. They did: soft, heavy seven- and eight-weight fiberglass rods of the sort you always see in K Marts and hardware stores, loaded with five-weight level lines. Under the best of conditions, I am a lousy caster; you should have seen me using one of those outfits, trying to cast heavily weighted nymphs and BUB Flies (a Chuck Tryon creation, the Big Ugly Black Fly is sort of a gonzo Girdle Bug with rubber-band legs, antennae, and forked tail). Amazingly, I managed to catch a few rainbows.

That trip has become relatively well known in Missouri fly-fishing circles. It is usually referred to in shorthand as "the tequila trip" (the reference being to my consumption one night of three-fourths of a bottle of the distilled extract of agave, the remainder of which is still maintained in the Tryon household under shrinelike conditions). I prefer to think of it as "the hogmolly trip," because it marked the first time I'd ever seen a northern hog sucker (and Spence still can't believe I spent several minutes staring into the water at it, ignoring a brief feeding blitz that was going on under some nearby willows at the time). Either way, it burns on vividly. Or maybe it's a case of absence making the heart grow fonder.

◆   ◆   ◆

The future is a crap shoot, but the way things are going, I think I may finally find my home water around and among the Florida Keys. The variety of fish available, the incredible blue–green palette of the waters, the beauty of the parts that haven't yet been trashed by development—these are like siren song to me. But my youngest daughter just graduated from college, and that means staying in the city for a while to build up a little nest egg.

You probably think I've become a flats-fishing addict. Nope; not yet, anyway. Every time I've tried to fly-fish the flats for bonefish or permit, it has blown too hard. When the surface is too riffled, the fish can see me before I can see them. That means casting to spooked fish. Not to mention what the wind does to my casting. Fly-fishing the flats successfully requires that you be able to cast quickly, accurately, delicately, and far. These are pretty much mutually exclusive propositions in my personal experience. Putting two or more of them together requires a little luck. In a stiff wind, I can't put one of them together. No, my best Keys fly-fishing so far has come in two different and quite disparate environments: offshore in the biggest, wildest river of them all, and hard up against the shoreline.

I love to while away the hours, wading along the shore in swim trunks, casting flies around canal-inlet jetties and the little rock groins that shoreline landowners mistakenly erect to save their little beaches, both of which create wonderful microhabitats for inshore species. I cast small, usually shrimp-imitating, flies and take schoolmasters, mangrove, and other snappers, baby jacks of several species, needlefish. If I use a wire or heavy mono tippet, I can take barracudas, which hit a fly with incredible savagery.

Except for the clumsiness of handling and protecting a long fly rod in the typical sportfisherman's cockpit, blue-water fly-fishing is a snap. My friend Ray Madeo, who lives on Cudjoe Key, raised both eyebrows when he saw me carry a fly rod on board his boat the first time. It was a windy day, the water was choppy, and he wasn't planning to do any chumming. On the way out, he asked me how much offshore fly-fishing I'd done. "None," I replied. "But you know me: always ready to experiment." Unlike most blind dates and a lot of my angling experiments, this one worked out well.

There weren't many weed lines out in the Gulf Stream that day, and we trolled past every little patch we could find. Finally, one of the rods went down. "Dolphin!" someone shouted as the brilliant blue-gold-and-green fish burst from the surface in the grandest of jetés. We got the trolling rigs in and grabbed for the spinning rods. There were four of us on board—the writer Jack London, who lives on Summer-land Key, the Connecticut outdoor-writer Ed Ricciuti, Ray Madeo, and me—and we each fished something different. One rod was rigged with cut ballyhoo, another with a small spoon, yet another with a bucktail jig. I was using a small Sevenstrand Clout, my favorite light-tackle offshore lure because it can be cast, trolled, or jigged. After I had caught a couple of fish, I decided to try the fly rod. I had already tied on a green-and-yellow Lefty's Deceiver, and it turned out to have been a happy choice.

At the end of each twenty- or thirty-foot sidearm cast, I usually had two or more fish contending for the fly. As soon as one grabbed the Deceiver and felt the hook, it would get airborne—typically about six feet up and fifteen to twenty feet out. Until I had to stop using the fly rod, I was catching fish that were slightly bigger than those being taken on the spinning rods (no one could figure out why). I had to stop fly-fishing because I had disassembled and cleaned the reel the night before, and I had reassembled the drag wrong. When I tried to adjust the drag wheel, the whole thing started loosening up. Finally, I had to lay the fly rod down for fear the Alvey reel would come apart and fall to the deck in pieces, and that I'd lose some of the parts out the scuppers. But it was wonderful while it lasted, and the fly rod has now become my dolphin tackle of first choice.

I already have my Keys fly-fishing agenda made out: bonefish and permit on the flats, tarpon and blacktip sharks in the passes between the flats, sailfish and blackfin tuna and wahoo offshore, jacks chummed up from under buoys, snook and redfish and sea trout and ladyfish in the backcountry.

◆   ◆   ◆

My daughter Juliette just graduated from Columbia University, and she knows that if she decides to go to graduate school, she's going to have to do it without much help from her fishing-bum father. He's going to be too busy pitching flies and woo in home water he has been looking for all his life.

CONTRIBUTORS' BIOGRAPHIES

◆ ◆ ◆

A writer of both scholarly and popular works, and a prize-winning poet, **Justin Askins** is an assistant professor of English at Radford University in Virginia. He formerly taught at Hunter College, Baruch College, and the College of Staten Island, where he took his bachelor's degree. He also holds a master's from Boston University and a Ph.D. from the City University of New York.

◆ ◆ ◆

After ten years at *Sports Afield,* **Lionel A. Atwill** moved to *Field & Stream* in 1990 as a contributing editor. Earlier, he had edited *Adirondack Life* and *Backpacker* magazines. The son of actor Lionel Atwill, Tony played lacrosse and football (linebacker) while at Duke University. During his four years as an airborne ranger in the army, he served as a reconnaissance platoon leader with the 1st Division in Vietnam, earning a Purple Heart and two Bronze Stars. His book, *Sporting Clays: An Orvis Guide,* was published in 1990.

◆ ◆ ◆

A native of Idaho, **Dennis Bitton** has an advertising agency in Idaho Falls, where he also publishes *FlyFishing News, Views & Reviews,* edits The Federation of Fly Fishers' quarterly magazine, *The Flyfisher,* and works to maintain and restore the South Fork of the Snake River.

◆ ◆ ◆

Stephen J. Bodio lives in the boondocks near Magdalena, New Mexico, where he writes "Bodio's Review" for *Gray's Sporting Journal* as well as books and articles on fishing, falconry, pigeons, and the other facets of life that interest him. His books include *A Rage for Falcons*, *Aloft*, and the recently published memoir *Querencia*.

◆   ◆   ◆

A celebrated novelist since 1947, **Vance Bourjaily** for more than two decades taught at the University of Iowa Writers Workshop. Outdoor sportsmen came to know him through his many articles and columns in *Esquire* and other magazines and through his 1973 book, *Country Matters*.

◆   ◆   ◆

Richard Brautigan (1935–84) began his writing career as a poet in the late 1950s. A flower child of San Francisco's Haight-Ashbury District, he became a countercultural hero of the turbulent 1960s. His career peaked early, with *Trout Fishing in America* (1977). Reportedly depressed with his languishing career, he apparently took his own life in 1984. His friend and publisher, Seymour Lawrence, called him "a true American genius in the tradition of Twain and Lardner."

◆   ◆   ◆

President Jimmy Carter has been an outdoorsman all his life, but is a fairly recent convert to fly-fishing. "On Turniptown Creek" appeared in only slightly different form as the last chapter in his eighth book, *An Outdoor Journal*. As president, Jimmy Carter presided over an administration that was one of the best friends that outdoor sportsmen, conservationists, and free-flowing rivers ever had. He remains active in environmental issues through Global 2000, Inc. He founded the Carter Center at Emory University in Atlanta and directs its consultations on world issues.

◆   ◆   ◆

Russell Chatham has had a dual career as artist and writer. His paintings are highly prized by collectors of modern landscapes, and his writing on fishing, which he often said was pay-the-rent hackwork, has enduring charm and power. Among his best-known books: *The Angler's Coast*, *Striped Bass on the Fly*, *Silent Seasons*, and *Dark Waters*. His answers to questions on the *Contemporary Authors* questionnaire exemplify his iconoclastic nature: Politics, "Smash the State"; Religion, "Salmon Fishing"; and "I write and paint for money; fish, cook, shoot pool, and chase women for fun."

◆   ◆   ◆

After working in and around his native New York City as a writer, private investigator, public-relations representative, and commercial fisherman, **John N. Cole** emigrated to Maine. He spent twenty years there editing four different newspapers, including *The Maine Times*, which he founded. He has written nine books, including *Striper, Fishing Came First*, and the recently published *Tarpon Quest*. His journalistic efforts have won numerous awards, including the Missouri Medal for Journalism, the EPA's Environmental Achievement Award, and the New England Academy of Journalism's Yankee Quill Award. He and his wife, Jean, now divide their time between Brunswick, Maine, and Key West, Florida.

◆   ◆   ◆

Formerly a veterinarian, **Tony Dawson** is best known as a photographer, although he broke into the outdoor field by writing articles for *Field & Stream*'s regional pages. He and his wife, Kathy, operate a successful photography business out of Anchorage, Alaska. Their photos have appeared in numerous national magazines, from *Field & Stream* to *Audubon* to the newsweeklies. "The Creek" is set in the Blue Mountains of Oregon.

◆   ◆   ◆

A college professor since 1957, **John Engels** has published several books of poetry, a book on the poet William Carlos Williams, and (with his father) two books on writing and literature. He also writes short fiction on fishing, an example of which is included here. He was born in South Bend, Indiana, and was educated at Notre Dame, the University of Dublin, and the University of Iowa.

◆   ◆   ◆

Jeanette Foster lives in Hawaii where she and her husband, Rick Gaffney, travel around the globe in search of "the perfect fishing hole" for their free-lance magazine articles. She has fished the Atlantic, Pacific, and Indian oceans, from twenty-eight different islands, in nine nations, and on five continents, managing along the way to capture two world records. She was formerly a reporter for wire services and daily newspapers.

◆   ◆   ◆

Born in Illinois, **John Gierach** moved to Colorado and took up fly-fishing in 1969, the year he graduated from Findlay College in Ohio with a degree in philosophy. He lives on the St. Vrain River near the town of Lyons, where he writes a weekly outdoor-sports page for the *Longmont Daily Times-Call*, articles for numerous magazines, and books that have already become classics of angling literature, among them, *Trout Bum, The View from Rat Lake*, and *Sex, Death, and Fly-Fishing*.

◆   ◆   ◆

Caroline Gordon (1895–1981) was a native of Kentucky, which served as the setting for her first two novels, including *Aleck Maury* (1934), from which the selection in this book was adapted. Although fiction, the book was based on her father's reminiscences. The writer of several novels, numerous short stories, and books on literature, she was for a time married to the poet Allen Tate. She lectured on creative writing and the novel at Columbia University and the Universities of North Carolina, Washington, Virginia, Utah, and Kansas.

◆   ◆   ◆

Elevated to the peerage by King George V in 1916 as the first **Viscount Grey of Fallodon,** Edward Grey (1862–1933) was the scion of an English family with a long tradition of public service. He served in Parliament and the British cabinet, as ambassador to the U.S., and as chancellor of Oxford University, from which he had been sent down in 1894 for "laziness." While serving as foreign secretary (1905–16) he worked long but fruitlessly to avoid war. His best-known books were *Fly Fishing, Fallodon Papers*, and *The Charm of Birds*.

◆   ◆   ◆

Steven A. Griffin has been a full-time free-lance writer and photographer since 1975, contributing to a wide range of regional and national magazines and newspapers. Since 1987 he has been teaching a course in magazine and feature writing at Central Michigan University.

◆   ◆   ◆

Born and educated in England, **Roderick L. Haig-Brown** (1908–76) became a wilderness logger in the western U.S. and Canada by the time he was twenty. He settled in British Columbia, fished his beloved Campbell River, farmed, wrote, and presided as judge of the provincial court in Vancouver for thirty-four years. Besides his many famous fishing books, he also wrote two novels. He received many awards for his writing, his conservation work, and his public service.

◆   ◆   ◆

Stewart Hardison wrote several articles in *Wildlife in North Carolina* while a student at North Carolina State University in the early 1970s. "Into Big Timber Creek" was one of them.

◆   ◆   ◆

A dedicated fisherman who was brought up on the rivers of Cumberland, the Englishman **John Waller Hills** (1867–1938) called his biography *My Sporting Life.* He also wrote *The River Keeper, A History of Fly-Fishing for Trout,* and *A Summer on the Test,* his best-known book from which was taken the piece in this anthology.

◆   ◆   ◆

For many years a senior writer for *Time* and *Sports Illustrated,* **Robert F. Jones** now lives and writes in southern Vermont. Besides his many free-lance articles on hunting, fishing, conservation, and life, he has written four novels. His most recent, *Blood Tide,* was published in 1990.

◆   ◆   ◆

Ted Kerasote writes both the "Outdoor Skills" and "EcoWatch" columns as well as feature articles for *Sports Afield* and has contributed articles to many national publications. He is the author of *Navigations,* a collection of essays on wilderness travel, and is currently working on a book about the psychology of hunters. He has been an instructor and course director for the Colorado Outward Bound School, taught creative writing at the University of Colorado, and

traveled widely in the Americas, Europe, Asia, East Africa, Green-
land, and New Zealand.

◆   ◆   ◆

Stephen Leacock (1869–1944) was born in England, but emigrated to
Canada with his parents in 1876. Educated at Canadian and U.S.
universities, first in languages, then in economics and political science, he earned his Ph.D. in 1903 and became a professor of economics at McGill University. Famous both as an economist and a
humorist (and as a biographer of Charles Dickens and Mark Twain),
he is often credited with having set the standard for modern wit.

◆   ◆   ◆

Born in New York City, **Michael Levy** grew up in Indiana and Connecticut and graduated from the University of Connecticut. But he
seriously took up fishing and began writing about the outdoors in New
Jersey, during his four years as the only reporter on the *Princeton
Packet.* In 1969 he moved to upstate New York, as a general-
assignment reporter with *The Buffalo News.* For the past ten years he
has also served as the paper's outdoor editor. His free-lance contributions have appeared in various regional and national outdoor magazines.

◆   ◆   ◆

Although he never flaunts his erudition, **Nick Lyons** took a bachelor's
degree at the University of Pennsylvania, did graduate work at Bard
College, and earned master's and doctoral degrees at the University of
Michigan. A Renaissance man, he taught English at Hunter College
in New York for more than twenty-five years, during which time he
also spent more than a decade as executive editor of Crown Publishers,
wrote, edited, or ghost-wrote several books and the "Seasonable Angler" column for *The Fly Fisherman,* and founded Nick Lyons Books
(now Lyons & Burford) in 1978. Among his own books: *Bright Rivers,
Fishing Widows, The Seasonable Angler, Fisherman's Bounty,* and *Con-
fessions of a Fly Fishing Addict.*

◆   ◆   ◆

One of the best-known novelists of the past two decades, **Thomas
McGuane** writes and ranches in Montana, with occasional screen-

writing and directing forays to Hollywood and fishing trips to Key West. His first novel, *The Sporting Club,* was set in one of those North Woods clubs favored by monied sportsmen from the Detroit suburbs. The adversaries of his next novel, *Ninety-two in the Shade* (which was made into a movie), were flats guides in the Florida Keys. Several of his essays on fishing and hunting were collected in *An Outside Chance: Essays on Sport.*

◆   ◆   ◆

Steven J. Meyers is a free-lance writer, photographer, and graphic-arts consultant who lives in Durango, Colorado. After receiving a bachelor's degree in psychology from Wheaton College and a master's in photography from the Illinois Institute of Technology, he moved to Colorado in 1975 and began working for a Denver publisher. He also spent five years as a photo-interpreter and control-survey team member with a photogrammetry firm in Durango. "Lime Creek" was adapted from his *Lime Creek Odyssey,* which was published by Fulcrum in 1989.

◆   ◆   ◆

While still in college at Louisiana State University, **Harry Middleton** began free-lancing for *Sports Illustrated.* A "military brat" who was born in Germany, he lived in many different places, but got hooked on trout fishing while growing up in the Ozarks. For six years he worked for Time, Inc. (now Time-Warner), writing for *Southern Living, Southern Accents, Southpoint,* and other magazines in the Southern Progress group. His books include the award-winning *The Earth Is Enough* and the recently published *On the Spine of Time,* from which his contribution to this book was adapted.

◆   ◆   ◆

The daughter and granddaughter of fishing forebears, **Judy Muller** began her journalistic career as a reporter for two newspapers in New Jersey. She switched to radio in 1977 at WHWH/WPST in Princeton, moving to Denver in 1979 as anchor and reporter for KHOW-AM. From 1981 to 1990, she was a news correspondent with CBS News in New York, anchoring her own morning and midday radio news-commentary shows, substituting for Charles Osgood on "The Osgood File," and contributing reports to Charles Kuralt's "CBS Sunday Morning" TV show and anchoring "For Our Times" for CBS-TV. In

1990 she moved to Los Angeles, where she is a television correspondent for ABC News, contributing reports to "World News Tonight with Peter Jennings," "Prime Time," "Good Morning, America," and "Nightline."

◆   ◆   ◆

W. H. H. Murray (1840–1904), a Yale-educated cleric, was a pastor in Greenwich and Meriden, Connecticut, and at the Park Street Congregational Church in Boston. He resigned his pastorate in 1874 to devote himself to business pursuits, writing, playing the horses, and preaching to independent congregations.

◆   ◆   ◆

Although he grew up on the northern coast of the Gulf of Mexico (where he still maintains a house), **Geoffrey Norman** has lived in Vermont for the past fifteen or so years. Formerly *Esquire*'s outdoors editor, he now free-lances for many magazines. He has written six books; the most recent, *Sweetwater Ranch,* is a novel set in the Florida Panhandle.

◆   ◆   ◆

The holder of a master's degree in English, **Margot Page** taught college writing for three years before getting into publishing. She worked for a time at Nick Lyons Books in New York, where she met her husband, Orvis's Tom Rosenbauer. She free-lances now from Vermont for such publications as *The New York Times, American Health, New Woman, Trout,* and *Fly Rod & Reel.* She also edits the American Museum of Fly Fishing's quarterly journal, *The American Fly Fisher,* and its newsletter, *Greenheart Gazette.* She is the granddaughter of Alfred W. Miller, who was better known as Sparse Grey Hackle.

◆   ◆   ◆

Thomas R. Pero says he "ran away from Massachusetts to be closer to steelhead." Now he lives in Bend, Oregon, "in a cedar house with large glass windows looking out at ponderosa pines and distant volcanoes." He has been editor of *Trout,* the award-winning magazine of Trout Unlimited, for a decade and a half. He collects fly rods, salmon flies, shotguns, and Charlie Parker records.

◆   ◆   ◆

Harry Plunket Greene was a well-known opera and concert singer in his day. But he is remembered today for his one angling book, *Where the Bright Waters Meet*, a memoir of his love affair with the River Bourne in Hampshire. It was first published privately in 1924.

◆   ◆   ◆

A man of diverse talents, **William Cowper Prime** (1825–1905) practiced law in New York City from 1846 to 1861, at which time he became part owner of the *New York Journal of Commerce*, which he edited until 1869. In 1874 he became a professor of art at Princeton, his alma mater. He wrote several books, among them *The Old House by the River* and *I Go A-Fishing*.

◆   ◆   ◆

Having retired after a diplomatic career in the State Department, **Datus C. Proper** now writes from his home in the Gallatin Valley of Montana. He has formerly claimed home streams in Yellowstone, Pennsylvania, Virginia, New Mexico, Ireland, England, Brazil, and Portugal. His articles have appeared in many fishing and outdoor magazines, but he may be best known for his books: *What the Trout Said* and *Pheasants of the Mind*.

◆   ◆   ◆

A Rhodes Scholar with a graduate degree in literature from Oxford, **David Quammen** has worked as a river guide in Montana, where he now lives. Perhaps best known for his "Natural Acts" column in *Outside* (which won the 1987 National Magazine Award for essays and criticism), he has written three novels and is a regular contributor to *Audubon* and other magazines. Several of his columns and articles have been collected in *Natural Acts: A Sidelong View of Science* and *The Flight of the Iguana*. He is presently working on a book about "island biogeography and the problem of fragmented habitats on the world's mainlands."

◆   ◆   ◆

A native of Los Angeles and a graduate of Washington State University, **Paul Quinnett** lives in the woods near Cheney, Washington. He has been director of Adult Services at the Spokane Community Mental Health Center since 1971. He also maintains a private counseling practice and serves as a consultant to several corporations and an inpatient chemical-dependency hospital. His professional books include *The Troubled People Book*, the best-selling *Suicide: The Forever Decision*, and the recent *On Becoming a Health and Human Services Manager*. Quinnett also writes essays, columns, and humor articles (mostly on the outdoors) for a wide range of national magazines. His son Brian is a professional basketball player in the N.B.A.

◆   ◆   ◆

George Reiger, the widely read conservation editor of *Field & Stream* (and formerly its saltwater fishing editor), has also been Washington editor of *Audubon* and senior editor of *National Wildlife* and *International Wildlife* magazines. Among his many books are *Profiles in Saltwater Angling*, *The Wings of Dawn*, *The Wildfowler's Quest*, and the Pulitzer Prize nominee *Wanderer on My Native Shore*. After serving in Vietnam as a navy intelligence officer, he was a translator and interpreter to Ambassador Henry Cabot Lodge at the peace talks in Paris.

◆   ◆   ◆

Edward R. Ricciuti, who attended Notre Dame on a boxing scholarship and Columbia University's Graduate School of Journalism as a Sloan–Rockefeller Advanced Science Writing Fellow, has written three dozen books on nature, conservation, and the outdoors. His latest book: *The Natural History of North America*. His articles have appeared in many national magazines. He is also executive editor of World Wrestling Federation publications, and formerly was editor and publisher of *Connecticut Audubon* as well as editor of *Animal Kingdom* (now called *Wildlife Conservation*) and curator of publications for the New York Zoological Society. He lives outside Killingworth, Connecticut, where he "frequently breaks knots and rod tips."

◆   ◆   ◆

When he isn't out hunting or fishing somewhere, **Jack Samson** can be found writing in his boyhood home—Santa Fe, New Mexico. Formerly editor of *Field & Stream* and outdoor columnist for The Associated Press, he now serves as editor-at-large for *Western Outdoors* and as saltwater fly-fishing columnist for several magazines. The author of seventeen books and thousands of magazine articles on the outdoors, he was formerly a wire-service war correspondent and flew with General Claire Chennault's Flying Tigers in China. He has been a board member of several organizations and presently serves as a representative to the International Game Fish Association.

◆   ◆   ◆

Fly-fishing, wildlife conservation, and national parks are **Paul Schullery**'s passions. He was a ranger–naturalist and historian at Yellowstone National Park, 1972–77, and for the next five years was executive director of the American Museum of Fly Fishing. Since 1982 he has been writing about trout and fly-fishing, and consulting on park matters. He has edited numerous books on natural history, national parks, wildlife conservation, and the outdoors. His best-known books among anglers are *Freshwater Wilderness: Yellowstone Fishes and their World* (with John Varley), *Mountain Time*, and *American Fly Fishing*.

◆   ◆   ◆

David Seybold is a free-lance writer and editor whose short stories and articles about fly-fishing have appeared in many magazines. He is the editor of the anthologies *Seasons of the Angler* and *Boats* and coeditor of *Waters Swift and Still* (with Craig Woods) and *Seasons of the Hunter* (with Robert Elman), and is presently working on three other books. He lives in New Hampshire with his wife and daughter, close to a small lake that has been his home water for twenty years.

◆   ◆   ◆

Gary Soucie, an editor for *National Geographic Magazine*, and formerly the executive editor of *Audubon*, is the author of *Hook, Line, and Sinker* and *Soucie's Field Guide of Fishing Facts*. For four years he taught a graduate course in environmental reporting at New York University. He also served as the first eastern field representative of the Sierra Club, executive director of Friends of the Earth, president of the Environmental Policy Center, and vice chairman of the League of Conservation Voters.

◆   ◆   ◆

Both a writer and a photographer, **Ron Spomer** has published articles and photographs in more than sixty publications. He grew up near the South Dakota–Nebraska border and worked for *Kansas Wildlife* magazine before moving to Idaho and full-time free-lancing.

◆   ◆   ◆

A lifelong Californian, **Peter Steinhart** writes for numerous newspapers and magazines, including *Audubon* where he is a contributing editor and writes the "Essay" column. Before becoming a full-time free-lance writer in 1987, he taught writing at Stanford University. His books include *Tracks in the Sky* (on waterfowl conservation in the Pacific flyway) and *California's Wild Heritage* (on that state's endangered species).

◆   ◆   ◆

Chuck Tryon lives in Rolla, Missouri, where he ties flies, and writes, teaches, and speaks on fly-fishing. A fly-fisher from the age of seven, he was formerly a wildland hydrologist with the Forest Service. **Sharon Tryon** (1938–1991) began fly-fishing later in life, but her dedication to the sport and to cold-water stream preservation were second to none. Her death from cancer in November 1991 left a big hole in Missouri fly-fishing and conservation circles. Chuck and Sharon coauthored *Fly Fishing for Trout in Missouri* and *Figuring Out Flies: A Practical Guide*.

◆   ◆   ◆

Born on a farm near Girard, Kansas, **Charles F. Waterman** attended what was then called Kansas State Teacher's College, did "some small-time professional wrestling," and taught in a one-room country school for one term. He wrote his first outdoor columns in 1934. During World War II he became officer-in-charge of a combat photographic unit in what was known as the Steichen Group, named for its commander, the great photographer Edward Steichen. He moved to Florida in 1952, where he has written thousands of articles and some fifteen books. He presently is a regular masthead contributor to six outdoor magazines.

◆   ◆   ◆

W. D. Wetherell has twice won the O. Henry Award for his widely published short stories and was the 1981–82 recipient of a National Endowment for the Arts fellowship in fiction. His novel, *The Man Who Loved Levittown,* won the Drue Heinz Literature Prize in 1985. Several of his stories were collected in *Hyannis Boat and Other Stories.* Besides fiction, he has written *Vermont River* and *Upland Stream.*

◆   ◆   ◆

Unfortunately, the editor has been unable to find any biographical information on **J. P. Wheeldon,** whose "The Vicar's Pool" was pub- lished in 1894 in *Sporting Facts and Fancies.*

◆   ◆   ◆

Formerly a writer for the Massachusetts Department of Fish and Game, in recent years **Ted Williams** has become the gadfly of the conserva- tion movement. His articles and columns in *Audubon* (of which he is a contributing editor and for which he writes the "Incite" column) and *Fly Rod & Reel* (of which he is conservation editor) have earned him numerous writing awards, the admiration of most readers, and the enmity of a few whose oxen were gored. Between his agency stint and his free-lance career, he served as senior editor at *Gray's Sporting Journal.* He is the author of *Don't Blame It on the Indians: Native Americans and the Mechanized Destruction of Fish and Wildlife.* He is often confused with The Splendid Splinter, who is also an avid fly- fisherman. But this Ted Williams writes better even though he doesn't bat as well.

◆   ◆   ◆

Henry Williamson (1895–1977) was truly a multitalented man: nov- elist, essayist, short-story writer, journalist, biographer, nature writer, autobiographer, editor, radio broadcaster, farmer. He enlisted in the British army at age seventeen and served as an infantryman and officer during World War I, returning at age twenty-three gray-haired, de- pressed, drinking too much. He was briefly a journalist in London, then moved to Norfolk where he farmed and wrote. During the 1930s he broadcast a farm-news radio show. His dozens of highly regarded books include the "Flax of Dreams" tetralogy of novels and the non- fiction books *The Old Stag, Tarka the Otter, Salar the Salmon,* and *The Phasian Bird.*

◆   ◆   ◆

Formerly an associate editor at *The Fly Fisherman*, **Craig Woods** now lives in Dorset, Vermont, where he writes books and articles and edits *Stratton* magazine. He helped develop and edited the first issues of *Walking* magazine. "Battenkill Seasons" was adapted from two of the essays in his book *The River as Looking Glass and Other Stories From the Outdoors*. He also wrote *The Fly Fisherman's Streamside Handbook* and coedited (with David Seybold) *Waters Swift and Still*.